UNDERSTANDING
KOREAN
POLITICS

೪

SUNY series in Korean Studies
Sung Bae Park, Editor

UNDERSTANDING
KOREAN
POLITICS

AN INTRODUCTION

EDITED BY

Soong Hoom Kil
and
Chung-in Moon

STATE UNIVERSITY OF NEW YORK PRESS

Published by
State University of New York Press, Albany

For information, address State University of New York Press,
90 State Street, Suite 700, Albany, NY 12207

Production by Diane Ganeles
Marketing by Patrick Durocher

Library of Congress Cataloging-in-Publication Data

Understanding Korean Politics : An Introduction / edited by Soong Hoom Kil, Chung-in Moon.
    p. cm. — (SUNY series in Korean studies)
    Includes bibliographical references and index.
    ISBN 0-7914-4889-4 (alk. paper) — ISBN 0-7914-4890-8 (pbk. : alk. paper)
    1. Korea (South)—Politics and government. 2. Korea (North)—Politics and government.
    I. Soong Hoom Kil. II. Moon, Chung-in. III. Series

    JQ1725 .U53 2001
    320.95195—dc21   00-033895

10 9 8 7 6 5 4 3 2 1

Contents

Tables

1

Introduction: Understanding Korean Politics

Soong Hoom Kil
and
Chung-in Moon

South Korea drew worldwide attention as it experienced two dramatic events in December 1997. One was the collapse of the Korean economy and the subsequent $57 billion bailout arranged by the International Monetary Fund (IMF), and the other was the nation's first peaceful transfer of political power from the ruling to opposition party through the election of Kim Dae Jung as the new president. South Korea, once touted as a model for third world economic development, had been able to convince the world of its successful path from periphery to core through admission to the Organization for Economic Cooperation and Development (OECD) in 1996. Yet while cheers abounded for its economic performance, as always, Korea's politics were subject to disdain and ridicule due to chronic authoritarian rule and failed democratic reforms. A first-rate economy and fourth-rate politics were Korea's trademarks—a shared understanding among Koreans and international observers. However, the two events of December 1997 completely reversed this traditional view. Now, Korea may well be known for its first-rate politics and fourth-rate economy.

Understanding Korean Politics: Four Legacies

Traditional South Korean politics is deserving of such a negative portrait. Four decades of soft and hard authoritarianism, frequent military interventions in civil politics, and the politics of personalism, factionalism, and regionalism have impaired any potential for political development and stable democracy. Despite the democratic opening of 1987, actual democratic reforms have been delayed, and former presidents Chun Doo Hwan and Roh Tae Woo, as well as the second son of former President Kim Young Sam, were put in jail under charges of corruption. Past political practices have left four legacies from which South Korea still suffers.

The first legacy is the narrow ideological spectrum. Immediately following national independence in 1945, the Korean peninsula enjoyed a wide ideological spectrum ranging from ultraright to far left. However, national division and American military occupation paved the way for the triumph of right-wing conservative forces, and the progressive forces were purged from the political scene. The narrowing of the ideological spectrum was unavoidable, given the ideological confrontation between the now-divided two Koreas, which was initiated and reinforced by the logic of Cold War bipolarity. The outbreak of the Korean War and its aftermath further consolidated the power of conservative forces and stamped out all progressive movements. Anticommunism emerged in the South as a hegemonic ideology; no alternative ideological postures were allowed. Socialist discourse was legally forbidden, and even social democratic ideals were dealt with suspicion. The overwhelming continuity of such monolithic ideology narrowed the space for ideological plurality and flexibility in governance and policy, ultimately undermining any further democratic developments.

To some extent, the democratic opening of 1987 lifted the unidimensional ideological overlay from Korean politics, as evidenced by the sharp surge in liberal and progressive discourses and movements. However, this trend did not last long. The grand conservative ruling coalition formed in 1990 dealt a critical blow to the progressive camp, and the historical clock again reversed towards the conservative direction. For all its campaign pledges and earlier efforts at reform, the Kim Young Sam government, which was the first civilian government since 1960, was also swept by recurrent waves of the conservative ideology. It remains to be seen whether the new reformist leadership of Kim Dae Jung can successfully cope with the subtle tradeoff between democratic mandates in order to expand the ideological spectrum and economic imperatives required by IMF neoconservative conditions.

The second legacy is authoritarianism. South Korea has a long history of authoritarian rule. While traditional Confucian culture forced conformity to authoritarian values, Japanese colonial rule carved out a critical base for authoritarian governance. With the exception of a brief political albetura in 1960, South Korea was never able to escape from the grip of autocracy and authoritarianism for four decades. Park Chung Hee's developmental dictatorship during the Third and Fourth Republics succeeded Syngman Rhee's autocratic rule of the First Republic. Park's tragic death in 1979 was not the end of authoritarianism in Korea; Chun Doo Hwan, seizing political power through a military coup in 1980, continued the politics of repression and intimidation. South Korea went from authoritarianism to authoritarianism where the garrison state became the prevailing image of governance. This protracted authoritarian tradition caused South Korean politics to be downgraded, despised, and ridiculed by its own people and the international community.

Yet authoritarian rule in South Korea was not to last forever. Popular uprisings in June 1987 opened the way for democratic transition. Two factors account for the opening and transition. One was the people's continuing belief in liberal democracy. Ideals of liberal democracy, first transmitted to Korea through American missionary workers and later through academic circles, are not foreign to Koreans. These ideals have had a profound impact on traditional political culture as well as on political institutions and practices, laying the ground for democratic opening. The other factor was economic development. Rapid economic development accompanied both structural and cultural changes. Economic growth realigned the structural foundation of Korean politics by expanding the middle and working classes; a higher educational level, spread of mass media and communication, and urbanization, all closely associated with economic growth, entailed concurrent cultural shifts toward political liberalism and pluralism. The confluence of structural and cultural changes offered a critical catalyst for democratic opening and consolidation in the late 1980s and the 1990s.

The third legacy is the bureaucratic state. Modern democratic politics is characterized by a system of checks and balances among the three branches of the government. In South Korea, this hallmark of democracy does not exist. The executive branch has always prevailed over the legislative and judiciary branches—the National Assembly is effectively nothing but a rubber stamp, the judiciary remains politically ineffectual. Beyond this one-branch dominance, the Korean state subjugated political and civil society to its corporatist control. Such executive dominance was possible due to the institutional arrangement framed around a presidential system as well as the traditional political culture and authoritarian mode of governance. This severely damaged democratic political processes by excluding the citizens, and it deformed the institutional balance among the three branches. Administration from the top eliminated real politics from below.

Still, it is precisely this bureaucratic state that often has been singled out as a key determinant of South Korea's impressive economic performance. Executive dominance, bureaucratic unity and competence, monopoly of policy instruments and resources, strategic intervention in the economy, and insulation of policy-making machinery from contending social and political pressures, which are all essential features of the bureaucratic state, are believed to have ensured efficient, coherent, and consistent formulation of economic policy and its effective implementation. Indeed, the bureaucratic state made significant contributions to steering and enhancing economic performance. But the recent economic downturn points to the fundamental limits of the "visible hands" of the bureaucratic state. In a brave new world of democratic opening and economic liberalization, there seems to be no place for the bureaucratic state.

Finally, Korean politics has been obsessed with the legacy of the myth of "revolution from above." The study of Korean politics has focused solely on the study of political leadership. In the political space of South Korea, only political leaders exist. Yet preoccupation with leadership has neglected other important ingredients of contemporary democratic politics, namely, people, interest groups, political processes, and coalition dynamics. For transitional democracies such as South Korea, political leadership occupies the preeminent position, but it needs to be balanced with other political actors.

It is through these four legacies, among others, that South Korean politics has been portrayed as a dismal enterprise. But recent political changes, manifested through the election of Kim Dae Jung as the fifteenth president, portend a new era for democratic politics in South Korea.

Structure of the Book

The present volume is designed to offer readers a comprehensive overview of Korean politics over the past five decades by recasting the four legacies discussed above as well as forecasting the future of Korean democracy in light of recent changes.

The book is composed of nine chapters. In chapter 2, Woon-Tai Kim presents a comprehensive overview of the ecology of Korean politics. Kim examines the historical context, geopolitical setting, economic development, social changes, and political culture of Korea, and traces how these environmental settings have influenced the evolutionary dynamics of Korean politics. Kim argues that although the ecological variables surrounding Korean politics have not always been favorable, they have served as major catalysts for enhancing democratic change and national survival. Chapter 3 by Soong Hoom Kil provides a rich overview of the development of Korea for the past five decades with a specific focus on democracy and economic development. Kil argues that the sole achievement of Korean politics is the basic introduction of liberal democracy in Korea. He also points to the fact that democratic opening and consolidation since 1987 was a paradoxical outcome of economic development which past authoritarian regimes engineered in order to enhance their political legitimacy. He concludes that despite sporadic setbacks and transitional uncertainties, South Korea will soon reach the desired stage of a mature liberal democracy. He offers a detailed analysis of democratic reforms under the Kim Young Sam government.

In chapter 4, David C. Kang provides a framework of analyzing continuity and change in Korean politics by examining its institutional foundations. By utilizing theories of principal-agency and transaction costs, which are the two main analytical trends of new institutional economics, Kang offers a persuasive explanation for continuing corruption and political crises in South Korea. He ascribes the current institutional deformity to the concentration of executive power, weak legislature, and unstable party system. In order to overcome the stalemate, Kang suggests that there must be an end to the patrimonial politics of the "three Kims" as well as the strengthening of the National Assembly as a decision-making institution.

With the revelations of corrupt and illicit acceptance of political funds in unthinkable amounts by past leaders, especially Chun Doo Hwan and Roh Tae Woo, chapter 5 by Ki-shik S. J. Hahn on political leadership is relevant. Hahn reviews the past leaders and examines their achievements in national building, economic growth, and national security with a focus on personality, behavior, and political philosophy. Hahn also presents an interesting survey of administrators and legislators who served from the First to Sixth Republics (1948–1992). Despite the risk of being a conservative interpretation, Hahn's chapter provides a rich account of leadership profiles in contemporary Korean politics.

In chapter 6, Jung Bock Lee offers an excellent analysis of political processes in South Korea, focusing on electoral institutions, political parties, interest groups and other leading social forces, such as students, the military, and mass media. Due to the prevalence of authoritarian rule, political processes could not draw scholarly attention, especially nongovernmental processes focusing on political and civil society. However, Lee's chapter fills the gap by presenting thorough empirical accounts of the historical evolution of nongovernmental processes. His analysis is balanced and informative. In chapter 7, Dong Suh Bark provides a concise analysis of the history of the administrative process in South Korea, beginning from the patrimonial bureaucracy of the Chosun dynasty, moving on to the bureaucratic administration of the authoritarian Third to Fifth Republics, and ending with the promises of reform and change in the Kim Young Sam government. Bark concludes that while the administrative process in Korea has faced some major obstacles, there are promising signals for the future settlement of democratic governance and administration. Chung-in Moon and Sunghack Lim, in chapter 8, present a political and institutional account of the rise and decline of the Korean economy. They attribute impressive economic performance during the 1961–1987 to favorable international environments, market-conforming economic policies and institutions, effective functioning of the developmental state, and social and policy networks. However, they argue that the very determinants of economic success turned out to be the primary causes of the recent economic downturn and crisis. The structure of vulnerability resulting from a deep integration into the world economy, dismal corporate performance, deformed developmental state, and network failures are regarded as factors precipitating economic crisis in South Korea.

In chapter 9, Byung Chul Koh offers a penetrating analysis of the foreign and unification policies of the Republic of Korea. He identifies the quest for legitimacy, security, and development as the major themes of South Korea's foreign and unification policies, and traces how such themes have dictated the nature and direction of South Korea's policies. The dynamics of South Korean politics cannot be appreciated without reference to North Korean politics, since both have interacted in mirror images. Sung Chul Yang's chapter

10 is devoted to the analysis of the North Korean political framework. He casts the North Korean political system in comparative socialist studies perspectives and delineates common and idiosyncratic elements of the North Korean political system. His analysis sheds an important insight into understanding the foundations of North Korean politics.

The present volume was originally intended as a textbook on Korean politics. We believe our intention is well served, although some chapters go beyond an introductory level. We hope our readers will find this book, a part of the State University of New York's monograph series on Korean studies, useful in understanding contemporary Korean politics. We would like to express our cordial thanks to Professors Sung Bae Park and Sung-taek Cho for encouraging us to undertake the project and being patient with the delayed submission of the manuscript. Robert Siegel, managing editor of the monograph series, also deserves our gratitude for his generosity and patience. Several colleagues and research assistants helped us in translating some chapters into Korean and making editorial improvements. We thank Professor Jongryn Mo, Dr. Kisoek Kim, Judy Eun-ju Chung, Yoonkyung Lee, Eun-sun Hwang, Eunsook Kim, Minuk Kim, Hyun-sook Heo, Song-hyun Chon, and Angie Kim for their comments and assistance. We are also grateful to the Institute of Korean Political Studies at Seoul National University and the Center for International Studies at Yonsei University for their institutional and logistic support.

2

৵

Korean Politics:
Setting and Political Culture

Woon-Tai Kim

While the end of the Second World War brought about national liberation for Korea from Japanese colonial rule, it did not assure the nation full autonomy and independence. Power politics between the United States and the Soviet Union led to the division of the peninsula along the thirty-eighth parallel, which deepened the ideological and military confrontation between North and South Korea. This superpower intervention and subsequent national division have worked to steer both Koreas along divergent paths of political, economic, social, cultural, and military development. While the South followed a path aiming for Western-style democracy and capitalism, the North's was a process of Sovietization in which proletariat dictatorship and socialism became the principles of political and economic governance. National division was soon followed by the outbreak of the Korean War in June 1950, traumatizing the entire Korean population. Mass killings and the destruction of war were immense on both sides, which further aggravated inter-Korean relations.

Since the late 1980s, however, the global system has undergone a profound transformation. Mikhail Gorbachev's *glasnost* and *perestroika* not only fostered the collapse of the Soviet Union, but also precipitated revolutionary changes in the political landscape of Eastern Europe, including the German unification. All this brought a sudden end to the Cold War system, expanding the space for diplomatic maneuvering by South Korea while significantly limiting that of North Korea. South Korea normalized diplomatic ties with Russia and China through assertive *nordpolitik*. Yet the irony has been in the inability to use the end of the Cold War as a means to bring about positive dividends for peace and security on the peninsula. The national division of Korea apparently has evolved into its own peculiar conflict dynamics as dictated by the interplay of geopolitics, ideology, and domestic politics.

Likewise, the evolution of Korean politics has been influenced by multiple variables involving international, inter-Korean, and domestic dynamics. This unique aspect of Korean politics makes it difficult to capture the essence of Korean politics through an application of Western paradigms. Alternative methods are needed to conceptualize Korean politics. First, Korean politics should be approached from holistic and integrative perspectives. An analytical segmentation of Korean political reality can only yield a sterile portrait. Second, historical approaches should constitute an integral part in studying Korean politics. Today's political reality is an extension of its past, and an adequate understanding on the reality cannot be realized without elucidating the historical context that has been shaped by the dynamic interplay of constant foreign invasions and persistent national resistances. Third, the study of Korean politics should be anchored in nationalism. For Koreans, nationalism is not fictional, but real. A strong feeling of national identity and national community has long served as a principal ethos of political development in Korea. National division and a yearning for a unified Korea have made nationalism all the more salient. Finally, the study of Korean politics needs to be policy-relevant. A nation's rise and fall depend on effective political management, which is predicated on relevant policy choices and their implementation. Thus, discourses on Korean politics should not be left to the domain of rhetoric, but extended to the domain of policies to cope with mounting internal and external challenges and crises.

Against this backdrop, this chapter is designed to present an overview of the geopolitical, economic, social, and cultural setting of Korean politics.

Geopolitical Setting

Geopolitics has long been an important subject of scholarly debates in political science.[1] Its relevance seems more pronounced in Korea than in other parts of the world, since Korea's geographic location has constantly influenced the destiny of its people. Frequent foreign invasions, rivalry on the peninsula among major powers at the turn of the century, and more recently, national division in the vortex of the Cold War confrontation all underscore the importance of geopolitics in Korean politics. Additionally, climate and natural resources have played equally significant roles in shaping the evolutionary dynamics of the Korean people and politics.

Geography

Korea is located on the eastern tip of the Asian continent, composed of the Korean peninsula and 3,305 islands (see map 1). Its area covers 220,000 square kilometers, South Korea accounting for 98,000 square kilometers. The northern border of the Korean peninsula is demarcated from China and Russia by the Yalu and Tumen Rivers. Its eastern, western, and southern borders are surrounded by sea. The Korean peninsula traditionally served as a bridge linking the Asian continent in the north with Japan in the south. During the late nineteenth century, Japan and the Western powers viewed Korea as a springboard from which to project their power and influence into Manchuria, while China and Russia used the peninsula as a stepping stone in their attempts to expand into the Northern Pacific. Korea, the crossing-point of two conflicting forces—the continental power and the maritime power—was trapped in the vortex of geopolitical rivalry. Thus, it is no exaggeration to claim that foreign invasion was an inseparable part of Korea's historical destiny.

The inverse relationship between Chinese unity and Korean hardship underscores this point relatively well. Unification of China was always followed by invasions into the Korean peninsula. The Han dynasty, which unified China for the first time, invaded and colonized the northern part of the peninsula for over four hundred years. Similarly, the Shu dynasty also set out, after unifying China, to conquer the Korean peninsula, only to be defeated by General Euljimunduck of the Koguryo dynasty. Also Tang, Wen, and Ching all invaded Korea after they unified China. Of more recent times, China under Mao Zedong engaged in the Korean War by dispatching massive ground forces to Korea. All this implies that whenever China experiences internal unity, it has a natural propensity to expand into the Korean peninsula. The same may be said of Japan: times of internal unity and national strength led to attempts to conquer the peninsula for use as a springboard to expand the Japanese sphere of influence into the Asian continent.

The Japanese invasion of Korea in the late fifteenth century, as well as the Japanese annexation of Korea in 1910, is the testimony to this trend. Still, even after the end of the Second World War, Korea could not escape the trap of its geopolitical destiny, as evidenced by the national division and the Korean War.

However, its geopolitical setting could be viewed as a mixed blessing, since it has not always posed constraints on the Korean peninsula. The post–Cold War era gave the Korean peninsula the potential ability to emerge as a regional center of economic, financial, and cultural interactions. Within a two-hour flight from all major cities in the region, Korea, whether unified or divided, could be a vital regional center in years to come with its growing regional economic, social, and cultural interdependence that will demolish contrived barriers of regional interactions.

Climate

Korea displays an interesting climate pattern. An intersecting point of continental and maritime climates, Korea has four distinct seasons. Spring and fall are moderate, summers are hot and humid, and winters are cold. Since long ago the climatic pattern has produced a sedentary agrarian society, cultivating a sense of fatalism and compliance with nature.[2] Such cultural traits rendered Koreans as conservative and hierarchical. Also lacking empathetic capacity, Koreans tend to follow a dualistic logic of black and white, while defying persuasion and compromise. Progress in science and technology has, however, gradually diminished the impact of climate on politics. Nonetheless, it cannot be denied that the climate pattern and resulting social and economic organizations have been instrumental in the evolutionary dynamics of Korean society and culture.

Natural Resources

Survival and prosperity of a national population depend on the availability of natural resources including food, water, energy, and nonfuel minerals.[3] It is axiomatic that a rich endowment of natural resources can ensure national survival as well as strengthen national power. Yet rich natural resources also can work adversely: the people may lack the motive for achievement, thereby leading to the weakening of national will and power. Korea was endowed with poor natural resources; nonetheless, it was a victim of colonial powers in search of natural resources. Japan was known to have annexed Korea not only because of its strategic location for colonial expansion into China and Manchuria, but also because of its rich agricultural resources (rice) and minerals. For Korea, its poor resource endowment later proved to be a driving force of economic development.

Since the 1960s, South Korea has undergone a major transformation. Assertive pursuit of modernization and economic development has entailed a serious dilemma for natural resources. While population and consumption have grown, natural resources and inhabitable space have considerably diminished, jeopardizing South Korea's ecological carrying capacity. This ecological dilemma has posed dual challenges. Internally, it has intensified social conflicts over the distribution of resources. Increasing income inequality, urban congestion, and shortage of housing have bred acute social tensions. Externally, South Korea's dependence on foreign supplies of strategic resources, such as oil, steel, copper, and even food, has greatly deepened. The adoption since the mid-1970s of an energy-intensive heavy-chemical industrialization strategy has further aggravated the situation and has made South Korea more vulnerable to external shocks. The two oil crises and rollercoaster effects of international primary commodity markets have severely undermined South Korea's economic security. Likewise, Korea's natural resource endowment has had a profound impact on its domestic and external politics.

Economic Setting

Politics cannot be understood separate from economics. Economic dynamics can influence the pattern of political development in several ways. As modernization theorists hypothesize, the level of economic development is closely correlated with the level of political development.[4] The higher the level of economic development measured in Gross National Product (GNP), the higher the level of political development and the lesser the level of social and political instability. The hypothesis is plausible because economic development creates a large middle class, whose existence is indispensable to maintaining political stability. As Mancur Olson warns, however, rapid economic growth can also disrupt social and political order and stability by too rapidly altering old social and class structures.[5] Ample empirical evidence supports his thesis; political and social unrest and the subsequent rise of authoritarian regimes in Latin

America, Asia, and the Middle East coincided with periods of rapid economic development. In view of this, the impact of economic development on politics can be bidirectional. And South Korea is not an exception to this general rule.

Economic Profile

South Korea was one of the poorest countries in the world in the 1950s; its per capita income was less than US$100. The economy was primarily agrarian, and its imports were financed mostly by American aid. Poverty and underdevelopment were pervasive. Several factors account for the economic backwardness. First, poor resource endowment and an expanding population significantly constrained potential for economic development. Second, Japanese colonial exploitation and national division critically impaired the structural foundation of the Korean economy. Third, the Korean War that lasted three years (1950–1953) devastated the national economy by destroying most of the physical and social infrastructures as well as industrial facilities. Finally, incompetent political leadership, corruption and rent-seeking, and social and political chaos in the 1950s delayed postwar reconstruction and economic development.

Since the early 1960s, however, South Korea has shown remarkable economic performance. In less than three decades, it has emerged as one of the most successful developing economies in the world. Its economy grew at an average annual rate of 10 percent; its per capita income rose from $100 in 1960 to $10,000 in 1995. Its share of world exports accounted for 1.2 percent in 1995, making South Korea the world's twelfth largest exporter. South Korea's industrial structure has also transformed from agrarian to industrial. As of 1995, almost 70 percent of exports were composed of semiconductors, automobiles, steel, consumer electronics, and petrochemical products.[6] More important, South Korea was officially admitted to the OECD in 1996 and formally elevated to the status of developed country. Unlike other developing countries, rapid economic growth did not, however, impede overall social development. South Korea's physical quality of life index (measured by the combination of life expectancy, literacy rate, and other basic human needs) is one of the world's highest. While excessive economic concentration in the hands of big business conglomerates, and a skewed distribution of wealth, remain as grave social and economic problems, income distribution has gradually improved over time, especially since the democratic opening in 1987. Owing to this impressive economic performance, South Korea was touted as a model for third world development.

As chapter 8 by Chung-in Moon and Sunghack Lim discusses in depth, several factors account for South Korea's economic miracle: human capital investment and the availability of qualified manpower, American security commitment and economic assistance, a timely transition to an export-led growth strategy, an international economic environment favorable to the export drive, and effective political leadership and competent bureaucrats. In late 1997, however, the South Korean miracle was shattered by an unprecedented economic crisis. A sequence of foreign exchange and financial crises drove the South Korean economy to the edge of default and eventually placed it under the economic trusteeship of the IMF. The economic downfall damaged national pride and cast bleak prospects for the Korean economy.

Economic System and Management Style

After liberation from Japan and national division, North and South Korea followed different paths of economic transformation. North Korea adopted a socialist path; South Korea adopted a capitalist one. However, South Korean capitalism was not an orthodox laissez-faire type, but an Asiatic mode of capitalism in which market, plan, and culture were intertwined.[7] As recent debates on the capitalist developmental state illustrate, South Korea's initial economic success can be seen as a product of an ideal combination of the state and the market. While the market was employed as the principal operating vehicle of the Korean economy, strategic government intervention facilitated its effective functioning. Intervention ranged from medium-term economic planning (five-year economic plans) to sector-specific industrial policies affecting the microeconomic decisions of individual firms. In light of this, the Korean economy was more than a mixed economy as envisioned by Keynsian structuralists. As Robert Wade and Alice Amsden elucidate, South Korea's economic system resembled *dirigisme,* or state-guided capitalism.[8]

Several factors explain the rise of such a peculiar economic system. First, there is the matter of constitutional arrangement. The Constitution of the First Republic, which was modeled partly after the German Weimar Constitution, incorporated socialist ideology in its provisions on economic management. Chapter 6, article eighty-four, of the Constitution stipulated that the "Well-being and order of the Republic of Korea should be based on the realization of socialism and the development of balanced national economy that can satisfy basic needs of all citizens."[9] The constitutional provision provided the government with a legal foundation to intervene in and guide the national economy. Second, the transmission of ideas from the outside world also facilitated state management of the national economy. In the late 1950s, newly independent nations underwent the first wave of political change. Idealistic Western liberal democracies were overthrown by military coups, and modernizing oligarchies began to emerge as the dominant form of governance in many parts of the third world.[10] These modernizing oligarchies set economic development as the ultimate goal and adopted government intervention through economic planning as a pronounced policy tool in fostering modernization, economic development, and industrialization. The military government under Park Chung Hee aggressively adopted and implemented such practices, paving the way for rapid economic development.[11] Finally, expansion of college education and growth of military organizations also facilitated the supply of qualified manpower as well as the formation of national ethos, both essential for state-guided economic development.

The most pronounced aspect of South Korea's state-guided capitalism consists in the formulation and implementation of five-year economic plans. The plans not only mapped out the nature and direction of economic development, but also served as effective macroeconomic guides for private firms. The first five-year economic development plan, initiated in 1962, was a failure due to excessively ambitious goals, poor harvest, and economic mismanagement involving currency conversion. With the second five-year plan (1967–1971), the South Korean economy began to pick up. During the third (1972–1976) and the fourth (1977–1981) five-year-plan periods, there was an acceleration of industrial deepening, and South Korea emerged as the forerunner of the Newly Industrializing Economies with its export dynamism. Yet an expansionary macroeconomic policy during the third and fourth periods, which disregarded inflationary consequences, resulted in a major economic crisis during 1979–1980.

The fifth five-year plan (1982–1986) was qualitatively different from previous ones; the style of economic management underwent fundamental realignments. Realizing the pitfalls of excessive government intervention, the plan emphasized the primacy of the market over government, and the French style of indicative planning was formally introduced. Along with this, the government undertood neoconservative reforms comprising macroeconomic stabilization and structural adjustment. Price stability, distribution, and balanced economic and social development were emphasized throughout the plan period. The fifth plan was successful in revitalizing the Korean economy, which showed steady growth amid price stability while achieving a record-high balance of payments surplus. Gradual implementation of economic liberalization and the expansion of the private sector diluted the importance of the sixth (1987–1991) and the seventh (1992–1996) five-year plans. While the government's strategic intervention through industrial policy has noticeably diminished, liberalization, deregulation, globalization, and rationalization have emerged as the new guiding principles of economic management since the sixth-plan period.

Challenges of the Korean Economy

Despite its remarkable performance in the past three decades, the South Korean economy encounters three major political and economic challenges. The first is related to economic concentration and its political implications. The South Korean government utilized *chaebol* (big business) as agents of export drives and heavy-chemical industrialization. In doing so, the government extended enormous preferential treatment to *chaebols*, such as policy loans, tax incentives, and various forms of administrative benefits. Consequently, *chaebols* have gótten larger, while small- and medium-size firms have been pauperized. Lax enforcement of fair trade and antimonopoly laws have further aggravated the problem of economic concentration. Excessive *chaebol* ownership, market, and business concentration has not only weakened the international competitiveness of the Korean economy, but also undermined the free and fair rules of the market economy. The 1997 economic crisis and IMF bailout can be attributed to the reckless corporate expansion of *chaebols* with borrowed money.

The second challenge concerns the distribution of wealth and the quality of life. Unlike many other developing countries, South Korea's rapid growth did not entail a serious tradeoff between income and wealth equality. Owing to steady economic growth and expansion, the unemployment rate decreased from 7.4 percent in 1965 to 2.7 percent in 1995. The ratio of absolute poverty stratum in the entire national population was also substantially reduced from 40.9 percent to 7.7 percent in 1990. The urban-rural income gap has narrowed over time. The average rural income in 1969 was less than two-thirds of the average urban income (100: 65.3). In the 1970s, however, rural income rose to a level almost equal to those of urban workers. The government's grain subsidy policy and the New Village Movement were instrumental for the leveling-off of rural income. Sporadic changes notwithstanding, the ratio of urban-rural income has remained stable throughout the 1980s.[12] Nevertheless, the distribution of wealth still appears to be problematic.

As with most rapidly growing economies, economic development in South Korea caused several other social problems. Compared with other advanced industrial countries, crime and drugs are less problematic in South Korea. However, environmental degradation, chronic housing shortages, and other social and welfare issues have become visible. Rampant industrialization supported by a "growth first" policy has severely deteriorated environmental quality; rapid urbanization has caused serious urban congestion problems involving traffic jams and housing shortages. Furthermore, citizens have become increasingly concerned about social welfare issues such as pensions, medical insurance, and occupational safety. Issues related to the quality of life have been gaining enormous political attention in recent general and presidential elections.

Finally, the export-led growth strategy, the secret of Korea's economic miracle, cannot escape the law of diminishing returns. It is well known that South Korea's outward looking development strategy has been blended with extensive neomercantile practices. As South Korea has reached a higher level of economic development, however, it can no longer rely on such practices. Settlement of the Uruguay Round, coupled with bilateral pressures from the United States, has forced South Korea to open its domestic markets in all sectors including agriculture, manufactured goods, and even services. Admission to the OECD has added more pressure on financial and capital market liberalization. Deprived of protective shields, Korean firms are now burdened with fierce international competition. Reorienting economic agents from mercantile protection to open competition requires enormous adjustment efforts and social costs. Opening of domestic markets also bears serious political repercussions. Import market liberalization has severely undercut the interests of farmers, small and medium firms, and workers; assuring their economic interests through structural adjustment has emerged as a major political task of the new democratic government. In fact, the recent economic downturn can be viewed as an inevitable outcome of the failure to effectively manage the transition from mercantile protection to free market competition.

Social Setting

A striking aspect of Korean politics is the perpetual primacy of the state over the civil society, presenting a stark contrast to Western countries where the state emanated from the civil society. Recently, however, a growing number of scholars have paid closer attention to the social foundation of Korean politics.[13] Given that political interactions are ultimately embedded in social structure, it is essential to explore the social setting that surrounds Korean politics.

Social Groups and Political Function in Korea

When viewed from cultural tradition and social composition, social groups in Korea can be classified into three distinct categories. They are blood-tie groups, local-tie groups, and interest groups. Primary groups involving blood, school, and local ties have been traditionally strong in Korea. However, the process of modernization has led to a rise in secondary groups based on an association of interests. These social groups have significantly influenced the political process and policy formulation in South Korea.

The most distinct social organization is a group formed through blood ties. *Hyulyonjipdan* (blood-tie group) is composed of two subgroups, namely, family and kinship. Although the process of modernization and urbanization has transformed the traditional structure of the extended family into that of the nuclear family, the Korean family still retains traditional family norms of *"hyo"* (filial piety) and *"sanghobujo"* (mutual self-help).[14] Such norms bind family members together by transcending physical separation. The same can be said of kinship relations. Despite extensive social transformation, kinship members in Korea tend to maintain strong bonds by living in the same villages. Even when apart, they hold strong organic ties through such kinship rituals as annual worshipping of their ancestors. The organic bond shaped by blood lineage has been instrumental in sustaining a strong kinship community.[15] However, the primary group composed of family and kinship has often been blamed for the creation of a backward political culture characterized by familism, collective egoism, authoritarianism, and exclusivism. *Jiyonjipdan* (local-tie group) has been the most controversial element in Korean politics. Since the mid-1960s, localism or regionalism has served as the most reliable predictor of electoral outcomes. Despite modernization, industrialization, urbanization, and structural differentiation, local or regional identity is still regarded as a significant political parameter. Regardless of social status, education, and income, Koreans have shown voting behavior bounded by local or regional origins. Political parties or factions within them are also framed around regional ties rather than ideology and policy. Politicization of regionalism has thus hindered the settlement of a stable democracy. *Jiyonjipdan* is primarily formed through administrative boundaries involving *li* (basic rural unit), *dong* (basic urban unit), *myon* (smaller rural township), *eup* (larger rural township), *gun* (county), *si* (city), and *do* (province). However, the administrative units, especially at the provincial level, are anchored in historical, cultural, and even linguistic (i.e., local dialects) differentiation. Synchronization of administrative boundaries with a natural community of sociocultural homogeneity has cultivated politicized localism or regionalism in South Korea. The regional rivalry between the Kyongsang and Cholla provinces presents the epitome of negative regionalism in Korean politics.

The rise of *iikjipdan* (interest or pressure group) is closely related to modernization, structural differentiation, and political development. Individuals form groups to advance their private or public interests in political processes.[16] In a society where primary groups are dominant and pluralistic politics is foreign, interest groups as a social organization are less likely to flourish. According to one survey, there were 426 interest groups as of August 31, 1959.[17] Another survey conducted in 1963 shows some 600 interest groups approved by the government.[18] The figure rose to 1,034 in 1974 and to 1,322 in 1984. Since the democratic opening in 1987, interest groups, both private and public, have phenomenally increased as the government legally assured the freedom of association.[19]

Iikjipdan in Korea cannot be regarded as being identical to those in the United States or elsewhere. During past authoritarian rule, interest groups were under the tight corporatist control of the state. Most peak organizations were organized, subsidized, and controlled by the government, with other interest groups also under government guidance and control. The state's corporatist control has in turn produced a large number of "illicit" or "dissenting" public interest groups that have engaged in extensive antigovernment campaigns. Thus, civil society in South Korea has been polarized into two blocs of interest groups, pro- and antigovernment. Another distinctive aspect is that Korean interest groups form weak links with political parties in articulating their interests and that the legislative branch seldom becomes the target of lobbying by interest groups. This is due not only to executive dominance over legislature, but also to the lack of an institutional arrangement for lobbying. Unlike the United States, legislative lobbying is not legally allowed in South Korea, one reason why there has been more political corruption in South Korea than in other countries.

Family Structure, Demographic Dynamics, and Urbanization

The family is the basic unit of social organization in Korea. The number of households rose 2.6 times from 4.36 million in 1960 to 11.36 million in 1990. Predictably, during the same period, rural households decreased from 2.35 million to 1.96 million, while urban households increased to 9.4 million in 1990 from 2 million in 1960. The average member of each household has also visibly decreased from 5.7 in 1960 to 3.8 persons in 1990, approximating the level of advanced industrial countries such as Japan (3.1) and the United States (3.2).

In the process of modernization, the traditional extended family structure transformed into a nuclear one. The nuclearization of family structure has had a profound impact on the Korean society. The advent of the nuclear family has gradually altered the pattern of political socialization by weakening the traditional authority structure and facilitating individualistic traits among the younger generation. This is precisely because of the gradual erosion of patrimonialism associated with the Confucian culture. The head of a household now has less influence and control over social behavior of family members. Equally important is the diminishing social value of the family. In the past, the origins of the family were closely related to social status; in the present, the family is a less important factor in determining social status. The most profound impact involves the changing role of female family members. The social participation of female members, who are no longer confined to the household, has expanded phenomenally. For instance, only 36.5 percent of females held jobs outside the household in 1965, but

in 1990 this figure increased to 47.1 percent, approximating that of
males (73.9 percent).[20] Women's social and economic participation
has naturally led to a higher level of political participation, especially since the democratic opening in 1987. The changing social
role of Korean women can be attributed to the weakening of conservative, antifeminist Confucian values as well as to shifting labor
market conditions that demand more female labor.

South Korea has also undergone a major demographic change.
In 1949, a year after its birth, the population of the Republic of
Korea was 20.2 million, while North Korea's was 9.7 million. By
1984, South Korea's population had doubled to 40 million. Demographic transition in the South has shown a pattern similar to
advanced industrial countries; in the 1950s, average annual population growth rate was 3 percent, typical of developing countries.
However, the government's systematic family planning, along with
improved economic conditions, slowed the population growth rate.
Since 1984, it has been kept below 1 percent, comparable to most
advanced industrial countries. Yet its small geographic area has
burdened South Korea with a high population density—440 people
per 1 square kilometer.[21]

Of developing countries, South Korea is one that has experienced the fastest rate of urbanization. Despite the devastating
aftermath of the Korean War in the 1950s, the rural population constituted a lion's share, accounting for 75.4 percent, while the urban
area's share was 24.5 percent. Such rural-urban ratio continued
throughout most of the 1960s. Since the 1970s, however, the ratio
radically reversed. In 1975, the rural-urban ratio was changed to
38.2 percent versus 61.8 percent. By 1990, the rural population
accounted for only 21.4 percent; the urban population for 78.6 percent. Urban migration was unavoidable in the process of modernization and industrialization. As of 1990, 33 percent of the nation's
population was concentrated in two metropolitan cities, Seoul and
Pusan. Six major cities (Seoul, Pusan, Taegu, Inchon, Kwangju, and
Taejon) accounted for 59.7 percent of the entire population in
1990.[22]

Social Stratification

Social stratification can be defined as a hierarchical ordering
of social forces by the level of income and wealth, education, and
social status. The pattern of social stratification is not uniform but
varies across nations and over time.[23] During the Chosun Dynasty,

Korean society was highly stratified, being heavily influenced by the Confucian feudal order, in which *yangban* (gentry class), *jungin* (middle class), *pyongmin* (commoners), and *chunmin* (lower class) maintained a distinctively hierarchical relationship. Japanese colonial rule, however, radically altered the feudal social order. The collapse of the Chosun Dynasty and the Japanese appropriation of land virtually destroyed the ruling status of the gentry class, which derived its social status from its Confucian authority and land ownership. Japanese colonial land policy also transformed middle farmers into peasants by buying out their small tracts of arable land. The Korean War and two rounds of land reforms in 1948 and 1957 further eroded the traditional social stratification based on the pattern of land ownership.

Since the 1950s, the ruling class in South Korea has evolved into different configurations. The 1961 coup and the consolidation of political power by the military elevated the military to the core of ruling elite. The military's dominance continued through the 1980s as it renewed political control through another coup in 1980. Although the Kim Young Sam government was successful in civilianizing the military since 1993, the military still occupies a strategic position in the Korean society. Rapid economic growth has also transformed big business into important elements of the ruling class, with recent democratization and economic liberalization likely to strengthen their position. Along with this, politicians, intellectuals, journalists, and bureaucrats constitute the mainstay of the ruling class in South Korea.

A remarkable aspect of Korean society is the expansion of the middle class. According to a social survey conducted in 1991, 61.3 percent of respondents identified themselves as middle class.[24] This reflects a sharp increase from 40 percent in 1980.[25] While the concept of the middle class in South Korea is still controversial, it is accepted to be composed of owners of small- and medium-size firms, merchants, farmers, and white-collar workers. Also, blue-collar workers often perceive themselves of being middle class. Several factors account for the expansion of the middle class: rapid physical and perceptual erosion of traditional social stratification, expanded space for upward mobility through education and new job opportunities, and improved living conditions that have narrowed the gap between the rich and the poor.[26] Of these, education and upward mobility appear to be the two most important factors in realigning the perceptual foundation of Koreans. In South Korea, education is essential for upward social mobility. Being accepted into top universities assures a shortcut to the upper class. Regardless of social, regional, and economic origins, educational opportunities are open and fair. It involves an extremely competitive process, creating an image of the "examination hell" similar to that of Japan. It is through this educational process that Koreans can easily transcend the existing barriers of social structure and portray themselves as members of the middle class.

The middle class in South Korea is often characterized by an ambivalent political orientation. Having served as the mainstay of conservative forces, the middle class once favored the status quo. However, as the case of democratic opening in 1987 illustrates, the middle class can no longer be considered to be conservative. Defying its previous conservative posture, a great majority of the middle class supported and even participated in student protests against the ruling regime. White-collar elements were especially instrumental for shifting the middle class attitudes on politics. The middle class has now become more vigilant and taken a lead in shaping public opinion. This changing attitude can be attributed in part to the consummate objection of authoritarian rule and in part to the overall culture shift in favor of democratic values, while rejecting conservative and authoritarian ones. In the age of democratic opening and consolidation, the middle class is likely to play a more crucial role in crafting South Korea's political terrain.

According to a 1988 survey, the top 20 percent of the population accounted for 42.2 percent of national income, while the bottom 20 percent accounted for only 7.4 percent.[27] The figures indicate that South Korea still has a larger population base of the lower class. Objectively speaking, blue-collar workers, the urban poor, and peasants can be classified as members of the lower class. Nevertheless, they, especially blue-collar workers, do not identify themselves as belonging to the lower class. Thus, it can be said that South Korea is closer to approaching a social structure similar to that of advanced industrial countries. A substantial reduction of the absolute poverty group as noted above further confirms a thinner boundary separating the lower class.

Political Culture

So far we have examined the overall geopolitical, economic, and social setting surrounding Korean politics. Yet it is equally essential to elucidate political culture in order to understand its ethos. Political culture is critical since it affects people's political attitude and behavior, and ultimately maps out the process of political socialization. There have been extensive scholarly debates on political culture in South Korea, and most argue that it has several distinct traits that cannot be easily captured by using Western concepts.[28]

Three factors can be identified as contributing to the formation of political culture in Korea. First is traditional values and sociocultural evolution, such as native shamanism, the Confucian tradition, and historical experiences. Second, Japanese colonial rule also is a factor in molding the foundation of a more recent political cultural template. While the repression of national identity during the Japanese colonial occupation cultivated resistance as an integral part of Korea's political culture, the militaristic bureaucratic rule was partly responsible for the advent of authoritarian regimes. It also left a cultural legacy of internal division, distrust, and coercive governance. Finally, the process of modernization has accelerated a culture shift by spreading individualism, mass consumption, and pluralistic values. Thus, formation of political culture can be conceived of as being a product of dynamic interplay of these three factors. Now let us turn to some distinctive features of political culture in Korea.[29]

Communitarian Identity

The most distinguishing aspect of political culture in South Korea lies in communitarian identity. Having shared the same racial, historical, cultural, and linguistic legacies, Koreans possess a strong feeling of covariance or a sense of common destiny. Being descendants of one ancestry, *Tangun*, they consider themselves as part of an organic whole, the Korean nation. Korean communitarian identity is best summed up in the idea of *taidongjuui*, which posits Koreans as one large whole, regardless of social, economic, and regional differences. The idea of *taidongjuui* justifies the primacy of group over individuals, who cannot exist in separation from the community. It is through this orientation that Koreans share a highly cohesive nationalism.

The communitarian identity affects political behavior in two ways. On the positive side, it reinforces a strong social bond and solidarity as well as promoting cooperation and mutual self-help by emphasizing social obligations, loyalty to the community, and a sense of collective indebtedness to society. It also helps social exchange, as opposed to economic exchange, to be the dominant pattern of social interactions. In the process of modernization, such cultural traits served as the major driving forces in forging national unity and in mobilizing the people toward national goals. On the negative side, however, the primacy of collective identity has contributed to justifying the rise of authoritarian state corporatism in which individual human rights were often violated in the name of the state and nation. It has also impeded diffusion of political and social pluralism, which are essential for a stable democracy. Exclusive and often xenophobic nationalism, a natural byproduct of excessive collectivism, has delayed the process of globalization and liberalization.

Authoritarian Value

Another salient trait of political culture in Korea involves an orientation toward authoritarian values. Conformity, compliance with authority, and acceptance of a hierarchical social order have long characterized the patterns of political socialization in Korea. Several factors have contributed to the formation of authoritarian values. While a patriarchical tradition has routinized children's conformity with the father in the family structure, the Confucian culture emphasizing people's compliance with the heavenly mandate and hierarchical order has cultivated a social fabric conducive to authoritarian value. In addition, the centralization of power and the dominance of bureaucracy during the Chosun Dynasty, the lingering legacy of Japanese colonial bureaucratic rule, and the longevity of bureaucratic authoritarian regimes in the postindependence era have all socialized Koreans to comply with authoritarian values.

Authoritarian political culture has often been blamed for fostering and even legitimizing political deformity in Korea. As can be seen in North Korea, such value orientation paved the way to the rise of Kim Il Sung's personality cult and totalitarianism. The politics of personalism in South Korea, which centers around key political figures such as the "three Kims" (Kim Young Sam, Kim Dae Jung, and Kim Jong Pil), can also be understood as an extension of this value orientation. It has also bred several dysfunctional political attitudes and behaviors such as blind obedience to authority, paralysis of critical thinking, permission of arbitrary rule by superordinates, and political apathy. Sustained authoritarian rule and the rise of the abusive state in the four decades after national independence resulted partly from the authoritarian values prevalent among Koreans.

However, there are some positive aspects arising from the presence of conservative authoritarian values. Order and stability in Korean society have been ensured through the spread of these values; Korea otherwise could not have easily escaped from the social anarchy and trauma associated with its major political upheavals—national independence, the Korean War, revolution, and two military coups. Some scholars even ascribe the South Korean economic miracle to the Confucian authority structure, which is believed to produce harmonious working relationships between the government and people as well as between managers and workers.[30]

Factionalism

As manifested in the idea of *taidongjuui*, Koreans constitute one nation, and national unity is a salient trait. Yet under the fabric of one nation, fierce competition exists among factions. Primordial affinity has made factionalism an inseparable part of Korean life, and Koreans cannot exist without associating themselves with the groups to which they belong. Individuals are considered asocial or deviant. Political parties, firms, schools, the military, and most social organizations are composed of factions; factions can be said to be the basic unit of social and political interactions. As briefly noted above, factionalism in Korea takes several forms. The most rudimentary is the *munbol* (kinship clan), which is formed through blood ties. In the past, especially during the Chosun Dynasty, the kinship clan was the most important factor in determining social upward mobility. Social stratification was determined by family names, which led to the spread of illicit practices of family name selling. Although kinship ties are still important, the process of modernization and urbanization has weakened its overall influence on political and social life.

The second type of factionalism involves school ties (*hakyon*). Old-boy networks formed through school ties are not new—they date back to the Chosun Dynasty during which political power struggles took place among contending schools of Confucian thoughts. Political fortune often depended on which school one went to since the rise and decline of scholarly factions was directly linked to the rise and decline of political power. In contemporary Korea, school ties have become less important, but still serve as a significant variable in determining elite recruitment, social mobility, and business opportunities. Senior-junior relationships formed in schools continue even after graduation. For example, during the Chun Doo Hwan and Roh Tae Woo regimes, graduates of the Kyongbuk High School in Taegu used to be the major beneficiary of positional and material benefits, coining a new expression, "T-K (Taegu-Kyongbuk) mafia." Key elite figures in both the Chun and Roh governments were recruited from graduates of that school. During the Kim Young Sam government, graduates of Kyongnam High School in Pusan and Kyongbok High School in Seoul virtually monopolized key governmental and political positions, thus replacing the "T-K mafia" with the "P-K (Pusan-Kyongnam) mafia." Graduates of these schools enjoyed benefits because President Kim himself was a graduate of Kyongnam High School, while one of his influential sons was a graduate of Kyongbok High School. Regardless of regime types, graduates of such prestigious high schools as Kyonggi High School and Seoul High School enjoyed benefits by forming implicit or explicit factions based on school ties. School ties are more critical at the local level in social and political interactions. Though weaker than high school ties, factional patronages derived from college ties also exist in every corner of Korean society involving the government, business, and military. Graduates of Seoul National University, Yonsei University, and Korea University form the three dominant college factions in Korean society.

Finally, regional and local ties are also deeply rooted in Korean society. Hometown networks or localism are prevalent and important in social and political life. As noted before, localism is the most reliable predictor of electoral outcomes in Korea. To a large extent, factions in political parties or government circles are formed primarily through local networks. The Cholla and Yongnam regions are the two primary rivals emanating from regional confrontation. Other regions, such as Chungchong, have also increasingly shown local identity in political behavior.

Factionalism has both positive and negative aspects. On the positive side, factionalism can foster the formation of social networks and trust that can reduce transaction costs, facilitate flow of information, and ultimately enhance efficiency in society.[31] However, negative effects appear to outweigh the positive ones. Rent-seeking, corruption, irrational pattern of recruitment, and the politics of exclusion, all of which are closely associated with factionalism, have undermined political development and economic efficiency.

Formalism

Formalism can be defined as the politics of face-saving, reputationalism, and legitimacy. Its origin dates back to the neo-Confucian tradition of the Chosun Dynasty, which emphasized the primacy of form over contents, ethical code over substance, and legitimacy over pragmatism.[32] Formalism has led Koreans to redefine the essence of politics by refuting the Machiavellian concept. In Korean politics, power is a necessary, but insufficient condition for governance. Without good name or legitimacy, no one can become a good ruler. Despite impressive achievements, Park Chung Hee is still viewed an unacceptable ruler by many simply because of illicit seizure of political power through military coups and authoritarian rule. Formalism, while it makes political behavior more predictable, also reveals a myriad of negative aspects. While the dualistic logic of black and white rigidifies political life, excessive emphasis on ethics and form undermines substance and practical values.

We have examined four distinctive features of political culture in Korea. However, communitarian identity, authoritarian value, factionalism, and formalism do not present the entire picture. There are several other factors, such as the spirit of resistance, fatalism, dualism, civic minds, and egalitarianism. Discussion of these cultural traits will be left for another future opportunity.

Conclusion

In view of the above discussions, Korean politics is quite complex. Its evolutionary dynamics has constantly been influenced by several exogenous variables. While geopolitical setting and frequent foreign invasions have armed Korea and its politics with a defensive nationalism, poor resource endowment has driven Koreans to look outward. A capitalist path to economic growth has also had a profound impact on the historical trajectory of Korean politics. Its earlier phase of modernization and industrialization closely associated with developmental dictatorship, the mature stage of economic development, and subsequent structural and cultural changes, paved a way to democratic opening and consolidation. Indeed, South Korea has confirmed the thesis of modernization theorists that development fosters democracy.

The process of modernization and industrialization has also

been accompanied by structural differentiation and social mobilization. Massive urban migration, expansion of the middle class, and new configuration of the ruling class have significantly reshaped the landscape of South Korean politics. Equally critical is the political culture. The dynamics of Korean politics can be appreciated more accurately by cultural variables than by sociological ones. Dialectical blending of traditional and modern values has greatly influenced the pattern of political socialization in South Korea. Despite its impressive economic growth and internationalization, South Korean politics displays a unique blend of tradition and modernity.

All this implies that Korean politics cannot be fully understood by looking into political variables alone. As politics shapes other domains, geopolitics, history, economy, society, and culture dictate the political dynamics of South Korea. It is for this reason that we need to employ a historical and holistic approach to Korean politics.

Notes

1. On the origins of geopolitical debates, refer to works by Jean Bodin and F. Ratzel. Also see C. L. de S. Montesquie, *De l'esprit de lois*, vols. 14–16.

2. Politics in Asian agrarian societies was once very sensitive to climate patterns. A poor harvest followed by an excessive drought or a heavy flood was usually considered to be due to the lack of virtue on the part of the ruler. Thus, a ruler's virtue was closely interrelated with the climate pattern.

3. See Dennis Pirages, *Global Eco-Politics* (North Scituate, Mass: Duxbury Press, 1979); Harold and Margaret Sprout, *Foundations of International Politics* (Princeton, N.J.: Van Nostrand, 1962).

4. See S. Martin Lipset, *Political Man* (New York: Doubleday, 1958).

5. Mancur Olson, "Rapid Growth as a Destabilizing Force," *Journal of Economic History* 23 (1963), pp. 530–531. This hypothesis was also echoed by Karl Deutsch, see "Social Mobilization and Political Development," *American Political Science Review* 55 (1961), pp. 493–514.

6. Byongrak Song, *Han'guk Kyongjeron* [The Korean Economy] (Seoul: Bakyoungsa, 1992), 3rd ed.; Office of Statistics, *Chuyo Kyongje Sahoe Chipyo* [Major Social and Economic Indicators] (Seoul: Office of Statistics, 1996).

7. For debates on the nature of Korean capitalism, see Byongrak Song, op. cit., pp. 61–62.

8. On the developmental state, see Robert Wade, *Governed Market* (Princeton: Princeton University Press, 1990); Alice Amsden, *Asia's Next Giant* (Oxford: Oxford University Press, 1989); Chung-in Moon and Rashemi Prasad, "Beyond the Developmental State: Politics, Institutions, and Networks," *Governance: International Journal of Administration* 7:4 (October 1994).

9. Woon-Tai Kim, *Hyondae Han'guk Chongchisa—Che 1 Konghwaguk* [Contemporary History of Korean Politics Vol. 2—The First Republic] (Seoul: Sungmungak, 1986), pp. 267 and 316.

10. See Gabriel Almond and D. Coleman, *Politics in Underdeveloped Areas* (Princeton: Princeton University Press, 1960), pp. 572–573.

11. Stephan Haggard, Byung-kook Kim, and Chung-in Moon, "Transition to an Export-led Growth in South Korea," *Journal of Asian Studies* 50:4 (November 1991).

12. These data are from Song, *Han'guk Kyongjeron*, op. cit., p. 507, tables 10–14 and p. 695, tables 13–14.

13. Hagen Koo, ed., *The State and Society in Contemporary Korea* (Ithaca: Cornell University Press, 1991).

14. Haeyoung Lee, "Kajok [Family]," in Haeyoung Lee and Taehwan Kwon, eds., *Han'guk Sahoe III: Inkuwa Palchon* [Korean Society III: Population and Development] (Seoul: Seoul National University Press, 1978), pp. 753–814.

15. Jae-sok Choi, "Chongjok Jipdanui Chojikkwa Kinung [Organization and Functions of Kinship Groups]," *Minjokmunwha Yonku* 2 (1966); Doo-heon Kim, *Han'guk Kajok Chedo Yonku* [A Study of Korean Family System] (Seoul: Seoul National University Press,1969).

16. Harmon Zeigler, *Interest Group in American Society* (Englewood Cliffs: Prentice Hall, 1964), pp. 30–31.

17. Mun-kyu Park, *Han'guk Chongburon* [Korean Government] (Seoul: Pakyoungsa, 1963), pp. 557–559.

18. Haekyun Ahn, "Han'gukui Iik Chipdane Kwanhan Charyo Yonku [A Study of Research Materials on Interest Groups in Korea]," *Haengjung Ronchong* 3:1 (1965), pp. 320–335.

19. See Hyong-sop Yoon, "Han'guk Chongchi Kwajong [Political Process in South Korea]," in Woon-Tai Kim et al., *Han'guk Chongchiron* [Korean Politics] (Seoul: Pakyoungsa, 1989), 2nd ed., p. 532; Young-rae Kim, *Han'gukui Iik Chipdan* [Interest Groups in Korea] (Seoul: Daewangsa, 1987).

20. Song, *Han'guk Kyongjeron*, op. cit., p. 507.

21. Ibid., p. 501.

22. Woon-Tai Kim, et al., *Han'guk Chongchiron*, op. cit., p. 81; Song, *Han'guk Kyongjeron*, op. cit., pp. 503 and 861.

23. Melvin M. Tumin, *Social Stratification* (Englewood Cliffs: Prentice Hall, 1967), p. 6.

24. Korean Statistics Association, *Han'gukui Sahoe Chipyo* [Social Indicators of Korea] (1992), p. 317.

25. "Tukjip—Han'gukui Chungsan Chung [Special Issue on the Middle Class in Korea]," *Minjok Chisung* [National Intellectualism] 2:20 (October 1987), p. 30.

26. Ibid., p. 38.

27. Nyonghoon Kwon, "Han'guk Kyongjerul Wihan Tawonjuuijok Sinkyongje Chongchaek [Pluralistic New Economic Policy for the Korean Economy]," in The Academy of Korean Studies, ed., *Han'guk Chabonjuuiui Chindan* [A Diagnosis of the Korean Capitalism] (Seoul: Academy of Korean Studies, 1992), p. 105.

28. Heesop Lim, *Han'guk Sahoeui Palchonkwa Munhwa* [Development of Korean Society and Culture] (Seoul: Nanam, 1987), p. 227; Chung-si Ahn, "Han'guk Chongchi Munhwaui Tuksongkwa Pyonhwa [Characteristics and Change of Korean Political Culture]," Institute of Korean Politics Studies, *Han'guk Chongchi Yonku* [Research on Korean Politics] (Seoul: Seoul National University, 1987); Woon-Tai Kim, *Han'guk Chongchiron*, op. cit., pp. 136–182; Bae-ho Hahn, "Kaehwaki Ihuui Chonchewa Chongchi Munhwa: Segaeui Inyomhyong [Polity and Political Culture since Opening of the Nation: Three Ideal Types]," *Han'guk Chongchi Hakhoebo* [Korean Political Science Review] 10 (1976), pp. 23–39.

29. For a detailed discussion, see Ji-hoon Lee, "Han'guk Chongchi Munhwaui Kibon Yoin [Basic Determinants of Korean Political Culture]," *Han'guk Chongchi Hakhoebo* [Korean Political Science Review] 16 (1982), pp. 112–113; Myongsoon Shin, "Chongchi Munhwawa Minjujuui [Political Culture and Democracy]," in Korean Political Science Association, ed., *Contemporary Korean Politics* (Seoul: Bubmunsa, 1987).

30. Lucian Pye, *Power and Authority in Asian Politics* (Cambridge: Harvard University Press, 1986).

31. See Peter Evans, *Embedded Autonomy* (Princeton: Princeton University Press, 1995); Francis Fukuyama, *Trust* (New York: Free Press, 1996).

32. Woon-Tai Kim, *Chosun Wangjo Haengjongsa* [Administrative History of the Chosun Dynasty] (Seoul: Bakyoungsa, 1981), pp. 49–50.

3

ᄙᆞᄀᆞ

Development of Korean Politics—
A Historical Profile

Soong Hoom Kil

This chapter is designed to provide an overview of Korean political development since 1945, the year of Korea's liberation from Japanese colonial rule. It is well known that Korea has experienced frequent crises of constitutional order and political instability. From 1948, the birth year of the Korean constitution, to 1987, no less than six republics were established. During this thirty-nine-year span, the constitution was revised nine times (see Appendix 1),[1] and those republics were ruled by presidents with military backgrounds from 1961 to 1992. On taking office on February 23, 1993, Kim Young Sam registered a genuine civilian democratic government under a true civilian president. A more significant development is the selection of Kim Dae Jung as president in the December 1997 presidential election—the first peaceful transfer of power from the ruling to the opposition party in the history of South Korean politics.

Despite its turbulent path of political development, South Korea has achieved two cherished goals. One is the democratic change, and the other is the economic development. After more than three decades of hard and soft authoritarianism, the Republic of Korea has finally realized democratic transition and consolidation. The democratic opening, which was engineered by the people's uprising in June 1987, has evolved into the crystallization of democratic consolidation through the election of Kim Dae Jung in December 1997. Although a major economic crisis placed its economy under the economic trusteeship of the International Monetary

Fund (IMF), South Korea has shown remarkable economic performance in the past three decades. From a colonial legacy, the rubble
of the Korean War, and a vicious cycle of poverty and underdevelopment, the South Korean economy was able to emerge as the
twelfth largest economy in the world. This chapter aims to recast
the developments of democracy and economy by looking into the
historical context of political evolution in South Korea in the last
fifty years.

American Occupation and the
First and Second Republics (1945–1960)

Korea built the First Republic with relatively "modern" political institutions after liberation from Japanese colonial rule (August
15, 1945) and from political struggles under the American military
occupation (until August 15, 1948). The capitalist system, the cornerstone of Korea's high economic growth in the 1960s and 1970s,
was also instituted during this period. The First Republic under
Syngman Rhee, which was founded in 1948, was toppled in 1960 by
the April 19 Student Revolution, giving birth to the Second Republic under Chang Myon. The Second Republic did not last long, however, ending with the military coup by Park Chung Hee on May 16,
1961. The fall of the Second Republic implied a failure of the dream
of establishing an authentic parliamentary democracy. Against this
brief sketch, we will examine the historical development of Korean
politics from 1945 to 1960, with a special focus on constitutional
order, legislative and party politics, and the genesis of capitalist
economic institutions.

The Politics of Constitution Building

Amid the various political parties[2] competing for power immediately after liberation, Syngman Rhee and the Korean Democratic
Party (KDP) emerged as the central actors in leading the construction of the First Republic in 1948. Other political factions were
debilitated due to loss of leadership or refusal to join the building of
a "divided government" between North and South Korea. The chief
task of the first national assembly, often referred to as the "constitutional national assembly" and formed through the May 10 General Election in 1948, was to draft a new constitution (see Table
3.1). The political factions surrounding Syngman Rhee desired a

presidential/unicameral power structure, while the KDP proposed a parliamentary, bicameral system. Compromise resulted in a mixture of an American-type presidential system, based on the division of power, and a unicameral legislature, with parliamentary features such as a prime minister, cabinet council, executive legislation, and a ministerial report to the National Assembly.[3] Syngman Rhee was elected as president of the National Assembly following the constitutional principle of indirect presidential election.

The new constitution suffered from the political crises of the "Balchwe (Selected) Constitutional Amendment" (July 7, 1952) and the "Sasaoip (Rounding-off) Constitutional Amendment" (November 29, 1954). The government proposed the Balchwe Amendment after Syngman Rhee lost the support of the KDP, which was essential for his reelection in the National Assembly. The constitutional amendment sought to replace the indirect presidential election system with a direct presidential election system. However, the January 18, 1952 vote of the National Assembly, resulting in 19 approvals and 143 rejections, blocked Rhee's amendment plan. Rhee seemed doomed to lose his elected office. The government, however, resubmitted the amendment bill to the opposition-dominated National Assembly, setting off what came to be known as the "Pusan Political Crisis." In order to get the bill passed with a two-thirds majority, the government imposed a marshal law around the temporary capital city of Pusan. National Assemblymen were subjected to political terrors pressing them to vote for the bill. In the subsequent vote, 163 out of 166 participants voted in favor of the bill, with only three abstentions.[4]

The "Sasaoip Amendment" was to clear the way for Syngman Rhee's third-term and eventual life-long tenure of power. When National Assembly members voted on November 27 of 1954, the outcome was 135 approvals, 60 rejections, and 7 abstentions. Although at first rejected by the government for being one vote short of the two-thirds majority, the bill was later passed on the basis of the round-off rule.[5]

During the First Republic, additional political coercion shaped and formed political institutions and the general political atmosphere. For instance, the ruling Liberal Party (LP) held rigged elections to safeguard two-thirds of the parliament seats required for constitutional revision. In addition, there was an attempted assassination of vice president Chang Myon, who was likely to succeed the aging Syngman Rhee. Furthermore, the National Security Law, passed in the National Assembly on February 24, 1958, led to the

Table 3.1
Summary of Constitutional Amendments

	Date of Promulgation	Main Contents	Causes	Notes
Constitution	July 7, 1948	*Presidentialism *Indirect presidential election in NA *Unicameralism, 4-year term	*Establishment of Republic of Korea	Proposal of parliamentary system turned into indirect presidential election system due to rejection of President Rhee
1st	July 7, 1952	*Direct presidential election *Bicameralism (Lower House: 4-year term; Upper House: 6-yearterm)	*Reelection of Syngman Rhee	Political crisis due to *Balchwe* Amendment; Promulgation of martial law; Imprisonment of NA men
2nd	Nov. 29, 1954	*Repeal of limit on number of reelections	*Third reelection of Syngman Rhee	Two days after announcement of rejection on November 29, correction announcement of pass (*Sasaoip* Revision)
3rd	June 15, 1960	*Parliamentarism *Presidential election by NA, 2 five-year terms allowed	*April 19 Revolution	Birth of DP government
4th	Nov. 29, 1960	*Punishment of antidemocratic actors & illegal fortune collectors	*April 19 Revolution	Retrospective legislation
5th	Dec. 26, 1962	*Presidentialism *PR system *Unicameralism; 4-year term	*May 16 Military Coup	Establishment of DRP Government

(continued on next page)

Table 3.1 (*continued*)

	Date of Promulgation	Main Contents	Causes	Notes
6th	Oct. 27, 1969	*Allowed third presidential reelection	*Third reelection of Park Chung Hee	Anomalous pass at third annexed building of NA
7th	Dec. 17, 1972	*Guiding presidentialism (no limit) *Indirect presidential election at NCR *Appointment of *Yujonghoe* member by president	*Park Chung Hee lifetime seizure of power (*Yushin*)	Promulgation of martial law
8th	Oct. 27, 1980	*7-year single term *Indirect presidential election by electoral college *PR system, 4-year term	*Rise of new military group after December 12 Incident	National martial law except for Cheju; new military group nullifies agreed proposal of constitutional amendment of direct presidential election
9th	Oct. 29, 1987	*Direct presidential election, 5-year single term *Revival of parliamentary inspection of administration	*June Resistance *June 29 Declaration	First agreed on constitutional amendment; Direct presidential election system in 15 years

February 4 Political Crisis between the ruling and the opposition parties. The law contained potentially dangerous elements that could be abused by the government to oppress civil liberties and freedom of expression.[6] The LP also carried out a large-scale rigged election on March 15, 1960, to reelect Syngman Rhee and Lee Ki Poong as president and vice president, respectively. In short, the constitutional history of the First Republic was tumultuous. Political corruption manifested through the rigged March election, coupled with prevailing social and economic crises,[7] ignited mass uprisings led by students in April 1960. The April 19 Student Revolution toppled the Rhee regime and paved the way for the Second Republic. Meanwhile, the United States, which had been a firm supporter of the Rhee regime, repealed its support, and the Korean military declared its neutral stance in domestic politics.

In the aftermath of the April 19 Student Revolution and the collapse of the First Republic, the Huh Jung caretaker cabinet emerged as a transitional government. Although LP members still dominated the National Assembly, the cabinet undertook a constitutional amendment that adopted the parliamentary system on June 15, 1960. It was the third revision of the constitution. The Huh Jung cabinet later gave way to the Chang Myon cabinet as a result of the general election for the establishment of the Second Republic on July 29, 1960.

The third constitutional amendment transformed the government from a presidential to parliamentary system by turning unicameralism into bicameralism, instituting direct election of local governments, and declaring the political neutrality of the police force.[8] This new constitution stipulated that the National Assembly would elect the president and prime minister and that the president was to be merely a national symbol, while actual political power would rest with the prime minister. The constitution reflected the people's desires that presidential dictatorship should not be allowed again.

On the basis of the new constitution, Korea held a general election on July 29, 1960. The outcome of the election was a great victory for the conservative Democratic Party (DP), which had struggled under the dictatorship of the Syngman Rhee regime. The DP won 175 out of 233 (75 percent) Lower House seats and 31 out of 58 (53 percent) seats in the Upper House. The National Assembly meeting following elected Yoon Bo Sun and Chang Myon as president and prime minister, respectively. However, as theorists of "stable democracy" point out, the drastic transition from a dictatorship to a democracy entailed dangers of social disorder and political instability.[9] The Second Republic was by no means an exception. The ruling DP was divided into the Old and New factions over conflicts regarding the distribution of key governmental positions. The Old faction eventually defected to form the New Democratic Party (NDP). While the power struggle within the ruling circle virtually paralyzed the politics of the establishment, the proliferation of interest groups and their radical demands, such as the "neutralized reunification" of divided Korea, instigated social disturbances. Students, the principal agents of democratic changes through the April 19 Revolution, echoed sound and fury, discontented with the ruling regime's conservative ideology, and rushed into the streets calling for radical reforms. More important, student leaders formed the Student League for National Unification on May 5, 1961, and declared that they would engage in direct talks with North Korean student leaders in Panmunjom. Korea was at the brink of anarchy. The ruling DP regime could not cope effectively with the turmoil. Chang Myon's weak political leadership, internal division among the ruling elite, failure to consolidate power, and the widening gap between people's expectations and actual satisfaction crippled the effective functioning of the Second Republic, and it fell prey to the 1961 May 16 military coup.

The Second Republic undertook the fourth constitutional amendment on November 27, 1960, as a response to severe popular and legislative protests over a series of generous court sentences given to those who were responsible for the March 15 rigged election as well as those who had illicitly accumulated wealth through political connections under the First Republic. Despite the fear of setting a bad precedent for political retaliation and retrospective legislation, the government undertook a constitutional amendment, paving the way for the drafting of retrospective special laws such as the "Punishment Act of the Participants in the Rigged Election," the "Civil Rights Restriction Act," and the "Punishment Act of Illicit Wealth Accumulators." However, their implementation was suspended by the May 16 military coup.[10]

Legislative Politics and the Role of Political Parties

The first Korean National Assembly was founded through the May 10 General Election in 1948, and was named the "constitutional assembly" because it drafted the first constitution. At the time, the assembly was endowed with strong power and authority;

the Korean public felt that it should function as the central arena for political activities. Thus, in addition to its ordinary law-making functions, it exercised extensive power and authority, such as legislative oversight of the executive branch, public hearings, impeachment of public officials including the president, appointment of main executive posts, approval of foreign policy, and election of the president.[11]

This legislative empowerment gradually eroded for two major reasons. One was the increasing limitations on its power due to constitutional amendments, such as the *Balchwe* and *Sasaoip* amendments. The second reason involved the LP's dominance in the Assembly. The support of the KDP was a significant factor behind Syngman Rhee's presidential election. In 1951, however, he separated himself from the KDP (and its offspring, the Democratic National Party [DNP]) and organized the LP. At the time of the May 20 general election in 1954, the two major parties (the ruling LP and opposing DNP) moved one step further toward standard party politics by adopting a system of official party endorsement of candidates. In the 1954 general election, the LP won the majority (114 out of 203 seats) in the National Assembly for the first time, and continued to dominate it until the downfall of the First Republic. Meanwhile, the DNP, with only fifteen seats, failed to form a negotiating body.

The power and authority of the National Assembly was revived in the Second Republic, which adopted bicameralism. The Lower House consisted of 233 legislators elected in the single member district for a four-year term. The Upper House consisted of 58 members elected from the large districts, such as Seoul and other provinces, for a six-year term. Revival of legislative empowerment in the Second Republic was manifested in terms of its mandate to elect the president (a symbolic figure) as well as prime minister.

In tandem with the precarious nature of legislative politics, the political party system also suffered growth pains. Like other newly independent countries, Korea lacked institutionalized legal apparatus or regulation concerning the organization of political parties at the time of the liberation. As noted before, any group of three people, a simple report, and registration at a government office were enough to set up a political party.[12] Not surprisingly, hundreds of political parties flourished. One observer of Korean politics reported that at its peak, the number reached 422.[13] Some significant groups included the KDP (extreme right), the Korean Independence Party (moderate right), Working People's Party (moderate left), and the South Korean Worker's Party (extreme left). The KDP, the landowners' party, represented the nationalist camp by encompassing a wide range of right-wing political groups. Under the aegis of the American military government, it successfully extended political influence and played a leading role, along with Syngman Rhee, in establishing the independent government in South Korea. The Korean Independence Party was organized by Kim Koo, a supreme nationalist leader, who led the provisional government in Shanghai during the Japanese colonial period. Although representing the right wing as the KDP, it took a more independent line from the American military government by initiating talks with the North Korean leadership. The moderate left Working People's Party was organized by Yo Un-hyong and the members of Committee for the Establishment of the Korean State. It was also joined by the Coalition Committee under American military rule. Finally, the South Korean Worker's Party was the successor of the Choson (Korean) Communist Party established in 1925. It was rebuilt by Park Hon-yong after liberation and led various strikes and riots in South Korea. After 1946, however, the anticommunist policy of the American Military Government forced it to go underground.[14]

Among all of these groups, only the KDP members, pro-KDP independents, and supporters of Syngman Rhee participated in the election held on May 10, 1948. Other parties boycotted the election in opposition to the establishment of a divided government in North and South Korea. As a result, the Constitutional National Assembly was composed of fifty-five members from Rhee's *Toklipchoksunghoi* (National Society for the Rapid Realization of Korean Independence), twenty-nine members from the KDP, and sixty pro-KDP independents who temporarily withdrew from the unpopular KDP for electoral purposes.[15] Thus, the First Republic was created with the KDP and the pro-KDP legislators dominating the Constitutional National Assembly and electing Syngman Rhee as president. In other words, the First Republic was governed by extreme right conservatives. The Korean War further reinforced the conservative and right-wing nature of Korean politics.[16]

Indeed, the Korean War had a profound impact on the development of Korean politics. A tragic incident between South-North Korean brethren, the war was wrapped in an ideological conflict between communism/socialism and anticommunism/capitalism. Consequently, the war naturally resulted in the consolidation of an anticommunist, capitalist political order in South Korea. Postwar

Korean politics swung back to the extreme right to the extent that even discourses on the Marxist ideology were no longer allowed. The Korean War provided the participants of the May 10 election with the momentum to consolidate their political standing at the expense of nonparticipants. The purge of Cho Pong-am exemplified the right-wing campaign to wipe out its ideological foes. In the 1956 presidential election, Cho, the candidate of the moderate leftist Progressive Party, was successful enough to defeat the incumbent Syngman Rhee in 25 out of 125 electoral districts.[17] Later, he was framed as a pro-North Korean sympathizer and was hung under the Anti-Communist Law, his death marking the literal end of progressive ideology in South Korea. The Korean people were conservative enough to tolerate this absurd political concoction.[18] The conservative nature of political parties was sustained even during the transition from the First Republic to the Second Republic. This was possible simply because the political power of the LP was passed on to the Democratic Party, the heir to the conservative KDP line. In the July 29, 1960 election that established the Second Republic, the LP collapsed, the DP won a sweeping victory, and the moderate leftist parties could garner only a small number of seats.[19]

While anticommunism united political parties in their ideological outlook, real politics divided them into two opposing camps: prodemocratic and antidemocratic forces. This polarization was an unavoidable outcome of Syngman Rhee's autocratic rule. While the supporters of the authoritarian Rhee regime were branded as "antidemocratic," opposition parties, such as the KDP and the succeeding DNP and DP, constituted prodemocratic forces. Rhee originally opposed organizing a political party on grounds that political parties sought the parochial interests of political factions rather than the interests of the whole nation. Yet after the loss of KDP support early in the First Republic, he realized the importance of creating his own political party; thus, in 1951, Rhee founded the LP as the ruling party.

The KDP, reorganized into the DNP in February 1949 by forming a coalition with the Shin Ik-hee and Lee Chung-chun factions, was not successful in gaining popular support. It won just twenty-four seats in the May 30 General Election in 1950 (see Table 3.2). Such poor performance resulted from its failure to clean up its perceived image of being the feudal landowners' political party.

Several years later, the DNP encountered the political crisis of the *Sasaoip* Amendment in November 1954. After this incident, the DNP changed its name to DP and adopted the "democratization of politics" as its first tenet. At that time, citizens were angry over Rhee's frequent violations of the rules of the political game, and consequently switched their support to the DP, which promoted an antidictatorship slogan.[20] The DP won 79 seats in the fourth general election of 1958, adding a significant presence to the National Assembly which had 126 members from the LP, one from the Unification Party, and 27 independents. The Korean political party system began to take shape as a two-party system, composed of the dictatorial LP and the opposing DP. In the July 29, 1960 general election, which was taken after the fall of the First Republic, the DP was able to win majority seats in both houses: 175 of 233 in the Lower House, and 31 of 58 seats in the Upper House (see Appendix 2). Yet the oversize DP could not maintain its internal unity. The conflict between the two competing factions—the old faction composed of politicians with KDP and DNP background, and the new faction composed of politicians with other backgrounds—exacerbated and eventually split the party into two, the Democratic Party and the New Democratic Party on February 20, 1961. Both parties ceased to function with the military coup in May 1961.

Forging a Capitalist Economic System

South Korea showed one of the highest economic growth rates in the world from the 1960s to the 1980s. As Bruce Cumings argues, the origins of South Korean development can be traced back to the period of Japanese colonial rule.[21] But equally important was the rise of a new political and economic order under the American military government, which not only blocked the socialist path to development, but also reduced the power and influence of landlords through land reforms. Moreover, it is through the American window that South Korea was able to integrate into the capitalist world system. Were it not for this historical conditioning, South Korea's developmental trajectory could have taken a different orbit.

South Korea's selection of the capitalist development path can be seen as a trick of history. At the time of national liberation in 1945, socialist forces were on the rise. They were more well organized and enjoyed greater potential for mass mobilization, owing to the strategic position they cultivated during the independence movements against Japanese colonial rule.[22] Leftist groups such as the Committee for the Establishment of the Korean State and the South Korean Workers Party literally dominated the political arena after liberation. Leftist intellectuals, released from prisons after

Table 3.2
Partisan Distribution of Seats in the National Assembly

(Seats)	
Constitutional Assembly (200)	1) Independents (85) 2) National Society for the Rapid Realization of Korean Independence (55) 3) Korean Democratic Party (29) 4) Great Korea Democratic Youth Alliance (12) 5) Chosun National Youth Corps (6) 6) Peasant's Alliance for the Rapid Realization of Korean Independence 7) Korean Labor Alliance (1) 8) Chosun Democratic Party (1) 9) Korean Youth Corps (1) 10) Korean Independence Party (1) 11) Association of Education (1) 12) Dan People's Party (1) 13) Society for Big Success (1) 14) Confucian Doctrine Party (1) 15) Headquarter of National Unification (1) 16) Chosun Republican Party (1) 17) Pusan 15 Club (1)
2nd Assembly (210)	1) Independents (126) 2) Korean Nationalist Party (24) 3) Democratic Nationalist Party (24) 4) Nationalist Association (14) 5) Korean Youth Corps (10) 6) Korean Labor Alliance (3) 7) One People Club (3) 8) Social Democratic Party (2) 9) Alliance for National Freedom (1) 10) Society of Korean Housewives (1) 11) Buddhists (1) 12) Female Nationalist Party (1)
3rd Assembly (203)	1) Liberal Party (114) 2) Independents (67) 3) Democratic Nationalist Party (15) 4) Nationalist Association (3) 5) Korean Nationalist Party (3) 6) Association of Constitutional Assemblymen (1)
4th Assembly (233)	1) Liberal Party (126) 2) Democratic Party (79) 3) Independents (27) 4) Unification Party (1)
5th Assembly	Lower House: 1) Democratic Party (175) 2) Independents (49) 3) Social Mass Party (4) 4) Liberal Party (2) 5) Korean Social Party (1) 6) Unification Party (1) 7) Other (1) Upper House: 1) Democratic Party (31) 2) Independents (20) 3) Social Mass Party (1) 4) Korean Social Party (1) 5) Other (1)
6th Assembly (175)	1) Democratic Republican Party (88+22=110) 2) Democratic Justice Party (27+14=41) 3) Democratic Party (8+5=13) 4) Liberal Democratic Party (6+3=9) 5) Nation's Party (2)
7th Assembly (175)	1) Democratic Republican Party (102+27=129) 2) New Democratic Party (28+17=45) 3) Public's Party (1)

(continued on next page)

Table 3.2 *(continued)*

(Seats)

8th Assembly (204)	1) Democratic Republican Party (86+27=113) 2) New Democratic Party (65+24=89) 3) Nation's Party (1) 4) Public's Party (1)
9th Assembly (219)	1) Yujunghoe (73) 2) Democratic Republican Party (73) 3) New Democratic Party (53) 4) Unification Party (2) 5) Independents (19)
10th Assembly (231)	1) 1) Yujunghoe (77) 2) Democratic Republican Party (68) 3) New Democratic Party (61) 4) Unification Party (3) 5) Independents (22)
11th Assembly (276)	1) Democratic Justice Party (90+61=151) 2) Democratic Korean Party (57+24=89) 3) Korean Nation's Party (18+7=25) 4) People's Right Party (2) 5) Democratic Social Party (2) 6) New Government Party (2) 7) Peaceful People's Party (1) 8) Democratic Peasant Party (1) 9) Independents (11)
12th Assembly (276)	1) Democratic Justice Party (87+61=148) 2) New Democratic Party (50+17=67) 3) Democratic Korean Party (26+9=35) 4) Korean Nation's Party (15+5=20) 5) New Justice Social Party (1) 6) New Democrats Party (1) 7) Independents (4)
13th Assembly (299)	1) Democratic Justice Party (87+38=125) 2) Peaceful Democratic Party (54+16=70) 3) Democratic Party (46+13=59) 4) New Democratic Republican Party (27+8=35) 5) One Nation Democratic Party (1) 6) Independents (9)
14th Assembly (299)	1) Democratic Liberal Party (116+33=149) 2) Democratic Party (75+22=97) 3) Unified Nation's Party (24+7=31) 4) New Government Party (1) 5) Independents (21)

Source: 1–13th National Assembly: Chungang Songo Kwanliwiwonhoe, *Taehanminguk Sonkosa* [History of Election in the Republic of Korea] vol. 1 (1973), p. 613; Woon-Tai Kim, *Han'guk Chongchiron* [Korean Politics], 2nd rev., (Seoul: Pakyongsa, 1989), p. 494; 14th National Assembly: Chungang Songo Kwanliwiwonhoe, *14 dae Kukhoeuiwon songochongram* [General Information on the 14th Parliamentary Election] (March 24, 1992), p. 112.

liberation, returned to their hometowns and organized and mobilized socialist movements. Their political activities became visible and forceful as evidenced by various peasant and workers' movements that swept across the Korean peninsula.[23] Establishment of a communist government in the North furthered the socialist wind in the South. It was in this context that the American military government laid the foundation of capitalist development by wiping out socialist groups, while assisting right-wing groups in consolidating their political power. The advent of the Cold War and the containment of communist expansion helped South Korea enjoy the fruits of capitalist growth, while avoiding socialist entrapment.

The capitalist path to economic growth could not have been possible without corresponding changes in social structure. As Barrington Moore has documented so well, the transformation of a feudal system into a capitalist system is bound to encounter enormous social and political resistance from the landlord class.[24] Mancur Olson even argues that the elimination of feudal lords is a prerequisite for capitalist development.[25] South Korea was successful in removing the power and influence of the landlord class, and, thereby, opening the way for capitalist growth. Obviously, the demise of the Yi Dynasty and subsequent Japanese colonial rule precipitated the erosion of the feudal landlord class. Yet some elements survived[26] and founded the KDP after liberation. The move, in fact, was designed to protect their interests at the time of transitional uncertainty with the help of the American military government.[27] The KDP also supported Syngman Rhee with the hope of retaining their privilege and power. Though elected president with KDP support, Rhee soon detached himself from the party and thus weakened it. Forming the first cabinet in 1948, he assigned only two ministerial positions to KDP members, Kim Do-in to the Ministry of Finance and Lee In to the Ministry of Justice, and managed to pass the Land Reform Act in the 1949 National Assembly. As a result, the size of large landlords dwindled, while independent farmers were on the rise. The number of independent farmers rose from 17 percent in 1947 to 51 percent in 1951, underscoring a significant downfall in landlords.[28] The Korean War, subsequent land reforms, and industrial transformation led to the shrinking of landlords' power and contributed to solidifying capitalist development.

Finally, despite the sociopolitical instability and economic deformity that followed Japanese colonial rule and the Korean War, South Korea encountered a relatively favorable external economic environment. Geopolitical location, poor resource endowment, and chronic underdevelopment helped South Korea escape the trapping structure of dependency that is often seen as a major source of poverty and underdevelopment in Latin America and elsewhere.[29] American security interests in light of Cold War confrontation with the Soviet Union opened a window of opportunities for South Korea. The United States provided South Korea with extensive economic assistance, and induced it to adopt an export-led economic development strategy in the 1960s. Ensuring economic growth and prosperity was regarded as serving American national interests.

Adoption of a capitalist growth path, removal of the landlord class, and American economic assistance did not produce immediate outcomes. Both the First and Second Republics suffered from low growth, chronic inflation, and severe unemployment. However, they all served as crucial catalysts of economic growth when South Korea began to pursue an export-led growth strategy in the early 1960s.

In the Heart of Darkness: Political History of the Third through Sixth Republics

The Third through Sixth Republics, spanning from the downfall of the Second Republic in 1961 to the end of the Roh Tae Woo regime on February 25, 1993, had two main political and economic features. First, Korean politics experienced the rise and fall of authoritarian regimes led by the three presidents of the military clique: Park Chung Hee, Chun Doo Hwan, and Roh Tae Woo, eventually leading to democratic opening in June 1987. Second, while South Korea enjoyed unprecedented economic growth during this period, economic growth propelled by "developmental dictatorship" enhanced the political consciousness and power of Korean people, ultimately contributing to its demise.[30]

Constitutional Foundation of Authoritarian Politics

As with the two previous republics, constitutional order was not stable throughout the period of the Third through Sixth Republics. It was subject to frequent alterations and manipulations. There were all together five additional amendments of the constitution during this period: the fifth revision (December 26, 1962) giving birth to the Third Republic after the May 16 military coup; the sixth revision allowing a third presidential term for Park

(October 27, 1969); the seventh revision establishing the *Yushin* regime (December 27, 1972); the eighth revision (October 27, 1980) establishing the Chun Doo Hwan regime; and finally, the ninth revision (October 29, 1987) amending the terms of presidential election (see Appendix 1).

Immediately after the May 16 coup, the military replaced the existing constitution with the Law on Extraordinary Measures for National Reconstruction, and launched the Supreme Council for National Reconstruction (SCNR). Coup leaders declared anticommunism as the leading national doctrine and stressed political stability and economic reconstruction. They placed "old politicians" under a political ban by enacting the Political Purification Act and began to prepare the inauguration of the Third Republic. The fifth constitutional amendment bill was enacted on December 17, 1962 with a 78.8 percent approval of effective votes in the national referendum.

The gist of the new constitution was as follows: shift of power structure from parliamentarism to presidentialism; restoration of unicameralism in the National Assembly; reinforcing the official party endorsement for National Assembly candidacy; and loss of seats in the event of defection from a party or change of party affiliation.[31]

The constitutional amendment was followed by a presidential election in 1963. Park Chung Hee, the candidate of the newly organized Democratic Republican Party (DRP), defeated Yoon Po Sun, the unified candidate of the opposition parties, by a narrow margin. In the November general election, the DRP safeguarded the majority in the National Assembly by getting 110 (62.9 percent) of the 175 seats.[32] President Park was reelected in the October 17, 1967 presidential election. Instead of stepping down after his second term, he prolonged his political power through the '*Samson* Amendment' (which allowed for the third term) on September 9, 1969. Park played at will with the constitution to consolidate his power and elongate his rule. But the worst was yet to come.

On December 17, 1972, Park put the notorious *Yushin* Constitution into effect through the seventh amendment, which allowed him to remain as president indefinitely by not only abrogating the three-terms limit, but also by institutionalizing indirect election of president through the National Council for Reunification. The Park regime justified the *Yushin* amendment with reasons of national security. In light of heightened military threats from the North amid an eroding American security commitment, it argued that a stronger political system was necessary. With this, President Park convened an extraordinary cabinet meeting on October 17, 1972, and proclaimed marshal law, terminating the authority of the existing constitution. He also promulgated extraordinary measures, such as the dissolution of the National Assembly and a ban on political parties and their activities. The meeting passed the draft of constitutional amendment on October 27 and enacted it through the national referendum on November 21 by getting 91.5 percent approval. On December 23, the National Council for Reunification, which was newly formed as an ad hoc governance body, unanimously reelected President Park.[33] Official promulgation of the *Yushin* regime on December 27 was the most tragic day in the constitutional history of South Korea.

The *Yushin* constitution can be differentiated from previous ones by three important accounts. The first is with regard to the power of the newly established National Council for Reunification. The Council was endowed with power and authority to elect the president, to elect one third of National Assemblymen, and to make decisions on constitutional amendments proposed by the National Assembly. Second, it institutionalized imperial presidency by giving extraordinary power to the president, such as the right to dissolve the National Assembly, the extra-constitutional power to enact special measures, and the right to nominate one third of the National Assemblymen. Additionally, it stipulated the six-year presidential tenure without term limits, securing Park's life tenure in presidency. Finally, the power of the National Assembly was considerably weakened with the terms of session shortened and legislative oversight over the executive branch eliminated.[34] The *Yushin* system, intended to enhance national security and economic prosperity by replacing the "luxurious and inefficient" parliamentary politics with an efficient presidential system, ended on October 26, 1979, with the assassination of President Park by his trusted aide.

The demise of the *Yushin* regime did not lead to democratic opening and consolidation. A brief democratic opening in the spring of 1980 was shattered by another round of military intervention. Weak political leadership of the transitional government under Choi Kyu-Hah, internal division among political leaders, and social and economic crises, all reminiscent of the Second Republic, provided the military with an excuse to intervene in civil politics. After consolidating power in the military through a mutiny on December 12, 1979, the new military group, led by General Chun Doo Hwan and his followers, extended marshal law in May 17, 1980, and imposed a ban on political activity. In contrast with the 1961 military coup, the Korean people strongly opposed this attempt at military rule, as illustrated by the May 18 Kwangju uprising.

Chun brutally repressed the Kwangju uprising and other popular protests, and took power by forcing Choi Kyu-Hah to step down. General Chun (then lieutenant general) was elected president in a perfunctory election at the National Council for Reunification. The Council for Constitutional Amendment drafted a new constitution and enacted it through national referendum on October 27, 1980. It was the eighth constitutional amendment following the *Yushin* Amendment. The new constitution endowed the president with the power to form the temporary National Security Legislative Council, which would later pass the Reform Law of Political Climate to ban the activities of politicians. In February 1981, the presidential electoral college, which was similar to the National Council for Reunification under *Yushin*, elected Chun as president. In March, the Fifth Republic began with the general election. The new constitution was different from the *Yushin* in several respects. The president was limited explicitly to a seven-year single term, and the power of the National Assembly was also revived. However, the constitution also gave the president strong powers, such as the ability to disband the National Assembly, impose extraordinary measures, and submit constitutional amendment bills as well as laws.[35]

Like his predecessors, Chun also deliberated on extending his presidential tenure through a constitutional amendment toward the end of his term. However, his plots were revealed and triggered an avalanche of public protests.[36] Faced with such challenges, President Chun gave up and announced the April 13 Declaration regarding the preservation of the existing constitution. It was a strategic move to nominate and support his successor in winning the presidency without competition through the existing constitutional rule of indirect election of president. Public outcry escalated, and the streets bustled with student demonstrations. Opposition political parties formed a coalition with students and *chaeya* (antigovernment activists) and intensified public protests. This coalition and its actions would bear fruit, but not before several radical actions. In May 1986, four students of Seoul National University burned themselves to death calling for the "overturn of the Fifth Republic regime." In January 1987, the report of college student Park Jong-chul tortured to death shocked citizens. In May 1987, another college student from Yonsei University, Lee Han Yol, fell prey to violent police repression, precipitating the June uprising. At this point, finally, the silent majority of Korea, namely the middle class, began to join in on the antigovernment protests. This forced the Chun regime to yield and accept Roh Tae Woo's proposal, the June 29 Democratization Declaration. The Declaration was the fruit of combined efforts by the NDP, students, antigovernment activists, and the silent majority; on October 29, on the basis of the agreement among the three political leaders—Roh Tae Woo, Kim Young Sam, and Kim Dae Jung—the ninth *Jiksonje* (direct presidential election) Amendment was implemented.[37]

The ninth Amendment gave Koreans the hope of realizing a civilian government. As the two civilian political leaders, Kim Young Sam and Kim Dae Jung, failed to produce a single candidacy, this hope vanished, and Roh Tae Woo, an ex-military general, was elected as new president. The Sixth Republic under Roh was relatively democratic, but was still criticized for its politics of public security, T-K mafia dominance, and the politics of *Hanahoe* (a clandestine organization of military elite). Actual civilian rule would not occur until Kim Young Sam won in the presidential election of December 18, 1992.

National Assembly and Party Politics in the Dark Age

As noted before, the constitution of the Third Republic, which was amended in December 1962, revived the presidential system blended with unicameralism. Until the end of the Fifth Republic, the South Korean legislative was nothing but an appendage to the "administrative state." Appointment of cabinet members, including the prime minister, no longer required legislative approval.[38] A two-member district system allowed for the simultaneous election of candidates from both ruling and opposition parties. Executive dominance over the legislative branch was further institutionalized with presidential power to nominate one-third of the *Yujonghoe* (National Assembly members). The *Yushin* constitution also abolished the parliamentary inspection of the administration and limited the term of parliamentary sessions to 150 days a year.[39] The political role of the National Assembly during the *Yushin* period was emasculated, acting as nothing more than a rubber stamp.

The National Assembly under the Fifth Republic more or less regained its political roles. The *Yujonghoe* was disbanded; instead, the same number of legislators were to be assigned to political parties according to the principle of proportional representation. The formula of proportional representation automatically assigned two-thirds of the legislators to the ruling party. In fact, the opposition parties were fabricated and controlled by the government. Legislative investigation of the administration was revived on some limited issues, although it never went into full effect during the Fifth Republic. The National Assembly remained the "maid of the executive."[40]

The parliamentary system of Korea became more democratic only after the June 29 Democratization Declaration in 1987. The constitution of the Sixth Republic annulled various premiums of the ruling party, and the National Assembly became powerful. While legislative inspection of the administration was fully restored, national assemblymen were assertive in lawmaking as well as other activities as evidenced by holding a hearing of the Fifth Republic that brought former president Chun Doo Hwan to testify on his abuse and misuse of power during his reign.

Regarding party politics, South Korea experienced frequent institutional changes during the Third to Sixth Republics. The constitution and laws of the First and Second Republics contained no clauses on political parties.[41] After the May 16 military coup, some provisions were made in accordance with the "Kim Jong Pil plan."[42] They include party endorsement of national assembly candidates, deprivation of seats in the case of defection or change of party affiliation, and prohibition of independent candidacy for the National Assembly. These institutional arrangements provided the president of the Third Republic with de facto power to dominate the National Assembly through the strong ruling party. The Political Party Law, the progeny of the Third Republic's Constitution, prescribed stricter requirements for the organization of a political party. To be legally recognized, a political party was required to have branches in more than the one-half of the total electoral districts (131 districts at the time). Furthermore, branches had to be spread among more than five major cities and provinces, including Seoul and Pusan, and each branch had to have at least 100 qualified members.[43] Along with the single-member small-district system, these requirements blocked the advent of small or radical parties, while facilitating a conservative two-party system. In the Third Republic, the system of a strong ruling party and fragmented opposition parties merged into a two-party system composed of the ruling Democratic Republican Party (129 seats out of 175) and the opposing New Democratic Party (45 seats, and 1 seat from the People's Party). In the seventh National Assembly molded in 1971, the DRP and the NDP shared 204 total seats, a proportion of 113 to 89.

The Korean political party system lost many of its features in 1972 with the introduction of the *Yushin* system. Among other changes, the *Yushin* constitution relaxed the requirements for the organization of a political party. For instance, the minimum number of required branches was reduced from one-half to one-third of the total number of districts and the number of required members of a branch dropped from 100 to 50 people.[44] President Park's phobia of political parties and the powerful National Assembly were significant factors contributing to the new institutional arrangement. He preferred loyalist groups such as high-level bureaucrats, the intelligence agency, *Yujonghoe*, the organizations for *Saemaul Undong*, and presidential aides to political parties as his agents.[45] Consequently, the role and size of the ruling DRP during the *Yushin* period were considerably curtailed. State dominance over the ruling party were solidified, and the dynamics of political society vanished.[46]

An institutional outlook of the two-party system, however, was kept even in the *Yushin* system. Due to the crippled DRP, the opposing NDP was given relatively more political weight. The moderate wing, led by Lee Chul-seung, who favored "compromise and bargaining," prevailed in the opposition camp. The image of being a struggling opposition party was greatly improved when the NDP outvoted the DRP by a margin of 1.1 percent in the tenth general election. Kim Young Sam, a hard-liner against the ruling party, was elected as the leader in May 1979.[47] From that point on, the party politics of Korea polarized, precipitating social and political instability and contributing greatly to the assassination of President Park on October 26, 1979.

The revised Political Party Law of November 25, 1980, rejuvenated political parties and encouraged the multiparty system.[48] The National Council for Reunification was replaced with the Presidential Electoral College, and party endorsement became a requirement to qualify for presidential candidacy. Deposit money for the party-endorsed candidates was also substantially reduced. Additionally, the requirements to form a political party were relaxed: the required number of branches dropped from one-third to one-fourth of the total number of districts, the minimum number of projectors of a party was reduced from "more than thirty people" to "more than twenty people," and the required minimum members of a branch were decreased from "more than fifty people" to "more than thirty people." Hence, the eleventh National Assembly was composed of the Democratic Justice Party (DJP: ruling party), the Democratic Korean Party (DKP), and the National Party (NP). The New Democratic Party (NDP) was added to the list in the twelfth National Assembly.

However, one should be careful in attaching too much political meaning to the above institutional modifications, since the Fifth Republic's military government was illegally established and based on fear, intimidation, and repression. The ruthless crackdown of the Kwangju uprising is a telling evidence. Moreover, President Chun was elected through the so-called Gymnasium Election devoid of fair competition. Hence, political party rejuvenation faced serious limitations. The policy of encouraging a multiparty system was merely a different version of the previous conservative two-party system without progressive or radical parties. Despite this manipulation of party politics, the rise of the NDP in the twelfth National Assembly deserves attention. While the eleventh National Assembly was composed of the ruling and government-manufac-tured opposition parties, a major change took place. Only two months after its formation, the NDP entered the twelfth general election race in February 1985 and won the second largest number of seats in the National Assembly only next to the ruling DJP. The NDP afterward played a key role in leading democratic movements and obtaining a compromise from Chun, which resulted in democ-ratic opening in June 1987 and the collapse of the authoritarian Fifth Republic.

Developmental Dictatorship and Economic Performance

While constitutional order, legislature, and party politics were subjected to authoritarian control and manipulation, the South Korean economy showed remarkable performance during this period. South Korea's per capita income was less than US$100 in 1960, but rose almost to $10,000 by the end of the Sixth Republic. Despite sporadic dismal performance, growth rates recorded aver-age annuals of more than 10 percent from 1961 to 1987. By the end of 1987, South Korea emerged as one of the top twenty largest economies in the world. In particular, its export drive alarmed the world. Until the recent economic crisis and economic IMF trustee-ship, South Korea had been touted as a model case of economic development, becoming the forerunner of the Newly Industrializing Economies. Given the vicious cycle of poverty and underdevelop-ment of the First and Second Republics, economic performance during the period from 1961 to 1987 may well be labeled a "miracle." What factors are responsible for South Korea's economic performance? Perhaps the most important is the timely sequencing of the development strategy. South Korea pursued import substitution industrialization in the 1950s, which deepened economic stagnation. When Park Chung Hee seized political power through a military coup in 1961, he made a drastic transition to an export-led growth strategy. The transition was made due to dismal economic performances, American pressure, and leadership commitment. In the 1960s, labor-intensive light industries such as clothing, footwear, and electronic appliances were singled out as strategic sectors. During the 1970s, however, the target sectors shifted to heavy and chemical industries involving steel, shipbuilding, automobile, heavy machinery, electronics, petro-chemical, and nonferrous metal. In 1979–1980, the big push based on heavy-chemical industrialization encountered a major crisis due to overinvestment, duplication, and hostile international economic environments. Nevertheless, these sectors became the primary source of the second coming of the Korean economy in the mid-1980s.

Equally important was the labor control policy. The Third through Sixth Republics consistently repressed wages below the level of labor productivity in order to enhance international competitiveness. Some variations are observable between the periods of the 1960s and the 1970–1980s.[49] During the 1960s, low wages and extended working hours were induced primarily through the market mechanism. This was possible due to the massive exodus of labor from rural areas, facilitated by a series of government policies favoring the modern urban sector. The excessive supply of labor functioned as the market mechanism that maintained low wage and long daily hours of labor. Rapid expansion of export industries during the late 1960s and the early 1970s, however, altered labor market conditions, causing excessive demands of labor and, consequently, lack of labor. The market mechanism could no longer effectively sustain the low-wage policy. The Korean government decided to stick to the low-wage policy by relying on "coercive" measures. The *Yushin* political system was instituted partly for maintaining low wages through control of the labor sector. The incessant struggles of industrial labor, as manifested in such incidents as the self-burning of Chun Tae-il and the arson of the KAL building, were byproducts of the low wage policy and labor repression. Yet the Chun regime continued to repress labor, and tensions between state and labor heightened. Nevertheless, continuing low wages, secured through systematic exclusion of the popular sector, allowed South Korea to enjoy international competitiveness and the fruits of economic growth. But the democratic opening in 1987 opened wide the window of opportunities for workers, so that they could increase their wages through political bargaining.

Apart from development strategy and labor, there are several other factors that contributed to South Korea's economic growth. First is leadership commitment. While Park Chung Hee pushed for modernization and industrialization with the unprecedented "can-do" spirit, Chun Doo Hwan overcame the economic crisis of 1980 by implementing macroeconomic stabilization without interruption. For both leaders, economic growth was an essential prerequisite for national security and political legitimacy, and thus, they elevated developmentalism as a hegemonic ideology. Second, state structure also mattered. While executive dominance freed economic policy-making from legislative intervention, competent and relatively meritocratic bureaucrats, recruited through a highly competitive examination system, guided the national economy.[50] Finally, insulation of economic policy-making from contending social and political pressures allowed the formation of efficient, coherent, and consistent policies and their effective implementation. Indeed, state strength and autonomy played a critical role in shaping economic performance during 1961 through 1987. But these two elements of success were by and large a result of authoritarian mode of governance. In other words, it cannot be denied that impressive economic growth under the Third to Sixth Republics emanated from developmental dictatorship, posing a profound tradeoff between political liberty and economic growth.

While developmental dictatorship shaped an internal landscape favorable to rapid economic growth, external environments also were, in essence, conducive to the South Korean economy during this period. An export-led development strategy is predicated on a deeper integration in the international economy. The integration entails both opportunities and constraints. For relatively small countries like South Korea, the costs of integration can be higher than its benefits. Yet South Korea under the Park and Chun regimes successfully turned risks into opportunities and paved the way for economic transformation.

Three factors deserve to be highlighted in this regard. First is Park's strategic maneuver founded on his nationalist disposition. President Park at times adopted the doctrines of "dependence on the U.S." or "pro-Japanese stance" for economic purposes. He was, however, also staunchly nationalist. After the normalization of diplomatic relations with Japan in 1965, the Park regime induced Japanese capital and funneled it into exports.[51] In doing so, Park preferred loans to direct investment until the mid-1970s, when the capacity to return the principals and interests reached its uppermost limits.[52] The move was designed to reduce dependency on foreign capital. In the 1970s, Park also pushed the heavy-chemical industrialization plan against the will of the Japan and the United States. This was partly due to Park's obsession with the defense industry. Second was the geopolitical factor. Despite potentially damaging boomerang effects, the United States drove South Korea to adopt an export-led growth strategy, allowed South Korea's free-riding in American domestic markets disregarding the reciprocity principal of the GATT, and helped it access international capital. The United States compromised its economic interests in pursuit of military security. Comparativists of East Asian economic success and the stagnated Latin American economies explain the different outcomes with the concept of the Grand Area.[53] Finally, luck also mattered. At the time of South Korea's transition to an outward-looking strategy, the world economy was under a boom cycle, facilitating export market expansion. South Korea's labor-intensive export promotion in the mid-1960s coincided with the Vietnam boom, opening export markets for military uniforms, blankets, and other military supplies. The oil crisis of 1973–1974 undermined the South Korean economy, but the Middle East construction boom helped the Park regime survive through hard times. The Chun regime also benefited from the boom and bust cycle of the international economy. "Three lows" (interest rates, oil price, and currency rate) facilitated Chun in securing the economic recovery in the mid-1980s.

In view of the above, economic performance under the Third to Sixth Republics was a result of the dynamic interplay of developmental dictatorship and favorable external environments.

Broken Promises: Politics and Economy under the Kim Young Sam Government

After three decades of military and authoritarian rule, South Korea gave birth to a genuinely civilian government through the fourteenth presidential election held in December 1992. Kim Young Sam was elected president by winning slightly over 40 percent of votes. Inauguration of the Kim Young Sam government marked a triumphant page in the modern history of Korean politics. As noted before, Kim Young Sam, along with Kim Dae Jung, was a champion of democratic causes and antigovernment movements since the First Republic. Yet in 1990, Kim departed from the opposition circle and formed a grand conservative coalition with the ruling Democratic Justice Party (DJP) along with Kim Jong Pil's National Party (NP). After fierce internal struggles, Kim Young Sam managed to win a party nomination for the fourteenth presidential race, and defeated Kim Dae Jung and Chung Ju Yung in the presidential election. Although Kim Young Sam won the presidency through fair competition, he was confronted with the burden of forming a coalition with former enemies he had fought so hard against in the past. Partly to offset such negative image, and partly to expedite the process of democratic consolidation, the Kim government undertook sweeping political, social, and economic reforms.

Immediately after inauguration, Kim undertook a series of political reforms.[54] His reforms were framed around two major themes. One was to restore authentic "civilian" (*munmin*) politics, and the other was to clean dirty politics.

"Civilian" politics denotes the construction of a power structure based on the outcome of the fourteenth presidential election by removing old legacies of military culture from Korean politics. Indeed, Korean politics has been infested with military legacies: authoritarian rule, vertical command, abuse and misuse of security apparatus, politicization of the military, and prevalence of regional politics.

In order to undertake reforms targeting these military legacies, President Kim appointed the reform-minded to key presidential staff posts. He also recruited such former antigovernment figures as Han Wan-sang, Kim Dukryong, Oh Byung-moon, Hwang San-sung, and Lee In-je to cabinet posts.[55] Kim took drastic measures to depoliticize national security organizations that had been misused for regime security. Surprisingly, he chose Kim Duck, a professor of international relations, as the head of the Agency for National Security Planning (former KCIA), and restructured the agency by banning its intervention in domestic political affairs as well as by reducing its size. The notorious Korean National Security Command (NSC), which served as the most important instrument of political surveillance and intimidation during the Chun regime, was also subject to substantial restructuring, downsizing, and alteration of its functions. The NSC was no longer permitted to interfere with civilian affairs, and its role was strictly delimited to the military domain. The rank of its commander was lowered from lieutenant general to major general, and direct reporting to the president was prohibited with the rearrangement of its chain of command and report through the Minister of National Defense.[56]

Perhaps one of the most significant achievements of Kim's democratic reforms was the civilianization of the military. Chronic military intervention in civil politics, as manifested by Park and Chun, was due partly to intramilitary factionalism. Since the days of Park Chung Hee, *Hanahoe* (Society for Oneness), emerged as the dominant faction in the military whose members enjoyed special treatments in promotion and assignments. Membership surged and was more prominent in the Fifth and Sixth Republics as it was founded by Chun Doo Hwan and Roh Tae Woo. The faction demoralized military officers and heightened the opportunities for military intervention in civil politics. Against this backdrop, President Kim began to purge and disband *Hanahoe*. He dismissed its members from key military posts, such as Chief of the Staff of the army, commander of the NSC, and other strategic commanding posts. Its members were also eliminated from the promotion list. Despite initial concerns, purification of the military was undertaken with no negative spin-off, and the opportunities for military intervention in civil politics were fundamentally curtailed.

Another negative legacy of three decades of military rule was the regional monopoly of positional values in Korean society. All three military leaders—Park, Chun, and Roh—came from the city of Taegu in the province of Kyongsangbuk. They recruited and appointed people from the Taegu-Kyongbuk area to important political and administrative posts, resulting in the formation of the T-K mafia during the Third through Sixth Republics. Thus, removing the T-K mafia from the political and government circle posed a major task of democratic reform under Kim, and the Kim government made good progress in this regard. Of fifty key government posts, only three were allocated to those from the T-K area in the initial phase of cabinet formation.[57] However, the problem arose with the T-K mafia gradually being replaced by the "P-K" mafia (the Pusan-Kyongsangnam region). The P-K area is the stronghold of President Kim Young Sam, and like his predecessors, Kim also recruited heavily from his own province. In light of this, his reform efforts to remove regionalism were tainted.

Along with civilian politics, "clean politics" constituted another pillar of Kim's democratic reforms. Initiated with the "cam-

paign to clean the upper stream," its rationale was clear: dirty political practices would not disappear without first cleaning up the ruling elite. On March 4, 1993, President Kim declared that he would
not collect a single penny for political funds.[58] Along with this declaration, he banned the traditional practices of raising and distributing slush funds within the political circle. As part of the campaign, he refused to meet business leaders and made public his
personal assets. He also forced all high-ranking government officials, including ruling party members of the National Assembly, to
annually open their assets to the public. As a result, it has become
easier to monitor changes in personal assets held by these officials.

The system worked. Several high-ranking officials had to
resign under charges of illicit wealth accumulation. The new government finally reached an agreement with opposition parties to
put the Public Officials' Ethics Law into effect on May 20, 1993,
which obligated the disclosure to the public and registration of
1,167 high government officials' personal assets.

As part of the "clean politics" campaign, President Kim implemented the real-name financial transaction system through an
emergency decree on August 12, 1993. The system—designed to
prevent illicit financial transactions as well as to raise tax revenues
by obligating real-name bank deposits—was originally conceived by
Chun Doo Hwan, but opposition from the business community and
the political circle had aborted it. Roh Tae Woo also adopted its
immediate implementation as his election campaign pledge, but
had failed to deliver it. The real-name financial transaction system
brought about several positive outcomes.[59] Not only did it contribute to severing corrupt ties between politicians and businessmen, the arrest of former presidents Chun and Roh offered a critical momentum. The new system helped government authorities
trace their slush funds—each had amassed an astronomical
amount of slush funds exceeding 50 trillion won during their
respective reigns—illicitly taken from businessmen. Jailed under
charges of corruption, their arrest also implicated chief executives
from leading *chaebols*. Even opposition political leaders confessed
to taking illicit political funds.

In the wake of the arrests of two former presidents, President
Kim launched another campaign, the campaign for correcting past
history. Upon his inauguration, President Kim made it clear that he
would investigate the political wrongdoings of those who were
involved in the mutiny on December 12, 1979, the illicit seizure of
political power in May 1980, and the violent repression of the

Kwangju uprisings, including Chun and Roh. The disclosure of the slush funds allowed Kim the opportunity to not only investigate but also to indict the two former presidents under an additional charge of treason and to arrest all those involved in the military coup of 1979 and 1980. This was truly an unintended consequence of the democratic reforms.

The "clean politics" campaign also touched on electoral campaign issues. In the past, political corruption occurred because of the high costs of election campaigns. In tandem with the real-name financial transaction system, President Kim pushed for reforms of campaign and political funds. As a result, the National Assembly passed two laws, the Integrated Election Act and the Political Fund Act, in its 166th temporary session on March 4, 1993. Both acts aimed at establishing institutional mechanisms to guarantee inexpensive, or fair elections. Although the legal limit of campaign funds was 120 million won, loose enforcement of the law allowed candidates to spend several billion won. The new act delimited the amount to 53 million won per candidate, installed a strict mechanism of monitoring and enforcement, and required candidates to open their personal assets to the public. Punishment for violating the law was severe.[60] By institutionalizing the rule of fair competition, the reforms also significantly curtailed the premiums of the ruling party, such as support from the administration, virtual monopoly of political fund, and easy access to mass media.[61] Although there were some deviations, these reform measures were relatively well observed throughout the local elections in 1995, the general election in 1996, and the presidential election in 1997. The stunning victory of the opposition parties in the 1995 local election and the 1997 presidential election offer eloquent testimonial.

Despite this impressive political reform effort, the Kim Young Sam government was dealt a critical blow with the Hanbo scandal, severely damaging the image of "clean politics." In December 1996, Hanbo Steel went bankrupt after borrowing almost 5 trillion won from banking and financial institutions. Its delinquent loans paralyzed several commercial banks and drove hundreds of subcontractors to the brink of collapse. It was later disclosed that Hanbo had secured banks loans through political connections. Kim Hyun-chol, second son of President Kim; Hong In-gil, the most trusted presidential aide; and several others, including cabinet members, were indicted and eventually put in jail. The developments implied that Kim's "clean politics" campaign was nothing but a fiction. Investigation of Kim Hyun-chol revealed another important fact: that

President Kim had also amassed a considerable amount of slush funds for the 1992 presidential election. Kim's achievement in democratic reforms was shattered, and his public apology was televised nationally.

Kim's reforms were not limited to the political domain, but also extended to social and economic issues. From the beginning, the Kim Young Sam government faced two contradictory tasks: enhance international competitiveness while accommodating popular demands for equality and improved quality of life.

As a way of improving international competitiveness, President Kim undertook a globalization campaign, designed to free South Korea from parochial nationalism and defensive mercantilism and to prepare for infinite competition in international market places. The Kim government liberalized domestic markets by ratifying the Uruguay Round in the name of globalization. It also fostered an admission to the OECD, resulting in greater liberalization of domestic financial and capital markets. As government regulations emerged as a major barrier to international competitiveness,[62] deregulation was also accelerated.[63] Furthermore, the globalization campaign pushed for privatization of public enterprises and banks, and for liberalization of interest rates. The purposes were, no doubt, to encourage private investment in the manufacturing businesses, to carve out the corruption caused by the tradition of government initiation, and to promote competitive market activities by enhancing market competition. The ultimate goal was to place South Korea among the Group of Seven (G-7) members by the early part of the twenty-first century. To this end, new economic targets were set to increase the GNP per capita from $7,000 in 1992 to $15,000 in 1997, by maintaining an average annual growth rate of 7–8 percent per year, and to boost trade volume from $158 billion in 1992 to $400 billion in 1998.[64] However, facing the nation's worst financial and foreign exchange crises, the Kim Young Sam government filed for national economic bankruptcy with the IMF, requesting a $57 billion bailout. Through this action, President Kim transformed national pride in the economic miracle shaped by developmental dictatorship into national shame and despair. Kim's popularity declined from over 90 percent in 1993 to a low single digit in 1997.

As a way of enhancing equality and the quality of life, President Kim paid the utmost attention to, among others, labor and small- and medium-size firms, but was unable to fulfill his original pledges in these areas. In the beginning, Kim sought progressive labor reforms by appointing Lee In-je, a reform-minded lawyer and national assemblyman, as labor minister. Lee favored a progressive labor policy such as "no work-partial wage" (i.e., employer supports the fundamental expenses of labor such as traffic and meals during strikes) as well as multiple unions and unions' political activities.[65] Yet evident through the passage of the labor reform bill in December of 1996 are the considerable concessions the Kim Young Sam government made to the business community, including the permission of flexible layoffs with two-year probation. The Kim government's original plan to revive small- and medium-size firms, while diffusing the economic concentration of *chaebols*, was never realized.

Conclusion: Toward a New Political Horizon

This chapter is intended to trace the historical trajectory of South Korea's political development and economic changes over the last half century. Presenting an overview of fifty years of development in a single chapter is a presumptuous task. South Korea's political landscape is full of fractured pains, despair, and hopes. Democratic opening in 1987 and the subsequent process of democratic consolidation gave Koreans high hopes for a mature democracy. Yet democratic reforms begun under Kim Young Sam remain unfinished. Economic success, which has been South Korea's trademark, was undeniably enhanced by developmental dictatorship. Democratic changes, while associated with the economic downturn, did not impede its growth path.

Two stunning changes occurred after this chapter was written: an acute economic crisis and subsequent IMF rescue financing, and the election of Kim Dae Jung as president. The occurrence of both events were unthinkable to the minds of Koreans. Koreans were not concerned or aware of the depth of the economic crisis due to healthy macroeconomic indicators. No one believed that Kim, who had already previously run for president three times, would win the election—not only due to deeply rooted regional animosities, but also because of the structural disadvantage associated with being a candidate from the opposition party.

The two events bear paradoxical implications. South Korea was once touted as a model of economic development for the third world, while being criticized for its political backwardness. The trend now seems to be in reverse. The election of Kim Dae Jung as president underscores the first peaceful transfer of power between the ruling and opposition parties in the modern history of South Korean politics. Democratization consolidation is no longer rhetoric, but a reality. After a long, uncertain process of political development, South Korea is truly reaching a new horizon of democratic politics. Meanwhile, South Korea's economy has fallen into default. IMF conditionalities have produced an increasingly difficult economic situation involving mass corporate bankruptcy, high unemployment, and grave distributional consequences. This mismatch of democratic triumph and economic downturn is sure to pose formidable constraints on the political leadership of Kim Dae Jung, and it is yet to be seen how Kim undertakes IMF demands without undermining democratic ideals.

Notes

1. Of the nine revisions, five were amendments made by Presidents Syngman Rhee, Park Chung Hee, and Chun Doo Hwan to prolong or seize political power illegally. Four of the revisions were undertaken to establish a new government after the collapse of the previous regime. All nine revisions purported to establish or consolidate presidential power, except in the case of the Second Republic, when the revision was made to establish parliamentarism.

2. Due to Article 55 of the Act of American Military Rule that defined a political party as "any group that is engaging in political activities in any way with more than three members," political parties proliferated. For instance, the number of political parties registered with the Public Information Bureau of the U.S. Military Government Office totaled 107 in June 1946 and 344 in 1947. The number of South Korean political parties and social groups registered as the counterpart of consultation in the Common Council of the United States and Soviet Union was 422. See Hyong-sop Yoon, "*Han'guk Chungchi Kwajong*" ["Political Process in Korea"], in Woon-Tai Kim et al., *Han'guk Chongchiron* [Korean Politics] (Seoul: Pakyongsa, 1982), p. 387.

3. The distribution of seats in the May 10 General Election in 1948 was: the National Society for Independence Promotion (pro-Syngman Rhee), fifty-five; KDP, twenty-nine; and the majority of remaining seats were won by independent candidates. However, about sixty independent elects were pro-KDP. See Chang-song Moon, "*Hanmindangun odero kana?*" ["Where Goes the Hanmin Party?"], *The Shinchonji* (August 1948), p. 26.

4. For details of the crisis surrounding the *Balchwe* Amendment, see, Byungsik Shin, "Pusan Chongchi Padongkwa Syngman Rhee Chejeui Hwagrip," in *Kuyongrok Kyosu Hoegap Kinyom Nonmunjip* [Collection of

Theses to Honor Professor Yongrok Ku] (Seoul: Bopmunsa, 1994), pp. 567–599; Keunsik Yoon, *"Han'guk Chongchihyongtae: Che 1 Konghwaguk"* ["Political Form in Korea: The First Republic"], in Kim, et al., *Han'guk Chongchiron*, op. cit., pp. 246–262.

5. Keunsik Yoon, Ibid., pp. 256–257.

6. Ibid., p. 258.

7. Growth rates of GNP were 8.7 percent in 1957, 7.0 percent in 1958, 5.2 percent in 1959, and 2.1 percent in 1960, and the unemployment rate in 1960 was 20 percent. Hochul Sonn, *Towards a Synthetic Approach of Third World Political Economy: The Case of South Korea* (Unpublished Ph.D. Dissertation, University of Texas at Austin, 1987), p. 244.

8. Keunsik Yoon, "Han'guk Chongchihyongtae: Che 2 Konghwaguk" ["Political Form in Korea: The Second Republic"], in Kim, *Hanguk Chongchiron*, op. cit., pp. 263–273.

9. For instance, see Gabriel Almond and Sidney Verba, *The Civic Culture* (Princeton: Little, Brown and Co., 1963), ch. 13; Samuel P. Huntington, *Political Order in Changing Societies* (New Haven: Yale University Press, 1968).

10. For details of the processes of the fourth constitutional amendment, see Sung Joe Hahn, *Che 2 Konghwagukkwa Han'gukui Minjujuui* ["The Second Republic and the Korean Democracy"] (Seoul: Chongrosochok, 1983), ch. 7.

11. For evidence of strong parliamentary power during the early First Republic, see Yoon, op. cit. pp. 260–261.

12. See note 2.

13. Ibid.

14. For details of the activities of political parties during the three years after the liberation, see Soong Hoom Kil, *"Chongdang Chongchiui Taedongkwa Ku Chongae"* ["The Origin of Political Party System and Its Development"], in Han'guk Chongchi Yonkuso [Institute for Korean Politics], ed., *Han'gukui Hyondae Chongchi: 1945–1948* [Contemporary Politics in Korea: 1945–1948] (Seoul: Seoul National University Press), pp. 187–203.

15. Feudal landowners that constituted the mainstay of the KDP made great contributions to the independence movement against Japan but failed to gain mass support. Thus, they attempted to form a coalition with members of the provisional government camp or the Syngman Rhee camp. See Bruce Cumings, *The Origins of the Korean War* (Princeton: Princeton University Press, 1981), vol. 1, ch. 6.

16. See note 3.

17. Hahn, *Che 2 Konghwagukkwa Han'gukui Minjujuui*, op. cit., p. 84.

18. The DP's lack of sensitivity to Cho's plight can be attributed partly to sheer political calculation. Cho's Progressive Party had a broad support base in the urban area, undercutting the DP's constituency. See Yoon, op. cit., p. 258.

19. In the Lower House, the Social People's Party and the Korean Society Party won 4 seats and 1 seat, respectively. In the Upper House, each party won one seat. (See Table 3.1.)

20. See Byung-young Ahn, *"Han'gukui Chongdang Chejewa Chong-dangnaeui Pabolhaengtae"* ["Political Party System in Korea and Intra-party Factionalism"] in *Kim Woon-Tai Kyosu Hwagapkinyom Nonmumjip: Han'guk Chongchi Haengjongui Chekye* [Collection of Theses to Honor Professor Woon-Tai Kim: Administrative System of Korean Politics] (Seoul: Pakyongsa, 1982), p. 83.

21. Bruce Cumings, "The Origins and Development of the Northeast Asian Political Economy," *International Organization* 48:1 (Winter 1994), pp. 25–27.

22. The *Shinganhoe* Movement in 1927 offered the momentum of left-ist dominance in independence movements by weakening the base of right-wing nationalists. Duk-kyu Chin, *Han'guk Chongdangsahoeui Konryokgu-joe Kwanhan Yonku* [Research on Power Structure of Korean Political Party Society] (Ph.D. Dissertation, Yonsei University, 1977), pp. 155–158.

23. The number of leftists released from the prison reached approximately 16,000. See Cumings, op. cit., p. 73.

24. Barrington Moore, *Social Origins of Dictatorship and Democracy* (Toronto: Beacon Press, 1966).

25. Mancur Olson, *The Rise and Decline of Nations* (New Haven: Yale University Press, 1982), ch. 1.

26. Chin, op. cit., p. 160.

27. Ji-yon Shim, *"Posuyadangui Ppuri, Hanmindangui Konggwa"* ["The Root of Conservative Opposition Party, Hanmindang"], in Hanguk Ilbosa, ed., *Hangukûi Chôngdang* [Political Parties in Korea], p. 170.

28. According to data that shows the patterns of the ownership of land at the time, the ratio of independent farmers was 17 percent in 1947, 37 percent in 1949, and 51 percent in 1951. Ahn, op. cit., p. 214.

29. Andre G. Frank, "The Development of Underdevelopment," in James D. Cockcroft, A. G. Frank and Dale L. Johnson, *Development and*

Underdevelopment: Latin America's Political Economy (Garden City, NY: Anchor Books, 1972), pp. 3–17; Immanuel Wallerstein, "The Rise and Future Demise of the World Capitalist System: Concepts for Comparative Analysis," *Comparative Studies in Society and History* (September 1974), pp. 387–415.

30. See Chung-in Moon and Yong-cheol Kim, "A Circle of Paradox: Development and Democracy in South Korea," in Adrian Leftwich, ed., *Development and Democracy* (Cambridge: Polity Press, 1996).

31. Yoon, "Han'guk Chongchihyongtae: Che 3 Konghwaguk" ["Political Form in Korea: The Third Republic"], in Kim, op. cit., pp. 273–283.

32. See Appendix 2.

33. Woon-Tai Kim, "Han'guk Chongchihyongtae: Che 4 Konghwaguk" ["Political Form in Korea: The First Republic"], in Kim, op. cit., p. 291.

34. Ibid., pp. 291–297.

35. Woon-Tai Kim, "Han'guk Chongchihyongtae: Che 5 Konghwaguk" ["Political Form in Korea: The Fifth Republic"], in Kim, op. cit., pp. 307–310.

36. For details of the debates on constitutional amendment at the time, see Jae-hee Nam and Kwan-yong Park, "Minjuhwanun Kwonryokbunsanuro" ["From Democratization to Diffusion of Power"], *The Monthly Chosun* (April 1986), pp. 124–135; Min-woo Lee, "Kaehonun Umjikilsuopun Kukminui Hapui" ["Constitutional Reform is Unmovable National Consensus"], *The Shindonga* (June 1986), pp. 212–219; Young Sam Kim, "Kaehonun Hungjongui Taesangi Anida" ["Constitutional Reform is not the Object of Bargaining"], Ibid., pp. 238–247; Chul-seung Lee, "Naegakchaekimjenun Chehoniraeui Sosin" ["My Faith in Parliamentary System"], Ibid., pp. 248–255; Chul Kim, "4·13 Kaehon Yubogyoldankwa Chongguk Panghyang" ["The Delay of Constitutional Reform and Political Atmosphere"], Ibid., pp. 158–165.

37. Min Kang, "Che 6 Konghwaguk Minjuhwaui Kujojuk Hankyewa Chongchisanghwangui Nonri" ["Structural Limit of Democracy of the Sixth Republic and the Logic of Political Situation"], in Korean Political Science Association, ed., *Han'guk Chongchiui Minjuhwawa T'ongil P'angan* [Democratization of Korean Politics and Alternatives for National Unification] (Seoul: Ulyumunhwasa, 1990), p. 28.

38. Yoon, op. cit., p. 280.

39. Kim, *Han'guk Chongchihyongtae: Che 4 Konghwaguk*, op. cit., pp. 291–297.

40. Ibid., pp. 307–313.

41. Yoon, op. cit., pp. 280–281.

42. The "Kim Jong Pil plan" was to establish a political party system in which political parties undertake every significant political activity such as the election of the National Assemblymen, official endorsement, and the roll-call vote in the National Assembly following the model of the British party system. Su-young Choi, *"Konghwadanggwa Kim Jong-pil Plan"* ["Republic Party and Kim Jong-pil Plan"], *The Sasanggye* no. 119 (March 1963), pp. 178–183.

43. Yoon, *Han'guk Chongchi Kwajong*, op. cit., p. 369.

44. Ibid.; Kim, *"Han'guk Chongchihyngtae: Che 4 Konghwaguk,"* op. cit., pp. 294–295.

45. *Chungang Songo Kwanriwiwonhoe*, ed., *Taehanminguk Chong-dangsa: Che 1 jip* [History of Political Parties in ROK 1945–1972], vol. 1 (1981), p. 392.

46. Ibid.

47. Korean voters in the 1960s and 1970s contributed to the formation of a two-party system with their reluctance, in the hope of having a unified opposition party, to support the independent candidates. See Ahn, op. cit., p. 94.

48. Woon-Tai Kim, "Han'gukj Chongchihyongtae: Che 5 Konghwaguk" ["Political Form in Korea: The Fifth Republic"], op. cit., pp. 314–315.

49. Hyuck-baeg Im, *The Market, the State, and the Democracy: Korean Democratic Transition and Theories of Political Economy* (Seoul: Nanam, 1994), pp. 41–42.

50. Ezra F. Vogel, *Japan As a Number One: Lessons from America* (Cambridge: Harvard University Press, 1979), ch. 7; Roy Hofheinz, Jr. and Kent E. Calder, *The East Asia Edge* (NY: Basic Books, 1982), pp. 113–114.

51. *Nihonkeizaichosakai, Kankokukeizaino Zitsuzyo* (Tokyo: Keizaio-raisha, 1964), pp. 140–146.

52. Foreign loans, despite the repayment burden of principal and interest, tend to be less externally dependent than direct investment since the recipient country retains autonomy in distribution.

53. See note 36.

54. For an overview of political reforms and globalization under the Kim Young Sam government, see Chung-in Moon and Jongryn Mo, eds., *Democratization and Globalization in Korea: Assessments and Prospects* (Seoul: Yonsei University Press, 1999).

55. For details of President Kim's personnel management policy, see, *The Sisa Journal* (February 28, 1993).

56. *Donga Ilbo*, March 31, 1993.

57. *The Weekly Toyosinmun*, March 10, 1993.

58. *Donga Ilbo*, March 5, 1994.

59. Kwang Choi and Jong-bum An, "Kumyungsilmyongje: Nonriwa Chongchaek Kwaje" ["Real Name System: Its Logic and Future Tasks"], Korean Political Science Association, ed., *Munminjongbuwa Chongchigaehyok* [Civil Government and Political Reform] (December 1993), pp. 147–148.

60. *Donga Ilbo*, March 4, 1994.

61. *Chosun Ilbo*, March 11, 1994.

62. Kim Young Sam, "Naui Singongje Kusang" ["My Plan on the New Economy"], *2000 Sinhanguk* [2000 New Korea] (Seoul: Tonggwang Publishers, 1992), p. 234. This article was based on the address at the Forum on Economic Reform on November 16, 1992. He confessed that he was upset about the fact that the building of an enterprise requires 312 documents for sixty stages for three years and emphatically defined the "New Economy" as an economic system in which "citizens' participation and creativity instead of government's planning and regulation can be the ground of economic development."

63. *Donga Ilbo*, May 27, 1994. The Inspection Team for the Deregulation of Executive Control led by the chief economic aide to the president deregulated 809 (79.2%) out of 966 targeted items during the year following the commencement of Kim Young Sam's rule and pushed for second-stage deregulations.

64. *Hankook Ilbo*, March 20, 1993.

65. Young-il Lim, "*Singyongje 1nyonul Toedolabonda: Imkum Mitt Nodong Chongchaek*" ["Retrospect of New Economy: Analysis of Wage and Labor Policy"], *Daehaksinmun* [University Newspaper], May 16, 1994.

4

༄

The Institutional Foundations
of Korean Politics

David C. Kang

In recent years, scholars have turned increasingly to new institutional economics (NIE) as the source of theorizing about comparative politics.[1] Working from within the traditions of the NIE, I attempt in this paper to clarify the limitations and also to extend the applicability of the NIE. This paper takes one relatively recent phenomenon—the use of agency theory—and proposes merging it with a larger framework of transaction costs theorizing. Precisely because agency theory focuses theoretical attention on *ex ante* institutional mechanisms for oversight, its ability to explain *ex post* governance structures and maladaptation costs is minimal. By complementing agency theory with the transaction costs approach, governance at both the design stage and the adaptation stage is addressed. My contribution is also substantive. Most of the recent scholarships on South Korea's democratic transition has examined what have been different since the 1987 opening.[2] By examining the institutional foundations of Korean politics, I provide a framework that emphasizes continuity as well as change in postliberation South Korean politics, and also offer an institutional explanation for the endemic "constrained collusion" between the South Korean government and business elite.

The last two years have seen the emergence of two major corruption scandals in Korea that resulted in: the convictions of two former presidents, Chun Doo Hwan and Roh Tae Woo; the conviction of the son of former President Kim Young Sam; jail sentences for numerous politicians and businesspeople; and early retirement of a number of military officers. An additional set of government investigations reopened the issue of the 1979 coup d'état by Chun Doo Hwan, resulting in punishments in the name of correcting past history.[3] While numerous observers have professed to be shocked (!) at these revelations, in reality such scandals are recurrent themes in Korean political history, and the exchange of money for political influence was common knowledge.[4] However, the current situation presents an opportunity to put Korean political history into a larger analytic context. Indeed, woven into the story of Korean economic success is an underside of systematic influence-peddling and corruption. Yet the roots of corruption are as organic to Korean politics as are the roots of economic success, and both reflect substantial continuity in the institutional foundations of pre- and post-1987 South Korean politics. The current scandals raise a number of questions. Why has corruption occurred so regularly in Korea? Why has it taken the form it has? And has the nascent turn toward genuine democracy since 1987 augured lasting change?

In this chapter I make one overarching claim: that the post-liberation imposition of democratic institutions on a society already in turmoil led to an inversion of control. This inversion from bottom-up to top-down has had serious, but predictable, consequences: constrained collusion between state and business; recurrent political crises; a weakened legislature; and an unstable party system. As such, I will argue that there remains substantial continuity in South Korea's deeper political patterns and institutions. Understanding these recurrent patterns and the institutions that foster them will provide a larger, more comprehensive and general understanding of Korean politics and of corruption in particular, and the process of democratization.[5]

This chapter is organized into three major sections. In the first section I introduce a theoretical approach based on the new institutional economics that merges agency theory and transaction costs theorizing. I then provide a brief overview of Korean politics as viewed through the institutional lens. Using these insights, in the second section I briefly discuss how Korean politics inverted the political relationship, examining the executive, legislature, and parties. In the final section, I discuss the issues of regionalism and corruption in Korean politics, and argue that both are functions of the structure of Korean politics.

Institutions and Politics

If we define politics as "group decision-making," then it is institutions that serve to connect society to political choices. "Society" can be interest groups, individual voters, politicians, or organizations; institutions are the enduring structures that serve to link, filter, and constrain society's decision processes. Institutional theories differ from sociological or behavioral theories in that they view politics as more than the sum of competing interests.[6] Other approaches emphasize the cultural or historical milieu in which politics is conducted as central to understanding politics. While not directly in opposition to any of these approaches, an institutional perspective focuses on the constraints on actor's decisions. As James Alt and Kenneth Shepsle wrote: "One main theme (of institutional analysis) centers on replacing the assumption of purely decentralized exchange among individuals with models involving collective action, collective decisions, and, thus, collective choice processes, rules, and procedures."[7]

This chapter takes as its starting point two insights into politics drawn from the literature on the NIE.[8] First, that politics involves *exchange* between actors—whether informal agreements, promises, or voting. Second, that formal hierarchic relationships are subject to opportunism. The NIE emphasizes that creating, monitoring, and enforcing long-term exchange is inherently impossible, and therefore long-term or iterated exchange is risky.[9] The NIE thus examines the search for institutions that reduce the costs of exchange, and the basic insight is that institutions evolve in order to minimize these transaction costs and in order to make exchange more stable. Using the NIE as a lens with which to view politics leads to a focus on the types of exchanges political actors make. In politics, actors frequently make agreements with each other. This can involve log-rolling between politicians, campaign promises and agreements between elite and supporters, and decisions about both the substance and the implementation of public policy. Two problems arise immediately: such agreements are frequently to be implemented in the future—and hence are subject to revision—and such agreements are often unenforceable. Thus political actors—like economic actors—are concerned about opportunism and reneging, and they search for institutions and mechanisms by which they can reduce the potential for opportunism by others.

Principals and Agents

A popular strand of the NIE focuses on principal-agent analysis. A principal-agent model ("agency theory," hereafter "AT") consists of two hierarchically related actors, a principal and an agent. In these models the principal hires the agent to perform some task, for which the agent receives compensation. As Jonathan Bendor writes, "The agent knows something the principal does not and there is a danger that the agent will exploit this edge strategically. A key question is whether the principal can devise incentives that will induce the agent to act in the principal's interest."[10] This basic contractual problem lies at the heart of all politics: it is possible to think of many principal-agent relationships in politics: voters and their representatives; executives and bureaucrats; parties and politicians. In each of these cases the principal (voters, executive, or party) is in a hierarchical relationship with an agent (representative, bureaucrat, or politician) and in each case a contract (explicit or implicit) exists: the politicians do what their parties elect them to do; bureaucrats pursue the desires of their executives. The problem is that controlling agents is difficult, because information is poor and sanctioning is difficult. Thus the generic political problem is a search for ways to minimize these agency problems.

A stylized view of a democratic polity has a clear direction of agency relationships: voters with similar interests gather together and form a political party that aggregates their various interests in a coherent manner. That political party then selects a politician to represent their interests in the national government. Depending on whether a parliamentary or presidential system, either the parties or the voters then select an executive who best represents the interests of the nation as a whole. By winning enough votes at elections that are held at regular intervals, a democratically elected ruler or party earns the right to rule the country (see Figure 4.1).

This process is in essence a trade: voters give candidates votes, in return for which candidates promise to confer benefits on voters. This transaction is relatively secure: if the candidate fails to confer enough benefits on a large enough group of voters, at the next election he will lose his office. Democratic systems in this sense are a well-developed political "market," whereby many potential rulers compete among each other for the favor of many voters.[11]

A Gentle Critique of Agency Theory

While AT first provides a good approximation of the political process, viewing politics only in terms of agency theory can lead to an analytic dead end: when the institutional relationships drift out of alignment, AT leads the analyst back to the actors and their ini-

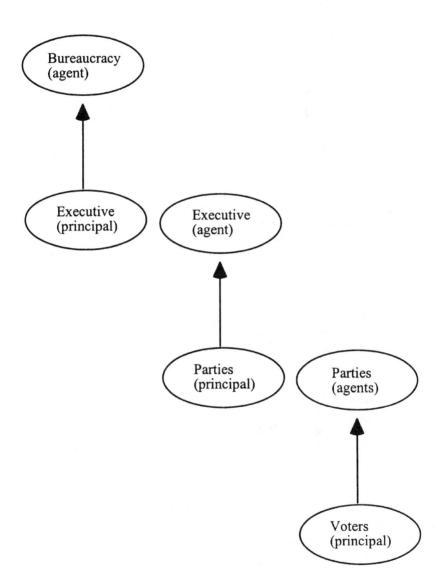

Figure 4.1
The Expected Direction of Control in a Democracy

tial *ex ante* bargaining. "Drift" in this context means any gradual change in the actors, either changes in their incentives, resources, or even the introduction of new actors. Thus any initial agreement will face pressures for change at the next stage, and an AT approach would lead the scholar back to bargaining over a new contract. This may not be the most useful way to view politics, for two reasons. First, as Terry Moe points out, many times actors are presented with institutions, and do not in any meaningful way create, or bargain over, the institutions themselves.[12] The average citizen of any country is presented with a set of rules, norms, and laws; only in extreme cases of emigration or attempts to overturn institutions is it meaningful to think of actors as actually engaged in the process of bargaining or renegotiating along the lines suggested by agency theory. It is also difficult to think of many political relationships as having been bargained over by two autonomous actors that can choose not to engage in the transaction if the agreement is unsatisfactory. Second, AT implies that if an actor is capable enough, he can design an institutional structure that will resolve the shirking problems—and hence the actor himself is unimportant once the institution is in place. This is mechanistic and seriously underestimates the role that political leadership plays in politics.[13] It is rarely the case that politicians and leaders are unimportant and merely manage a smoothly running system.

A transaction costs approach offers a way out. While transaction cost economics (hereafter "TCE") shares a number of assumptions with AT, transaction costs can be distinguished from agency theory in its analytic focus and its emphasis on *ex post* as well as *ex ante* concerns. Much of the agency theory literature focuses on the steps by which a principal can design a relationship such that an agent will willingly enter the transaction. Even if actors at some point did make a contract, there are many other contractual problems that do not necessitate an entirely new bargain; these contractual problems occur during the implementation stage. Oliver Williamson writes "*Ex post* costs of contracting take several forms. These include (1) the maladaptation costs incurred when transactions drift out of alignment, (2) the haggling costs incurred if bilateral efforts are made to correct *ex post* misalignments, (3) the setup and running costs associated with governance structures (often not the courts) to which disputes are referred, and (4) the bonding costs of effecting secure commitments."[14] Reducing costs through judicious choice of governance structure, rather than merely realigning incentives and pricing them out, is the distinctive TCE orientation.[15] In fact, much of politics occur at the implementation stage, as political actors struggle over bureaucratic missions, voters compete with each other for access to decision makers, and politicians attempt to compromise with themselves. Neither AT nor TCE is a prior—or more fundamental—analytic perspective. Sharing many assumptions, but with different analytic foci, agency theory and TCE are both singular and yet complementary. (See Figure 4.2.)

Merging AT and TCE

In an AT approach, the problem is largely one of institutional design and construction, and a nation's constitution formally ensures that politicians can control bureaucracies, and that voters can control politicians. However, what if agents become principals? What if principals begin actively working to manipulate voters and their incentives? As agents gain more resources and more autonomy, and in some cases as agents actively work to change the principals or modify the principals' interests, an AT approach becomes increasingly less analytically useful. Initially, an AT approach would emphasize that this is "agency slack." However, in theory, putative principals can become agents, and while the *institutions* remain formally the same, the actual relationship has inverted. While TCE handles this easily by not imputing who is the principal and who is the agent, an AT approach has difficulty theorizing about *when* such an inversion is likely to occur. What if "design" is not the issue, but rather the transactions themselves are the issue? Politicians and voters may agree on their institutional structure, but disagree over how to manage their relationship. Merging AT

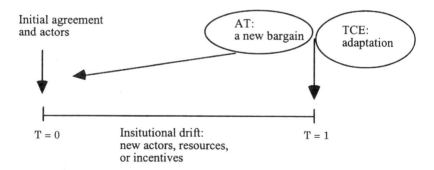

Figure 4.2
Agency Theory and Transaction Cost Economics

and TCE theorizing offers an analytically tractable way of answering these questions, as well as an overall framework that can incorporate both democratic and authoritarian regimes.

While most work using AT and TCE have focused on democracies, in authoritarian states the basic transaction remains the same, although in a more crude form: an aspiring dictator offers supporters various benefits if they support his attempt to capture control of the state. However, lacking regular elections and effective ways to monitor the ruler's behavior, it is difficult for society to sanction him once the ruler gains power. The costs of removing him from office are relatively large compared to similar costs in a democratic society.[16] Powerful interest groups can constrain an authoritarian ruler, but the process is neither as smooth nor as transparent as in a democracy, and the potential costs in attempting to influence an authoritarian ruler are much higher. That is, replacing an authoritarian ruler is neither easy nor quick—one risks getting shot in the process. Thus although the basic trade between ruler and constituents is similar in both authoritarian and democratic states, the *institutions* of democracy make problems of monitoring and sanctioning political agents lower than in an authoritarian state. That is, transaction costs are higher in authoritarian regimes.

Within this framework, TCE offers a lens on adaptation. It makes no presumption about who the principals or agents are, realizes that formal structures are always incomplete, and that actors realize this and take steps to ameliorate the situation. This framework has three theoretical implications for the study of Korean politics that lead to three empirical expectations. First, institutions that do not reflect the bargaining and resource strengths of the actors will be unstable; that is, as the abilities and resources of political actors drift out of alignment with the institutions, we would expect to see recurrent political crises. Second, as the transaction costs rise from this disjuncture, the putative principals will have a harder time enforcing their relationship with the putative agents: politics will be inverted and the agents may become principals. Interests will not necessarily be aggregated from below, and agents will have increasing autonomy and influence. Finally, the costs of running the system will be greater than in an institutional polity that accurately reflects the strengths and resources of the actors: both principals and agents will have to "pay more" for access to and policies from the institutions. Applied to the Korean case, this has had predictable results: increase of opportunism. Collusion between government and business to the detriment of voters (the putative principals) increased. Political parties, the legislature, and society at large had a difficult time restraining the executive, and in fact political elite form parties with the purpose of mobilizing support. Political crises are endemic to Korea as voters attempt to restrain leaders, and leaders attempt to manipulate voters.

A Brief Overview of Korean Politics

The main institutional feature of Korean politics has been the imposition of democracy by the United States after World War II, and the subsequent inversion of polity by continued streams of Korean political elite. Yet, ironically, it was U.S. policies and decisions that helped to undermine Korean democracy in the decades following liberation. Imposed elections in 1948 resulted in the election of Syngman Rhee. After the military coup in 1961, Park Chung Hee initially declared that after order had been achieved the military junta would step down and return to civilian democratic rule. As late as 1987 the United States supported democratic moves, making it clear to Chun Doo Hwan during the "spring crisis" that military intervention was not an option.[17]

While democratic institutions were imposed on Korea from the outside, there was a battle within domestic politics over who would have final and ultimate authority. Following the Japanese surrender in 1945, the USAMGIK (U.S. Army Military Government in Korea) took total control of the southern half of the Korean peninsula. Three years of Cold War posturing resulted in elections in the South, the formal creation of the Republic of Korea, and the withdrawal of American troops. While the full story has been told elsewhere, the initial American legacy was the wholesale transposition of U.S. institutions onto Korean society.[18] The USAMGIK created democracy with a system of checks and balances, an independent judiciary, and other institutions for the nascent South Korean state. Syngman Rhee immediately set about subverting the political process.

Ironically, the Americans helped subvert the very democratic process that they had instituted. Scholars of all persuasions are in general agreement that Rhee did not have a popular mandate after the first election in 1948, and that only by currying favor with the Americans was he able to wrest executive power from a more centrist or even leftist populace. By stifling all opposition on the left, and siding with Syngman Rhee in the period just after liberation, the USAMGIK began a process that gave the executive significant power and began to invert the agency relationship.

This democratic structure, inconsistent with the preferences of Korean civil society, created institutional tensions. Political struggles erupted over control of the executive, legislature, and bureaucracy. Although democracy was imposed from above, actors on the ground in Korea attempted to circumvent and manipulate the electoral process. Serendipitous events gave the executive in Korea access to varied and deep sources of informal and formal power.

Thus even from the beginning, while the United States imposed democracy on Korea, American political interests and the Korean War crushed the left, limiting the political "space" in which to operate. The executive was further strengthened by the amount of economic power that became vested in its office, and the social turmoil—and U.S.-inspired land reform—that destroyed the landed class weakened what little organized opposition might have faced Rhee. Neither political parties nor the legislature constrained the executive, and in fact became tools of the executive for organizing society from above.

Institutional Foundations of Korean Politics

The executive in Korea began its existence with numerous factors that gave it more power than expected. This section will examine how the executive subverted that relationship over time. I focus first on how executives—Rhee, Park, and Chun—were able to legally and illegally manipulate political institutions even further. I then examine how actors struggled to operate within this mangled democratic process by focusing on the institutional foundations of weak parties and legislatures. I then discuss how the executive was able to retain control over the bureaucracy, and conclude by showing how a vibrant and contentious civil society continually attempted to exert its voice despite institutional barriers.

Executives and Legislatures:
Subverting the Agency Relationship

The pattern of executive dominance was set early in the life of the new republic. Not surprisingly, given the tremendous advantage with which the executive branch began its life, political leaders in Korea have been able to continuously arrogate more and more power to themselves. Also not surprisingly, those early traits were those that became institutionalized. In any political system, the incumbent has an advantage, by dint of superior institutional resources and the "glow" of office. The Korean executive formed parties that were weak, used those parties to further strengthen political control, and organized society from above.

Even before the first constitution in 1948 was promulgated, a struggle over presidential or parliamentary system occurred. In 1947, a constitution committee of some thirty members, headed by Dr. Yu Chin-o, began to draft the Republic of Korea's first constitution. Although they initially decided on a cabinet-responsible system of government, on June 20, 1948, Rhee called the drafters of the constitution to his mansion and pressured them to adopt a presidential system.[19] This initial system had numerous checks and balances—the president had strong powers but was elected by two-thirds of the National Assembly. Two-thirds of a two-thirds quorum could override a presidential veto.

As Gregory Henderson wrote, "It soon became apparent that in 1948 the fault lay less in the constitution than in Rhee's—and Korea's—inability to live with any concept of the balance of powers."[20] Between September 1948 and April 1949 over 89,000 people were arrested on various charges of disturbing state tranquillity. The Assembly twice passed resolutions calling for the resignation of the entire cabinet; both were ignored. Facing almost a certain defeat in the 1952 elections, Rhee began to push for the more easily manipulable popular elections. On January 18, 1952, the Assembly voted this proposal down 143 to 19. Only after Rhee arrested the entire Assembly on charges of "communist conspiracy" and forced them at gunpoint to vote for the amendment did he obtain popular elections.[21]

The Korean War (1950–1953) created a strong military and justified repression of almost any sort along the "national security" or "anticommunist" lines. By being fully incorporated into the larger Cold War between the United States and the Soviet Union, South Korea gained a perhaps too healthy dose of U.S. resources. Distribution of "vested properties" left behind by the Japanese were controlled by the government, giving the executive enormous influence over future economic life in Korea.[22] U.S. aid accounted for 70 percent of Korea's government spending in the 1950s, 75 percent of total fixed capital formation between 1953 and 1960, and aid funds accounted for 73 percent of the central government's borrowing requirement.[23] Furthermore, this aid was channeled through the executive, again giving Syngman Rhee far-reaching influence over economic life. Imposed land reform (ironically, this was initially opposed by Rhee) weakened the traditional oligarchic landlords, and the social upheaval resulting from the war and colonialism also weakened existing social structures, thus allowing the president to further centralize power. Thus instead of representing a broad constituency, President Rhee was able to organize society from above with an increasingly narrow support base. This is the source of Korean authoritarianism and where we begin our analysis of the inverted agency relationship.

Park Chung Hee acted similarly in his relationship with the legislature. After the military coup in May of 1961, Park made vague promises to turn the country over to civilian and democratic leadership "when the time was right." For two years the country was run by the Supreme Council for National Reconstruction (SCNR), which vigorously purged politicians, civil servants, and businesspeople. In late 1962, Park reversed course, saying that the time was not ripe for democratic elections.[24] It was only after the threatened cutoff from U.S. aid that Park actually decided to implement elections. In response to Park's wavering, the United States again put pressure on Korea to hold elections, withholding economic aid until Park held elections. In March of 1962, James Killen, USAID director to Korea, began withholding portions of aid in an attempt to push the South Korean government to undertake economic reform. President Kennedy personally protested to Park with a note, while the State Department withheld $25 million in economic aid to "underscore the determination to bring constitutional government to Korea."[25] The economic situation in 1962 was severe, as Korea faced inflation, balance of payments crises, and surging interest rates. Park's initial attempts to find funding in Europe and private international sources were unsuccessful. Forced to rely on the United States to stabilize the economic situation, in 1963 Park acquiesced to U.S. demands and held elections.

Park Chung Hee proceeded to manipulate and intimidate the National Assembly more blatantly than Rhee. Whether this had an economic or developmental rationale is another question—when looking at how institutions affected the conduct of politics in Korea we continually return to the fact that putative agents (in this case, the executive) have been in a position to manipulate the larger institutional context to their favor. Park, like Rhee before him, was no great fan of democracy, yet because democracy was imposed by the United States, Korean leaders were forced to work within the confines of a democratic facade. For Park this facade became continually more mangled—in 1972 he declared martial law and reconstituted the *Yushin* constitution to make himself virtually dictator for life.[26]

In 1980, Chun Doo Hwan, seizing power through a military coup, promulgated the Fifth Republic with election of the president still coming from an "electoral college" composed of 2,525 members who were not appointed by political parties or the National Assembly. On August 16, 1980, the electoral college voted 2,524 to 1 to elect Chun. Gregory Henderson calls this a "Pyongyang-style majority."[27] In a practice dating to the First Republic, the president has always appointed the Chief Justice and the Supreme Court Justices—the justices not requiring National Assembly approval.

Thus, over time, the Korean executive branch has been able to arrogate power into its hands by outright coercion, manipulation, and adroit use of the military. Although South Korea has seen regular elections since 1948, this did not constrain the executive branch in any meaningful way. At this point an AT approach would emphasize "unusual" agency slack, but also note that within an AT approach, such a result is not necessarily surprising. For democratic theorists, however, such agency slack has serious implications. In the next section I discuss political parties, and show how political leaders have turned the tables on society. One particularly important result of executive dominance has been the manipulation of the party structure and electoral process, an issue to which I now turn my attention.

Why Have Not Political Parties Restrained the Executive?

When we move beyond the executive, we see how the entire chain of agency relationships in Korea has been inverted. Political parties have always been weak in Korea; they have not become institutionalized, nor have they served to connect voters with actual policy choices. Rather, parties have functioned to organize and manipulate society from above. In this section, I explore the institutional causes of a weak party system and consider the political ramifications of a manipulated electoral process. Given a strong executive branch supported by the United States and endowed with significant resources, the implication is that political parties will be organized from above rather than from below and will be weakly institutionalized. Scholars tend to view parties as institutions that aggregate diverse interests and represent them to the national government, yet in Korea this process has been reversed: parties created from above were designed to organize society and extend influence downward.[28] Since voters had no real power to select or sanction the executive, and yet since the executive was forced by the United States to provide a show of democracy, parties tended to reflect the interests and goals of the politicians, not voters.

A Weak Party System

Political parties in Korea have never had much influence. Ever since liberation, politicians have created political parties to further their own interests. Whatever organic political parties existed in the first heady days of liberation were quickly stifled by repression and a polarized atmosphere between North and South Korea. Parties existed in the first place to further their interests "from above," rather than to respond to interests expressed from below.

As a result, political parties live and die depending on the success of their creators. The Liberal Party, formed by Syngman Rhee in 1951, disappeared after he fled from office in 1960. Originally formed to serve Rhee's electoral needs, the party was heavily engaging in the entire political-economy of the Rhee period. Even though Rhee was quick to use outright coercion and manipulation, such actions still needed to be supported by a political machine that could actually gather and funnel funds to and from various sources and run candidates in the elections. By granting special privileges to certain businesses, the Liberal Party generated bribes that could be used for electoral purposes to shore up the vote. Thus because of the state's access to capital, and the need for elections, the Liberal Party became engaged more in machine-style rent-seeking than in any type of actual interest representation. And, predictably, when Rhee left office, and the source of power shifted to a new executive, the raison d'être for the Liberal Party disappeared, and with it the party itself.[29]

In 1963 Park Chung Hee created the Democratic Republican Party (DRP), again in order to mobilize the vote. Created by Kim Jong Pil, Park's nephew-in-law and head of the KCIA, the party was imposed from above. The DRP enhanced Park's executive power rather than limiting it. Park Chung Hee staffed the party with personal patrons: in the initial days top positions in the civilian government were filled by thirty-nine prominent members of the coup, twelve colonels, and only three high-ranking civilians. Like Rhee's Liberal Party before him, the DRP evaporated after Park Chung Hee died in 1979, as power shifted to a new center of gravity. Similarly, Chun Doo Hwan, after taking power in 1980, created the Democratic Justice Party (DJP), which disappeared after Roh took power in 1988. The DJP was staffed by many ex-military cronies of Park Chung Hee. Table 4.1 lists those ex-military officials in the National Assembly.

From 1963 to 1988 the electoral system returned a disproportionate number of National Assembly seats to the majority party. Justified in terms of "stability in the face of a North Korean threat," the system virtually guaranteed that the incumbent party would win any election. Although the details have been enumerated elsewhere, multiple-member districts with numerous "at large" or "national" seats in the National Assembly created a situation whereby the majority party could win one-third of the popular vote but retain two-thirds of the National Assembly seats.[30] This "proportional representation plus premium" system, combined with a gerrymandered system that increased the representation of the countryside against the cities, created a situation in which the government party could ensure its dominant electoral position.[31] Table 4.2 shows these results for the elections held since the Korean War. In all cases the ruling party received more votes than its popular electoral results, while in most cases the opposition parties were

Table 4.1
Former Military Officers among National Assemblymen and Committee Chairmen (percentages)

Sessions:	1963–67	1967–71	1971–72	1973–78	1978–79	1981–85
Assemblymen:	17.7a	21.1	17.2	22.4	16	9.4
	31b	37	35	49	37	26
Chairmen:	41.7	37.5	38.5	34.6	46.2	50
	10	9	5	9	6	13

Source: Kwang Woong Kim, *Hanuk-ui gwallyoje yongu: inae rul wihan gukkaron-jok chopkun* ([Research on the Korean Bureaucracy] [Seoul: Taeyong Munhwasa, 1991], pp. 10–11).

a: percentage
b: absolute number

Table 4.2
National Assembly Election Outcomes
(% of overall vote/% of national assembly seats)

	Government	Opposition		
1954	LP (37/56)			
1958	LP (42/54)	DP (34/34)		
1960		DP (42/75)		
1963	DRP (34/63)	DPP (20/23)	DPC (14/14)	
1967	DRP (51/73)	NDP (33/26)		
1971	DRP (48/55)	NDP (44/44)		
1973	DRP (39/67)	NDP (33/26)		
1978	DRP (32/63)	NDP (33/26)		
1981	DJP (36/55)	DKP (22/29)	KNP (13/9)	
1985	DJP (35/55)	NKDP (29/24)	DKP (20/13)	
1988	DJP (34/42)	UDP (24/20)	PPD (19/23)	NDRP (16/12)
1992	DLP (—/49)	DP (—/32)	UPP (—/10)	

LP: Liberal Party; DP: Democratic Party; DRP: Democratic Republican Party; NDP: New Deomcratic Party; DPP: Democracy and Peace Party; DJP: Demoratic Justice Party; NKDP: New Korea Democratic Party; DLP: Demoratic Liberal Party; PPD: Party for Peace and Democracy; DKP: Democratic Korea Party; UDP: Unification and Democracy Party.

(*Source:* Chon Soohyun, "The Election Process and Informal Politics in Korea" [East-West Center Working Papers no. 4, 1994], p. 4.)

significantly underrepresented. Also of interest is the rapid rise and fall of parties according to the rise and fall of the fortunes of their leaders.

Thus another reason for the weakness of the party system was the weakness of the legislature itself. Being unable to articulate or influence policy in any meaningful way, power and attempts for influence flowed naturally to the executive. Thus parties in Korea have traditionally not been the source to which people turn for political help.[32]

Causes of a Weak Party System

Parties and elections remain weakly institutionalized for two basic reasons. First, power has flowed down rather than up. Predominant power in the executive branch lessened the impact parties might have had. For almost forty years, the personalized political party system led to elections that were so heavily biased in favor of the incumbent party that it is impossible to call them "representative elections." Parties have remained weak for another related reason. The threat from the North—and the resulting competition between both halves of the peninsula—has looked balefully over the shoulder of the entire postwar South Korean political process. This North Korean threat has turned South Korean politics into essentially a "primary" where the competition in the South has been over who will lead the South in its ideological campaign against the North.[33] This is just a metaphor, of course.

Competition with the North has been intense on all fronts: diplomatic, military, economic, and political.[34] This has restricted domestic politics in South Korea to a rightist, pro-American stance. Any politician or party that strayed too far to the left on any agenda was subject to being labeled a communist or Northern "sympathizer," and thus the political space within which parties operate has remained constricted. Even after the turn toward democracy, the Northern issue has not been resolved, and thus politics, despite its new openness, remains truncated. In the National Assembly elections of April 1996, for example, Northern provocation provided a convenient excuse for the ruling New Korea Party to claim that it was the bulwark against the northern threat, and to emphasize the potential left-leanings of the opposition party led by Kim Dae Jung.[35]

The effect is that parties and electoral competition in South Korea are essentially a "primary" election of the rightists, with the winner then confronting the true leftist party, the Korean Workers Party of North Korea. This has had various political implications. First, voter choice in South Korea has essentially been obliterated, with all parties and politicians constrained to a rightist stance. Second, competition with North Korea led to the suppression of labor movement. The absence of a labor party in South Korea is an evidence of both the lack of voter choice and also the extent to which democratic politics must still evolve. While the previous authoritarian governments had suppressed labor for their own ruling purposes, one key reason that no labor party has emerged has been that to be too close to any "left" politics is dangerous.[36] Until conflict with the North is resolved, it is unlikely that this will change. Thus the structure within which parties operate in South Korea is heavily influenced by the existence of a competing North Korea. No labor party can emerge, candidate choice is truncated, and the issues are not truly debated.

This discussion has been superficial, and has ignored many dynamics of Korean party behavior. Korean parties are highly factionalized, personalistic, and top-down. Nominations for office are controlled by party leaders, and the allocation of nominations for National Assembly seats is balanced among competing factions. For our purposes, however, the general structure of Korean party behavior is top-down and created by the structure within which these parties operate.

The U.S. influence and the North Korean threat are essentially exogenous to my model—they only change the actors and the incentives—but a TCE framework puts such ad hoc factors into a framework that allows us to trace their effects in a systematic manner.

Results of a Weak Party System

The effect of a weakened party system has been to further subvert the chain of influence in the opposite direction: instead of voters aggregating interests through the party and then selecting an executive, weak and uninfluential parties furthered the power of the executive. Parties formed around an individual and would then disintegrate if the politician was unsuccessful. Some noted scholars have attributed this to Korea's atomistic political culture that brooks no alternate source of power save the state itself.[37] While this is certainly the case, the institutional situation within which Korea became enmeshed after liberation also lends insight as to how that system both sustained itself and also changed over time.

Although it is expected that they would serve as the function of aggregate interests, parties in Korea served only as instruments of politicians, furthering their individual interests. This resulted in politicized rather than institutionalized parties. Because of a highly manipulated electoral system, no election was definitive, and thus citizens either ignored the results or considered them illegitimate. Yet parties lacking institutionalized foundations may have other political functions. Absent strong party loyalty and routinized systems of interest aggregation, parties affected outcomes only through the effect of showmanship. Even the formation of parties themselves was a top-down affair—party leaders had the ability to nominate the lists of candidates for office—in order to even run for office one generally needed to engage in bribery of officials. Parties did not reflect platforms, ideological differences, or economic interests, nor did they legitimate election results, influence policy formulation, or restrain the executive branch. Parties are not the creation of voters with similar goals, but rather of politicians looking to perpetuate their power. A recent survey by the *Donga Ilbo* found that 49.1 percent of Koreans had no party affiliation at all.[38] However, parties do provide a means by which the state can extract rents from the capital class in exchange for favored economic policies.

Why Did Not Society Constrain the Executive?

Given this institutional setting, there have been limited ways in which voters or interest groups outside this inner circle could attempt to influence policy or make their preferences known. Voters dissatisfied with the status quo had a choice between acquiescence and increasingly violent or dangerous mass protests. Working within the system meant accepting a marginal role. Voters could attempt, against great odds, to defeat the incumbent in elections that had to be held. Such is the case in 1971, when Kim Dae Jung almost beat Park in the presidential election. Alternatively, voters could "take to the streets," attempt in a broad and dangerous way to remove the president from office, and try and change the entire system. Such was the case in 1960 (*Sa-Il-Gu*) and 1980 in Kwangju, and finally with success in 1987.

Despite executive manipulation of the constitutional process, attempts to subvert the electoral process, and outright coercion, civil society in Korea has been active and has been able to take a stand against the putative leaders in Korea. Hagen Koo notes that "despite the state's unusual strength and pervasive presence, civil society in the South has never been completely stifled but has always demonstrated a subversive, combative, character."[39] The continuous and recurrent popular movements belie any notion that Korean society is passive in nature.

Political Implications for Korean Politics

The implications of a weakly institutionalized party system and yet imposed democratic constraints are fairly straightforward: recurrent political crises with major effects on both economic policy and political rule. In addition, imposed democracy has meant that authoritarian leaders have had to finance big parties, and hence court big business. Political leaders in Korea faced major opposition from various sectors of the populace, in both mass protests and electoral results. Parties were top-down and served elite interests. An AT approach that retains a rigid distinction between principals and agents is not as useful as a TCE approach that emphasizes adaptation and bargaining *within* an institutional framework. Transaction costs were so high in Korea that executives were free to be opportunistic—as shown previously, this turned political leaders' attention away from labor, consumers, and other social groups to that of big business. This unstable environment led leaders to internalize their rule through easily manipulable institutions: parties that only served their purposes, and big business that sustained both party and leader.

The need to develop extensive networks of business-government support also derive from nominal democratic institutions in Korea.[40] With episodic regularity, South Korea has been rocked by corruption scandals. Compared to Taiwan, where KMT dominance was accepted by the United States, in Korea, leaders needed to develop and sustain political parties. This led to the need to finance parties—the role of big business. This also had implications for economic policy. In Korea, business has been more influential than in Taiwan due to the need of the political party to court business for electoral purposes. The erratic nature of economic policy and the extensive corruption can be seen as an outcome of this effort to build these bases of business support.

This has led to a concentration of both political and economic power, what I call a "mutual hostage" situation.[41] State control over the financial sector had enormous consequences for the organization and conduct of business in Korea. The state could, in fact, control business through its control over the flow of finance. Since Korean companies were highly leveraged, they were vulnerable to state control. Paradoxically, this weakness became a source of strength relative to the state. The Park regime—intentionally or unintentionally—actively encouraged the centralization and enhancement of economic power in the *chaebol* (see Table 4.3). From Park's initial decision in 1961 to pardon the "illicit wealth accumulators," to the bailout of highly-leveraged firms in August 1972, to the 1976 decision to promote general trading companies, there have been continuous policy moves by the state to encourage the rise of the *chaebol*.[42]

By encouraging the formation of large conglomerates that accounted for large percentages of the Korean economy, the state and *chaebol* in effect became "mutual hostages." Each needing the other, yet neither able to fully gain the upper hand, state and *chae-*

Table 4.3
Mutual Hostages, Part I
Sales of top *chaebol* as a percent of GNP, 1974–1984

Chaebol (ranking)	1974	1980	1984
1	4.9	8.3	12.0
top 5	11.6	35.0	52.4
top 10	15.1	48.1	67.4

(*Source:* Alice Amsden, Asia's Next Giant [Oxford: Oxford University Press, 1989], p. 116.)

Mutual Hostages, Part II
Debt/Equity ratio of manufacturing
firms in selected countries
1972–1984 (percent)

Year	Korea	U.S.	Taiwan
1972	313.4	—	—
1975	339.5	60.6	99.3
1980	487.9	177.0	82.5
1984	342.7	134.5	110.1

(*Source:* Adapted from Danny M. Leipziger, "Industrial Restructuring in Korea." *World Development* 16 (January 1988), p. 128.)

bol were forced to work together. The cause was high transaction costs: this relationship of small numbers of business and governmental elite was easier to sustain and monitor than the political elite having to deal with dispersed and diverse small businessmen.

Influence-peddling and Quasi-taxes

Yet a mutual hostage situation did not result in politics following the formal institutional lines set out by the constitution; rather, mutual hostages meant that the fate of government and business were inextricably bound together, against the larger wishes of the populace as a whole. This has resulted in consistent pressure by the political elite for donations by private business, a process that dates back to liberation. Government officials expected such large and regular business contributions that they became known as *jun jo-seh*, or "quasi-taxes." Most large *chaebol* made contributions at New Year's and *Chusok* (a traditional Korean holiday) as well as at other times calling for special needs or demands.

Park Byeong-seog writes, "The political funds system impedes financial support by certain social groups while encouraging and even subsidizing support by competing forces."[43] Under Park Chung Hee this financial system of exchanging policy for bribes became quasi-institutionalized. Four leading members of the DRP were in charge of political fund-raising: Chang Ki Young, Kim Hyung Wook, Kim Sung Kon, and Lee Hoo Rak.[44] These members of Park's inner circle had clear fund-raising duties: one dealt with personal connections, another with the parties, and others with big business. Allocation of bank loans, foreign loans, import licenses, and other policy decisions were based on a political funds system that required donations from the capitalists.

During the 1960s, businesspeople or politicians with close connections to Park were able to import or smuggle in Japanese products at windfall prices. Woo Jung-en notes that "the Japanese picked up the tab for launching the governing party in Korea."[45] Under Park Chung Hee, the expected "donation" in order to receive loans was formalized at between 10 and 20 percent of the value of the loan.[46] After Park's assassination, Kim Jong Pil was reported to have amassed over $150 million, and sought refuge in the United States for a few years in the 1980s.

Under Chun Doo Hwan this pattern continued at an even greater rate. The best example is the furor over the Ilhae Foundation ("Ilhae" for a pseudonym for Chun). Purportedly founded as a research institute to memorialize those cabinet members killed in Burma in 1983, the foundation was financed almost entirely by business contributions. The president of the Federation for Korean Industries, Chung Ju Yung, was put in charge of gathering the contributions, and many turned over up to $15 million.[47] All told, Ilhae received about $90 million in "donations."

One of the few businesspeople that turned down Chun's directive was Yang Chung-mo, founder of Kukje. In 1985 the Kukje group was dismantled, and all accounts point to Kukje being destroyed precisely because it did not play the political game.[48] In 1985 the Kukje group, with 38,000 employees, was the seventh-largest *chaebol* in Korea, and like all *chaebol*, was highly leveraged with significant loans from the government. However, Kukje's president, Yang Chung-mo, had seriously offended President Chun Doo Hwan by refusing to contribute significant sums to quasi-governmental organizations such as the Ilhae Foundation and the *Saemaul Undong* ("New Village Movement"). As a result, the state refused to loan money to Kukje and refused to honor its checks. Within weeks Kukje could not service its debt and had to declare bankruptcy.

The 1995 Scandal

This scandal is merely one more episode in a long-running Korean drama. In the fall of 1995, an opposition member of the National Assembly, Park Kye-dong, made charges that ex-president Roh Tae Woo had accepted millions of dollars in bribes during his tenure, which he had distributed to various businesspeople for safe-keeping. On October 27, Roh admitted to having collected over $650 million in corporate contributions that he had set into a personal political slush fund. The investigation widened to include ex-President Chun Doo Hwan and leading businesspeople, and ardent opposition leader Kim Dae Jung admitted accepting 2 billion won ($28 million) from Roh in 1992. Dozens of political and business careers were sidetracked by the scandal, which consistently revealed new culprits. In early March 1996, Chang Hak-ro, a personal assistant to ex-President Kim Young Sam, resigned after admitting to accepting bribes.

While the public expressed outrage and numerous political analysts in Korea howled in anger, the reality is that such collusion was inevitable and has long historical roots. The institutions that led to corruption and collusion under Rhee and Park were not significantly different under Kim Young Sam—the judiciary was only partially independent, the National Assembly continued to have truncated powers, and state influence in the economy was pervasive. This trend was evidenced even under the Kim Young Sam government. Kim's second son, Hyun-chol, and his most trusted aides including Hong In-gil were convicted and put into jail under corruption charges in the wake of the Hanbo scandal in early 1997.

Regionalism and the Future of Korean Politics

As democracy became more routinized, Korea has seen the emergence of *jibang-seh*, or regionalism. Most observers of Korean politics see regionalism as a major factor in determining electoral outcomes, and decry it as destabilizing at best, and undemocratic at worst.[49] In recent years these regional tendencies have manifested themselves in the form of the "Three Kims": Kim Dae Jung, from the Honam, or Cholla provinces; Kim Jong Pil, from the Chungchong provinces; and Kim Young Sam, from the Yongnam, or

Kyongsang provinces. All three of these regional leaders draw the overwhelming majority of their support from their respective home regions.

Many studies have shown that regional ties have become a major source of voting behavior for the Korean polity. In 1992 Kim Dae Jung received 89 percent of the vote from the Cholla provinces and only 9 percent of the vote from the Kyongsang provinces. Kim Young Sam, on the other hand, received 69 percent of the vote from Kyongsang and 5 percent of the vote from Cholla. In addition, polling data by Research and Research indicates that in 1994 "regional affiliation" was by far the best predictor of how a person would vote.[50]

In explaining the rise of regionalism, analysts have focused on three major variables: the excessive underdevelopment of the Cholla region compared to Kyongsang; the biased recruitment of elites by the military regimes, and manipulation of regional sentiment by political elites.[51] Regional bias has deep roots in Korean culture, extending as far back as the "three kingdoms" period, when *Silla* (now Kyongsang province) and *Paekche* (now Cholla province) consistently clashed. More recently, the phenomenon comes from the Park Chung Hee era of 1961–1979. Park, from the Southeast Kyongsang province, put his men in positions of power, and also skewed economic development toward the Pusan-Seoul axis.[52] There were both economic and political rationales for Park's actions. Economically, Pusan, the closest port to Japan, facilitated international trade. Similarly, placement of industrial sites at the southern end of the peninsula protected them from a possible North Korean invasion. Politically, Park Chung Hee—and Chun and Roh after him—needed to provide patronage posts to reward supporters and keep their power. Perhaps the most dramatic incident that helped fuel regional passions was the Kwangju incident of 1980, when the military violently suppressed a protest movement in the Cholla provincial capital.

Regardless of the causes, however, the effect has been slower political and economic growth in the Cholla provinces. And bias does exist: while economic development has lagged behind the southeastern provinces, tax collection has jumped ahead. Even though Kwangju's per capita income is lower than Taegu's, Kwangju residents generally paid more taxes to the government through the 1980s (see Table 4.4).

Yet these explanations of regionalism are at odds with the analysis presented in this chapter. The common explanations for

Table 4.4
Per Capita Total Tax Payment
in Kwangju and Taegu (won)

	Kwangju	Taegu
1980	820,088	487,615
1981	889,021	672,222
1982	910,605	988,183
1983	1,006,199	1,144,307
1984	1,062,923	940,109
1985	1,152,877	953,059
1986	1,241,285	951,371
1987	1,374,456	950,998
1988	1,647,319	1,173,778
1989	1,989,176	1,722,823

(*Source:* Park Jong Il, "Sodeuken Yongnami opgo Sekumen Honami Donenada [Income Is higher in Yongnam and Taxes are higher in Honnam]," *Shindonga* May 1990, 266–275.)

regionalism focus on the bottom-up preferences of voters and their desires, while this chapter has emphasized the inversion of that process and the top-down nature of Korean politics. Thus why did regionalism appear instead of other potential cleavages, and how does this relate to our institutional view of Korean politics?

The first explanation is that regionalism is a substitute for many other sincere voter interests—antigovernment, economic deprivation, and resentment for past discrimination. Korean society is in a state of long-term flux. Regionalism may "pick up" a number of other concerns among the electorate. In this sense regionalism is a function of weakly institutionalized parties responding to a generation of political leaders that all began their careers in the 1960s. More fundamentally, regionalism exists precisely because these other avenues of expression have historically been absent, and even in the present a wide range of voter choice is impossible—political parties are weak and provide no voter choice, power and policy making still revolve around the executive branch and its collusive ties to big business, and leaders of all parties are still forming rather than responding to constituent bases of support.

This institutional view was again confirmed in the 1997 presidential election, but with slightly different implications. Kim Dae Jung won the election with a narrow margin of 1.6 percent of the vote. Predictably, he received landslide support from the Cholla provinces (97.3 percent from Kwangju, 92.3 percent from North Cholla, and 94.6 percent from South Cholla), underscoring the issue of unresolved regionalism. But coalition with his old enemy, Kim Jong Pil, helped him perform well in the latter's stronghold, Chungchong provinces, leading to his victory.[53] It was the first interregional coalition building with a profound political implication of the peaceful transfer of power from the ruling to opposition bloc. Kim Dae Jung may redress the most obvious issue of regional bias against Honam. But he will do so with prudence. The election of Kim may not be able to solve the intermediate problem of regionalism in general, or the fundamental problem of reverting South Korean politics to a situation where voters have true choices. Nonetheless, his presidency could offer important momentum for resolving the dilemma of regionalism in Korea.

Until competition between parties generates choices for the electorate, and until parties serve to connect voters with what a government is likely to do, the "agents" in Korean society—president, party leaders, National Assembly representatives—will continue to hold more power and influence society in a more direct way than the putative principals in any democracy, the voters. For Korean politics to truly change, two things must occur. First, the older generation of leaders needs to be replaced by younger politicians of national stature and credibility. The three Kims all began their political career in the 1960s in the Park Chung Hee period, and all are irrevocably linked to certain political stances and attitudes. Until a newer generation of political leaders arrives on the scene, Korean politics will be dominated by old methods. The election of Kim Dae Jung as president can be interpreted as the end of the three Kims politics.

Second and more important, the locus of decision-making power must be widened to include the National Assembly as an institution. As long as parties do *not* connect voters with policies, there will be little incentive to form interest-based parties that transcend regional differences. There has been widespread sentiment to reform the system in Korea, and this has occurred at a fitful pace. In 1994 Kim Young Sam oversaw new election rules: the campaign law increased government subsidies to parties, increased allowances for candidates at all levels, and slashed the legal limit for campaign funds with severe penalties for violations—the candidate can forfeit victory even if relatives or staff members were responsible for violations. Also, businesses are now allowed to anonymously donate up to 30 million *won* (about $37,500), so as to protect them from government reprisals. Forbidding fictitious names also came about, making it fairly difficult to exceed campaign expenditure limits. The electoral reforms yielded positive dividends. The 1997 presidential election was the cleanest, most transparent, and least expensive in the modern history of Korean politics. Yet ultimately regionalism and money politics will continue to exist as long as parties remain weak, big business remains strong, and the president remains to be considered as *daekwon* (presidential power).[54]

The Institutions of Korean Politics since 1996

I have traced the institutions of Korean politics from the inception of the Republic in 1948 to 1996, part of the Sixth Republic as ratified by the National Assembly on October 27, 1987, and subsequently approved by national referendum. The basic constitution of the Republic of Korea provides for basic rights, checks and balances, and oversight (see chapter 3 by Kil).

The president is elected by direct popular election once every five years and cannot serve more than one term. The president cannot dissolve the National Assembly and is also prohibited from issuing emergency decrees covering the whole range of state affairs. However, the president can still proclaim martial law and grant amnesty. In fact, President Kim Young Sam granted amnesty to Chun and Roh on December 26, 1997, in consultation with president-elect Kim Dae Jung. The president appoints a cabinet consisting of twenty-three posts, among them prime minister, deputy prime minister (also the Minister of Finance and the Economy), deputy prime minister (and National Unification Minister), and twenty other ministry posts (see the appendix on formal structure of the Korean government).

The National Assembly consists of 299 seats, three-quarters elected from single-member districts, elected for terms of four years. The latest election was held in 1996, and the next election will be in the year 2000. The National Assembly elects a Speaker of the Assembly and two Vice Speakers, which in reality means that the majority party determines who the Speaker will be. The president, although he can veto National Assembly legislation, can be overridden by the Assembly by a two-thirds majority.

While Korea's political parties change names and identities quite often, in 1996 there were four major parties. The ruling party was the New Korea Party (NKP). The NKP was formerly the ruling

Democratic Liberal Party (DLP), but since Roh Tae Woo was tied to that party, party leaders changed the name to the NKP when he was arrested. Returning to politics in 1995, Kim Dae Jung created a new political party, the National Congress for New Politics (NCNP), in 1995. The two smaller opposition parties are the United Liberal Democrats (ULD) headed by Kim Jong Pil after he bolted from the ruling DLP in 1995, and the Democratic Party, headed by Li Ki-taek and later Cho Soon. In the process of the 1997 presidential race, however, there was another round of renaming and realignment of party politics. As former President Kim Young Sam relinquished his association with the ruling NKP, NKP leadership changed its name to the Grand National Party (GNP) and incorporated Cho Soon's DP. Lee In-je, who lost the NKP's presidential nomination to Lee Hoi-chang, also bolted from the ruling party and founded his own party, the New Party by the People (NPP).

The judicial branch consists of the Constitutional Court, the Supreme Court, and lesser courts, such as the Family Court and the District Courts. The president appoints the Chief Justice and Justices of the Supreme Court with the consent of the National Assembly. Judges other than the Supreme Court justices are appointed by the Chief Justice with the consent of the Conference of Supreme Court Justices. There is no jury system. The Constitutional Court, consisting of nine members, is appointed by the president (3 members), the National Assembly (3 members), and the chief justice (3 members).

Conclusion

While this chapter emphasizes the continuities in Korea's political history, there have been small steps toward genuine change: Kim Young Sam was the first nonmilitary president to take office since 1961; fraud and manipulation of elections has become virtually nonexistent; real reform of campaigns, finances, and the bureaucracy took place; and Kim Dae Jung was elected president. However, there remain significant barriers to the heart of democratic politics—voter choice. As long as parties fail to provide genuine alternatives from which voters can choose and continue to be run on personalistic and paternal bases, voters in Korea will lack a true vehicle for expressing their opinions and desires to the government.

Until competition between parties generates choices for the electorate, and until parties serve to connect voters with what a government is likely to do, the "agents" in Korean society—president, party leaders, members of the National Assembly—will continue to hold more power and influence society in a more direct way than the putative principals in any democracy, the voters. For Korean politics to truly change, two things must occur. First, the older generation of leaders needs to be replaced by younger politicians of national stature and credibility. Until a newer generation of political leaders arrives on the scene, Korean politics will be dominated by old methods.

Second and more important, the locus of decision-making power must be widened to include the National Assembly as an institution. If I am correct in focusing on institutions and not individuals, as long as parties do *not* connect voters with policies, there will be little incentive to form interest-based parties that transcend regional or personalistic differences. As long as North Korea remains a convenient bogeyman, and the judiciary remains subject to executive influence, true voter choice will not emerge. As a result, business will continue to seek presidential influence rather than party influence, and the basic contours of Korean politics will remain quasi-democratic in form but subject to abuse by the president.[55]

This chapter has also made a minor addition to the theoretical literature by highlighting the limits on the naive use of agency theory in political science. The rough model developed here incorporates both agency theory and transaction costs theory in a manner that allows for application to empirical cases. While both theories are rigorous in their own respect, a combination of them provides for a much richer treatment of politics.

Notes

1. See, for example, Frances Rosenbluth and Mark Ramseyer, *Japan's Political Marketplace* (Cambridge: Harvard University Press, 1993); Steven L. Solnick, "The Breakdown of Hierarchies in the Soviet Union and China," *World Politics* 48:2 (January 1996), pp. 209–238; Matthew D. McCubbins and Gregory Noble, "The Appearance of Power: Legislators, Bureaucrats, and the Budget Process in the United States and Japan," in Peter F. Cowhey and Matthew D. McCubbins, eds., *Structure and Policy in Japan and the United States* (Cambridge: Cambridge University Press, 1995); Philip Roeder, *Red Sunset: the Failure of Soviet Politics* (Princeton: Princeton University Press, 1993); Victor Nee and Peng Lian, "Sleeping with the Enemy: A Dynamic Model of Declining Political

Commitment in State Socialism," *Theory and Society* 23 (April 1994); Edgar Kiser, "Markets and Hierarchies in Early Modern Tax Systems: A Principal-Agent Analysis," *Politics and Society* 22 (September 1994), pp. 284–315; and Michael Chwe, "Why Were Workers Whipped? Pain in a Principal-Agent Model," *The Economic Journal* 100 (December 1990), pp. 1109–1121.

2. Masao Okonogi is representative of those who emphasize the change in Korean politics following 1987: "In the six months from the 29 June 1987 announcement . . . South Korea experienced a major political upheaval, one that rivals the events of 1960 and 1961 in its significance." Masao Okonogi, "South Korea's Experiment in Democracy," *Japan Review of International Affairs* 2:1 (1988). For similar views, see Jin Park, "Political Change in South Korea: The Challenge of the Conservative Alliance," *Asian Survey* 30:12 (1990); Hong-nack Kim, "The 1988 Parliamentary Election in Korea," *Asian Survey* 29:5 (1989); James Cotton, ed., *Politics and Policy in the New Korean State: from Roh Tae Woo to Kim Young-sam* (New York: St. Martin's Press, 1995); and Hak-joon Kim, "New Political Development with a Vision for the 1990s and Beyond," *Korea and World Affairs* 14:1 (1990). Robert Bedeski argues that there has been significant institutional change in South Korea since 1987—I will argue that the changes are superficial in nature. Robert Bedeski, "State Reform and Democracy in South Korea," *Journal of East Asian Affairs* 6:1 (1992).

3. For good overviews of the current scandals, see Ahn, *"Bijagumgwa Daekwonyokui Chuakhan Janchi"*; Yong-suh Kim, *"No Tae U Gusokkwa YS ui Sontaek"* ["The detention of Roh Tae Woo and Kim Young-sam's choices"], *The Monthly Sisa* (December 1995), pp. 56–65; Yong-jun Joh, *"Yukgong Chongsan No Tae U Kwiyang?"* ["The liquidation of the Sixth Republic and the exile of Roh Tae Woo?"], *The News Plus* (November 2, 1995), pp. 12–14; and Jae-hoon Shim and Andrew Sherry, "Cutting the Knot," *Far Eastern Economic Review* 158:48 (November 30, 1995), pp. 66–72. On the 1979 coup and the Kwangju uprising, see Il Kim, *"Miguk, Kwangju Haksal 'P'angjo/Sungin' Haetta"* ["The United States gave approval and assistance for the Kwangju incident"], *The Sisa Journal* (March 7, 1996), pp. 26–33.

4. For expressions of outrage, see Ahn, op. cit.; Kim, "No Tae U Gusokkwa YSui Sontaek"; and Joh, op. cit. While my discussion parallels the scholarship on Japanese corruption to some extent, I differ in both my theoretical focus and also the implications for continued political success. On Japan, see Chalmers Johnson, "Tanaka Kakuei, Structural Corruption, and the Advent of Machine Politics in Japan," *Journal of Japanese Studies* 12 (Winter 1986), pp. 1–28; and Yayama Taro, "The Recruit Scandal: Learning from the Causes of Corruption," *Journal of Japanese Studies* 16 (Winter 1990).

5. For treatments of democratic transitions in general, see Stephan Haggard and Robert Kaufmann, *The Political Economy of Democratic Transitions* (Princeton: Princeton University Press, 1995). For a good review, see Doh-chull Shin, "On the Third Wave of Democratization: A Synthesis and Evaluation of Recent Theory and Research," *World Politics* 47:1 (October 1994), pp. 135–170.

6. For example, see Mancur Olson's seminal work, *The Logic of Collective Action* (Cambridge: Harvard University Press 1965); James Buchanan and Gordon Tullock, *The Calculus of Consent* (Ann Arbor: University of Michigan Press, 1962); and James E. Alt and Kenneth A. Shepsle, eds., *Perspectives on Positive Political Economy* (Cambridge: Cambridge University Press, 1990). For approaches to Korean politics that emphasize societal interests, see James Cotton, "From Authoritarianism to Democracy in South Korea," *Political Studies* 37:2 (1989); Jae-hyon Choe, *"Han'gukui Chungsanchung: Oe Pigop Hanga?"* ["Why Is the Korean Middle Class Afraid?"], *The Monthly Chosun* (April 1987), pp. 354–363; and Won-mo Dong, "The Democratization of South Korea: What Role Does the Middle Class Play?" *Korea Observer* 22:2 (1991).

7. James E. Alt and Kenneth A. Shepsle, "Editor's Introduction," in Alt and Shepsle, eds., op. cit., p. 3.

8. For excellent introductions to the NIE, see Terry Moe, "The New Economics of Organization," *American Journal of Political Science* 28 (1984), pp. 739–777; Alt and Shepsle, eds., ibid.; Erik Furubotn and Rudolf Richter, "The New Institutional Economics: An Assessment," in Furubotn and Richter, eds., *The New Institutional Economics* (College Station: Texas A&M Press, 1991). For longer works, see Oliver E. Williamson, *The Economic Institutions of Capitalism* (New York: The Free Press, 1985); and Benjamin Klein, Robert Crawford, and Armen A. Alchian, "Vertical Integration, Appropriable Rents, and the Competitive Contracting Process," *Journal of Law and Economics* 21 (October 1979), pp. 297–326. For critiques, see Mark Granovetter, "Economic Action and Social Structure: The Problem of Embeddedness," *American Journal of Sociology* 91 (November 1985), pp. 481–501; Richard Posner, "The New Institutional Economics Meets Law and Economics," *Journal of Institutional and Theoretical Economics* 149 (March 1993), pp. 73–121 (with replies from Ronald Coase and Oliver Williamson); and Ronald Dore, "Goodwill and the Spirit of Market Capitalism," *British Journal of Sociology* 34 (1983), pp. 459–482.

9. I am emphasizing one strand of the NIE, that known as "transaction cost economics." See Pranab Bardhan, "The New Institutional Economics and Development Theory: A Brief Critical Assessment," *World Development* 17:9 (1989), p. 1389.

10. Bendor, op. cit., p. 363.

11. For seminal work in this tradition, see Anthony Downs, *An Economic Theory of Democracy* (New York: Harper, 1957). See also Buchanan and Tullock, op. cit.

12. Terry Moe, "Towards a Theory of Public Bureaucracy," *Journal of Law, Economics, and Organization* 7 (1991), pp. 106–129.

13. Gary Cox, *Managerial Dilemmas* (Cambridge: Cambridge University Press, 1993).

14. Oliver Williamson, *The Economic Institutions of Capitalism: Firms, Markets, Relational Contracting* (New York; London: Free Press; Collier Macmillan, c1985), p. 21.

15. Oliver Williamson, "Corporate Finance and Corporate Governance," *Journal of Finance* 43:3 (July 1988), p. 572.

16. For a discussion of why democracies lower transaction costs, see Douglas North, "A Transaction Costs Theory of Politics," *Journal of Theoretical Politics* 2 4 (1990), pp. 355–367. Most of the AT literature does not explicitly deal with authoritarian regimes. For one view, see Solnick, op. cit.

17. On the 1987, or *"minjung"* movement, see Hagen Koo, "The State, Minjung, and the Working Class in South Korea," in Hagen Koo, ed., *State and Society in Contemporary Korea* (Ithaca, NY: Cornell University Press, 1993).

18. The best and most comprehensive work on this period is by Bruce Cumings, *The Origins of the Korean War*, 2 vols. (Princeton: Princeton University Press, 1981, 1989). See also Gregory Henderson, *Korea: The Politics of the Vortex* (Cambridge: Harvard University Press, 1968).

19. See John Kie-Chiang Oh, *Korea: Democracy on Trial* (Ithaca, NY: Cornell University Press, 1968), p. 204.

20. Gregory Henderson, "Constitutional Changes from the First to the Sixth Republics: 1948 to 1987," in Ilpyong Kim and Young Whan Kihl, eds., *Political Change in South Korea* (New York: Paragon, 1988), p. 27.

21. For details of this incident (the *"Balchwe* Amendment"), see Byungsik Shin, *"Pusan Chungchi Padongkwa Syngman Rhee Chejeui Hwagrip," Ku Yong-nok Hoegap Kinyom Nonmunjip* [Collection of Theses to Honor Professor Yong-nok Ku] (Seoul: Bôpmunsa, 1994), pp. 567–599.

22. See Dae-keun Lee, *Han'guk Chonjaengkwa 1950 nyondae Chabon Chukjok* [The Korean War and Capital Accumulation in the 1950s], (Seoul: Seoul National University Press, 1987); and Byong-jik Ahn and Nakamura Tetsuo, *Kundae Choson kongophwaui yonku, 1930–1945* [Studies of Korea's Modern Industrialization, 1930–1945], (Seoul: Ilchokak, 1993), especially chapter 8.

23. Bank of Korea, *Kyongje T'onggye Yonkam* [Economic Statistics Yearbook], various issues.

24. The junta that conducted the coup experienced a fair amount of internal maneuvering, and it was not initially clear whether Park would emerge as the outright leader.

25. From Stephan Haggard, Byung-kook Kim, and Chung-in Moon, "The Transition to Export-led Growth Strategy in South Korea 1954–1966," *Journal of Asian Studies* 50:4 (November 1991).

26. For more on the *Yushin* constitution, see Song-guk Go, "1970 nyondae Chongchi Pyondonge Kwanhan Yonku" ["Research on Political Changes in the 1970s"], in Jang-jip Choi, ed., *Han'guk Chabonjuuiwa Kukga* [Korean Capital and the State], (Seoul: Hanul, 1985).

27. Gregory Henderson, "Constitutional Changes from the First to the Sixth Republics: 1948 to 1987," in Kim and Kihl, eds., op. cit., p. 33.

28. On political parties, see Woon-Tai Kim, et al., *Han'guk Chongchiron* [Korean Politics] (Seoul: Pakyongsa, 1982), p. 387.

29. Some key Liberal Party members were arrested and punished after the *Sa-Il-Gu* (April 19th movement) that felled Rhee. This undoubtedly hastened the LP's demise.

30. See also David Brady and Jongryn Mo, "Electoral Systems and Institutional Choice: A case study of the 1988 Korean Elections," *Comparative Political Studies* 24 (January 1992), pp. 405–429; and Tun-jen Cheng and Mihae lim Tallian, "Bargaining Over Electoral Reform during the Democratic Transition," in Heemin Kim and Woosang Kim, eds., *Rationality and Politics in the Korean Peninsula* (Seoul: International Society for Korean Studies, 1995), pp. 17–52.

31. In the 1985 National Assembly elections, for example, Seoul accounted for 15.2 percent of contested seats, although it accounted for 24.9 percent of all eligible voters. See B. C. Koh, "The 1985 Parliamentary Election in South Korea," *Asian Survey* 25 9 (September 1985), pp. 883–897.

32. This is an oversimplification: many parties have provided selected benefits, such as holiday gifts and local hiking clubs, although they have not served to transmit interests to the center. In this way political parties in Korea function similarly to those in Japan, where the personal support networks (*koenkai*) are more important than party labels.

33. Gordon Flake originally made this point.

34. For good discussion of this issue, see Young Whan Kihl, *Politics and Policies in Divided Korea: Regimes in Contest* (Boulder: Westview Press, 1984); and Sung Chul Yang, *The North and South Korean Political Systems: A Comparative Analysis* (Boulder: Westview Press, 1994).

35. See, for example, n.a., "Kim warns against NK Provocation," *Korea Times*, April 5, 1996; and "'DMZ' Emerges as hot issue in campaign," *Korea Times*, April 7, 1996.

36. On labor in Korean politics, see Hagen Koo, Chang-jip Choi, Frederic Deyo, and Jongryn Mo.

37. See Henderson, *Korea: The Politics of the Vortex* (Cambridge: Harvard University Press, 1968).

38. *Donga Ilbo*, January 1, 1996,

39. Hagen Koo, "Strong State and Contentious Society," in Koo, ed., *State and Society in Contemporary Korea*, p. 232.

40. For a more full explication of the comparison between Taiwan and South Korea, see Tun-jen Cheng, Stephan Haggard, and David Kang, "Institutions, Economic Policy, and Growth in Korea and Taiwan" (m.s., UC San Diego, 1995).

41. This label is derived from the NIE literature on business organization. A "mutual hostage" situation exists whenever two actors have significant vulnerability relative to each other. In this situation, each side thus has an incentive both to continue the relationship, and also the incentive not to take advantage of the other party. For more, see Williamson, *The Economic Institutions of Capitalism*, op.cit.

42. The literature on the political economy of Korea is vast. The best works are by Haggard and Moon; Tun-jen Cheng, Alice Amsden, and Pyongyun Park, *Chaebolkwa Chongchi* [Chaebol and Politics] (Seoul: Hanguk Yongusa, 1982).

43. Byeong-Seog Park, "Political Corruption in South Korea: Concentrating on the Dynamics of Political Parties," *Asian Perspective* 19:1 (Spring 1995), pp. 163–193.

44. Young-Suk Lee, "Sonko Chakumgwa *Chaebol*" ["Political Funds and *Chaebols*"], *The Monthly Chosun* (November 1987), pp. 222–239.

45. Jung-en Woo, *Race to the Swift: State and Finance in Korean Industrialization* (New York: Columbia University Press, c1991), p. 107.

46. Joungwon A. Kim, *Divided Korea: The Politics of Development, 1945–1972* (Cambridge: Harvard University Press, 1985), p. 243.

47. For more on this, see Donald Kirk, *Korean Dynasty* (New York: M. E. Sharpe, 1994), pp. 269–272.

48. On page 15, Amsden uses *Kukje* as an example of economic considerations driving government support or sanctions.

49. See, for example, "*Chibang Sonkoinka Taesoninka, Tasi bulbutun Kimdului Chonjaeng*" ["Whether a Regional Election or Presidential Elec-

tion, Once Again the War of the Kims Is Sparking up"], *The Sisa Journal* (June 29, 1995), pp. 16–21.

50. Unpublished poll conducted by Research and Research in July 1995.

51. See Peter Rimmer, "The Political Geography of Transport Infrastructure Development in South Korea," in James Cotton, ed., *Politics and Policy in the New Korean State: from Roh Tae Woo to Kim Young Sam* (New York: St. Martin's Press, 1995); and Eui-yong Yu, "Regionalism in the South Korean Job Market," *Pacific Affairs* 63 (1988), pp. 24–39.

52. Of those military men involved in the 1961 coup, the first to be purged were from North Korea, followed by those from Cholla provice. This left men from Kyongsang province comprising the major group.

53. *Donga Ilbo* (December 20, 1997).

54. For an excellent discussion of *daekwon* in Korean politics, see Sung-Chul Yang, "An Analysis of South Korea's Political Process and Party Politics," in James Cotton, ed., *Politics and Policy in the New Korean State*; Manwoo Lee, "South Korea's Politics of Succession and the December 1992 Presidential Election," in Cotton ed., Ibid., and Manwoo Lee, *The Odyssey of Korean Democracy: Korean Politics, 1987–1990* (New York: Praeger, 1990).

55. Yong-shik Byun writes that "the failure to create an institutional framework that can check the far-reaching power of the president may result in recurrent abuse of presidential power in the future." Byun, "*Daekwon* (Presidential Power)," *Chosun Ilbo* December 7, 1995.

5

࿐

Political Leadership
in Korean Politics

Ki-shik S.J. Hahn

The purpose of this chapter is to examine the leaders of past administrations from 1948 to 1992 (the First to the Sixth Republic); the role they played in state building and modern history, and how their achievements and leadership can be evaluated.[1]

The personality, behavior, and political philosophy of Korea's leaders receive the most attention in this chapter. The social backgrounds of administrators and legislators, especially political leaders, are also surveyed. I exclude the judiciary because their contribution to Korean political development cannot clearly be identified. However, those members of the judiciary who went on to pursue careers in the executive or legislative branch are included in this study.

Although it helps to understand the social backgrounds of the Korean power elite, they are not the critical variables in explaining either their record or their pattern of leadership. In describing and analyzing the behavior of the leaders, I provide background information only. For convenience, I have grouped together the First and Second Republics, the Third and Fourth Republics, and the Fifth and Sixth Republics.

Focusing on political leaders or holders of governing power has a long tradition in political research. The role of the power elite is absolutely essential, especially in the modernization and political development of newly independent nations. Harold D. Lasswell commented that political science is a field that studies "who gets what, when and how."[2] If we reinterpret this as "who contributes what, when and how," we can see why a leadership approach holds promise in political research.[3]

107

The Political Leaders of the
First and Second Republics

Syngman Rhee and Chang Myon

While president Syngman Rhee of the First Republic and premier Chang Myon of the Second Republic can be contrasted in many respects, they cannot be compared on an equal basis. Rhee ruled Korea as an autocrat for twelve years from August 1948 until April 1960, when he was forced out of office during a student uprising. We cannot evaluate Chang in the same way because he lasted only eight months as prime minister before being forced out by a military coup in May 1961.

The two leaders, both fervent anticommunists, worked together closely to establish an independent South Korean government in 1948. Rhee received degrees in political science at George Washington, Harvard, and Princeton, while Chang obtained a Ph.D. in education at New York's Manhattan College. Rhee was an arrogant and stubborn leader; Chang listened to other people so much that he was perceived by his supporters as irresolute and incompetent.

It is not difficult to see why Rhee looked down on Chang, who was twenty years his junior. It was Rhee who raised Chang to high positions in government and fostered his political career.[4] Chang was no match for Rhee in terms of family background, activity in the independence movement, or especially in political capability and leadership. Chang became prime minister under a parliamentary system in the postauthoritarian environment, reflecting popular and especially, elite disenchantment with an overly authoritarian leader like Rhee.

Rhee, born March 26, 1875, studied Chinese classics in his childhood and entered Paejae School in 1893. Here, he was editor of an English language newspaper under the guidance of Seo Jaepil. This experience helped him to pursue a journalistic career, and he went on to become a notoriously controversial editor. He was arrested and sentenced to life imprisonment for his antigovernment activities, including his active participation in the Independence Association. Freed after seven years in 1904, he was sent to the United States by government leaders Min Yungwhan and Han Kyuseol to prevent the Japanese attempt to annex Korea. Rhee met President Theodore Roosevelt and Secretary of State John Hay but failed to persuade them. Realizing the inevitability of the Japanese annexation of Korea, he decided to remain in the United States and pursue his education.[5]

Rhee briefly returned to Korea after receiving his doctoral degree, but went back to the United States in 1911 after the Japanese annexation of Korea. In 1919, he became president of the Korean Provisional Government based in Shanghai, China. After resigning from presidency, Rhee was based in Hawaii and acted as the North American representative of the Provisional Government. In this capacity, he warned against Japanese expansionist ambitions for world domination in international conferences that he attended and in his newspaper articles and his meetings with government officials. He continued these activities for thirty years; his central message being that world peace could not be maintained so long as Japan occupied Korea. However, few were persuaded.

Korea became independent in 1945. Rhee demonstrated his political capacity and persistence by establishing the Republic of Korea in 1948 after an extended struggle against the leftist forces that were dominant at that time. In 1948, when he was seventy-three years old, Rhee was elected president by the First National Assembly.[6] He ruled for the next twelve years, often criticized by his people for his dictatorial style. He was eighty-five years old when he was forced out by the April 19 Student Revolution in 1960. He would be exiled to Hawaii, where he died five years later.

Rhee's contribution to Korean political history was the protection of his country from the communist threat during its early independence. The political ideology that he pursued was anti-Japanese and anticommunist; during his rule, many violations of democratic rules brought on legitimacy crises. One wonders why Rhee used the word *democracy* so often when his actions lacked democratic principles. Was it because the democratic allies of Korea preferred it to the word *nationalism*? Did Rhee feel uncomfortable with using nationalistic language when he declared himself to be a defender against communism? Perhaps he believed that he could not strictly follow the rules of democracy until the communist threat disappeared. One thing is clear, however: Rhee was an avowed nationalist who at the same time possessed many characteristics of an internationalist.

When Rhee was studying at Princeton, Woodrow Wilson, then president of the university, used to introduce him half-jokingly as "the future savior of Korean independence." In fact, Rhee lived his life only for Korean independence: everything else was secondary. Rhee did not consider Korea to be fully independent so long as

North Korea remained under the communist rule. He raised a slogan, "March North for Unification," sincere in his belief that no one other than himself could reunify the two Koreas. That seems to be the reason why he refused to relinquish power despite his age. But although he continued his long rule with purpose and devotion, he ultimately was expelled.

Although Rhee possessed unusual intellect, there is little evidence that he thought deeply about why Korea had to regain independence from Japan and why communism was wrong. He appears to have been too emotional and action-oriented to spend time writing his views on those questions. He did not seem to possess an intellect creative enough to provide highly persuasive arguments for an independent and unified Korea. Consequently, Rhee was not a leader who could inspire in his people a sense of a true character of the Republic of Korea.

The main instrument with which Rhee sought to accomplish his political objectives was diplomacy. He relied on the power of the United States to gain and maintain Korean independence and to reunify the divided nation. He was an internationalist in that he thought it was in the United States' interest to help Korea achieve its political objective. His internationalism was based on strong self-interest because he wanted to use foreign power for the interest of his nation. I do not agree with many analysts who view him as pro-United States and criticize his pro-U.S. policy. Rhee did not live for the United States; it is more accurate to say that he felt the United States existed for him to use. This is not surprising because from his point of view, Korean and U.S. interests coincided, and his own personal interests were similarly aligned.

Because his main interest was in diplomatic issues, he tended not to take much interest in domestic problems or administrative details. Moreover, he knew little about administration and national development, having had no administrative experience since his youth. Had he become president at a younger age, he might have better adapted himself to the new environment. However, Rhee, at the age of seventy-three, was too mentally and physically exhausted to learn how to govern a new republic.

The authoritarianism, incompetence, and corruption of Rhee's Liberal Party (LP) government not only alienated many people but also raised hostility. Nevertheless, his egotistical and narcissistic personality seems to have rendered Rhee unable to understand why people were discontent with him and his government. He apparently thought that if people were virtuous and honest, they would respect and follow him, no matter what he believed in and did. Therefore, he appears to have thought that the protest against his government was manipulated by a small number of demagogues.

However, Chang, who resisted Rhee's authoritarian rule, expressed in his memoirs his feelings about being forced out by the May 16 coup:

> Because of our long experience in the opposition, we understood the position of the governed too well. Having experienced Syngman's relentless oppression and persecution, we made it our principle not to follow Syngman's path. Needless to say, there were many difficulties keeping that promise . . . I regret that I did not have the time to put into action my plans for economic and social stability after having done all the preparatory work . . . I would like to say that if we had had a few more months, we could have built the basic framework for our country . . . what can I say to those . . . who did not give us that opportunity and tried to topple my government only eighteen days after inauguration?[7]

Those who reject the legitimacy of the May 16 military coup may wish to accept this recollection as is, but to those who support the coup, it is an unjustifiable excuse. The latter believe that the situation would have worsened if such a feeble prime minister had stayed in power for longer. Since Koreans are generally impatient, the Chang government was stripped of its opportunity to govern.

The Chang government had bureaucrats as competent as those of the Liberal Party. However, the public saw them competing for cabinet posts as if they were trophies. Even if Chang had shown resolute leadership, things would have been the same unless these attitudes had changed.

Political Leaders' Social Backgrounds
and Behavioral Patterns

CABINET MEMBERS OF THE LP GOVERNMENT. We can divide the members of the first cabinet into three groups. First, there were those chosen for their contribution to Rhee's victory: Chang Taeksang, Yoon Chi-young, Ahn Ho-sang (One-People-Ideology theorist), Chi Chung-chun (Anti-Communist Youth Organization), and Chun Jin-han (Anti-Communist Unions). Second were those recruited for political considerations: Lee Bum-seok was appointed prime minister with the intention to check Hanmindang (Korea Democratic

Party); and Cho Bong Am's appointment as minister of agriculture was intended to induce prominent communist leaders to break away as well as to control his sharp tongue. Rhee's personal confidence explains the cases of Kim Do-yeon and Lee In, but it is possible that he sought to thus divide the Hanmindang.[8]

However, as Rhee's power base solidified, the criteria for cabinet selection changed from those who could help regime survival to those who could contribute to regime efficiency, the third group. This explains why many of the bureaucrats from the colonial period were appointed to the cabinet. Because Rhee left domestic politics to Lee Ki Poong in the late 1950s, his own preference became less influential in cabinet selection. Lee, who selected cabinet members on the basis of qualifications, was criticized by the left of recruiting Japanese sympathizers to top posts.[9]

The social backgrounds of the cabinet ministers under the LP governments were as follows. If we look at their age distribution, there were three under age thirty-nine (2.5 percent), eighteen under age forty-five (15.3 percent), twenty-six between age forty-five and forty-nine (21.0 percent), thirty between fifty and fifty-four (25.4 percent), thirty between fifty-five and fifty-nine (25.9 percent), and ten between sixty and sixty-five (8.5 percent). The average age was about fifty. Sixty-nine-point-six percent (82) of the cabinet ministers had received college education and 17.9 percent (21) technical education, for a total percentage of 87.5 percent having had received higher education. By country of education, thirty-one were educated in the United States, thirty in Japan, twelve in China, six in Britain, two each in Germany and France, and one in the Soviet Union. Seventy-one percent of LP cabinet ministers had finished their education abroad. By specialization, 31.9 percent has studied law, 10.7 percent, economics; 13.9 percent, philosophy; 9.0 percent, political science; 9.0 percent, natural sciences; 6.6 percent, military sciences; 4.9 percent, literature; and 9 percent, other fields.

Careerwise, 23 percent came from the bureaucracy; 16 percent from academia; 13 percent from political parties; 13 percent from the legal profession; 7 percent from the military; 6 percent from the medical profession; 4 percent each from banks and firms; 1 percent from religious organization; and 9 percent from other professions.

The pattern of regional backgrounds shows that 32.3 percent came from Seoul, 19.0 percent from Kyungsang, 12.6 percent from Kyunggi, 8.7 percent from Pyongan, 7.1 percent from Kangwon, 4.0 percent from Cholla, 3.2 percent from Hamkyung, 2.3 percent from Hwanghae, and 1.6 percent from other regions.[10]

According to Kim Kyu-taek and Han Bae-ho's research on religious backgrounds, 32.9 percent were classified as Protestants, 7.4 percent as Catholics, 16.2 percent as Buddhists, 17.6 percent as Confucianists, 0.3 percent as Chon-do, 18.3 percent as unknowns.[11] My research into their class backgrounds and living standards shows that 86.9 percent belonged to upper-middle class, 10 percent to the lower-middle class, and 3.1 percent to the lower class. This classification, however, is too subjective to provide objective evidence.[12]

SOCIAL BACKGROUNDS OF SECOND-PERIOD CABINET MINISTERS. If we divide the LP's twelve-year rule into two periods, we can see that the pattern of cabinet selection changed in the second period, which began with the end of the Korean War. Compared to the first period, second-period cabinet ministers tended to be younger, to have received their college education in the United States and Japan, and to have had administrative experience in the colonial government. This change can be explained by the emphasis placed on professionalism and pragmatism in view of the overriding objectives of postwar reconstruction and economic recovery.

Without exception, all second-period cabinet members graduated from college, technical school, or a military academy. Among the first-period cabinet members, twenty-four out of thirty-two college graduates got their degrees from Western universities. Among the second-period members, only seven out of forty-seven college graduates went to western nations. The rest of them had studied in Korea or Japan. The government favored bureaucrats with more pragmatic backgrounds over those who had received abstract education.

If we look at the occupation of second-period ministers' fathers, we find that the number from middle-class farming families increased while fewer came from large landowners. Although we may not want to believe cabinet members' statements about their fathers' occupation and social position, there is no question that second-period cabinet members rose to their position because they had above-middle-class family backgrounds.

There were hardly any ministers in the second period who fought for independence against the Japanese. Instead, we see a large increase in the number of bureaucrats who had administrative experience in the colonial government. One gets the impression that in the first cabinet, members were chosen on the basis of Rhee's personal confidence or network, but gradually administrative experience and functional specialization guided recruitment. Among the sixteen former colonial officials, fourteen had served in the judicial branch. In addition, there were twelve teachers, seven doctors, five bankers, and five officers from the Japanese military. The relative rise of practical administrators shows that the demand for modernization and functionalization was increasing.

Legislative and Party Administrators

LEADERS OF THE LIBERAL PARTY. Because Rhee always distrusted political parties, he consistently refused offers to make him party president or adviser after he returned to Korea from exile. He wished to be a leader of the people as a whole, not of a political faction. The only post he accepted was the presidency of the Peoples' Committee for Promotion of Korean Independence. He later had no choice but to give up his "antiparty" attitude and organize a political party of his own.

The number of Rhee supporters in the Second National Assembly was small (57). Even independents, whose number now rose to 128, often threatened Rhee's power base by working with Hanmindang to revise the constitution to adopt a parliamentary system.[13] When Rhee's intention to form a political party was known, two party organizations competed to recruit him as their president. One was the parliamentary faction led by Lee Kap-sung and Kim Dong-sung, which later became the building bloc of the Democratic Party (DP). The other was the nonparliamentary faction of the LP centered around prime minister Lee Bum-seok and Lee Jae-hyung. This second group advocated a strong presidential system. Rhee instead instructed Lee Ki Poong to reorganize the Liberal Party. It was at this time that Lee rose to the second spot in the LP government.[14]

As Rhee grew older, it was considered only a matter of time before Lee succeeded him as president. If Lee were to step aside, his successor would eventually rise to the top position. The struggle over the number-three positions was shaped by the conflict between hard-liners and soft-liners. Lee sided with the latter in the beginning, but sided more with the hard-liners as the conflict between the ruling and opposition parties deepened. The rigging of the March 15 election reflected this internal competition for loyalty.

LEADERS OF THE DEMOCRATIC PARTY. The center of the opposition, the Hanmindang, had played a decisive role in establishing the Republic of Korea in 1948. Yet it was excluded from the first cabinet by Rhee, and so began to lead an anti-Rhee movement. To expand the anti-Rhee forces, the Hanmindang absorbed other parties to create the Minkukdang (Democratic National Party), becoming the Democratic Party in 1955. The DP was divided into the Old Faction, consisting of prominent Hanmindang politicians, and the New Faction centered around the parliamentary faction. The Old Faction was composed of people with vested interests, such as landowners and businesspeople, while many members of the New Faction were professional bureaucrats with no outside interests. The conflict for party control between these two factions was intense. After the Old Faction lost Shin Ik-hee in 1956 and Cho Byung-ok in 1960, its power receded and the New Faction gained the edge.

Assessment of Official Recruitment and Governing Style

The basic responsibilities of government officials are first, to protect the life, liberty, and property of their people; second, to provide a high standard of living; and third, to foster a sense of national commonality. By doing so, they must establish social order in place of the lawlessness of the transition period.

In comparing the governing styles of the Rhee and Chang governments, the first thing to notice is that the ministers of this period possessed neither the capacity nor the qualifications necessary to carry out the basic tasks of government. The state and the government were preserved through the patronage, protection, and support extended by the United States. The most obvious example of this was the Korean War and postwar reconstruction. If the United States had not protected and supported the Korean government militarily, the Korean peninsula would have been unified with the South being absorbed by the communist North. Although the Chang cabinet had better personnel than the early Rhee cabinets, it was no better in terms of administrative experience and specialized knowledge.

Second, the Rhee government lacked legitimacy from the start. Many leaders who deserved consideration for cabinet posts, such as widely respected independence movement leaders and other civic leaders, were excluded. Many members of the first cabinet were unknowns, and the cabinet as a whole was considered third-rate by many of its contemporaries.[15]

In appointing posts, it would have been desirable to demonstrate political unity and solidarity by forming a coalition cabinet, transcending the president's personal influence. However, even the leaders and moderates of the right wing, who supported Rhee's line in Korea and abroad, were excluded from the first cabinet along with those on the left and at the center. For this reason, Rhee's government failed from the outset to win popular support and confidence.

Especially disappointing to many, and damaging to the legitimacy of the Rhee government, was that cabinet positions were filled not by independence movement leaders but by people with a record of collaboration with the Japanese. However, it was not because Rhee intended to give special treatment to pro-Japanese leaders, but seemingly due to the fact that the independence movement and resistance leaders did not have the necessary experience to govern.

In fact, few of those who led the independence movement were recognized for their contributions. Only Rhee in South Korea, Kim Il Sung in North Korea, and a small number of government officials around them were rewarded. More often than not, they were murdered, imprisoned or left in poverty. In contrast, those who collaborated with the colonial government were able to maintain and even improve their social position because of their education and administrative experience. Moreover, they were able to provide their children with the best education possible, and thus had a competitive advantage within the social and governmental hierarchy. To protect and improve their positions, they needed a charismatic leader like Syngman Rhee. Their show of respect and obedience to the old revolutionary gained them commensurate advancement. In contrast, the children of those independence fighters and revolutionaries who could not support their families economically did not receive even secondary education. It was their opposition to authority that kept them from positions of power.[16]

The Kim Il Sung regime in the North expelled and eliminated not only pro-Japanese Koreans but also members of the middle class who received more than primary education. By doing so, while they were able to entrench the antiimperialist, antifeudal people's government, modernization and development of North Korean society had to be delayed. Kim Il Sung was able to maintain his absolute rule because the poorer and less-educated people obeyed and worshiped him as a god. Herein lies the reason North Korea remained more backward than the South.[17]

The Political Leaders of the
Third and Fourth Republics

President Park Chung Hee

President Park Chung Hee was born on November 4, 1917, in a small village in Kyungbuk Province. Because he was the youngest of six in a poor family, he seems to have grown up feeling insecure or psychologically pressured for not contributing to the livelihood of his family.[18] As he grew up, he was not content with his simple life. He would have felt that the way to pay his debt to his family was to make a great contribution to the nation and society.

In April 1926, he entered elementary school. Always quiet and concentrated in his studies, the young Park did not mingle or play with other children.[19] Unimposing and diminutive, Park excelled in his studies, in constant competition for top place in his class. In 1932, he enrolled in the Taegu State School, graduating in 1937 to become a teacher at a school in a remote corner of Moon Kyung. He later entered the Manchu Military Academy, graduating at the top of his class and going on to complete a one-year program at Japan's Military Academy in 1944. He was a lieutenant when Korea became independent in 1945.

After independence, he returned briefly to his hometown before joining the army. He was commissioned as an officer in 1946 but, because he was implicated in the Yeosu-Soon-chon Military Rebellion, his promotion was slow. However, he was widely known as a competent officer free from corruption—rare among Korean officers—stern and responsible.[20] He placed himself in an even more difficult position by refusing orders to intervene in the March 15 election toward the end of the Liberal Party rule.

After the Rhee regime was toppled, a movement in the army began calling for the purge of military officers who had committed election fraud or engaged in corrupt activities in association with the Rhee government. Park emerged as the leader of this movement. The movement was suppressed, however, and the leaders court-martialed. Park, realizing that reform was impossible under the current social and authority structures, plotted a successful military coup.

Park Chung Hee's government, which ruled for eighteen years, was the most successful government in Korean history in terms of national defense, economic prosperity, and promotion of national pride. Why, then, do analysts critical of the Park government outnumber those that are supportive of his regime? Some cannot accept the third-term constitutional revision, though they accept the justification for the May 16 military coup. Others argue that the *Yushin* constitution and the May 16 military coup cannot be justified because they were both military interventions in politics and led to military dictatorship. However, the most important factor in explaining this negative assessment is that Korean analysts tend to value legitimacy over utility and efficiency.

Yet those who carried out the coup and the *Yushin* system wanted to place significant meaning on them. Park Chung Hee made the following comment:

> The May 16 coup spoke for the aspirations of our people for stability and prosperity in place of the disorder and pain of poverty; manifested the will of our people to pursue self-reliance and development in place of the pressures of dependence and stagnation; and instilled in us a mission to divorce ourselves from our history of ordeal and trial and pioneer a new history of pride and honor . . .[21]

Around the time of the inauguration of the Third Republic, new politicians joined the ruling party, advocating democracy and seeking to practice constitutional politics geared toward modernization. Opposition forces were composed of politicians who had been in opposition since the 1950s. However, they could not muster force in the face of the persecution by the executive authority and the interference of the Korean Central Intelligence Agency (KCIA). The Park government signed the Korea-Japan Normalization Treaty in spite of violent demonstrations and succeeded in strengthening the base of industrialization by implementing the First and Second Five-Year Economic Plans. Encouraged by these economic successes, Park planned a constitutional revision to grant himself greater power. He implemented the *Yushin* system in part because the number of opposition supporters rose drastically in the 1971 presidential election and a large number of opposition members won the election. The *Yushin* system weakened the power of the National Assembly while executive, administrative, and judicial power was concentrated in one person, the president.

The *Yushin* ideology was one of national revival under a one-man leadership system. The *Saemaul* (New Village) movement began as one of the regional developments emphasizing farmers' self reliance, but was in reality a cooperative national movement aimed at modernization. Ultimately, the *Yushin* ideology became one of bureaucratic authoritarianism and was criticized as a system allowing Park Chung Hee to exercise unrestrained power. Whether or not the *Yushin* system was a form of Latin American bureaucratic authoritarian regime was one of the main debates in academic circles in the 1980s.[22]

Cabinet Officials' Social Backgrounds
and Behavioral Patterns

THE PRINCIPLES OF CABINET SELECTION IN THE THIRD REPUBLIC. The first cabinet of the Democratic Republic Party (DRP) government consisted of eighteen members including five former military officers: Chung Il-kwon (foreign minister), symbolizing military unity, Kim Sung-eun (defense minister), representing the Marines, Lee Seok-jae (minister of government administration), representing the leaders of the May 16 military revolution, and two others from military medicine and research units. Of the civilians, most were former vice ministers or had held important administrative positions.

THE SOCIAL BACKGROUNDS OF CABINET MINISTERS. If we examine the social backgrounds of cabinet ministers during the period from December 1963 to December 1970, we find the following:

Age: The average age of cabinet ministers during that period was 51.6, slightly lower than the average age of 53.6 for those who served the LP government from 1953 to 1960. However, this figure was higher than the average age of cabinet ministers in the beginning (1948–1953) of the LP rule and the military government which were 43 and 43.9, respectively. This was because more experienced bureaucrats were appointed. For example, Paek Doo-jin, 44 years old when appointed finance minister and 45 when he became prime minister under the Rhee administration, was 62 years old when he returned as prime minister in the Democratic Republic government. Lee Ho also was a young cabinet minister (41 years old) under Rhee, but was reappointed justice minister at age 54 by Park Chung Hee. We should see this trend as reflecting not the influence of premodern culture but the maturation and growth of administrative experience. The average age of cabinet members during the Fourth Republic was 51.03 as the proportion of former legislators and party activists declined while that of professors, journalists, and bureaucrats increased.

Educational Backgrounds: Almost all members of the cabinet during this period received college or the equivalent level of education. Among the eighty-nine cabinet ministers, all except for four (4.5 percent) graduated from college, technical school or military academy. Among them were twenty-one military academy graduates, representing 23.6 percent of the total. Among the sixty-four college graduates, thirty-six (56.3 percent) were educated in Japan and Manchuria, eighteen (28.1 percent) completed their college or technical school education in Korea, and ten were trained in the United States or Europe. Among twenty-one military academy graduates, fourteen (66 percent) graduated from a Korean military academy, five (23.8 percent) went to the Manchurian military academy, and two (9.5 percent) graduated from a Japanese military academy. In the Fourth Republic, the number of cabinet ministers educated in the West increased and the number of graduates of Seoul National University's Law School also rose at a rapid rate.

Professional Backgrounds: Although the military government was dominated by former military officers, the number of military officials fell to twenty-six (41.3 percent) in the DRP government. The number of professors also increased. As for those with civilian backgrounds, forty-one out of sixty-three (69.2 percent) were bureaucrats, bankers, or managers, eight (9.6 percent) were self-employed professionals, and twelve (21.1 percent) fell into both categories.

Careers: The DRP government chose cabinet members on the basis of their aptitude, qualifications, and careers, more so than any previous government. The DRP government was able to fill cabinet posts with more qualified people than either the Rhee or Chang governments because they could tap into the growing pool of experienced bureaucrats. One obvious statistic after 1963 was the increase in the number of cabinet members who had previously served as vice minister or minister. Because the Park government, unlike the DP government, tried to make up for its lack of legitimacy with administrative performance, it was reluctant to recruit leaders of the DRP and instead, favored bureaucrats and military officers whose professions demand efficiency.

Social Backgrounds: The DRP government recruited a large number of high-ranking bureaucrats. Although we do not have precise data on cabinet ministers' family backgrounds, my investigation of forty-seven members reveal that twelve came from wealthy land-owning families, another twelve from small landowners, and eighteen from independent farmers. In other words, forty-two had middle- or upper-class backgrounds. Only five out of forty-seven (10.6 percent) came from poor families.

Regional Backgrounds: Twenty-two (24.7 percent) were natives of Kyungsang, fifteen (16.9 percent) were from Cholla, thirteen (14.8 percent) from Seoul, twelve (13.5 percent) from Chungchung, eight (9 percent) from Pyungan, six (6.7 percent) from Hamkyung, two each from Kangwon and Cheju. The number of North Korean natives exceeded that of not only Kangwon and Cheju but also Cholla and Kyonggi because there were many North Korean natives among right-wing and military leaders. During the Fourth Republic, the share of Kyungsang natives jumped to 35 percent while that of Honam natives fell.

Legislative and Party Officials

THE DEMOCRATIC REPUBLICAN PARTY. The DRP was founded in 1963 by Kim Jong Pil, then director of the Korean Central Intelligence Agency. Leaders of the coup rebelled against this unilateral move; many of them were forced to seek temporary refuge abroad. The DRP consisted of the Kim Jong Pil faction, holdovers from the LP (such as Yoon Chi-young, Kim Seong-kon, Kim Jin-man), former DP members (Oum Min-young, Paek Nam-uk, Park Joon-kyu, and Kim Jae-soon), and several military groups.[23]

Initially, a coalition of anti-Kim Jong Pil factions curbed the power of his supporters. After the Third-Term Constitutional Amendment, the party was taken over by the leadership team of Kim Seong-kon, Paek Nam-uk, Kim Jin-man, and Kil Jae-ho. However, following the introduction of the *Yushin* system in October 1973, the party was unable to check the executive branch. Kim Jong Pil was elected party president after Park was assassinated in October 1979, but the DRP was dissolved by Chun Doo Hwan in May 1980, seventeen years after its founding.

The opposition parties that had lost the 1963 general elections merged to create a unified party, the People's Party.[24] However the rivalry between Yoon Po-sun and Yu Jin-san intensified, and Yoon left to create his own New Korea Party when Yu took control. The two parties merged again in July 1967 into the New Democratic Party (NDP). Yu Jin-ho, former president of Korea University, was elected president of the NDP, and was succeeded by Yu Jin-san after the Third-Term Amendment. The conflict over party control in the opposition parties pitted politicians from aristocratic families against strategists with less affluent backgrounds, emphasizing the change in the character of the opposition party. Yu Jin-san lost power due to rumors that he had made a secret deal with the ruling party to raise political funds.[25] It was at this juncture, while in his forties, that Kim Young Sam first argued for a new leader. Kim Dae Jung and Lee Chul-sung soon joined the hegemonic conflict for party control, and it was Kim Dae Jung who was nominated presidential candidate in the party convention held on September 29, 1970.

Legislators and Party Leaders in the Fourth Republic

RESULTS OF GENERAL ELECTIONS AND LEGISLATIVE ELITES' SOCIAL BACKGROUNDS. In the tenth National Assembly election of 1978, the DRP lost to the NDP by 1.1 percent. Park Joon-kyu was named party chairman and became the second in line. However, Kim Jong Pil was elected party president after Park Chung Hee's death. The NDP under Yu Jin-san's leadership was divided over how to fight the *Yushin* system. When Yu Jin-san died in 1974, Kim Young Sam took control of the party[26] but this leadership resigned in 1975, having been attacked by both hard-liners and moderates. Afterward, Lee Chul-sung ran the party as a coalition consisting of Lee Chung-hwan, Yu Chi-song, and Lee Jae-kwan from the mainstream and Lee Chul-sung, Sin Do-hwan, and Ko Heung-moon from the opposition. Kim Young Sam resisted party leaders and organized the Committee for Recovering the True Opposition. After Kim was expelled from the National Assembly, demonstrations protesting his expulsion took place in Masan and Pusan. Kim Young Sam regained control of the NDP after Park's assassination.

The social backgrounds of legislators were as follows:

Age: Among the legislators elected from local districts in the ninth National Assembly election, 55 percent were between forty-one and fifty-one years old; 14 percent were in the fifty-one to fifty-five age group and 8.0 percent in the fifty-six to fifty bracket. In the tenth National Assembly, members forty-six to fifty-five years old comprised 52.6 percent and those forty-one to forty-five years old made up 17.5 percent.

Education: As the general level of education improved, so did that of National Assembly members. Among the directly elected members of the ninth National Assembly, 36.24 percent had graduate-level education while 25.3 percent had only college education.

Thus, a total of 88.5 percent had at least college education. In the case of the tenth National Assembly, 89.6 percent had college education or better; 31.8 percent received graduate education. This statistic can be attributed to expanded opportunities for higher education created by many new special graduate programs. Only 27 out of 226 (11.9 percent) legislators went abroad for their education, and their share dropped significantly. Seoul National University graduates comprised 29 percent, followed by Korea University (11 percent), Yonsei University (5 percent), military academies (12 percent), foreign universities (12 percent), and others (32 percent).

Careers: Professional politicians were the largest career group (26 percent) among the directly elected legislators, followed by bureaucrats (16 percent); businesspeople (15 percent); military officers (12 percent); journalists (8 percent); lawyers, judges, and prosecutors (5 percent); and others (8 percent). In selecting appointed legislators the criterion of functional expertise continued to be applied, as can be seen from the following distribution of career backgrounds: professors, 25 percent; military officers, 18 percent; bureaucrats, 14 percent; journalists, 14 percent; politicians, 11 percent; lawyers, judges, and prosecutors, 7 percent; businesspeople, 4 percent; and others, 8 percent.

*Evaluation of Recruitment of
Political Leaders and Governing Styles*

It has been said that there was no politics, only administration, under the Park regime. In fact, it is more appropriate to refer to him as a ruler than as a politician. He detested politics from the start, considering the DRP's role as being to elect him to presidency and his followers to the National Assembly. He allowed no autonomy to party politics beyond what was necessary. As a result, Kim Jong Pil was often forced to leave the party and his followers were regularly purged. Even after Kim left, the purging of the party continued and the role of the party shrunk accordingly. Furthermore, Park established nonelected legislators to check the DRP under the *Yushin* system. The suppression of the opposition parties was more thorough. On the one hand, Park disliked even meeting party leaders face-to-face. On the other hand, he enjoyed meeting and talking with the leaders of the *Saemaul* movement.[27] He made excessive use of the Korean Central Intelligence Agency to monitor each cabinet ministry and, ironically, was killed by the director of KCIA in October 1979.

In many respects, the cabinet of the Third Republic was the

one most considered in forty years of constitutional rule. Two developments deserve attention: under military rule, traditional status-oriented politics gave way to performance-oriented politics and many individuals with middle- or lower-class backgrounds gained high positions in the bureaucracy and military. In contrast, opposition leaders, who usually came from middle- or upper-class families, saw their social standing falling.

The debate on whether the May 15 Military Revolution was a revolution or a coup has recently reemerged. I believe it had elements of both. Because the basic character of the anticommunist, pro-American authoritarian government did not change after May 16, 1961, it can be viewed as a coup. On the other hand, it was revolutionary in several respects. First, it transformed within ten years a backward agricultural country into an advanced or midlevel industrial economy. As a result, rural population fell drastically while urban population rose rapidly, bringing about fundamental changes in the people's value system and social attitudes. Second, politicians became more achievement-oriented and less concerned with status. Finally, people developed confidence in their ability to catch up with the advanced countries. Therefore, one can argue that the May 16 Military Revolution was a coup in form, but a revolution in substance and consequences.

A final note should be taken on the change in Park Chung Hee's psychological condition during his rule. Initially, he was sincere and shrewd, governing the country calmly and solidly. However, when he gained absolute power and when his opponents were eliminated in the Fourth Republic, he became arrogant, violent, and decadent, especially after the death of his wife. The Park Chung Hee government made huge contributions to developing the economy and fostering a sense of self-confidence. Why is it that people continue to criticize his government? Perhaps because the brighter the light, the darker its shadow?

The Political Leaders of the Fifth and Sixth Republics

Leaders with Military Backgrounds:
Chun Doo Hwan and Roh Tae Woo

CHUN DOO HWAN. Chun Doo Hwan was born in Kyungnam, the fifth son of seven siblings.[28] His father, a farmer who moved his family to Manchuria to escape retaliation for the manslaughter of a Japanese policeman, returned to Taegu two years later. Chun, who could not attend elementary school regularly, enrolled in Taegu Technical Middle School in September 1947. In the middle of the Korean War, Chun entered the Army Military Academy in November 1951 along with Roh Tae Woo, Kim Bok-dong, and Paik Untaek.

On September 30, 1955, the first-ever graduates of the four-year program at the Military Academy were commissioned. Chun expressed his joy and emotion: "I did not graduate from the Military Academy with a distinguished record, but will become the best officer in the army." He wrote the phrase "Fearless Dash" on his official album. There would be no better word to describe his personality and attitude.[29]

When the May 16 Military Revolution began, Chun, then a captain, delighted Park Chung Hee by proposing to organize the military academic cadets to demonstrate in support of the revolution. Although Park invited him to work with him in his government many times, Chun refused and remained in the military. Chun, however, held nonmilitary posts including secretary of civil affairs to the chairman of the Supreme Council of National Reconstruction and director of personnel at the KCIA.

Chun was appointed commander of the Military Intelligence Command on March 5, 1979, and took charge of investigations of Park's assassination as the head of the Joint Investigation Headquarters. He went ahead with the execution of the assassin, Kim Jae-kyu, despite calls for his release. When General Chung Seung-hwa, the Army Chief of Staff and Commander of Marshal Law Administration did not cooperate with the investigations and prepared to transfer Chun to a post at the front-line, Chun sent his men to arrest General Chung. He took control of the military in the subsequent turmoil on December 12, 1979.[30] His victory over the marshal law commander in the power struggle was made possible through the cooperation of Chun's supporters in the military.

Chun's takeover of the government was the result of several factors. First, there was an implicit agreement among his classmates that they, being the first graduates of the military academy, should take over the military, and that they had to secure political power to do so. Second, the military as a whole harbored a deep distrust of civilian politics. Military leaders felt that in order to protect national security, they had to expel the "three Kims" from the political arena. Third, military leaders seem to have believed that a military coup could be justified if it replaced the one-person rule and systematic corruption of the *Yushin* system.

The contributions of the Chun government can be summarized as follows: first, there was an end put to the political turmoil following the assassination of Park and maintenance of some level of political stability, despite the fact that Chun had come to power through force. Second, the trade balance registered a surplus for the first time in history; he held a period of sustained economic growth by completing the heavy industry promotion program that Park Chung Hee had began but could not finish, and also by targeting strategic industries. Third, Chun extended Korean diplomacy, improving relations with other countries. In particular, we cannot underestimate the contributions to national prestige by successfully hosting the 1986 Asian Games and the twenty-fourth Olympiad in 1988.

ROH TAE WOO. Roh Tae Woo, born on December 4, 1932 in Kyungbook, was the eldest son of his family. He lost his father at the age of seven and had to play the role of the head of household. This may explain why he was quiet and grew up being praised for his maturity. His mother used to tell him "not to behave like a fatherless son."[31]

When he was preparing to apply for medical school in his third year at Kyungbuk High School, the war broke out. He was enlisted as a student soldier and served at the Military Police School. When the war reached a stalemate in 1951, he enrolled at the Military Academy.

During the May 16 Military Revolution he went to the Military Academy, along with his classmates, to persuade the cadets to parade in support of the revolution, revealing his political inclinations for the first time. He fought in the Vietnam War as a lieutenant colonel, earning the Hwa Rang Distinguished Service Medal.

Roh was the commander of the ninth Army Division when Park Chung Hee was assassinated and sided with Chun Doo Hwan against General Chung Seung-hwa. After serving as a martial law commander in the Seoul metropolitan area and head of the Military Intelligence Command, he retired as a four-star general in September 1981 after twenty-six years of military service in order to begin a political career. After holding various posts in the government and the party, he was nominated the presidential candidate of the ruling party. Roh defeated Kim Young Sam and Kim Dae Jung in the December 17 presidential elections and was inaugurated as the twelfth president on February 25, 1988.

Perhaps because he had lost his father at a young age, Roh was always cautious and treated everyone good-heartedly and kindly, gaining the confidence of his superiors and the respect of his juniors. He rarely pursued his goals aggressively because he preferred to prepare for all contingencies from the beginning to prevent any losses than to lose all by recklessly pursuing excessive gains.

Roh had developed at an early stage an ability to achieve his objectives quietly without being criticized and without quarreling with or being harmed by others. When faced with a difficult problem, he tended to wait for it to disappear or for people to lose interest. Although this leadership style meant nicknames like "water president" or "Water Tae Woo," we have to understand that it was a calculated move that had served him well before.[32]

He took full advantage of his dissembling and image-making skills in dealing with opposition leaders and the media. No one in Korean history had a more cooperative relationship with opposition leaders and maintained a more mutually beneficial relationship with the media than Roh Tae Woo. Unlike previous military leaders, he was conscious of his popularity and paid detailed attention to his image. On the one hand, due to his popular management ability, he was able to finish his term without a major crisis even though he did not make any special contributions. On the other hand, because of his obsession with popularity, he has been criticized for deserting friends like Chun Doo Hwan, Kim Bok-dong, and Chung Ho-young.

However, too much focus on the good-natured and smooth aspects of his personality, we risk bypassing other aspects. He possessed a willingness to take the risk when necessary: along with Chun Doo Hwan, he persuaded the cadets to show support for the military coup, he brought his troops to control key institutions during the 1979 power struggle; and he punished Hyundai to curb the power of the *chaebol*.

Although Roh Tae Woo usually cultivated an image of a gentle and democratic political leader, he was ruthless and brutal when punishing his political enemies. He was, if he decided to retaliate against a person, as brutal as any authoritarian leader and fully mobilized resources within his power such as the bureaucracy, the judicial branch and the media.

There is an anecdote that clearly contrasts the personality and leadership styles of Chun and Roh. When Chun was briefed about a problem and possible solutions, he would issue an order even before the briefing was finished. Roh in the same situation would not make a decision even after the presentation. It is possible that Chun often made mistakes in such hasty decisions. By comparison, Roh would rather wait patiently for the problem to resolve itself or for interested parties to become exhausted and lose interest than make a mistake by trying to bring about a quick resolution. In a way, this can be viewed as a sign of incompetence or shirking responsibility, but at least he could avoid the consequences of bad decisions.[33] In this respect Roh Tae Woo was a nearly perfect self-protector.

The list of Roh Tae Woo's achievements is as follows: first, he was instrumental in bringing about democratization in process. Since democratic process was ineffective in managing the excessive political participation of many interest groups as the centralized control of the authoritarian government weakened, Korean political development did advance as much as economic development in the last thirty years. Nevertheless, Roh Tae Woo implemented the democratization promises he made in his June 29 Declaration.

Second, by concentrating on *Nordpolitik*, he was able to reconcile and normalize diplomatic relations with communist regimes such as the Soviet Union and China. As a result, Korea was ready to carry out an omnidirectional, independent diplomacy.

The Social Backgrounds and
Behavioral Pattern of Administrators

THE PRINCIPLES OF OFFICIAL RECRUITMENT. The criteria for cabinet selection in the Fifth Republic were (1) strengthening regime legitimacy by recruiting civilians to the cabinet, (2) preference for bureaucrats, and (3) rewarding those who contributed to the founding of the regime. First, ministerial positions were filled with prominent civilian leaders. Regional backgrounds were also taken into account; many ministers such as Kim Sang Hyup, Chin Euijong, and Lee Han-ki were natives of Cholla province.

Second, many cabinet members were specialized professionals who accumulated experience in the Third and Fourth Republics. They were capable in their fields and contributed to expanding administrative capacity in the 1980s. However, one could not expect former bureaucrats to have the flexibility to overcome and resolve crises that required a high level of political judgment.

Third, few members of the core ruling group joined the cabinet: Roh Tae Woo, Park Se-jik, and Huh Moon-do were typical examples. Most instead occupied important positions in the National Assembly and Chong Wa Dae. Cabinet selection in the Sixth Republic was more or less modeled after the Fifth Republic, but was different in two respects. First, the Sixth Republic did not favor Cholla natives as ministers. Second, increasing numbers of Kyungbuk natives were appointed to positions with more power in the Sixth Republic.

If we examine the social backgrounds of cabinet ministers in the Fifth and Sixth Republics, we find the following:

Age: The age distributions of cabinet ministers in the Fifth and Sixth Republics were very similar. The average age of cabinet ministers during the two periods was 53.03 with the forty-one to sixty age group making up the 81 percent of the total. The average age went up to 56.2 in the Sixth Republic because many bureaucrats, academics, and journalists were recruited.

Education: The level of education of cabinet members continued to increase. The number of cabinet ministers with graduate education increased to 41.5 percent in the Fifth Republic from 28 percent in the Third and 23.8 percent in the Fourth Republic.[34] Eighty-three-point-three percent of those who studied abroad still went to the United States or Japan, although a greater range of educational institutions was represented. In the Sixth republic, the number of cabinet members who studied in Japan decreased while those in the United States increased.

Law and military science majors comprised 46.23 percent of cabinet members. The share of law school graduates, 26.4 percent, fell from the 34.9 percent of the Fourth Republic[35] but they dominated positions of power to such an extent that some called the DJP a party of generals and attorneys.[36] The assistance of law graduates was probably needed to justify the military rule, but this contributed to the further alienation of the people from the regime.

The percentage of Seoul National University (SNU) graduates continued to rise, from 30 percent in the Fourth Republic to 48 percent in the Fifth and 52 percent in the Sixth. It has been argued that the rise of the SNU share resulted from the effort to recruit qualified professionals. Nevertheless, the fact that more than 50 percent of cabinet ministers came from one university among 110 suggests the existence of bias. It is naive to think that the military authoritarian regime could improve its legitimacy by replacing the proportion of former military officers in the cabinet solely with SNU graduates.

The educational level of cabinet ministers also increased. Opportunities for reeducation expanded in general, and during the Sixth Republic in particular, highly educated individuals such as academics, bureaucrats, and journalists were more favored.

Why is it that the Sixth Republic had a record so much weaker than any of the previous authoritarian governments when it came to the appointment of more mature, highly educated, and experienced cabinet ministers? One possibility is that the quality of education may not have improved despite the increase in duration. It also suggests how decisive the leadership of the president is relative to the quality of cabinet ministers.

The number of cabinet ministers who studied in the United States continued to rise while the position of Japan as a place of education continued to fall and slipped to third place behind Britain. A large number of officials who were born in the late 1910s and early twenties went to Japan for education: they were now replaced by those who were born after the 1930s and were educated in the United States.

The distributions of college majors and alma maters did not change much from the Fifth to the Sixth Republic. Law and military science majors comprised 45.8 percent of the cabinet in the Sixth Republic, followed by 15 percent for economic, management, and political science majors. Other areas were insignificantly represented.

The fact that the Sixth Republic continued, like the military regimes, to favor law and military science majors indicates that the president's way of thinking did not change. It is notable that at a time when various issues were debated as a result of democratization, the cabinet was dominated by a small number of majors. Ministers lacking specialized knowledge cannot be expected to respond effectively to the complex problems of the real world.

Career Backgrounds: We also find that the share of cabinet ministers who had been legislators was only 5.7 percent; the others had been bureaucrats (31.13 percent), military officers (20.7 percent), professors (19.81 percent), and journalists (6.6 percent). It is reasonable to appoint professionals to the cabinet, but the appointment of a large number of bureaucrats widened the distance between the government and people, since they lacked sophisticated political skills.

Compared with the Fifth Republic, the Sixth appointed fewer military officials and more bureaucrats, professors and journalists.

However, the pattern of recruitment did not change, and the proportion of bureaucrats, professors and military officers together remained high, at 75.6 percent. It would seem natural that the cabinets of a democratic system should consist more of political and social interest group leaders than bureaucrats. These individuals are more suited to the task of mediating between conflicts of interest and translating social demands into policy than career bureaucrats. Presidents in the past favored career bureaucrats for important positions because they were efficient at implementing the leaders' intentions, but this practice does not help democratization. During the Sixth Republic, as the media became more influential, bureaucrats became overly sensitive and began to avoid media scrutiny and criticism. This trend among the bureaucrats hampered their ability to serve the country.

Regional Backgrounds: As in the Fourth Republic, the Kyungsang provinces, with their 30 percent population share were disproportionately represented at 33.01 percent. Cholla provinces, 11 percent of population, increased their share to 15.09 percent from 12.7 percent. In the Fourth Republic, Kyungbuk and Kyungnam had an equal share of 17.46 percent. But in the Fifth Republic, Kyungbuk received special consideration, alienating other regions; Kyungnam with a population share of 13.4 percent had 12.16 percent of cabinet ministers, but Kyungbuk with only a 16.9 percent population share claimed 20.7 percent of cabinet ministers.

The prejudice for the Kyungsang provinces deepened in the Sixth Republic. Compared to the Fifth Republic, the shares of Seoul and Kyonggi increased while that of Cholla natives further declined. Kyungbuk, in particular, had 19.6 percent of cabinet ministers, and it is clear that it was treated better than other regions, including Seoul and Kyonggi, even after taking into account its population share. This problem was more serious in terms of the regional distribution of positions of power.[37] It is difficult to deny that this one-sided recruitment contributed to regionalism that has distorted Korean political process for so long.

Evaluation of Political Leaders'
Recruitment and Governing Styles

The recruitment of government ministers during the Fifth and Sixth Republics shared several characteristics: first, the share of military officials was relatively large; former generals, Chun Doo Hwan and Roh Tae Woo, had many close associates of military background; second, there was a continued rise in the number of career bureaucrats, among whom SNU law graduates were dominant. The preference for military and bureaucratic officers was one of the factors sustaining the authoritarian system, since such officers tended to care more about gaining their superiors' confidence and attention than the people's interests and mood.

Third, regional, occupational, and school disparities continued to widen. The Fourth Republic did not hide its preferences for certain regions, career backgrounds and universities, and the Fifth and Sixth Republics intensified rather than corrected these biases. If it is true that Park Chung Hee and Chun Doo Hwan, who came to power by force, had felt threatened, then their preference for those from their home region is understandable. However, in the case of Roh Tae Woo, his natural cautiousness and distrust of other people are more plausible reasons as to why he reinforced the dominance of the Kyungbuk faction despite negative public opinion.

Every political leader relies on a group of advisers with whom he consults, known as his reference group. Chun Doo Hwan's reference group consisted of intelligence agencies and bureaucrats. Their administrative expertise was useful, but their participation often backfired and caused popular resistance because of their prejudices. Delegating responsibility to his juniors was one of Chun's strengths, as well as a limit of his governing ability.

President Roh Tae Woo was no different from Chun Doo Hwan in relying on bureaucrats and intelligence agencies. However, he appeared to give more weight to the opinions of media and opposition leaders. This was not because they were more valuable than or superior to those of bureaucrats and intelligence agencies; the opposite was often true. Roh seems to have believed that consulting the media and opposition leaders could protect him from criticism. In fact, he was often accused of trying to build a protective shield to escape political retaliation after leaving office.

It could be argued that the officials of the authoritarian system, whose motivation was to principally avoid the president's displeasure, helped to bring an abrupt end to the *Yushin* system and the Fifth Republic. Interestingly, none of these officials defended their leaders when, after their rule ended, they came under attack from the media.

Roh Tae Woo's efforts to open dialogue and cooperate with the opposition parties, dissident groups, and media resulted in a relationship better than any other past government. However, Roh lacked the leadership and responsibility to present a genuine political vision. Although he may have protected himself well, he was too accommodating toward the media, dissident groups, opposition parties, and the general public.[38]

Leadership is the ability to set a goal and lead the media and the opposition toward it; it does not mean pandering to or being led by them. Without that sense of direction, a president finds himself losing sight of his true role. A president should also possess a sense of responsibility; he is responsible for protecting the basic values of his country and achieving its objectives without succumbing to pressure from within or without. Although the Roh government survived in a difficult situation and was able to escape attacks and criticisms from the public, it fell well short of achieving its goals of political development, national harmony, and unification. Because it did not deal effectively with social and political disorder and economic stagnation, it has not been regarded highly.

Conclusion: Evaluating Political Leadership and the Patterns of Official Recruitment

Korean leaders, no matter how autocratic, will receive different evaluations depending on one's perspective. We can certainly give them a positive evaluation based on the fact that they founded an independent government, defended the country from a communist takeover, and transformed a backward, agrarian society into a dynamic industrial one in a remarkably short span. This is evidence that leaders and officials were both dedicated and capable.

Left-wing analysts paint a negative picture of the role of South Korean political leaders by accusing them of being responsible for national division and military confrontation with the North, all dictated by a grand conspiracy of the United States. The radical also argue that South Korea's economic development in the past four decades has been nothing but dependent, shaped by an American imperialistic plot to expand capitalism in East Asia. In my opinion, both accusations are wrong. It is the people and leaders of South Korea who are ultimately responsible for their situation, and South Koreans must not shift the blame to foreign countries.

Evaluations of political leaders in South Korea have been overly negative. As is often the case, people's evaluations of others tend to be extreme. North and South Korea are good examples. Assessments of South Korea's leaders have always been too negative, while North Korean leaders have been overvalued by their people. There are several reasons why South Korean leaders have been underestimated.

The standards people have set for political leaders have been unrealistically high because people expect and demand much from them. People compare their leaders with those of advanced industrial countries without taking into account the peculiar conditions of Korea, or judge their leaders harshly by comparing them with an ideal figure—a wise, morally virtuous, and sage king. This happens because the perspectives on evaluation standards are unrealistic and inappropriate. Most people in Korea have neither the realistic and appropriate evaluation standards nor a tradition of cherishing leaders, probably because of a short political history of the republic, combined with ideal values of Confucianism.

Korea's leaders have been often condemned because of their one-sided ideology, namely anticommunism. To those who like to label them as agents of imperialists or antinational reactionaries, no one but a communist leader is immune to such criticism. Reality is reality. In the face of real and acute offensive from communist North Korea, it might be natural for South Korean leaders to be armed with anticommunism.

It is difficult to form a rational judgment on recent history because the stress and unsatisfied desires accumulated through social turmoil and upheaval tend to make people denounce their leaders. The lower people's moral standards are, the more likely they are to develop a habit of speaking ill of leaders without any justification. Moreover, in the process of an intense ideological conflict after liberation from Japanese colonial rule, the conservative, right-wing forces maintained power by suppressing and excluding other political forces—center-right, middle, and left. As a result, political resentment and hostility have accumulated over a long period of time. Many of the intellectuals who were excluded from power found careers in academia, media, culture and arts, and publishing, and their negative opinion and evaluation of political leaders easily spread to the general public.

The spread of such negative images of political leadership cannot be separated from the dark side of political history in South Korea. Park Chung Hee's military coup on May 16, 1961, and the forced adoption of the *Yushin* regime and the advent of the Chun's new military regime through the suppression of the political *albetura* (opening) of Spring 1980; the May 17 suspension of constitutional order; and the violent repression of the

Kwangju uprising have implanted hostile feelings and distrust in the minds of Koreans.

Viewed from this backdrop, it seems quite understandable why Korean leadership has been held in much lower esteem than they deserve. This is a tragedy not only for those leaders, but also for the country as a whole. However, it must be noted that leaders are mirror images of the people. A low opinion of leaders may well represent the low intellectual capacity of the average citizen. Leaders do not exist in isolation: they come from and return to the masses. When most citizens are politically unwise and malicious, their leaders cannot be expected to be wise and virtuous.

Another chronic problem with political leadership and the power elite is that their rise and fall or turnover has been much quicker in Korea than any other country. Frequent change of political leadership deprives leaders of the opportunity to grow and mature. These changes are undesirable for both individuals and the nation. There must be a more innovative system of cultivating and recruiting leaders and officials. We divide officials into three classes—candidates, incumbents, and elders. Candidates can become officials only if they show ability and moral integrity during the candidacy. Incumbent officials with an outstanding record can be elected to the positions of elders who guide and advise the government. Institutionalization of this system could present a promising solution to the problems with official recruitment.

Democratic reforms under the Kim Young Sam government have resulted in the disqualification of most leaders in elder positions and the purging of many active officials. Exemplifying these reforms are the arrest of two former presidents and the intentional downgrading or alienation of elite who served in previous regimes. Even among candidates, there has been a significant change in composition. In the past, anticommunist, right-wing leaders oppressed, persecuted, and excluded their left-wing political opponents, causing distortions within the authoritarian system. Developments under Kim showed a reverse trend. Liberal, progressive elite, in strategic government positions, have systematically excluded and harassed right-wing, conservative leaders. To prevent the continuation of political instability that this vicious cycle of resentment and retaliation entails, we must fill positions of power with intellectually and morally superior officials. Citizens, in turn, must monitor political leaders and hold them accountable so that no authoritarianism, left or right, will strike the country again.

Notes

1. An analysis of the Kim Young Sam government was excluded.

2. Harold D. Lasswell, *Politics: Who Gets What, When, How* (New York: Peter Smith Co., 1995); Harold D. Lasswell, *The Political Writings of Harold D. Lasswell* (Chicago: Free Press of Glencoe, 1951).

3. Ki-shik S. J. Hahn, *Han'guk Chongchiui Chidojadul* [Leaders of Korean Politics] (Seoul: Dae-jung-jin, 1992), pp. 11–24; Ki-shik S. J. Hahn, ed., *Leadership Ironkwa Han'guk Chongchi* [Leadership Theory and Korean Politics] (Minjokjisung [National Intelligence] Sa, 1988), pp. 152–171.

4. Syngman Rhee not only sent Chang Myon to the 1947 UN General Assembly as the head of the Korean delegation but also appointed him as the first Korean ambassador to the United States and later as prime minister. Unseok Sunsaeng Kinyum Chulpan Ouiwonhoe [Publishing Committee for Memoirs of Dr. Chang Myon], ed. *Chang Myon Paksa Hoekorok-Hanaui Milali Chukji Ankonun* [Memoirs of Dr. Chang Myon—Unless a Grain of Wheat Dies] (Seoul:Yang-woo-dang 1967), pp. 29–36.

5. For biographies of Syngman Rhee, see Richard A. Allen, *Korea's Syngman Rhee—Unauthorized Portraits* (Vermont: Charles E. Tuttle, 1960); Robert T. Oliver, *Syngman Rhee: Man Behind the Myth* (NY: Dodd Mead, 1954); Wonsoon Lee, *Ingan Yi Sung Man* [Syngman Rhee as a Man] (Seoul: Shin Taeyangsa, 1965); Seil Sohn, *I Sung Man kwa Kim Ku* [Syngman Rhee and Kim Ku] (Seoul: Iljokak, 1970).

6. Election fraud in the March 15 election were not committed to help Syngman Rhee, who was expected to win easily. Rather, they resulted from factional competition within the ruling party to claim credit for electing Lee Kiboong as vice president.

7. Unseok Sunsaeng Kinyum Chulpan Ouiwonhoe [Publishing Committee for Memoirs of Dr. Chang Myon], ed. op cit. pp. 81–82; Do-hyon Kim, *Naui Insaeng Paekso—Haksan Hoekorok* [White Paper on My Life—Haksan Memoirs] (Seoul: Kang Woo Publishers, 1968), pp. 385–395.

8. Ki-shik S. J. Hahn, "Han'guk Chongchiui Kwonryok Elite" ["The Power Elite of Korean Politics"], in Woon-Tai Kim, ed., *Han'guk Chongchiron* [Korean Politics], 3rd ed. (Seoul: Pakyongsa, 1994), p. 441.

9. Before judging who was a Japanese sympathizer or collaborator and who was not, it is necessary to give a precise definition. If we adopt the definition specified in the Crime Against People Law rather than define Japanese collaborators as anyone who held official positions during Japanese rule, a significant number of power elites can be absolved of such charges. Ki-shik S. J. Hahn, et al., *Haebang Chunhusaui Changjomkwa*

Pyongka II [Issues and Assessments in Korean History around 1945 II] (Seoul Hyongsul Publishers, 1991), pp. 321–326; Ki-shik S. J. Hahn, "Chinilpa Sukchong—Namhanui Ilje Chanjae, Otoke Choridoeo Wanna" ["Purges of Japanese Collaborators—Japanese Legacy in South Korea, What to Do about It?"] *Chaengjom Han'guk Kunhyundaesa II* [Issues in Contemporary History of Korea] (Seoul: Center for Contemporary Korean History, April 1993).

10. Ki-shik S. J. Hahn, *Han'guk Chongchiui Kwonryok Elite* [The Power Elite of Korean Politics], op.cit., pp. 445–450.

11. Baeho Hahn and Kyu-taik Kim, "The Korean Political Leaders: Social Backgrounds and Skills," *Asian Survey*, 6:7 (July 1975), pp. 31–34.

12. From 1967 to the end of 1968, I collected social background data through literature survey, questionnaires, interviews and other indirect methods. Ki-shik S. J. Hahn, "The Political Leadership and Development in Post War Korea," Ph.D. dissertation, University of California, Berkeley, 1971.

16. When the Second National Assembly election was held in 1950, many of the politicians who did not run in the first election won, defeating Rhee supporters. In a way, the Korean War saved the Rhee regime because it broke out as Hanmindang forces, who were ignored in the selection of the first cabinet, began to mount opposition to Rhee's dictatorial rule. Ki-ha Lee, *Han'guk Chongdang Paldalsa* [History of Korean Political Development] (Seoul: Uihoe Chongchisa [Parliamentary Politics Publishers], 1961).

14. Soon-muk Lim, et al., *Chongchi Yahwa I* [Untold Stories of the Political World I] (Seoul: Hong Moon Publishers, 1966), pp. 287–289.

15. Kwan-sik Min, *Nakjesaeng* [A Plucked Student] (Seoul: Jeong-eum-kak, 1961), pp. 78–79. The press at that time called the first cabinet third rate. Compilation Committee on the History of the April Revolution, ed., *Sawol Hyokmyong Chongsa* [The History of the April Revolution] (Seoul: Sung-gong-sa, 1960).

16. Sung-joe Hahn, "Haebang Chonhuui Han'guk Chisong" ["Korean Intellectuals around the Time of Independence"], *Haebang Chonhusaui Chaengjomkwa Pyongka II* [Issues and Assessments in Korean History at the Time of Independence], 2 vols. (1989), pp. 317–345.

17. Sung-joe Hahn, "Han'guk Chongchiui Kwonryok Elite" ["The Power Elites of Korean Politics"], op. cit., pp. 462–463.

18. Park Chung Hee's biographies are: Mong-ku Chung, *Chonki: Pak Chong Hi* [Park Chung Hee: A Biography] (Seoul: Education Commentary Publishers, 1966); Dong-sung and Ko-ryung Shim, *Yomyongui Kisu* [A Flag-Bearer in the Twilight] (Seoul: Educational Culture Publishers,

1961); Chang-wan Han, *Han'gukul Umjikinun Inmuldul* [Movers and Shakers of Korea] (Seoul: Jung Kyung Bodosa, 1966); Kwang-mo Chun, *Chong Wa Dae* (Seoul: Eomoonkak, 1967); Jong Shin Kim, *Yomyongui Hoetbul* [A Torch in the Twilight] (Seoul: Hallym Publishers, 1967).

19. Dong-sung Park, op. cit.; Kwang-mo Chung, op. cit., p. 130.

20. Robert Ernson of AP described Park Chung Hee as follows: "He is one of the rare Korean military officers who have never played golf with US army officers. He is a man without a nickname and is an enigmatic person behind his sunglasses." Hak-su Lee, *Sobakhako Pakryokinnun Chidoja: Kkhaewoe Kijaka Bon Pak Chong Hi Taetongryong* [A Humble and Forceful Leader: President Park Chung Hee as Seen by Foreign and Domestic Reporters] (Seoul: Kwang Myung Printing Corporation, 1967); Ki-shik S. J. Hahn, "Han'guk Chongchiui Kwonryok Elite" ["The Power Elite of Korean Politics"], op. cit., p. 477.

21. *Pak Chong Hi Taetongryong Yonsolmunjip Il Chip* [Speeches of President Park Chung Hee], vol. 1 (Chong Wa Dae, 1971), pp. 157–58.

22. Min Kang, "Kwanryojok Kwonwijuuiui Han'gukjok Saengsong" ["The Rise of Bureaucratic Authoritarianism in Korea"], *Han'guk Chongchi Hakhoebo* [Korean Political Science Review], 17 (1983); Sang Jin Han, "Kwanryojok Kwonwijuuiwa Hankuk Sahoe" ["Bureaucratic Authoritarianism and Korean Society"], *Yi Man Kap Hoegap Kinyomnonjip* [A Collection of Essays in Celebration of Lee Man Kap's Sixtieth Birthday] (Seoul: Bupmoonsa, 1983).

23. Central Election Management Committee, *Taehanminkuk Chongdangsa* [The History of Korean Political Parties] (1989), pp. 291–435; The Democratic Republican Party, *Minjukonghwadangsa* [The History of the Democratic Republican Party] (1973), pp. 35–107.

24. Jong-sin Kim and Hang-eui Lee, "Minjungdangui Seryok Punpo" ["The Distribution of Power in the People's Party"], *The Monthly Sedae* (June 1966), pp. 258–349.

25. Jae-hee Nam, "Chongdang Unyongkwa Tang Chaejong" ["Managing a Political Party and Party Finances"], *Chongkyong Yonku* [Political Economy Research] (December 1967), pp. 132–137.

26. Hyung-seok Lee, *Yadang 30 Nyonsa* [Thirty Years of the Opposition Party] (Seoul: Ingansa, 1987), pp. 321–322.

27. Ki-shik S. J. Hahn, *Han'guk Minjujuui-Ironkwa Silje* [Theory and Practice of Korean Democracy] (Seoul: Hyongsul Publishers, 1984), pp. 249–89.

28. Keum-sung Chun, ed., *Hwangkangeso Pukakaji* [From Hwang River to Pukak] (Seoul:Donga Publishers, 1981), pp. 20–36.

29. Ibid., p.158

30. Sang-woo Lee, "12.12 Satae" ["The Event of December 12"], *The Shindonga* (January 1988), pp. 272–275.

31. Kyung-nam Lee, *Yongkiinnun P'otong Saram, No Tae U* [Common Man with Courage] (Seoul: Ulyoo Moonhwasa, 1987), p. 64.

32. Ho-jin Kim defined Chun Doo Hwan as reckless and offensive (a lion type) and Roh Tae Woo as defensive and adaptable (a fox type): "Roh Tae Woo's leadership style was status-quo protecting and follower-oriented. Although much of it was made up, he projected a follower-oriented image by making efforts to accommodate the wishes of the common man." Ho-jin Kim, *Han'guk Chongchi Chejeron* [Korean Political Systems] (Seoul: Pakyoungsa, 1991), pp. 278–280.

33. Ki-shik S. J. Hahn, *Han'guk Chongchiui Kwonryok Elite* [The Power Elite of Korean Politics], op.cit., pp. 510–511.

34. Byung Man Ahn, "Chongp'u Elitewa Ku P'yondong" ["Government Elites and Change"], *Hyondae Han'guk Chongchiron* [Contemporary Korean Politics] (Seoul: Bupmunsa, 1987), p. 331.

35. Ibid., pp. 132–186.

36. Dong-myong Park, "Minjongdangun Yukbopdanginka?" ["Is the DJP a Yukbopdang (party of army generals and attorneys)?"], *The Monthly Chosun* (May 1985), pp. 370–379.

37. Among the cabinet posts, TK members were appointed to Economic Planning Board, Home Affairs, Foreign Affairs, Trade and Industry, and National Security and Planning; people from other regions were assigned to politically weak posts like Agriculture and Post and Telecommunications.

38. Phillip Selznick, *Leadership in Administration: A Sociological Interpretation* (Evanston: Row, Peterson, 1959), pp. 142–151.

6

ဆ

The Political Process in Korea

Jung Bock Lee

While political processes include both nongovernmental and governmental processes, this chapter will focus on the nongovernmental processes in Korea. More specifically, the focus will be on political processes involving elections, political parties, students, the military, mass media, and interest groups.

Nongovernmental politics (input processes) have had an undeniable influence on Korean governmental policy (output processes). Even during the military regime, nongovernmental political processes restrained formal politics, tempering the military's human rights violations, driving the government to accomplish economic development in an effort to compensate for its perceived illegitimacy, and determining the direction of political development in Korea. The military *coup d'état* in 1961 marked the beginning of a thirty-year military regime. The struggle by students, the opposition party, and citizens against this regime ultimately resulted in a democratic constitution and the inauguration of a civilian president.

Korean political processes will be discussed according to three different analytical methods. The most widespread analytical method used is David Easton's input-output processes theory.[1] This perspective was popular in Korea among political scientists before the *Yushin* period who expected democratic processes to develop. However, Korean politics had become extremely authoritarian by the early 1970s. Since then, a considerable number of scholars have begun to analyze the political processes of Korea from a neo-Marxist perspective. Bruce Cumings has analyzed postliberation Korean politics from this point of view.[2] A third type of analysis, the "sectoral analysis," has been presented by Professor Han Sung Joo.[3] Han interpreted the Korean political processes of the 1960s as the confrontation between two opposed social sectors, which were incompatible with democratic politics.

However, all these theories have their weaknesses. Eastonian theorists have placed too much emphasis on Korean elections, political parties, and interest groups. Neo-Marxist theorists have underestimated the importance in Korean politics of nonclass factors such as students, the military, and regionalism. Han's "sectoral analysis" appears more realistic than the Eastonian or neo-Marxist theories, yet it is subject to arbitrary interpretation because objective criteria for evaluating sectoral forces and their oppositions have not been established. Additionally, it neglects elections and political parties as part of the political system.

This chapter employs none of the above analytical approaches, because generalizations derived from them could simplify or distort concrete political realities. Instead, the chapter aims at identifying major components of the political process in South Korea involving elections, political parties, students, the military, mass media, and interest groups, and elucidating their political dynamics from an objective perspective.

Elections in Korea

In the United States and Western European countries, the democratic system developed gradually from the eighteenth to the twentieth century. In Korea, universal suffrage was established in 1948. Koreans did not struggle for franchise: democratic elections were granted to the people in order to oppose the spread of communism during the American military occupation of Korea. However, democratic elections were not suitable to Korea, where democratic politics had never before been practiced and the per capita income was less than $100. In a sense, expecting a Western-style democracy to function in Korea was, as a western columnist in the 1950s wrote, almost like expecting a rose to blossom out of a trash can.

Against this backdrop, this section provides a general overview of how the electoral system, election climate, and the voting behavior of Korean voters have evolved over time. Special attention will be given to the presidential and parliamentary elections. Even though their results were repeatedly nullified by events like the April 19 Student Revolution in 1960, the May 16 Military Coup in 1961, the declaration of the *Yushin* constitution in 1972, and the May 17 Military Coup in 1980, elections have continuously been held since the establishment of the Republic of Korea. Local government elections, however, were only periodically enforced in 1952, 1956, and 1960. In 1991, local assembly elections were partially restored. In 1995, local elections, including those for provincial governors and the heads of local councils, were held at a national level.

The Electoral System

The electoral system is by and large contingent on constitutional order. The constitutional order can be divided into three periods: the first democratic constitutional period from 1948 to 1972; the authoritarian consitutional period from 1972 to 1987; and the second democratic constitutional period from 1987 to the present. The first democratic constitutional period can be further divided into three periods: the First Republic from 1948 to 1960, the Second Republic from 1960 to 1961, and the Third Republic from 1963 to 1972. Each republic had a different election system.

The First Republic was a unicameral system. The candidate winning the most votes in a single electoral district was elected assemblyman for a four-year term in a comparative majority system similar to those in England, Canada, and New Zealand. While its shortcomings included overrepresentation of the majority and underrepresentation of the minority, the system encouraged political stability.

Though no change occurred in the parliamentary elections of the First Republic, the presidential election was changed from an indirect to a direct election system by popular vote. The paradoxical indirect election of president was the outcome of a compromise between Rhee and the Korea Democratic Party (Hanmindang) that supported him but that favored a parliamentary system. During the third presidential election in 1956, a constitutional amendment was passed that nullified the two-term limit of the first president, Syngman Rhee. The ruling party succeeded in passing it despite the protests of the opposition party by employing methods of mass mobilization and use of force.

The First Republic elected a vice president (abolished after the Second Republic) on a separate ballot. The fact that the president and vice president belonged to opposing parties was ironic, especially considering the constitutional article that provided for the vice president to assist or substitute for the president in an emergency. This was the result of a political compromise between Rhee and his opposition.

The Second Republic adopted a parliamentary constitution in which the president was symbolic and elected by the National Assembly. The bicameral National Assembly was comprised of the *minuiwon* (Lower House) and the *chamuiwon* (Upper House). The latter's electoral system, the small district system with a comparative majority rule, the same as in the First Republic, consisted of the large electoral districts where Seoul and each province elected two to eight members. Restricted continuous voting, where voters in the large electoral districts could vote more than two candidates, was allowed. The candidate recommendation system was abolished and an absentee voting system was introduced to prevent voting by proxy. The recording of serial numbers of voter ballots was introduced to prevent relay voting. During this time, the minimum voting age was lowered from twenty-one to twenty.

The Third Republic reintroduced the presidential system in which the president was elected directly by the people for a maximum of two terms. Amendments to this constitution required a referendum as well as parliamentary approval—measures taken to prevent a prolonged dictatorship like that of Syngman Rhee. President Park Chung Hee, however, managed to amend the constitution and was reelected for a third term in 1971.

The parliamentary election during the Third Republic maintained the comparative majority system of the First and Second Republics, while introducing a system of proportional representation. In doing so, the Third Republic reduced the number of electoral districts from 233 to 131, and allocated one-third (44) of district seats to national district candidates in accordance with the proportional representation formula. However, proportional representation under the Third Republic differed from that of Western countries. First, people voted only for local district candidates. The total votes for each party's local district candidates were regarded as the votes for the national district candidates of each party. Voters could not elect national district candidates directly. Second, the allotment of national seats in the National Assembly was not proportional. In the case of the leading party, if the local district total voting rate was over 50 percent, national seats were allotted proportionally according to the number of votes obtained; but if it was less than 50 percent, half of the total number of national seats were allotted. In the case of the second party, when the number of votes obtained was more than two times the total number of votes for the parties below the third party, the remaining seats were allotted proportionally; otherwise, two-thirds of the remaining seats were allotted. A party with no more than three seats, or 5 percent of the total valid vote, from local districts was excluded from the national seat allotment. In contrast to Western countries, the first party was given excessive seats.[4] In the first general election of the Third Republic, the Democratic Republic Party of Park obtained only 33.5 percent of valid votes, but was allotted 22 national seats, 50 percent of total national seats. As a result, the DRP was able to secure 110 seats, 63 percent of total seats in the National Assembly. Although this system did not exactly reflect public opinion, it paved the way for political stability and a bicameral system.

In the Third Republic, registration of candidates for assemblymen was by party nomination only. Thus, candidates who did not belong to any party were not allowed to register. This system was unique to the Third Republic. In the operation of parliamentary elections, the election campaign management system was improved by creating joint speech rallies and allowing the publication of campaign pamphlets. The campaigns of individual candidates, however, were restricted.

The election system during the nondemocratic constitutional period from 1972 to 1987 can be divided into two periods: the *Yushin* period of the Fourth Republic and the Fifth Republic. The *Yushin* constitution did not provide for a direct presidential election. The president was elected without debate by the concurrence of more than half the members of the National Council for Unification. The members of the National Council for Unification were not politicians; about 2,500 of those elected were no more than government puppets. The presidential elections in 1972, 1978, and 1979 were held under this presidential election law. Park Chung Hee (twice), and Choi Kyu-Hah ran as single candidates. Park Chung Hee won 99.0 percent and 99.9 percent, and Choi Kyu-Hah 96.7 percent of the votes.

During the Fourth Republic, seventy-three electoral districts were created, each electing two people to six-year terms. The system allowed the ruling party to take the majority of seats from the seventy-three electoral districts. Of the remaining seats, the majority was taken by the largest opposition party. Thus, this system was nicknamed as the "sharing" election system. Nevertheless, local district elections were politically significant since they reflected popular support for the ruling and the opposing parties. In the 1978 parliamentary election, the opposing New Democratic party obtained 32.8 percent of the vote compared to the ruling DJP's 31.7 percent—proof of serious popular opposition to the *Yushin* regime. However, one-third of the assemblymen elected in the National Council for Unification were appointed by the president, signifying an extremely undemocratic system.

In principle, the system established by the Fifth Republic, the military regime, was almost identical. However, the president was elected to a lengthened term of seven years by the presidential electoral college rather than by the National Council for Unification. Although the members of the presidential electoral college were elected by ballot, 5,000 of those elected were government puppets from the National Council for Unification.

The parliamentary electoral system of the Fifth Republic comprised ninety-two electoral districts. Two assemblymen were elected in each district, and ninety-two national seats on the National Assembly were allotted proportionally according to election results. Although the president in the Fourth Republic appointed one-third of the assembly members, the president of the Fifth Republic could appoint only 22 percent, namely national seats allotted to the ruling party. The ruling Democratic Justice Party (DJP) had a total of 35.8 percent of the vote in the first parliamentary election and took 54.7 percent of the seats. As will be seen later, this election system had become meaningless since the opposition parties of the Fifth Republic had begun a semiruling party. Although the system of the Fifth Republic had various problems, it was the first system to reflect popular consensus. In the 1985 election, the opposing New Democratic Party won an overwhelming victory over the ruling DJP in the major cities taking 29.3 percent of the total vote to claim fifty of the local district seats. It immediately became the first opposition party and successfully promoted the movement for constitutional amendment for a direct presidential election system.

The Korean electoral system regained some democratic characteristics with the beginning of the second democratic constitutional period of 1987. The Sixth Republic limited the presidency to five years while leaving the local and national districts intact.

The Korean system today restricts the presidency to a single five-year term. In parliamentary elections, people do not have the right to choose their assemblymen in their national district as in the Third, Fourth, and Fifth Republics. Although the assignment methods of assemblymen to national districts have greatly improved, the seats are still assigned in proportion to the number of seats held in the Assembly, not by the voting rate.

Election Climate

The election climate refers to awareness and behavior of those involved in the election: government, political parties, candidates, election campaigners, and voters. The election climate of Korea since the First Republic has had problems of government interference, slander, negative publicity, and low political awareness of voters.

In the election of 1948, the major problem was one of ideological confrontation. *Namrodang* (the left-wing Workers' Party of South Korea) interfered with the election: they attacked election offices and officials, threatened candidates, raided polling stations, destroyed communication networks, and spread rumors under the direction of the Soviet Union and North Korea. The American military administration attempted to stop these maneuvers but the confrontation was too serious. Since these maneuvers were communist inspired, voters had to participate in the ballot in order not to be regarded as pro-Communist. The high voting rates during the First Republic—95.5 percent in the Constitutional Assembly election and 90 percent in the presidential and parliamentary elections—reflected this ideological confrontation.

Apart from the ideological problem, the Constitutional Assembly suffered from money disputes and government interference. Rumors about candidates taking bribes and withdrawing their candidacy circulated. It was alleged that some government officials forced their subordinates to vote for particular candidates.

Such interference in elections worsened from the second parliamentary election of 1950 to the fourth presidential and vice-presidential elections of 1960. What began as money spent merely to entertain voters developed into votes being bought. Government interference ranged from police maneuvering to partial vote-rigging. Election manipulation took many different forms: suppression of opposition party campaigns; refusing registration of candidates or suggesting resignation; and threatening voters with legislation. Vote-rigging methods included "phantom votes" (using enlisted soldiers, emigrants, the dead and infants); "dumping votes" (using ballots stolen from printing shops); and "piano votes" (double-stamp-ing ballots voted for the opposition). Opposition election proctors were bribed and threatened, and political gangsters were mobilized to threaten or attack opposition party candidates, election workers, and even opposition voters. The candidates of the ruling party were always overwhelmingly supported by the army.

The First Republic was strongly anticommunist, which appealed to the voters. The Syngman Rhee regime took advantage of this social atmosphere in the election. During the second parliamentary election, President Rhee announced that reelection of candidates who had boycotted the Constitutional Assembly election was dangerous, and advised voters to consider past history when voting. Police and public officials threatened that the district voters' political orientation would be under suspicion if the opposing party candidates were to be elected.

However, this kind of election climate could not prevent the growth of the opposition party. Excessive interference was not always advantageous to the ruling party. During the fourth parliamentary election of 1958, the opposing Unified Democratic Party obtained 34.2 percent of the votes and elected 79 candidates, compared to the ruling Liberty party, with 42.1 percent of the vote and elected 126 candidates. This was unprecedented for the Democratic Party. The Liberty Party lost significantly in large cities, including Seoul, and the DP won overwhelmingly. Political awareness of the voters in Seoul and other large cities was high; therefore, the influence of money and governmental authority were not as effective. The trend of ruling party victories in the rural districts and opposing party victories in the big cities continue to this day.

The Liberty Party also committed large-scale election fraud during the vice-presidential election in April 1960. That year's April 19 Student Revolution that overthrew the Liberty Party regime was a positive sign of the people's political awareness, which grew even in the nondemocratic election climate. Despite the corruption of the Liberty Party regime in the fifth parliamentary election, the subsequent election climate was generally fair. There was almost no government interference during this election: since they had been accused of involvement in the corruption of the previous election, the police and interior public officials did not get involved. The neutral transitional regime managed the election fairly.

The fifth presidential election climate of 1963 was also relatively fair. The military regime managed the election, and General Park Chung Hee, who masterminded the coup d'état, became the presidential candidate. Yet because the corruption of 1960 was fresh in the minds of the people, opposing party candidate Yoon Bo Sun's suggestion that the ideology of candidate Park was suspicious greatly influenced the election atmosphere.

Though the sixth parliamentary election climate was relatively fair, money and government authority played a role. Providing entertainment for the voters during elections had been a problem before, and it proved to be so again in the sixth election. The police and public officials surveyed the support rate for the ruling and opposing party's candidates in each district and analyzed public support for the president. They promoted regional projects after discussing matters with the ruling party's candidates, and attacked the opposing party's candidate. By doing so, they caused the opposing party's force to collapse. However, as no open bribing, threatening, or assaulting of the opposing party's candidates or campaigners resulted, one can say that the sixth parliamentary election climate was relatively fair.

Still, the sixth presidential, the seventh parliamentary of 1967, the seventh presidential of 1971, and the eighth parliamentary elections were as corrupt as those of the First Republic. The seventh parliamentary election in particular was unprecedented in its corruption. Bribing, purchasing of ballot papers, luring campaigners from the opposing team were widespread. Although campaign funds for the regional districts were set legally at around two million won at the time, some ruling party candidates spent more than 100 million won, and some opposing party's candidates in turn spent several tens of millions. This kind of money corrupted voters, who expected to receive incentives from the candidates. The president, cabinet members, administrative public officials, police, and district heads all strongly supported the ruling party's candidates. President Park campaigned for them, and cabinet members threatened to support regional improvement projects only if the ruling party's candidates were elected. Government offices threatened voters in the region and threatened entrepreneurs with audits who favored the opposing party.

Although the election atmosphere of the eighth parliamentary election was calmer on the surface than the seventh, corruption was still substantial. The voters' expectations of rewards from the candidates became more apparent, and public officials' use of patronage for political advantage and hampering of the opposing party's campaigns were widespread. As in the seventh presidential election, there was election campaigning which tried to appeal to the regional emotions of the southwestern and southeastern region.

Still, none of this hampered the growing strength of the opposition party. In the eighth parliamentary election, the NDP obtained 44.4 percent of the vote and elected 89 people compared to 48.86 percent and 113 for the ruling DRP. These results merit close attention compared to the 32.7 percent and forty-five seats in the seventh parliamentary election.

Although corruption was rampant, one should not underestimate the significance of the election system of this period. As mentioned earlier, the ruling party of the First and the Third Republic periods could not stop the growth of the opposing party by corrupting the election climate, and the opposing forces actually gained power. The prior voting of the First Republic period by the ruling party to prolong its regime, and the *Yushin* of the Third Republic period's President Park to abolish the democratic election system itself were all due to the realization that they could not prolong their regimes in a democratic election system.

The nondemocratic constitutional period was actually less corrupt than the democratic constitutional periods. The election system of this period was undemocratic and guaranteed the ruling force's regime, so the ruling party did not need corrupt elections. There was no presidential election during this period, and thus there was not much dispute regarding elections. There was only a struggle for electoral reform and for a return to a direct presidential election system.

The ninth parliamentary election of February 1973, the first of the Fourth Republic, was called the "mute election" or "blind election" as no one paid any attention to it. Since two assemblymen were elected in each district, competition between the ruling and the opposing party was not fierce. Though the ruling party had nothing to gain, illegal campaigning in the form of preelection campaigning, bribing of voters, and campaigning by public officials occurred.

The tenth parliamentary election of December 1978 revived competition between the ruling and opposition parties, and the election climate again became corrupt—more so than in any other election. The ruling party candidates went beyond distributing gifts to the voters; they gave out cash. The NDP obtained 32.8 percent of votes and sixty-one seats; the ruling DRP 31.7 percent and sixty-eight seats.

The eleventh parliamentary election in March, 1981 was similar to the first parliamentary election of the Fourth Republic, but this time money was more seriously involved. Although this election system also guaranteed victory for the ruling party, the difference from the previous elections was that for the first time in the history of Korean elections, the ruling party won in both the urban and the rural areas. This was possible since the election was held in a suppressed atmosphere, and the major opposing parties (such as the Minhandang and Kookmindang) were portrayed as semiruling parties. The twelfth parliamentary election of February 1985 was similar in its mood to the second parliamentary election of the Fourth Republic's *Yushin* period. The NDP, clearly an opposition party proposing the recovery of democracy, gained much popularity and won overwhelmingly in the major cities. In the twelfth assemblymen election again the ruled party won in the rural areas, the opposing party won in the urban areas.

Korea regained a democratic constitution and election system in 1987. Leaders of the democratic force during the nondemocratic constitutional period, Kim Young Sam and Kim Dae Jung greatly contributed in the fight against corrupt electioneering. However, the two Kims separated after winning this fight in 1987, and after their separation the election climate displayed strong regional characteristics. Voters from Pusan and the southeast areas supported the candidates from the party led by President Kim Young Sam, and the voters from the southwest areas supported the opposing party led by Kim Dae Jung. The fifteenth presidential election, which was held on December 18, 1997, deserves special note. As a result of sweeping reforms in the election campaign law, which not only limited campaign spending but also altered campaign methods from mass rallies to television debates among candidates, the fifteenth presidential election turned out to be the cleanest and least expensive in the history of South Korean politics.

Voting Behavior

The following will analyze the factors influencing voters in choosing candidates they support. Then, it will examine how the voters' socioeconomic backgrounds and political attitude, which are recognized as important independent variables in the study of voting behaviors in the United States and Western European countries, have influenced the voting behavior of Koreans.

In general, the voting rate of presidential elections is a little higher than that of parliamentary elections. Because hardly any presidential elections occurred during the Fourth and Fifth Republics, the voting behavior will be analyzed based on assembly elections. The voting rate of the Korean people is relatively high. The recent voting rates, 75.8 percent in the thirteenth and 71.9 percent in the fourteenth assembly elections, are much higher than those in America, and at the same level as Western European countries. Voting rates were particularly high—over 90 percent—during the First Republic, the preindustrial period when educational levels were very low. In Korea, the relationship between economic and educational improvement and the voting rate seems inversely related whereas in advanced countries it is positively related. This high voting rate during the First Republic partly reflects the ideological confrontation, but as asserted by Yoon Chun Joo, a pioneer in the study of voting behavior of Koreans, it is mostly due to conformity rather than interest in voting.[5]

Examining the voting rate by looking at the urbanization of electoral districts at a given time reveals that the lower the level of urbanization, the higher the voting rate in the region, and vice versa. The voting rates in Cheju province, Kangwon province, and Chungchongbuk province, where urbanization is relatively low, are higher than in other regions; the voting rate in Seoul is the lowest. In the sixth parliamentary election of 1963, the voting rates in the former three regions were 81.5 percent, 75.3 percent, 78.1 percent, and the voting rate of Seoul was 57.6 percent. In the eleventh election of 1981, the voting rates in these three regions were 85.3 percent, 88.0 percent, and 86.7 percent compared to 71.1 percent in Seoul. The gap in the voting rates between those three regions with low urbanization and Seoul was more than 15 percent, largely because of widespread conformity voting in those regions.

The gap in the voting rates due to urbanization dwindled markedly in the twelfth assembly election of 1985, which was the last during the nondemocratic constitutional period. The voting rates of Cheju, Kangwon, and Chungchongbuk provinces were 88.9 percent, 89.5 percent, and 90.4 percent compared to 81.1 percent in Seoul, and the gap in the voting rates between these two regions decreased to about 8 percent. The unprecedented high voting rate in Seoul in 1985 was due to the voters' interest in reinstating the democratic constitution. Although the voting rates of all of Korea dwindled again after that, the gap in the voting rates between Seoul and other regions or between urban and rural areas decreased compared to the 1950s, 1960s, and 1970s.[6] This is partly because the gap in political awareness between urban and rural voters has decreased, and also because of regionalism, which has been an important factor since the thirteenth election.

The most influential socioeconomic factor that affected Korean voters in elections from the First to the Fourth Republic was the urbanization of the electoral district. As mentioned earlier, voters of urban electoral districts tended to support the opposition party's candidates, and rural districts' support of the ruling party's candidates remained unchanged during these periods. In the fourth assembly election in the First Republic the ruling Liberal Party had only one assemblyman elected in the sixteen electoral districts of Seoul, whereas the first opposition Democratic Party had fourteen assemblymen elected. Also, in all 62 city electoral districts, including Seoul, thirteen assemblymen were elected from the Liberal Party and 43 from the Democratic Party. This recurred in assembly elections during the Third Republic. In the seventh election of 1967, the ruling Democratic Republican Party had only one candidate elected in one district out of a total of fourteen, while the opposition New Democratic Party had candidates elected in thirteen districts. In the eighth election, NDP candidates were elected in eighteen districts, whereas only one candidate from the ruling DRP was elected in a total of nineteen electoral districts in Seoul. From the late 1950s through the 1960s, the ruling party had hardly any candidates elected in Seoul.[7] This was fatal to the ruling party even though it retained more than half of the assembly seats. The pattern changed during the Fourth Republic as each electoral district elected two assemblymen.

Yoon Chun Joo attributed the tendency of ruling parties winning in rural districts and opposition parties winning in urban districts to a tendency toward conformity voting in rural areas; he attributed its disappearance to more voters voting in their own interests and fewer being manipulated by bribes or suppression, concluding that conformity voting has diminished.[8] However, regionalism is more responsible for the disappearance of the phenomena. In the fourteenth election, voters in the regions of Taejon/Chungchong, Taegu/Kyongbuk, and Pusan/Kyongnam (south-central and southeastern areas) strongly supported candidates from the ruling DLP, while voters in the Kwangju/Cholla region overwhelmingly supported candidates from the first opposing DP. In Seoul, whose population comes from all over Korea, voters from the former and the latter regions showed the same tendency.

In the Sixth Republic, there was little correlation between either or educational level urbanization and voting behavior. This is due to the conservative nature of major parties in Korea, as well as to regionalism. In the fourteenth election, southwestern voters supported the opposing DP and southeastern voters the ruling DLP.[9] A similar trend continued in the fifteenth general election held in 1996.[10]

The political attitude of voters is a more critical factor in their choice of candidates than socioeconomic factors. Research on how the attitudes of voters influenced their voting behavior was a priority of the Sixth Republic. In a survey conducted before the fourteenth election, 53.9 percent of respondents answered that the quality of individual candidates is the most important factor in choosing the candidate; 20.5 percent named the party, and 19.4 percent the issue.[11] This individual-oriented voting behavior has decreased compared to the 1950s and 1960s, but it is still strong compared with the United States and Western Europe. It can be attributed to the fact that Korean people do not identify themselves with any party since Korean parties have frequently switched alignments and changed their names accordingly. Instead, a considerable number of Koreans identify with individuals such as Kim Young Sam or Kim Dae Jung, who have led Korean politics for the past three decades.

The Political Parties of Korea

The advent of political parties in the United States and Western European countries has a close relationship with the emergence of civil society and the Industrial Revolution. Political parties were established amid crises of participation, legitimacy and integration, and developed on the basis of such socioeconomic changes as the development of transportation, communication and the market, and the enlargement of education.[12] Thinkers during the French Revolution, as well as U.S. president George Washington, were against the idea of political parties because they thought the parties would split into factions and would harm the solidarity and interest of the people on the whole.[13] Nevertheless, political parties in the United States and Western European countries became organizations necessary to the promotion of democracy.

The political parties of Korea were formed before the establishment of civil society, and before the mature development of transportation and communication, markets, and the educational system. In Korea, people over 21 obtained the right to vote with the establishment of the Republic of Korea in 1948, and establishment of universal suffrage became the condition for the formation of political parties. The first political parties in South Korea were established outside the National Assembly. The first president of Korea was against political parties before he became president, sharing George Washington's opinion that factionalism could harm the development of the nation.

Contrary to his opinion, Rhee organized his own party at the end of 1951. This was because not long after his inauguration he was confronted by the National Assembly, and he felt it necessary to have a party to secure an institutionalized legislative support. The Liberal Party obtained 114 seats out of a total of 203 in the third assembly election of 1954, the first in which the LP participated. With the emergence of the LP, the National Assembly developed into a party-oriented Assembly from a nonpartisan one consisting mostly of nonaffiliated members. The number of nonaffiliates was 85 out of a total of 198 assemblymen in the First Assembly of 1948, and 127 out of a total of 210 in the Second Assembly of 1950. After the emergence of the LP, the Democratic Party was organized in opposition. Korean politics became characterized by the confrontation between the ruling party and the strong opposition.

The average life of Korean political parties has not been long. New ruling and opposing parties were formed with each change of regimes. The ruling LP in the 1950s, the ruling DRP in the 1960s and 1970s, and the ruling DJP in the 1980s have all disappeared. Ruling parties in Korea do not exist in themselves: rather, they are created and maintained by political regimes. Opposing parties have also transformed with the change of regimes, but have been comparatively more durable.

The opposition DP of the 1950s, was reassembled as the New Democratic Party, the opposition party of the 1960s and 1970s. It was also reassembled as the New Korean Democratic Party (NKDP), the opposition party in 1985, and again as the Unification Democratic Party (UDP), the opposition party in 1987. Half of the members of the UDP were reassembled as the Democratic Party. Since opposing parties were voluntarily organized unlike ruling parties, they could last relatively longer.

Political parties of Korea remain at a semiparty stage.[14] According to Huntington's concept of institutionalization, the criteria determining development of a political party are adaptability, complexity, autonomy, and coherence. Based on these criteria, political parties in Korea show a very low level of institutionalization.[15]

Political parties in the United States and Western European countries are becoming less highly regarded because of the increasing role of private and public interest groups. Political parties in Korea for a long time did not play a central role in politics. Under military dictatorship for thirty years, ruling parties were no more than election organizations or propaganda machinery, and opposing parties functioned merely as protest organizations. Neither ruling nor opposing parties influenced the major policy decisions of the government, and they did not serve as institutions recruiting cabinet members. Despite the advent of a civilian government in 1993, the role of political parties has not yet been sufficiently developed.

Organizational Characteristics of Korean Political Parties

When discussing the organizational characteristics of a political party, we first ask whether it is a cadre party or a mass bureaucratic party. A cadre party is a political party, also called a party of celebrities. It originated from the early parties of Western European countries when the population was not allowed to vote. This party, consisting mainly of social figures, chose its congressional candidates from this group and the candidates paid their own election expenses. Due to the decentralized power structure, the power of the chairman of the party was limited and was instead distributed to the key members. In addition, most policies were conservative.

The origin of the mass bureaucratic party can be found in the socialist democratic parties of Western European countries, which developed after suffrage was given to the general public. These parties, while centered around party members, are actually operated by party bureaucrats. In the beginning, assembly candidates of these parties were not notables, and party funds originated from rank-and-file members. The party has a centralized power structure; therefore, the power of the president and other party leaders is strong and they control the assemblymen.[16]

In Korea during the past half-century, both ruling and opposition parties were cadre parties. Key members of parties consisted of noted politicians. Assemblymen candidates were selected among them, and they paid most of their own election expenses. The activities of the parties were centered around the assemblymen, and parties did not have extensive bureaucratic structure nor mass party members. However, political parties in Korea and cadre parties in the United States and Western European countries share no further characteristics. The decentralized power structure, a characteristic of the Western cadre party, cannot be found in Korean political parties.

This is not to say that political parties in Korea did not have internal factions, the basis for a decentralized power structure. In the case of the ruling parties, the LP in the First Republic had groups inside and outside the Assembly. The DRP in the Third and Fourth Republic had pro– and anti–Kim Jong Pil groups, and the DLP during the Sixth Republic had factions from the former Democratic Justice, Democratic, and National Parties. However, Korean factions, unlike factions in the Liberal Democratic Party of Japan, do not have organizations independent of the party chairman and leaders. In the case of the opposition parties, the DP in the First Republic had Old and New factions; the NDP in the Third and Fourth Republic had Kim Dae Jung, Kim Young Sam and Lee Chul Seung factions; the NKDP and the UDP in the Fifth Republic had a Kim Dae Jung faction and a Kim Young Sam faction; the DP in the Sixth Republic had a Lee Ki-taik faction, a Tongkyo Dong (i.e., Kim Dae Jung) faction, and a Democratic League faction. Ruling party factions have no power against the party president, who is president of Korea. In the opposition party, power is concentrated on the presidential candidate of the party and influenced by the power structure of the ruling party.

The president of the ruling party in Korea has more power than that of the mass bureaucratic party in Western countries. Beyond this, there is no similarity between the two. Leaders of Korean parties, unlike those in the Western mass bureaucratic parties, do not have an elaborate bureaucratic organization.[17] They do not even have the bureaucratic organization of cadre parties of Western countries or Japan.

Yet this does not mean that the Korean political parties do not have a bureaucratic organization. Both the ruling and opposition parties have central, city, district, and provincial level organizations. The party center has a formalistic bureaucratic structure, and the bureaucratic organization of the ruling party is much larger than that of the opposition party. No matter how large the bureaucratic organization is, however, political parties of Korea do not have a principle bureaucratic system as defined by Max Weber. Weber's bureaucratic system presupposes a paid bureaucracy, a stable hierarchy, specialization, standardization of role, official procedure, and promotional order, none of which can fully be found in the bureaucratic organization of political parties in Korea. Heads of mass bureaucratic parties in Western countries have powerful influence due to their control of the bureaucratic organization. However, party bureaucrats in Korea must be accepted by the party head in order to have power. Michels warned that the bureaucratization of such a mass party as the Social Democratic Party of Germany would bring about an oligarchy of party leaders, so that the party would serve the interest of its leaders rather than that of its members. However, Michels' warning is not applicable to Korean political parties because their level of bureaucratization is too low.

Italian political researcher Panebianco divides party support into party members and supporting voters. The latter are divided into floating and fixed supporting voters, while the former are divided into general and enthusiastic party members. Enthusiastic party members are further divided into believers and careerists.[18]

In Western countries, supporting voters can be classified according to socioeconomic class, religion, culture and race, urban versus rural areas, and so forth. In Korea, however, the supporting voters of a particular party are less easily classified. From the First to the Fifth Republic periods, the ruling party had stronger support from voters in rural areas than did the opposition party, which had stronger support from voters in urban areas. In two presidential and assembly elections under the constitution of the Sixth Republic, however, the region became the most important criterion in classifying supporting voters of the party. Candidates from the former Democratic, Democratic Justice, and National Parties, which constitute the previously ruling DLP, received overwhelming support in regions of Kyongnam, Kyongbuk, and Chungnam, respectively. In Seoul, people from the southeastern region tended to support the DLP, while those from the southwestern regions supported the DP.

According to Panebianco, the most important incentive that party leaders can use to obtain support from the majority of voters is the collective incentive of identity. Party leaders can also use such selective incentives as the conferment of funds, the distribution of positions in the party, and the public nomination of assemblyman candidates, yet they cannot provide these incentives to millions of voters. Party leaders, especially those of the opposition party without many selective incentives, use the collective incentive of identity to appeal to a larger target group.

Under the military regime in Korea, the opposition party provided voters with the collective incentive of democratization, which appealed more to urban than to rural voters. As a result, the ruling party won in rural areas and the opposition party in urban areas. After Korea regained the democratic constitution in 1987, however, regional parochialism replaced democratization as the collective incentive. Voters believed that their interests would be maximized if the political party with the leader from their region won, and voted accordingly. In the elections of the Sixth Republic, especially in the fourteenth and fifteenth presidential elections, the candidates did not overtly emphasize regional parochialism to voters, asserting that they represented the interests of all classes, and this failed to provide a collective incentive to any class. Ironically, in this situation, the only difference that distinguished one candidate from another was the regional base.

Recently, political parties in Western European countries, whether conservative or socialist, have turned into "catch-all" parties that appeal to many different classes. Nevertheless, since the parties in these countries have preserved the attributes of class-based parties for the past 100 years, they still maintain a fairly high rate of fixed support from the class that they originally represented. Even though one can define the parties of Korea as "catch-all" parties, they differ from those of Western countries by not having a class-based background.

Western political parties have a considerable number of enthusiastic members who act according to collective incentives. However, enthusiastic members of parties in Korea are mostly careerists, expecting selective incentives from party leaders, and changing allegiance if party leaders do not provide those incentives. Believers, rare in Korean political parties, are necessary to establish an image of a policy-making party.

The organizational principle of political parties in Korea is neither Weber's bureaucratic system nor Marx's class, but that of a patron-client organization between the assemblyman, the chairman of the party's district office, and the careerists. A patron-client relationship is also established between the party leader and assemblymen. The party leader takes care of the assemblymen, who are key members of the party, and the assemblymen are loyal to the party leader. This patron-client relationship is further reinforced by the party leader's domination of the right to nominate party candidacy for the national assembly seats.

Political parties of Western countries dominate the lives of fixed voters. They recruit party members with these supporters, and encourage them to participate in many group activities related to the party. Korean parties do not dominate supporters in the same way. Most Korean voters hesitate to participate in party activities, regardless of their support. Only the beneficiaries or would-be beneficiaries of the party participate in party activities.

The Political Party System of Korea

Sartori classifies political party systems as competitive and noncompetitive systems. Competitive political party systems are then classified into one-party dominant systems, two-party systems, moderate multiparty systems, and bipolarized multiparty systems. Noncompetitive political party systems are classified into hegemonic uniparty systems.

During the period from the foundation of the Republic of Korea to the Fifth Republic, a two-party system was maintained: the LP and the DP, the new faction and the old faction of the DP, the DRP and the NDP, the DJP and the NKDP (later UDP). This two-party system did not emerge until the later stages of the republic. Though several parties existed in earlier stages, they gradually became insignificant. In the middle to late period of the republics, the polling score of the opposition party tended to increase to that of the ruling party. The political party systems of the First, Third, Fourth, and Fifth Republics had the characteristics of a hegemonic system according to Sartori's definition.

Until 1995, Korea maintained a two-party system between the Democratic Liberal Party and the Democratic Party. Yet the two-party system of the Sixth Republic was a natural result of the election. The Democratic Justice line, the Democratic Republican (National Party) line, and the Kim Young Sam faction within the Democratic Party joined to create the DLP. The merger of the Peace Democratic Party and the Democratic Party led to the Democratic Party. From 1995, however, political parties in South Korea underwent a series of alignments and realignments. Kim Jong Pil bolted from the ruling DLP and formed his own party (ULD), drawing support from the Chungchong provinces. Kim Dae Jung also formed the National Congress for New Politics by separating from the Democratic Party. The ruling DLP was renamed the New Korea Party (NKP) in the wake of the arrest of former president and coalition partner Roh Tae Woo under corruption charges. The NKP itself was split into the Grand National Party and the New National Party for People as a result of intra-party division following the presidential nomination race in the summer of 1997.

In view of the above, the political party system in Korea remains unstable. However, a notable development of the fifteenth presidential election in December 1997 bears profound implications for party politics. Kim Dae Jung from the NCNP won the election by forming a coalition with Kim Jong Pil's ULD. This alliance has meant that the ruling party is unable to form a majority in the National Assembly, creating a mismatch of power between executive and legislative branches. Nevertheless, election of Kim Dae Jung is the first peaceful transition of power from the ruling to the opposition party, which can only be conducive to the development of party politics in South Korea.

Students, the Military, Mass Media, and Interest Groups in Korea

Most textbooks omit students, the military, and the mass media in their discussion of political processes. In Western nations, interest groups, which have played an important role, are more likely to be included, when discussing the overall political process. Relatively speaking, however, the students, the military, and the mass media of Western countries have played a less decisive role than in the shaping of the Korean political process.

Student movements in the 1960s and the 1970s greatly influenced politics in Western countries. In the United States, student protests against the Vietnam War forced President Johnson to abandon his candidacy for the presidential election of 1968. In France, the student demonstration of May 1968 hastened the retirement of President de Gaulle. Although the military in Western countries have been faithful to the tradition of professionalism and political neutrality, they have formally participated in policy decision making and have even broken their neutrality on occasion. In the latter period of the Fourth Republic in France, for instance, the military threatened a coup d'état in order to oppose Algerian independence. The mass media of Western countries has a stronger political influence than its Korean counterpart. For example, the resignation of President Nixon in 1974 was triggered by thorough investigation in the Watergate affair.

In the political process of Western countries, however, these elements played active roles within the systematic frame of democratic politics. By contrast, the students and the military in Korea have played a primary role in changing the political system. Students after liberation were divided into left and right, the latter contributing to the construction of democratic politics and a free enterprise system in South Korea. Later, South Korean students overthrew Syngman Rhee's dictatorship and thus contributed to the reestablishment of democracy. During the military dictatorship, students, the most powerful social force against the regime, played a decisive role in obtaining the free democratic constitution of 1987. The military also has played a major role in transforming the framework of Korean politics. A military coup d'état subverted free democratic politics in 1961 and again in 1979. Military leaders who overthrew democracy were more fearful of students than of the opposition party. Likewise, students feared the military as the greatest threat to democracy. The media too has played an important role. A considerable number of people engaged in media participated in the struggle for democratization. Although often criticized for supporting the military regime, the Korean media has at the same time undeniably contributed to the democratization of Korean politics. Its power and influence have become more pronounced after the democratic opening.

In the past, interest groups have not played as central a role in the political process of Korea as they have in Western countries. American collective theorists, such as Bentley and Truman, interpret the American political process as the conflict and compromise of interest groups.[19] Laski asserts that interest groups have come to have a significance comparable to the state, thus threatening state sovereignty.[20] Until recently, interest groups in Korea, whether composed of capitalists or workers, were organized under the permission and guidance of the state. Therefore, lacking independence, they had no choice but to support the ruling class. Korean interest groups conformed to Schmitter's theory of state corporatism.[21] Since the establishment of civilian government, however, interest groups became more independent. Workers were successful in establishing a more pluralistic interest representation with the launching of the second labor or democratic union movement. In addition, the activities of public interest groups, such as the Citizen's Alliance for Economic Justice, grew more active since 1987.

Meanwhile, the political significance of students and the military is decreasing and being replaced by interest groups. To many Koreans, however, the development of interest groups is viewed somewhat negatively because they are associated with the image of collective egoism.

Students

The education level of the general public is low in developing countries. As the most educated and modernized members of society, college students have often been agents of change. Korean students have demonstrated the characteristics of a social force more than their counterparts in any other developing country.

During the First Republic, Korean students supported the Syngman Rhee regime, which was faced with the threat of a North Korean attack. In 1953, even junior and high school students joined the protest against an armistice negotiation. However, resentment developed among students when Rhee planned for lifetime dictatorship through constitutional amendment. They protested against the corrupt election of March 1960 and finally toppled the Rhee regime.

In 1960 Korean college students numbered around 100,000. In comparison, there was a total of 7,800 college students in 1945, 34,000 in 1952, and 2.1 million in 1993.[22] Despite their small number, the students were able to successfully bring down the Rhee regime largely due to their protest having been approved and supported by the urban middle class and the U.S. government. Judging from the military's neutral attitude toward the student demonstrations, it can also be argued that the Korean military offered an indirect support.

Korean students enjoyed greater freedom of speech and political influence during the Second Republic. Chang Myon's government was extremely weak and vulnerable to pressure from students, who demanded severe punishment for those responsible for the corrupt election and for those who had opened fire during the student uprisings. Some even called for the withdrawal of the American forces from South Korea and the establishment of a student conference between South and North Korea.

From 1961 to 1987, students consistently maintained resistance against the military regime. As government grew increasingly authoritarian, the student movement became more radical. During the Third Republic (1963–1972), students advocated a return to democracy, and protested against both the Korean-Japanese diplomatic normalization and Park's effort to amend the constitution for his third term. During the *Yushin* period, they again demanded democratic politics. Under the military dictatorship of the Fifth Republic, the student movement developed a strong anti-American rhetoric and a doctrine of radical popular democracy. They finally achieved their goal of a democratic constitution in 1987.

The students who overthrew Syngman Rhee's dictatorship would have only been partially successful in 1987. Students did not receive wide support from the urban middle class before 1987. The

Third Republic ostensibly had a democratic system, so the urban middle class viewed the students' antigovernment movement as nothing more than conventional criticism. Although in favor of the students' causes, they did not accept the progressive nature of the student movement. After the Kwangju incident during the Fifth Republic, the middle class strongly supported the students' democratic aims but was dissatisfied with anti-Americanism and the idea of popular democracy.

After the return to a democratic constitution, especially after the civilian government was established in 1993, most students returned to the normal academic life. Yet student movements turned more radical, becoming the target of criticism by the urban middle class and even among students themselves. This radical movement may have grown out of grievances against the character of the current ruling party, or as a move to speak for the alienated classes represented by no other political organization. It could also be due to extreme radicalism, which has been dormant for the last thirty years.

The Military

The Korean Army was founded by the United States. The model used in establishing the army was that of a professional army along American lines. Despite opposition from those who served as fighters for national independence, the United States appointed officers from the Japanese Imperial army. From a nationalist viewpoint, it was disgraceful for liberated Korea to have these officers take central positions in the newly founded Korean army. However, America favored the former Japanese officers, who were better trained than the Independence Army soldiers. Besides sophisticated training and modern warfare experience, they had another advantage: strong anti-Communist ideology. North Korean communists and South Korean left-wingers denounced these officers as traitors.[23]

Due to its foundation, the Korean military of the First Republic was different from those of other newly born nations after World War II in that it had no strong nationalistic and ideological tendencies.[24] This suited the U.S. military advisory committee, which detested military involvement in politics. However, the Korean military of the First Republic cannot be totally excluded from politics. President Rhee used military police and the Counter Intelligence Corps as his political apparatus, and used the military for his advantage in every election. Although the United States wanted to foster the Korean military as a politically neutral professional army, the Korean military leaders had to cooperate with the ruling force.

The officers who led the 1961 coup d'état denounced the military leaders' involvement in the corrupt election and demanded their resignation. Their leaders were General Park Chung Hee and Lieutenant Colonel Kim Jong Pil. General Park had attended the Japanese Imperial Military Academy, but unlike other generals, did not speak English, and did not associate himself with the U.S. Military Advisory Committee. He was well acquainted with Korean military leaders, but he did not belong to the mainstream of the Korean military.

The mainstay of the Korean military in the First Republic consisted of those from Hamkyung province and Pyongan province, not those from Yongnam province. There were many generals from Yongnam (or Kyonsang) province who were purged during the early establishment of the army because of their involvement in the left wing riot incident inside the military. Park, who was from the Yongnam region, temporarily resigned from the army because of his involvement with the Yeosoo and Sunchun Rebellion, but later returned to the army with the patronage of top-ranking officers.

After Park took political power through the 1961 coup, the mainstream of the military camp consisted of generals with the Yongnam regional background, primarily through his personal support. Park especially supported *Hanahoe*, which recruited elite officers from the top 5 percent of each year's Military Academy graduates. Officers who belonged to *Hanahoe* were favored in advancement and assignment of positions during Park's rule. After the assassination of Park in 1979, *Hanahoe* members staged a coup to seize military power from their superiors. In 1980, they attempted a coup d'état to seize governmental power.[25] Whereas the 1961 military coup was staged by an alienated force inside the army, the 1979–1980 coup d'état was undertaken by a privileged group within the military. There was a substantial difference between the 1961 coup and that of 1980 in terms of public reaction. People responded rather positively to the 1961 coup as something for which they had been waiting, but most were terrified by the 1980 coup.

After President Kim Young Sam's civilian government began in 1993, most members in *Hanahoe* were purged. But this does not necessarily mean that the Korean military turned into a nonpartisan, professional army. Generals from Pusan and Kyongnam province, who were not members of *Hanahoe*, have taken over the power in the military. It can be said that those from the same region as President Kim worked to form another military faction.

Mass Media

Newspaper has served as the major media vehicle in the past half century in Korean politics. Television is also a growing influence in Korea, as evidenced in the fifteenth presidential election. However, Korean television is still not independent of the government. Among TV broadcasting stations, two are owned by the government and one by a cultural foundation which is controlled by the government. The newest station is owned by an individual who must cooperate with the government. With the exception of government papers, such as *Seoul Shinmun* and some large company papers, newspapers have tried to be independent of the government. On the one hand, newspapers depend on government regulations and advertisement income from businesses, but they also depend on the subscription of their readers. Therefore, they cannot grow without reflecting public opinion. Furthermore, Korean people expect the newspapers to play a role in the surveillance and restraint of government. Since reporters enter the field expecting to play these roles, newspapers cannot help but be faithful to the principle of neutrality. In the case of Korea, where the National Assembly could not faithfully carry out those roles as in Western countries, people's expectations of newspapers were even higher, and the newspapers could not go against these popular expectations.

Korean newspapers, in principle, are unbiased. Most European newspapers clearly express their political opinion, and American papers also reveal the party they support through the editorials. Each newspaper in Korea has a unique political tendency, but formally it maintains a neutral stance between political parities, and do not openly reveal the political force they favor. Secondly, Korean newspapers are prestigious and widely read. Newspapers in European countries are divided into prestigious papers such as the *Times*, *Le Monde*, and *Frankfurter Allgemeine* which have thousands of readers, and mass papers such as *Daily Express*, *Le Petit Parisien*, and *Bild-Zeitung* with a circulation of millions. In the United States, the *New York Times* and the *Washington Post* are differentiated from other newspapers. Educated Americans in other areas read these papers even though they are issued in New York City and Washington, DC. *Donga Ilbo* and *Chosun Ilbo* of Korea, which has each a circulation of more than 2 million are read both by well-educated individuals and by those with lower levels of education, as are the *Asahi* and *Yomiuri* in Japan. Because these newspapers have the characteristics of both prestige and mass papers, Korean newspapers play a more important role in the formation of public opinion than do Western papers.

Newspapers in the First Republic could be published only with government permission. There were a total of 40 daily papers in Seoul and local areas combined, but only *Donga Ilbo* and *Chosun Ilbo*, founded during the Japanese colonial period, could be run independently. Beside these two, there were the *Hankuk Ilbo, Kyunghyang Shinmun,* and a government newspaper, *Seoul Shinmun,* in Seoul. The total circulation of these papers was 7–8 hundred thousand in the late 1950s. Of the total income of these papers, advertisement income occupied 20–30 percent, and newspaper sale, income was 70–80 percent. Korean newspapers depended more on sales income in this period than in any other. Major daily newspapers in Seoul, including *Donga Ilbo,* were opposed to the Liberal Party regime, and thus became antigovernment newspapers. The antigovernment tradition of Korean newspapers was set up during the First Republic. The tradition is also closely related to the fact that *Donga Ilbo* was founded and run by the family of Kim Sung Soo, an opposition party leader in the early First Republic, and *Kyunghyang Shinmun* was run by Catholics who supported Chang Myon, the vice president from the opposition party. Also, newspapers' high dependence on subscription income fostered an antigovernment stance.

In the Second Republic, as newspaper publication switched to a registration system, the number of daily newspapers increased to 97, three times than that of the First Republic. During this period, press abilities and reporting standards were poor due to low standards of living. However, mass media enjoyed the greatest freedom in criticizing the government during this period.

The Park Chung Hee regime purged weak press organizations by invalidating the permit of newspaper companies without appropriate facilities. As a result, the Third Republic had only thirty-nine daily newspaper companies. The number decreased even more in the *Yushin* period of the Fourth Republic because of mergers between local papers. Major papers in Korea, like those in Japan, were issued twice: in the morning and in the evening. In the First and the Second Republic they were issued once a day. During this period, press companies diversified their business. *Donga Ilbo* operated Dong-A broadcasting, and *Kyunghyang Shinmun* newspaper operated the MBC broadcasting station. The Samsung group owned the *Joongang Daily* and *Donyang TV*, and *Chosun Ilbo* operated the Koreana Hotel.

Along with noticeable economic growth in the Third and the Fourth Republics, the circulation of newspapers also increased. According to the Korean Newspaper Association, total circulation of national dailies was 800,000 in 1960, 2 million in 1970, and 5.4 million in 1980. The newspaper subscription rate per family was one issue per 5.5 families in 1960, one issue per 2.9 families in 1970, and one issue per 1.5 families in 1980. During this period, there was also a change in the rate between newspaper sales income and advertisement income. In the case of *Donga Ilbo*, the rate was 6:4 in 1962 and 5:5 in 1970. After 1970, *Donga Ilbo* depended more on advertisement fees than on subscription fees.

The tradition of criticism in the Korean press was considerably restricted during the military regime of 1961 to 1963, but was revived in the Third Republic. However, under the *Yushin* regime of 1972–1979, the press came under severe government restriction. Reporters of the *Donga Ilbo* and *Chosun Ilbo* formed an opposition movement against these restrictions, but it was unsuccessful due to governmental suppression and opposition from company owners. Many reporters were fired. *Donga Ilbo* suffered advertisement suppression because of its anti-*Yushin* stance.

Newspaper reporters contributed to the democratization of Korean politics by resisting governmental suppression. Yet the Fifth Republic under Chun intensified suppression of mass media by enacting the notorious Basic Press Law. The ruling military force fired reporters who were against the regime and invalidated the registration of periodicals with an antiregime bias. Government persecution of the press took other forms, including: merging and unifying communication companies; requiring one local paper per province; separating management of newspapers and broadcasting; and placing broadcasting under public management. As a result, the number of national daily papers was reduced to twenty-eight, and broadcasting to two companies. Also by the management separation policy, *Kyunghyang Shinmun* and MBC, the *Joongang Ilbo* and *Donyang* Broadcasting of the Samsung Group, and *Donga* Broadcasting and *Donga Ilbo* were separated, and the broadcasting wings were merged into the government-owned Korean Broadcasting Service (KBS). Although newspaper subscribers continued to increase in the 1980s, mass media's dependence on advertisement income became more critical.

The democratic opening in 1987 accompanied the abolition of the Basic Press Law and facilitated the enactment of the Press Relations Law that eased governmental restrictions on press organizations. As a result, the number of daily newspapers sharply rose to 103 in 1991, four times larger than that in the Fifth Republic. However, this did not mean diversification of the press structure. The Korean newspaper market was dominated by six national daily papers including *Hangyoreh* founded in 1988. Of those six papers, *Donga Ilbo* and *Chosun Ilbo* dominated the market.[26]

Today, Korean newspapers enjoy more freedom of press than ever before, but they are not fully utilizing this opportunity. In the past thirty years, the raison d'etre of the Korean press has been the championing of democratic causes by way of criticism of authoritarian regimes. This type of editorial stance was also favored by the readers. Despite the democratic opening and consolidation, today's newspapers have not gotten out of the past inertia of blind and sensational criticism, which undermines their credibility. In tandem with democratic changes, there must be corresponding changes in media attitude toward professionalism.

Interest Groups

The number of interest groups in Korea rose from 426 in 1959, 600 in 1963, and 1,034 in 1974, to 1,700 in 1988.[27] They include labor unions, business associations, professional organizations, nonprofit organizations, social and cultural associations, athletic organizations, and religious organizations, among others. Not all are equally important; the politically significant groups include the Korea Federation of Trade Unions (*Hanguk Nochong*), the National Association of Democratic Unions (*Minnochong*), the Federation of Korean Industries (*Chunkyungryun*), and the Korean Federation of Teachers (*Hanguk Kyochong*). Since democratic opening in 1987, several public interest groups, such as the Coalition for Economic Justice (*Kyongsilryun*) and Coalition for Environmental Protection (*Hwankyung Undong Yonhap*), have become more pronounced.

The Federation of Korean Industries (FKI) was formed in 1964 through the reorganization of the Korean Business Association, which was organized in 1961. Under the recommendation of the military regime, thirteen conglomerate heads accused of illegitimate wealth accumulation formed the FKI. As a peak organization representing large corporations and industry associations, the Federation had a total of 434 members with the mandate to defend their rights and benefits. However, it was subservient to the governments of the Third and Fourth Republics. Since the Sixth Republic, however, it began to show signs of independence, and its formal budget in 1993 amounted to 10 billion won.

The Korean Federation of Teachers grew out of the Daehan Education Association, which was formed in 1947 to protect the rights and benefits of teachers. Until the late Fifth Republic, it was merely a government controlled union, but in the Sixth Republic, the Federation was challenged by the National Democratic Teachers' Union and now strives to achieve independence from the government. It is a peak organization representing the interests of teachers at all levels and maintains national networks with an approximate membership of 250,000.

The Coalition for Economic Justice is a nonprofit organization established in 1989 with the goal of improving efficiency and equality of the Korean economy. It has become one of the most influential citizens' groups in monitoring and lobbying government economic policies since the democratic opening. Its membership rose from around 500 in 1989 to 7,000 in 1993. It maintains branches in twenty cities nationwide, as well as in universities, where various research activities are carried out. Many university professors and intellectuals participate in these research activities.

The Korean Federation of Trade Unions, the FKI, the Korean Federation of Teachers, along with most interest groups used to be under the tight corporatist control of the government in previous authoritarian regimes. Since the Sixth Republic, however, they have become more independent and politically more influential. One positive development since democratic opening is the expansion of the civil society, fostering the proliferation of both private and public interest groups. The trend is likely to continue as Korea becomes a more mature democracy.

Conclusion

This chapter has examined the evolutionary dynamics of three important components of the political process in Korea, namely elections, political parties, and interest groups, including students, the military, and mass media. Compared with advanced industrial countries, the political process in South Korea still suffers from a lack of maturity and dynamism. This can be attributed partly to Korea's political culture, and partly to the relatively long duration of authoritarian rule. Since democratic opening in 1987, however, profound changes have taken place. A fair and competitive electoral system has been institutionalized as evidenced by the dramatic election of as the fifteenth president of Korea. Democratic consolidation has substantially weakened power and influence of two ad hoc political groups, namely students and the military, the latter having once played a paramount role in shaping Korea's political landscape. Meanwhile, it has led to the proliferation and strengthening of various interest groups, ostensibly a desirable development. Mass media has also become more influential than ever before, also a sign of a maturing democracy.

However, the political party system seems to remain problematic. Political parties in Korea lack clear-cut ideologies, party platforms, and organizational structures. Factionalism and personalized leadership still dominate the dynamics of party politics, including alignments and realignments. Given the political party's central role in aggregating and articulating interests from below, the deformed political party system can undermine the very process of Korea's political system. In order to institutionalize democratic consolidation and to ensure a stable democracy, there needs to a more mature party system in terms of ideology, policy, and organization.

Notes

1. David Easton, *A Systems Analysis of Political Life* (Chicago: The University of Chicago Press, 1965).

2. Bruce Cumings, *The Origins of the Korean War* (Princeton: Princeton University Press, 1981).

3. Sung Joo Han, *The Failure of Democracy in South Korea* (Berkeley: University of California Press, 1974).

4. Douglas W. Rae, *The Political Consequences of Electoral Laws* (New Haven: Yale University Press, 1967).

5. Chun Joo Yoon, *Chungp'opan Han'guk Chongchi Chekye* [The Korean Political System], Supplement ed. (Seoul: Seoul University Press, 1979), pp. 180–269.

6. Chun Joo Yoon, *Tup'yo Chamyowa Chongchi Palchon* [Vote Participation and Political Development] (Seoul: Seoul University Press, 1986), pp. 66–67.

7. Chun Joo Yoon, op. cit., pp. 451–473.

8. Chun Joo Yoon, op. cit., p. 302.

9. Jung Bok Lee, "Han'gukinui Tup'yo Haengtae: Che 14 Tae Chongsonul Chungsimuro" ["The Voting Behavior of the Korean People in the fourteenth General Election"], *Han'guk Chongchi Hakhoebo* [Korean Political Science Review] 26:3 (1993), pp. 116–119.

10. Sejong Institute, ed., *Che 15 Tae Chongson P'unsok* [An Analysis of the fifteenth General Election] (Seoul: Sejong Institute, 1996).

11. Jung Bok Lee, op. cit., p. 126.

12. Joseph LaPalombara and Myron Weiner, "The Origin and Development of Political Parties," In J. L. and M. Weiner, eds., *Political Parties and Political Development* (Princeton: Princeton University Press, 1966), pp. 7–21.

13. Giovanni Sartori, *Parties and Party Systems* (Cambridge: Cambridge University Press, 1976), pp. 10–13.

14. Sartori, refer to pp. 244–272. Sartori refers to as "quasi-parties" the political parties of the newly formed African countries, but the political parties of Korea are semiparties, which are at a higher development level.

15. Samuel P. Huntington, "Political Development and Political Decay," *World Politics* 17:3 (April 1965), pp. 386–430.

16. Maurice Duverger, *Political Parties* (London: Methuen & Co., 1967), pp. 63–71.

17. Robert Michels, *Political Parties* (New York: The Free Press, 1962).

18. Angelo Panebianco, *Political Parties: Organization and Power* (Cambridge: Cambridge University Press, 1988), pp. 21–32.

19. Arthur Bentley, *The Process of Government* (Cambridge: Belknap Press of Harvard University, 1967) and David Truman, *The Governmental Process* (New York: Knopf, 1971).

20. Harold Laski, *A Grammar of Politics* (London: George Allen & Unwin Ltd., 1950).

21. Philippe Schmitter and Gerhard Lehmbruch, eds., *Trends Toward Corporatist Intermediation* (Beverly Hills: Sage Publications, 1979).

22. The total number of students here is extracted from Central Education Council, eds. *Kyoyuk T'onggye Yonbo* [Statistical Yearbook of Education] (Seoul: Ministry of Education, 1991).

23. On the characteristics of the professional army, see Amos Perlmutter, *The Military and Politics in Modern Times* (New Haven: Yale University Press, 1977).

24. See Morris Janowitz, *The Military in the Political Development of New Nations* (Chicago: University of Chicago Press, 1964).

25. Yong Won Han, *Han'gukui Kunp'u Chongchi* [The Korean Military Government] (Seoul: Daewang Publishing Co., 1993).

26. Myung Koo Kang, *Han'guk Sinmun Sanop'ui Yoksajok Kochal* [Historical Investigation of Korean Newspapers].

27. Young Rae Kim, *Han'gukui Iik Chipdan [Interest Groups in Korea]* (Seoul: Daewang Publishing Co., 1987).

7

෪

The Administrative Process in Korea

Dong-suh Bark

Administration is a term widely used in the social sciences, but its interpretations have been diverse. The contextual differences of states by time and space have rendered it difficult to define the term in a precise manner. For all its diverse interpretations, *administration* can be defined in the Korean context simply as the "decision making and its materialization within state authority." State authority is included not only to differentiate the term from *management*, but also to signify the close link between administration and state power in Korea, due to its brief history of democracy. Decision making is included because in Korea, administration functions beyond its classical role as defined in the division of three powers—the executive, the legislature, and the judiciary.

Thus, while the scope of administration includes the overall decision-making process, we have to consider whether the president in a presidential system should be included as well. The president not only represents and governs a nation but also heads the administration. In Korea, the president exercises enormous executive power. Thus, it becomes essential to include the president in understanding administration in Korea.

History of Korean Administration: An Overview

Before a detailed discussion of the administrative process, it seems logical to briefly review the history of Korean administration, which will guide us toward a more comprehensive under-

standing on the current issues and characteristics of the bureaucracy. Although the Korean state has been in existence for four
thousand years, this chapter will delimit the historical scope of the
overview to the three periods that have most influenced the formation of the contemporary administration in Korea: the Chosun
Dynasty, the Japanese colonial period, and the period of the Republic of Korea.

Chosun Dynasty (1392–1910)

During the Chosun Dynasty, administration and politics were
indivisible, both structurally and functionally. Administration was
identical with politics, inclusive of all decision making.

Though the ideal objective of politics as well as of administration was to serve the people, people at the time lacked the means to
check the governance of the king. Though few, some kings provided
a rule of virtue. In most cases, the objective of administration during the Chosun Dynasty was to maintain the existing order and
royal authority and to control the general population.

Division of labor and power within the political structure is
essential in ensuring rational decision-making. During the Chosun
Dynasty, such division did not exist, not to mention the absence of
political parties or a parliament. Moreover, even in the administrative structure, the division of roles among agencies was not clear.
The basic structure was composed of *Ui-jung-bu* (state council) and
Yuk-bu (six branches of the cabinet system). Specialization of bureaucrats and chain of command and control were conspicuously nonexistent. Information and opinion sharing was hardly expected, and
due to the autocratic atmosphere, there was no room for the flow of
opinions from bottom to top. In such an environment, rational and
efficient decision-making was almost impossible.[1]

Nevertheless, the king was expected to consult a small number of close bureaucrats before making a decision. When kings
abided by this principle, decision making was made through consensus, though in a very limited manner.

As Chosun society was structured on a rigid social hierarchy
of class stratification, not all people were eligible to take the civil
and military service examinations. However, it is significant that
public servants were screened through an open, competitive examination known as *gwageo*.

Management of financial resources was through a basic quota
system; each board had to be self-sufficient. Yet in the use of gov-

ernment funds, there was no clear division between private and public.[2] Undoubtedly, mobilization and distribution of financial resources directed by the "unlimited" privilege of bureaucrats was far from rational decision-making and implementation. Underdeveloped transportation and communication infrastructure made monitoring and control of such bureaucratic corruption more difficult.

In view of this, the Chosun administrative structures and practices were similar to what Max Weber has called the "patrimonial bureaucracy." In a patrimonial state, the king considered the state to be his own hereditary property; there was no distinction between public law and private order, or between the right to reign and the right to possess. This was undeniably the case during the Chosun dynasty.[3] The following is a summary of the major features of the Chosun administrative system as a patrimonial bureaucratic state:[4]

- Bureaucrats behaved not in accordance with law but with tradition. Lower officials were required to obey their superiors, and ultimately to the personal order of the King.

- Division of power was not based on specialization but on the private decision-making of the king. Thus, power was privatized and inherited, resulting in the weakening of the monarchical authority. Proliferation and negative effects of in-law politics in the late nineteenth century exemplifies this trend quite well.

- The relationship between high- and low-ranking bureaucrats mirrored the class stratification, and tight and comprehensive control over the lower officials was relatively well maintained.

- Knowledge required for bureaucratic service was not specific, but general, as was the content of the high civil service examination. Thus, the Chosun dynasty cultivated bureaucrats as generalists.

- As with most bureaucratic states, the Chosun dynasty displayed low policy predictability not only because decision making was personalized in the hands of the royal court, but also because the legal system was subject to the king's arbitrary interpretations.

In an administrative structure such as that of the Chosun era, it was hard to expect flexible adaptation or reform. The system was bureaucratic and ineffective, existing not for the ruled, but for the ruler. It would be, then, more appropriate to refer to Chosun bureaucrats as "mandarins" rather than authentic bureaucrats in the modern sense as they had considerably more power than their European counterparts. Rule by mandarins was one of the factors that hindered modernization of the Chosun government and society, ultimately resulting in its demise through the forced annexation to Japan in 1910.

Japanese Colonial Period (1910–1945)

Administration under Japanese rule existed to serve the Japanese emperor. However, actual political power did not rest with the emperor, but with the oligarchy of bureaucrats, big business, and the military. Thus, the Japanese Government-General in Korea was under the control of this tripartite oligarchy, and its objective was to maintain and consolidate colonial rule, to reign the Korean population, and to extract all it could.

The partial economic modernization achieved by the Japanese administration in the late colonial period was solely for Japanese gain, partly for its preparation for the coming wars and the conquering of mainland China.[5]

During the Japanese Imperial era, parliament and political parties existed in Japan, though with limited political functions. This was unthinkable for Koreans, and only minor improvements in the administrative system were introduced by Japanese colonial rulers. The two fields affected were infrastructure and the qualification of bureaucrats. Through both quantitative and qualitative development of communications and the transportation system, bureaucrats' awareness regarding the importance of information flow was raised significantly. Though the colonial bureaucracy was not widely open to Koreans and existed basically to serve the colonial order, civil servants attained a basic knowledge of modern law and economics.

What most distinguished the administration of the Japanese colonial period from that of the Chosun era was the effective mobilization, allocation, and use of human and material resources.[6] Each civil servant was given specific tasks, and the budget was effectively allocated. Bureaucratic abuse of privileged power and related "black money" corruption were dramatically reduced during the colonial era. The salary system was also rationalized.

All these changes were possible because the Japanese bureaucracy was relatively less corrupt. Further, the ruler and the ruled in Japan had maintained loyalty to one other for more than seven hundred years during the feudal era. Finally, the Meiji Restoration offered a momentum for modernizing the Japanese administration, something that Chosun never experienced. Thus, during the colonial period, the Japanese administrative system was transplanted in Korea. Such an administrative structure or bureaucracy is similar to what Weber classified as "modern bureaucracy." The main features of this system can be summarized as:[7]

- The power of administration is defined by law; thus abuse of power is reduced while stability and predictability of bureaucratic performance increase.

- The power of high and low rank bureaucrats is distinguished; the latter is supervised by the former.

- All bureaucratic affairs are based on paperwork, commitment, and professional specialization.

- Stability of the administrative system is assured through legalization.

As listed above, the administration of the Japanese colonial era existed to maintain colonial rule and enforce surveillance and control of the Korean people. The sole difference from the Chosun period was increased output due to effective use of inputs. In its outer appearance, Korea seemed to be modernizing, but still it was a colony, not an independent state. The Korean people were ruled and suppressed, unable to participate in the modernization process. Strong resentment of the Japanese rulers, not modern citizenship, was all that developed among the Koreans during this period.

The Republic of Korea Era (1948–)

Korea was liberated from Japanese rule in 1945. Before the establishment of the Republic of Korea in 1948, Korea experienced a three-year American Military Occupation. During this period, the administrative structure underwent significant changes. However, the reforms proved to be short-lived, as they were not based on the interests of the Korean people.[8] By early 1955, not a trace of the American reforms could be found in the Korean administrative system.

Although the ROK was founded on democratic ideals, the changes were nominal. The minds of the general population as well as of the civil servants remained the same. Korean administration remained bureaucratic in nature. The dearth of real democratic change in Korea is due largely to the nature of its origins in Korea—not through a middle-class (or bourgeoisie) revolution, but rather through the import of foreign ideas by an elite group emphasizing state power over the balance of state and civil society.

Therefore, throughout the 1950s, the major function of the Korean administration was to maintain social order and to exercise control over the people. In the 1960s, economic development was added as another role of administration; in the 1980s, words such as *justice* and *welfare* emerged in government reports, but only as an euphemism to disguise military dictatorship. It was only after the democratic opening in 1987 that these "dead" words were resuscitated in administrative practices.

Administrative decision-making in contemporary Korea has been highly centralized. Although political parties and the parliament were set up as decision-making institutions, their influence over decision making has been fundamentally limited. Betraying the expectations of the Korean populace, the Syngman Rhee government insulated the decision-making process from civil and political society, a practice followed by subsequent regimes. While citizen participation in decision making was limited, the participation of specialized professionals in the administration has increased since the 1960s and, though slow, the qualification of public servants has also gradually improved.

Division of work among different executive branches was settled with the 1961 military coup by Park Chung Hee. However, the quantitative increase of human and financial resources of administration did not equate with the qualitative and effective use of resources. Coercion remained the basic way to make civil servants work, while rationalized methods of information and opinion sharing did not emerge. The conservative character of the birth of the ROK infused dualistic features in the administration: *ancien régime* in its structure, democratic in its ideal.

Since the 1960s new functions were added to the Korean administration: the mobilization of the people to unify them in the direction of economic development, and modernization of Korean society. Output increased dramatically compared to the 1950s, but in terms of realizing democratic governance and efficient use of input resources the administration still needed fundamental reforms.

Having reviewed the evolutionary changes of the Korean administration, the following features can be summarized: [9]

• There has been a quick shift in the objective of administration—from Confucian virtues to Japanese colonial ideology, and later to modern democratic ideals.

• However, the changes in the objective and structure of administration lacked coherence and continuity. No reform was initiated from within the government for administrative purposes.

• Up until the early 1980s, administrative restructuring was imposed from above, mostly by specific political motivations of the ruling group apart from the general interests of the people. Reforms did not start from the bottom, and so failed to reflect social and economic developments of the Korean society and popular demands. Democratic opening in June 1987 marked a watershed for true administrative reforms.

• Changes in the Korean administration have taken place in sequence; from its political ideology, to objective of administration, and finally its structure.

• Since liberation in 1945, the Korean administration has shown a mixture of modern democratic ideals, colonial structure, and Chosun-style bureaucratic division of labor. This triplex character has impaired bureaucratic performance in contemporary Korea.

Democratization of Administration

Political Development and Democratization of Administration

The history of the ROK is rather short, beginning only in 1948. This short history and its precarious paths to political development have considerably impeded the democratization of administration in Korea. Independence of, and checks and balances among, the three branches of the government have remained weak. Having been seldom checked by the other two branches, the executive has continued to dominate. This is due partly to three decades of protracted authoritarian rule and partly due to the constitutional design of the presidential system. However, democratic transition and the subsequent expansion of civil society since 1987 have increased legislative oversight over the executive, and the division among three branches has become more clear and concrete.

The check-and-balance system is essential for a democratic administration. However, this must be guaranteed not only by the constitution, but also by the balance of power between the people and public authority. In order for civil society to have a balanced share of power against the state, the democratic experience of the general population should be firmly secured through the formation of diverse interest groups and participation in the decision-making processes.[10]

Dynamics of Political Development in South Korea

Despite social unrest and political turmoil, the Rhee government provided universal education; all Koreans were eligible to a six-year elementary education providing literacy and other basic education programs. Though its quality was questionable, this basic education encouraged many young Koreans, driven by the Confucian emphasis on learning, to extend their studies to middle, high school, and some cases to college levels, even going overseas to advanced industrial countries for their studies.

It was this high level of education and relatively free media that made possible the overthrow of the corrupt regime of Syngman Rhee in 1960. Given the long tradition of patrimonialism and the short history of the ROK, the 1960 Student Revolution that toppled the Rhee regime seems quite significant. The success of popular resistance demonstrated through the April 19 Student Revolution stimulated a sense of responsibility among politicians. Obsessed with power struggles, Korean politicians had paid very little attention to the well-being of the people, but now they were forced to turn their eyes to economic development, democratization, and reunification with the North.

As a result of the April Student Revolution, the opposition democratic Party (DP) during the Rhee regime came to power. During its one year in power, the DP government laid an institutional foundation for more democratic and open politics than the First Republic. But factional struggles within the ruling circle, fragile government, and unending social and economic instability sowed the seeds of self-destruction. Amid political turmoil, a group of military officers, led by General Park, seized political power through a military coup. Apart from raising the question of whether the Chang Myon government under the Second Republic would have been capable of running a country suffering from a backward socioeconomic situation, the 1961 military coup marked the beginning of military intervention in civil politics through means of force.

The Third Republic banned local autonomy and tightly centralized political power. The ruling group was composed of those with Japanese military background as well as graduates of the Korea Military Academy, and shared a strong anticommunist sentiment. The regime started its drive for rapid economic development, suppressing the popular move for democracy and reunification. Some scholars attribute as causes for Park's drive for economic growth his desperate efforts to justify his illegitimate rise to power, and his poor childhood. However, we should not underestimate the political situation of the time. Park himself had witnessed the people's power in 1960 and realized that by failing to respond to the demands of the general public, a ruler would eventually be overthrown by the people. Despite the lack of legitimacy, Park had to promote economic growth and get the Korean people out of absolute poverty in order to enhance his popular support and secure his own survival. In addition, his sympathy for socialist ideals in his youth influenced him to be more concerned with the economic development of the nation.

The ruling group of the Third Republic launched Five-Year Economic Development Plans and mobilized human and physical resources for economic growth, utilizing the organizational management capabilities learned while in the military. However, the allocation of resources was concentrated in a small number of businesses—the *chaebols*; this was the beginning of Korea's notorious government-business collusion. Against the normal process of political development, power became more centralized and the economy was subordinated to political rationale.

Meanwhile, positive changes also took place underneath these negative developments; the rate of secondary education increased significantly. Though the authoritarian regime set up political institutions against democratic values, students were exposed to democratic values, such as freedom and equality, through formal educational processes. Another positive result of economic growth was the birth of the middle-class and of small- and medium-size companies. They were relatively less dependent on the regime and wanted more independence and social security.

At the beginning of industrialization, there was an immense

urban migration of the rural population, which in turn offered an unlimited workforce for urban factories. Though this young labor force had little education, they soon took notice of the increasing gap between rich and poor. Industrial workers became involved in labor activism and called for fair distribution of income and wealth. These groups—college students, the middle class, and industrial workers—emerged as the major force in challenging the authoritarian regime through the 1970s and the 1980s.

In the early 1970s, the clock of democracy in Korea reversed direction. The Park regime strengthened its iron rule by amending the constitution to prolong his stay in power. This precipitated intensifying tension and confrontation between the state authorities and the general population. Park's belief that strengthened iron rule would prolong the maintenance of his regime did not work; the regime's instability increased with the growing resentment of the people. The short-lived Fourth Republic came to an end with the assassination of Park by his close associate.

Despite their contribution to the modernization of Korea, former presidents Rhee and Park are accountable for the following shortcomings:

- The regime lost legitimacy due to the reckless pursuit of power maintenance.

- As time went by after their inauguration, they were disconnected from the flow of public opinion and information from below. The premodern structure of Korean politics, characterized by personalism and factionalism, blocked the inflow of information. Further, close associates of the president distorted facts and information that were supposed to be delivered to the president.

- Both were "one-strong-man" characters rather than personalities that valued the participation of and cooperation with others.

- Righteous and competent people refused to join and support the autocratic regimes as their rule became prolonged with strengthened authoritarian repression, which in turn further weakened the support of the general public.

The military, however, did not learn from the lessons of history. In 1980, General Chun Doo Hwan seized power through a military coup. Treason and the bloody suppression of civilian protests in Kwangju severely impaired the legitimacy of the Chun regime from its outset. Chun purged opposition politicians and put gangsters into quasimilitary camps, under the name of "social purification." It also abolished curfew and deregulated uniform-wearing of secondary school students and the academic management system of universities. On the other hand, the regime tried to revitalize the debt-laden Korean economy through macroeconomic stabilization and structural adjustment. In terms of popular participation, however, the situation remained unchanged. Authoritarian rule continued and alienated critical members of the developmental coalition that sustained Park's *Yushin* regime. Frequently coerced to provide political contributions, even *chaebols* began to express their dissatisfaction with the regime,.

Furthermore, in personnel appointments, all important government positions were filled with military and political figures from the Taegu-Kyongsang (T-K) region. Despite increasing resentment from the overall population, Chun did not put forth any political measures to settle the mounting problems. His attempt to retain the existing constitution of the Fifth Republic in April 1987 flamed public outrage; college students, intellectuals, church groups, and workers, in alliance with opposition parties, staged popular uprisings in protest during the month of June 1987. The silent middle class joined and supported the uprisings.

The public called for an immediate constitutional amendment that would allow direct election of president. They also demanded a wide range of reforms involving freedom of expression and association, fair distribution of income and wealth, greater political participation by the people, and deregulation and decentralization of government power. Chun was finally forced to accommodate the popular demands and avoided a violent repression of the uprisings. This was embodied in the June 29 Roh Tae Woo declaration on democratic reforms, which assured the desired constitutional amendment, freedom of expression and association, revival of local autonomy, release of political prisoners, and abolition of the Basic Press Law. Indeed, the popular uprising of June 1987 served as a formidable deterrent to military intervention in civil politics by demonstrating the people's power.

The inauguration of the Kim Young Sam government in 1993 marked another milestone in the history of Korean democracy. Kim, as a long-time opposition leader, was qualitatively different from former presidents in terms of political beliefs, background, and leadership quality. Based on his lifelong commitment to democratic politics,

President Kim launched a series of democratic and administrative reforms: the real-name financial transaction system, annual public disclosure of private assets of high-ranking officers and politicians, refusal to take political contributions from *chaebols* and streamlining of election campaigns and political fund-related laws. Although President Kim himself fell victim to them with the conviction of his son under charges of corruption, the reforms led to the arrest of former presidents, as well as an array of politicians and bureaucrats, and significantly contributed to cleaning up Korean politics.

Administrative Reforms

From the perspective of social change theories,[11] the factors of democratic transition in South Korea are found in universal education, the relatively freer mass media, economic and technological ties with advanced democracies, competition with the North, successful economic development, and the growth of middle-class and industrial workers. When compared with the political landscape in the 1970s, democratic opening and transition since 1987 can be seen as being as miraculous as Korea's economic performance. It is more so because of the election of Kim Dae Jung as new president in December 1997. Kim's election marks the first peaceful transfer of power from the ruling to the opposition party in the political history of South Korea, signifying its democratic maturity.

Colonial historians, dependency, and Marxist theorists all have failed in predicting this peaceful transfer of political power in South Korea. They believed that extreme ideological confrontation, the lingering memory of the Korean War, and thirty years of authoritarian rule would prevent South Koreans from developing into a mature democracy.

The history of Korean politics demonstrates that bureaucratic reform is viable only after political democratization. Education, a market economy and its development, and increased participation of the middle class can open the way for democracy. Democratic administration cannot be achieved without corresponding popular control over the government and participation in the decision-making process.

Functions of Administration

Administration basically aims at realizing national goals through good governance. To achieve the goals in a democratic and efficient manner, the executive branch should avoid monopolizing power. The three branches of the government should coordinate their functions in policy making and implementation. The following presents a brief review of national goals, administrative ideology, and the dynamics of policy making and implementation that have governed the Korean administration in the past.

Changing Goals of National Governance

Goals of national governance have changed over time as dictated by internal and external conditions. Since the launching of the Republic of Korea in 1948, however, the Korean government has worked hard to achieve three major national goals: nation-building, democratization and economic development, and welfare and unification.

NATION-BUILDING. With the division of the peninsula into North and South, only those living in the South came to be the subject and object of nation-building. A major means was universal education, which infused an anticommunist ideology. The division of the peninsula did not end at the thirty-eighth parallel but was extended to the mentality of each Korean. Extreme hatred toward each other made the building of one nation an increasingly distant dream.

In the South, the people's anti-North orientation was bred initially after an acute confrontation between left and right during 1945 to 1948. But the devastation that followed the Korean War further deepened anti-North and anticommunist sentiment. In addition, the failed attempt to punish and wipe out Korean collaborators during Japanese colonial rule brought about another impediment to the process of nation building. This was a grave mistake on the part of Syngman Rhee, who relied heavily on those who were educated, trained, and employed by the Japanese. In order to maintain social order and to secure his political survival, he excluded both nationalists and leftists, and instead recruited and coopted those who had served under the colonial administration.

The twin legacies of national division and unjustified tolerance over the collaborators have long haunted Koreans by posing a major barrier to nation-building. Thus, the Korean government has consistently attempted to foster nation-building by removing the barrier.

DEMOCRATIZATION AND ECONOMIC DEVELOPMENT. When the Democratic Party came to power as a result of the April 19 revolution, an institutional foundation was laid for more democratic and open politics, as evidenced in the Constitution of the Second Republic, and ambitious economic development plans were launched. Yet the overall environment was not receptive to the success of such reforms. Devastated by Japanese colonial rule and the Korean War, the public did not possess enough political awareness to consolidate democracy. Capital, technology, and human resources were also inadequate for effective implementation of the economic development plans. Along with this, internal friction and the weak governing capability of the Chang Myon government worsened the situation.

Park's coup in 1961, while it meant a retreat in political development, offered a new momentum for economic development. The tradeoff between democracy and economic development became all the more pronounced. Leadership commitment, management capability, well-educated labor forces, massive mobilization of and selective allocation of financial resources, and technology infusion from abroad contributed to fostering modernization and economic growth under the Park regime.

SOCIAL WELFARE AND UNIFICATION. A higher level of education, economic development, and democratic changes have driven the South Korean people to call for better social welfare policies as well as reunification with North Korea. Having gone through the dark days of the 1970s and the early 1980s, Koreans yearned for democracy, welfare, and reunification. The people's dream came to be realized, albeit gradually, with the democratic opening in 1987. Pressured by workers and farmers' demand for their share in the expanded economic pie, the government started to implement various welfare policies, including unemployment insurance and comprehensive medical care programs in 1994. Though the welfare system was institutionalized, the quality of welfare in South Korea remained unsatisfactory. But this situation is expected to improve, for democratization is always accompanied by a fair distribution of income and wealth as well as a better quality of life. Of course, the economic trusteeship of South Korea under the International Monetary Fund (IMF) could delay the satisfaction of welfare needs.

Regarding unification, the Roh administration made efforts to resume a sincere dialogue with the North Korean authorities. Based on its superior political and economic development, the South Korean government was quite active in revitalizing North-South relations, but little progress was made due to the reluctant attitude of the North Koreans. Moreover, the 1994 nuclear crisis, the submarine incident in 1996, and the ongoing food shortage in North Korea have all darkened the prospects of peaceful unification of the two Koreas.

Despite his initial pledges to welfare and unification, President Kim Young Sam failed to achieve any visible outcomes. While the IMF system severely undercut the quality of life with grave distributional consequences, Kim's erratic policy vis-à-vis North Korea resulted in one of the longest stalemates with the North. Having experienced the devastating performances of the Kim Young Sam government, people's expectations were high for Kim Dae Jung, whom they believed to be able to improve the quality of life not only through an improved social welfare system but also through the realization of a peaceful unification with the North.

Administrative Ideology

In a country where liberal democracy and capitalism serve as the institutional foundations of governance, administration ideology is bound to pursue democratic principles, legitimacy, efficiency, and effectiveness. South Korea is no exception. Unlike other advanced democracies, however, in South Korea, democratic principles and legitimacy were emphasized more because these ideals rarely had been observed. Throughout the past four decades, South Koreans have experienced constitutional crises and illegitimate regimes, due primarily to a relatively weak civil society against an overdeveloped state. However, the democratic struggle in June 1987 reversed the situation.

Efficiency and effectiveness became important administrative ideals as the size of the government grew and its functions became more complex along with expanded revenues. In the past, taxpayers paid little attention to the national budget as the sum of money spent, as well as tax, were rather insignificant. The rapid increase in the budget during the Korean War was due to American aid. When Washington reduced its aid to South Korea after the military coup in 1961, the Park regime launched its economic development plans, mobilizing domestic capital and inducing foreign aid.

Since the mid-1960s, taxpayers began to demand more efficient use of the national budget. The government tried to achieve the goals of the economic plans and enhance their effective execution by conducting quarterly and yearly assessments. Unlike in the private sector, evaluating administrative efficiency and effectiveness is not easy. The evaluation was made not to the general bureaucratic performance of the administration, but to specific branches that were responsible for economic development plans. Evaluating the efficiency and effectiveness of the administration was definitely new for the government, and the objectivity of the evaluation remained problematic as it was subject to a personal evaluation rather than an institutionalized one. In addition, the ideals of efficiency and effectiveness were exploited by the autocratic regime to justify its illegitimate and undemocratic governance.

Policy Making and Execution

In order to realize the national goals discussed above, policies need to be formulated and executed. Policy making includes legislating new laws and devising appropriate decisions and measures to execute them. In principle, the parliament is responsible for this, but the actual process varies across countries, depending on each political system. In reality, parliament has rarely involved in the policy-making process in South Korea, where drafting of new laws and important decisions have been primarily made by the administration. The primacy of the executive branch is well illustrated by the existence of a legislation agency in the administration and not in the National Assembly.

However, this does not mean that the National Assembly does not make any new legislation. Lawmakers draft new bills and submit them to the National Assembly to be reviewed and passed. Yet only in a few cases does this happen. The draft bill first goes to the ruling party for consultation. In this respect, the political system in South Korea is similar to the parliamentary system, and fairly different from the U.S. presidential system. The Korean presidential system shares little in common with the American system. The role of the ruling party is identical with that under the parliamentary system; the giant government party links the administration and the legislature. Yet the administration is not monopolized by the lawmakers of the ruling party as is the case under the parliamentary system. Only a few lawmakers are appointed to be ministers; the majority are nonlawmakers. In view of this, the Korean system seems to be a mixture of the presidential and cabinet systems.

This system has several merits: first, the president's fixed term of office contributes to the stability of the administration; second, the appointment of cabinet members is not limited to lawmakers of the ruling party but can be extended to include various professional bureaucrats and intellectuals; and last, the directly elected president and lawmakers of the government party, on the one hand, and appointed cabinet ministers on the other check and balance each other through consultation meetings. However, it is also true that the consultation meetings are not enough to harness the excessive power of the administration. The more fundamental problem in Korean politics is that despite the official checking of the executive, neither lawmakers nor political parties are respected nor trusted by voters.

When a draft bill is submitted to the National Assembly after going through a consultation meeting, the ruling and opposition parties review the bill. The vote in the National Assembly cannot be based on the personal opinion of each lawmaker but rather on the party's unified position. Some political analysts criticize this as a "rubber-stamp vote," but in a democratic system of party politics, this party versus party debate could be more effective than personal votes. In Korea, the real problem lies in the lack of thorough discussion and participation of lawmakers within the party when drafting a bill. Thus, democracy within the political parties rather than in the political system itself remains a more fundamental issue.

Considering the political culture in Korea, it will take time to democratize the political parties. Occasionally, the parties should allow each lawmaker to vote for or against a bill according to their own personal judgment.

Finally, when a bill is passed in the National Assembly, the administration takes responsibility over the execution and implementation of the policy. The work is divided among the central and local administration and public corporations. But due to the long history of centralized government in Korea, the relationship between central and local administration is not independent but rather hierarchical. This is different from the UK or United States, both of which have long histories of well-developed local autonomy. The participation of local residents is limited and considerations on local peculiarities for economic and social development are easily disregarded.

Pressured by popular demands to introduce local autonomy, authoritarian regimes in the past increased the number of local branches of the central administration. This became a source of conflict between local administrative bureaus and local autonomy organizations that still remains today. Many of the administrative policies are also executed by public corporations and their subsidiaries with different names. This public sector bears the great possibility of high inefficiency, which needs to be critically addressed.

Administrative Division of
Labor and Resource Mobilization

Administrative Division of Labor

Effective operation of administration requires coordination and cooperation of various personnel and sectors as well as huge mobilization of resources. Here, I would like to touch on the organization and resources of administration.

Organization refers to a system of division of labor, which is composed of division of work and coordination. Division of labor has two dimensions, vertical and horizontal. Central administration in Korea has a similar number of ministries and division of labor system as in most advanced democracies. What makes the Korean system distinct is the horizontal division of labor. The stratification is hierarchical and complex—president, prime minister, ministers, metropolitan mayor, provincial governor, mayor, county headman, district chief, and chief of smaller districts of *eup, myon,* and *dong.*

Korea is under a presidential system, but the prime minister is expected to lead and coordinate the cabinet. But in reality, the prime minister has little power since he is appointed by the president, and his work is in constant conflict with that of the president since the division of labor between the two heads is ambiguous and overlapping. If the prime minister is too actively involved in policy coordination, he might come into conflict with the president. This is why most Korean prime ministers remain passive and silent. In addition, because under the presidential system the president does not resign over a political mistake or crisis, it has often been the case for prime ministers to step down. Therefore, if it is too controversial to abolish the prime ministership, it would be productive to grant him more autonomy. More effective division of labor between the president and prime minister is strongly suggested.

Under the prime minister, there are many ministries, offices, and sections. The Finance and Economy and the National Unification Board ministers are deputy prime ministers and they coordinate the affairs of other ministries. These two ministries are superagencies, in charge of not only policy planning and coordination but also of overall implementation.

Though the excessive power of the Ministry of Finance and Economy is a source of conflict with other ministries, there is little prospect for reform due to the progrowth drive of Korean administrations. It is often argued that the Blue House Secretary on Economic Affairs alone cannot fully assist the president in making economic decisions; thus, the status and functions of the ministry seems likely to remain unchanged for the time being. However, the recent economic crisis and the IMF trusteeship could weaken the power of the Ministry of Finance and Economy, eventually leading to its demise.

The situation differs in the National Unification Board, however. The issue of unification is complex, requiring the cooperation and coordination of other ministries, including the ministries of foreign affairs, defense, and finance and economy. Although headed by a deputy prime minister, the National Unification Board does not have the authority to exercise control over other ministries. It is therefore necessary for the new government to consider the restructuring of the National Unification Board.

Another inefficiency in the vertical division of labor is found in its multistratified and overlapping structure, which is the source of lack of accountability and waste of resources. With the introduction of local autonomy in 1994, division of labor among metropolitan cities, provinces, counties, and districts became more elaborate. It is suggested that quasi-autonomy should be given to *eup, myon,* and *dong* to at least take responsibility over the welfare policies of local residents. Another option is to abolish the administrative division of *eup, myon,* and *dong*.

Once a bureaucracy grows into a massive organization, it is difficult to reduce its size and to improve coherence, as compartmentalization and factionalism may prevail in any bureaucracy. In Korean administrations, sectionalism and compartmentalization has relatively little influence in the centralized state. Challenging the highest authority has hardly been allowed. Under the "strong man" rule, such a challenge was unthinkable, and as a consequence the emergence of middle leadership has been suppressed.

True integration of an organization should be based on autonomy of each sector, which is absent in Korean administration. Koreans are accustomed to unity imposed from top to down, while the heads of each section lack responsibility and loyalty to the goals of the administration. Government employers, thus, are often more preoccupied with their own interests than those of the organization. Additionally, factions based on school, blood, and regional ties prevail over loyalty to the organization, leaving many negative repercussions on bureaucratic performance. What is urgently required is the need to promote national integrity, reflecting the level of socioeconomic development.

Resources Mobilization

In order to maintain a large bureaucracy and to execute policies, huge and diverse resources are required. These include not only human and financial resources, but also additional information, political support, and time. The increased realization of the importance of human capital has drawn the emphasis away from financial resources. Now, highly qualified, high-ranking officials, as well as middle- and low-ranking public employees, are needed in order to improve public services and to enhance bureaucratic performance.

PERSONNEL. Public careers, highly valued in Korean society, attract qualified people. But the quality and quantity of public employees needs to be improved by reforming the backward stratification of positions.

FINANCE. The national budget has increased drastically over the past thirty years. While economic development has benefited taxpayers, there are still shortcomings in the taxation system and in budget spending. The substantial increase in tax income has been offset by flourishing underground economy, poor quality of tax administration, and prevalent tax evasion. As long as international media headlines run stories regarding the flow of black money from Korean business to politicians, effective financial mobilization through the tax system will face problems. Another problem concerns excessive military spending, which has been criticized as contributing to underdeveloped social welfare system and inadequate employment conditions of public servants. Thus, how to reconcile the tradeoff between guns and butter will pose a major problem in dealing with financial mobilization.

INFORMATION. Only very recently has there been an emphasis on the importance of information, resulting in only minor investment in this field. The severe lack in the quantity and quality of materials of Korean libraries clearly reveal this serious problem. Fortunately, the recent rapid increase in use of personal computers indicates positive signs that Korea is entering the "information soci-ety." Yet the proficiency level of PC use is not very high. In adminis-tration, information related to tax and real estate management is all computerized. The computer database is expected to be extended to other fields in administration to improve bureaucratic efficiency. From the citizen's perspective, however, accessibility to government information and protection of privacy should be guaranteed.

POLITICAL SUPPORT. Most of the political regimes that emerged and perished in modern Korean history failed to receive political support from the people due to their illegitimate rise to power and corruption. Moreover, arbitrary exercise of political power, or even terror and violence, evoked further popular resistance.

However, since 1987, in particular since the inauguration of President Kim Young Sam and his anticorruption campaigns, the government's popularity has improved and the general public has shown a more cooperative attitude toward government policies. This change in political support is expected to penetrate the rela-tions between the bureaucracy and its beneficiaries. Public ser-vants should not depend on coercion to induce cooperation from the people. People will respond to sincerity with voluntary support of the administration.

TIME. The stiffer the competition among individuals, groups, societies, and states becomes, the more emphasis is placed on time as a decisive factor. Korean government employees spend most of their time in the office but the quality of office work is often ques-tionable. The job description for each person is very vague; high-ranking officials are too busy, preoccupied with nonproductive work, whereas middle- and low-ranking servants lack the auton-omy and authority in any decision making.

Another important point is that the administration should maintain a long-term perspective. When ministries set a priority for their works to be carried out, they are usually blinded by short-term, urgent tasks. Without long-term plans and projects, it is impossible to have coherence and consistency in policy.

Enhancing Bureaucratic Performance: Evaluation and Control

Once a policy is formulated, decisions are made and resources are mobilized and allocated. Execution falls in the hands of public servants. However, as public servants are humans and not machines, they vary in their values, sentiment, information, and capabilities. This is why there are always different results of any tasks carried out. Evaluation thus is an essential part of administrative processes to improve bureaucratic performance.

Promoting Bureaucratic Performance

There has been strong criticism against public servants in South Korea. "They are not democratic" and "they are all corrupt" cover just the tip of the iceberg. Of course, not all of them have been as bad. Young people apply to public positions because official careers are valued and their social status is stable in Korean society. Once employed, they work hard, and promotion follows almost automatically. However, their low income has been the source of corruption, with most public servants depending on "unofficial income." Every time a new political leader came to power, he launched anticorruption campaigns and purged officials with the worst bribery records. But this has proven to be a mere tactical treatment rather than a fundamental surgery.

Another serious internal problem of the Korean bureaucracy has been the lack of communication, especially from bottom-up, and the authoritarian manner of high-ranking officials. However, this did not severely harm performance as most officials, having been brought up in such an environment, are accustomed to it.

Changes have begun to take place since the 1980s, when the chance of promotion decreased and the source of "unofficial income" was reduced. Public servants now face similar competition like the rest of the society; the days when they were protected like plants in a greenhouse are over. Inevitably, only qualified government employees will survive and maintain office.

To improve bureaucratic performance and discourage bribery, however, official income for civil servants should be increased to a reasonable level. Low incomes are not due to the lack of budget but to lack of understanding on the quality of civil service. For this, a mechanism should be devised to make heard the voice of lower level officers. In this way, authentic democratization within the administration and public servants will be consolidated.

Self-Evaluation

Evaluation includes self-assessment and reforms in administration, and it is essential to improve bureaucratic performance.

This concept was first taught in the American military, and when Korean generals, trained by Americans, took power, they applied it to Korean administration. With democratic opening in late 1980s, this concept began to wane away, crippling the development of administration.

I suggest that a prime ministerial or presidential commission for bureaucratic assessment and reform should be set up. A key to success of this commission will be the composition of the personnel, which should not be monopolized by bureaucrats but shared by civilians. If the commission is filled with public servants, it will be hard to undertake administrative reforms that will eventually harm their own interests.

In bureaucratic assessment and reform measures, the improvement of democratization and efficiency in administration should serve as the basic guidelines. This needs to be more high-lighted since the Korean administration is in a different stage of development than other advanced democratic administrations. Without power sharing in the administration, it will be difficult to achieve efficiency. History tells Koreans that authoritarian power structure has often been the major impediment to efficient bureau-cracy. Waste of huge human and financial resources for the "regime maintenance" exemplifies it. Despite setbacks, political and admin-istrative reforms by the Kim Young Sam government, especially concerning political fund, shed bright light to the future of Korean administration.

Conclusion

The long history of autocratic rule gave birth to a huge bureaucratic administration in Korea. The administration was not an agent of the three branches of the government, but the principal by which it exercised enormous power. Only after the establishment of democratic constitution in 1948 did the Korean administration begin to take a modern shape, along with the formal division of the government into three branches. However, the Korean War, ideo-logical confrontation, with the North, and prolonged authoritarian rule prevented a fuller rooting of democracy in South Korea.

Yet democratization in Korean politics and the following reforms of bureaucracy has been as miraculous as its economic growth. Early introduction of universal education, combined with the Confucian heritage that emphasizes learning, was one of the most contributing factors for this change. Based on this well-educated labor force, economic development drive was accelerated, which eventually gave birth to the middle-class population in Korea. All this led to the political opening in 1987.

Along with various political reforms, accountability of office holders, including the president himself, has been improved. Kim Dae Jung's coming to power in 1998 not only meant a new page in Korean history of democracy but also a promising signal for reforms and changes in the Korean administration.

Notes

1. Woon-Tai Kim, *Choson Wangjo Haengjongsa* [History of Chosun Administration] (Seoul: Pakyongsa, 1970), pp. 177–208.

2. Ibid., pp. 229–230.

3. Sechang Lee, *Han'guk Chaejongui Kundaehwa Kwajong* [Modernization of Financial System in Korea] (Seoul: Pakyongsa, 1972), p. 17.

4. Aoyama, *Max Weber no Sakai Liron* [Social Theory of Max Weber] (Tokyo: Iwanami Shoten, 1956), pp. 168–169.

5. Dong-suh Bark. "Han'guk Haeangjongui Sajok Pyonchon Mohyong" ["Historial Paradigms of Korean Administration"] *Haengjong Nonchong* [Administration Journal]. vol. 5, no. 2, (1967), p. 25; Dong-suh Bark, "Iljongkwa Han'gukinui Chamyo Mitt Nungryok Palchon" ["Japanese Rule and Koreans' Participation and Development"] *Han'guk Chongchihakhoebo* [Korean Political Science Review], vol. 10 (1976), pp. 87–96.

6. Dong-suh Bark, *Han'guk Kwanryo Chedoui Yoksajok Chonkae* [Historical Development of Korean Bureaucratic System]. Han'guk Yonkuwon [Korea Research Institute], (1961), pp. 62–76.

7. H. H. Gerth and C. W. Mills (trans.), *From Max Weber* (NY: Oxford University Press, 1958), pp. 196–198.

8. Han-bin Lee et al., *Han'guk Haengjongui Yoksajok P'unsok* [Historical Analysis of Korean Administration] (Seoul: Korea Research Institute of Administration Issues, 1969), p. 531; Suck-hong Oh. "Mikunjong Sidaeui Urinaraui Insa Chedo" ["Personnel Management During the American Military Occupation"], *Haengjong Nonchong* [Administration Journal] 3:1 (1965), pp. 99–115; Suck-jun Cho. "Mikunjong Mitt Che 1 Konghwakukui Chungang P'ucho Kikuui Pyonchone Kwanhan Yonku" ["Study of the Structure of Ministries During the American Military Occupation and the First Republic of Korea"]. *Haengjong Nonjip* [Journal of Administration] 5:1(1967), pp. 121–162.

9. Dong-suh Bark, "Sajok P'aekyong" ["Historical Background of Korean Administration"] *Han'guk Haengjongui Yoksajok P'unsok* [Historical Analysis of Korean Administration] (Seoul: Korea Administration Research Institute, 1969), pp. 23–24.

10. Charles Tilly, ed., *The Formation of National States in Western Europe*. (Princeton: Princeton University Press, 1975); Dong-suh Bark, "Kwankwonkwa Minkwon" ["Authority's Power and People's Power"], *The Monthly Chosun* (April 1981), pp. 48–57.

11. Robert A. Lauer. *Perspectives on Social Change* (Boston: Allyn and Bacon, 1977), p. 123.

8

ৡ৶

The Politics of Economic
Rise and Decline in South Korea

Chung-in Moon
and
Sunghack Lim

South Korea had long been regarded as one of the poorest countries in the world. While high population density, poor resource endowment, technological backwardness, and rigid social structure served as endogenous barriers to its economic transformation, Japanese colonial domination and devastation followed by the Korean War (1950–1953) trapped South Korea in vicious cycles of poverty and underdevelopment. National division, protracted military confrontation with North Korea, and pervasive social and political instabilities had further constrained the potential for economic development in South Korea.

Despite all these obstacles, however, since the early 1960s South Korea has achieved remarkable economic success, transforming itself from an isolated agricultural society to a major industrial power within a single generation. A nation defined by its muddy subsistence farming economy was dramatically changed into one of the world's largest producers of ships, electrical appliances, automobiles, and memory chips. During the past four decades, its annual economic growth has averaged about 8 percent per year and per capita income rose from $80 in 1960 to $10,307 in 1997. Exports grew from $33 million in 1960 to $130 billion in 1996. South Korea has now become the world's eleventh largest country in economic size and the seventh largest in trade volume. Its unprecedented success has often been touted as a model for third world development.

However, South Korea's economic miracle was not to last. Declining international competitiveness, massive investments with borrowed money, pervasive moral hazard and rent-seeking, and some critical government failures, when combined with regional financial instabilities, drove its economy to the brink of default through acute foreign exchange and financial crises in November 1997. As a result, South Korea sought rescue financing from the International Monetary Fund (IMF), and was placed under its economic trusteeship. The economic crisis shattered the myth of the Korean miracle, endangering the East Asian model of economic development.

This chapter is designed to explore the political and institutional foundations of South Korea's economic rise and decline. The first section presents a brief overview of contending models of the political economy of South Korea's economic transformation. The second looks at a historical trajectory of its economic development since the 1950s. The third section delineates the determinants of South Korea's economic rise and decline, paying particular attention to the international system, market, the state, and networks. Finally, the chapter suggests some important theoretical and empirical implications for the study of the political economy of development in South Korea.

Contending Models of the
Political Economy of South Korea:
Market, the State, Networks, and the International System

In accounting for the dynamics of economic transformation in South Korea, four analytical perspectives have been suggested. The first is the market perspective, which attributes South Korea's economic success to an interplay of open economy, market conforming government policies, and assertive entrepreneurship by the private sector.[1] According to this view, South Korean economic performance cannot be seen as a miracle, but as a natural and spontaneous outcome of the application of classical economic principles. Unlike North Korea, South Korea took the capitalist path to economic development following national independence in 1945, which in turn assured the institutional foundation for private property ownership and operations of the free market system. It also shortened the duration of import substituting institutionalization (ISI), which is known to be a major barrier to the economic development of third world countries, and made a swift transition to an export-led industrialization. In addition to this structural framework for economic development, the South Korean government adopted and implemented extensive market conforming economic policies through macroeconomic stabilization, selective liberalization of foreign exchange and interest rates, and institutional reforms for export promotion. It is under this market-friendly institutional setting that private entrepreneurs were able to vigorously exploit their comparative advantage. At the same time, heavy investment in human capital, diligence and discipline of the work force, frugality, low taxes, and a high savings rate, all of which constitute neoclassical prescriptions for economic development, contributed to crafting South Korea's miraculous economic success.

The neoclassical perspective had long prevailed as the dominant paradigm in accounting for South Korea's economic transformation. Since the early 1980s, however, there were growing challenges to neoclassical interpretations. A group of political scientists, developmental economists, and sociologists, who belonged to the developmentalist state camp, refuted the wisdom and insights of the neoclassical paradigm.[2] Developmental statists argued that market forces alone cannot adequately explain South Korea's economic miracle. According to their critics, the South Korean state was not a minimalist state envisioned by neoclassical economists. It was neither a simple guarantor of the existence of a free and competitive market nor a passive and neutral container of contending social and political interests. It had its own developmental objectives framed around the ideology of "rich nation and strong army" which went beyond simple manipulation of the arsenal of macroeconomic parameters. The South Korean state made strategic intervention plans in the economy through plan rationale, industrial targeting, and mobilization and selective allocation of resources in strategic sectors. In other words, the state virtually dictated the nature and direction of market forces in order to achieve its objectives by effectively utilizing the reservoir of policy instruments available to it. As Alice Amsden observed, the South Korean miracle was a product of "getting the prices wrong," not "getting the prices right."[3]

The South Korean state was able to govern market forces effectively because of its unique organizational features. While executive dominance ensured a centralized decision-making structure, the relative autonomy of the state and its competent and meritocratic bureaucrats facilitated the formulation of efficient, coherent, and consistent economic policies and their effective implementation. In fact, rapid capital accumulation and efficient economic policy require restrictions on social demands, not only of labor or the popular sector, but of rent-seeking business groups. The South Korean government was able to overcome this collective action dilemma by insulating economic policy-making from these contending social pressures. Its economic miracle would have never been possible without the strategic intervention of a mercantilist and entrepreneurial state, which was relatively free from social capture.

The statist claims are by and large predicated on the dichotomy of state and society in which the state is assumed to prevail over civil society. But several scholars have criticized that such a binary distinction is an artificial analytical construct. They argue that the state and society are constantly interconnected through a myriad of formal and informal networks and that a country's economic performance depends on the nature of these networks.[4] In South Korea, state-society networks have been based on a vertical hierarchy that enabled the state to dictate to the society. However, such a hierarchy has been complemented by horizontal ties formed through formal (e.g., examination council) and informal organic (e.g., family, school, regional) networks. Vertical command and discipline were matched with horizontal consultation and consensus through shared corporate goals, producing harmonious relations between the state and the private sector, and enhancing trust and the exchange of knowledge essential for economic performance. South Korea's economic success can be ascribed to this rather unique state-society arrangement.

Finally, the international and regional system also factors in. Two contending views have emerged in linking South Korea's political economy of development to international and regional dimensions. One is the dependencia approach, and the other is the geopolitical explanation.[5] Despite its earlier claims that the South Korean economy has been trapped in the structure of dependent development, its impressive economic performance and admission to the Organization for Economic Cooperation and Development (OECD) have by and large falsified the validity of the dependencia approach. The geopolitical explanation has drawn greater empirical appeal. Throughout the 1950s and 1960s, South Korea benefited from a special relationship with the United States. This relationship was predicated on the geopolitical assumptions of American policy-makers, who saw South Korea as an important arena for

Cold War confrontation with the Soviet Union. American strategic interests in South Korea allowed it to enjoy hefty economic benefits in terms of aid, trade, capital, and technology from the United States.[6] It is widely acknowledged that South Korea could have not survived its economic hardships were it not for generous American assistance in the 1950s and South Korean access to its export markets since the mid-1960s. Such a geopolitical landscape, coupled with the expansionary world economy at the time of South Korea's transition to an export-led growth strategy, facilitated its economic ascension.

All four analytical perspectives are convincing. But forces propelling economic performance are multifaceted, and therefore, market, the state, networks, and the international system are not mutually exclusive, but complementary. Monocausal explanations are prone to commit the fallacy of reductionism. It thus seems essential to integrate all four variables in understanding South Korea's economic development. While the market and international system offer necessary conditions, the state and politics can be seen as sufficient ones. It is not only because the state and politics influence economic policy affecting the patterns of economic growth, but also because they determine the nature and scope of market and external transactions. Meanwhile, networks serve as facilitating or inhibiting variables between the above causal variables and economic performance. One caveat is in order, however. Market forces, the state, networks, and the international system are not static, but variable, and their shifting nature brings about profound impacts on economic performance. Economic success as well as economic decline and crisis can be accounted for by looking into the dynamic interplay of these four variables over time.[7]

Historical Trajectory of Economic Transformation: An Empirical Overview

Initial conditions for South Korea's economic development were extremely unfavorable. Thirty-six years of Japanese colonial rule, national division and three years of social and political chaos immediately after national independence, and the Korean War that lasted from 1950 to 1953 had virtually wiped out the material and institutional foundations of South Korea's industrial development. As Table 8.1 illustrates, per capita income in 1953 was $67, and current account deficits were $67.8 million. In addition, rampant

Table 8.1
Macroeconomic Indicators of Korean Economy

	GNP per Capita (US$)	GNP (Billion US$)	GNP Growth Rate (%)	Inflation Rate (%)	Interest Rate (%)	Rate of Savings (%)	Current Balance (million US$)	Export (million US$)	Foreign Debt (million US$)	Rate of Unemployment (%)	Gross Domestic Investment Ratio
1953	67	0.5		—		13.1	-67.8	39.6		—	
1955	65	1.4	4.5	10.5	12.0	10.3	-36.5	18	341		11.7
1960	80	1.9	1.1	5.8	10.0	9.0	-13.4	33	316	11.7	10.0
1965	105	3.0	5.8	13.5	26.4	13.2	9.1	175	206	7.4	14.1
1970	243	8.1	7.6	25.7	22.8	18.1	-622.5	882	2,245	4.5	24.3
1975	591	20.9	6.8	25.6	15.0	18.1	-1,886.9	5,003	8,456	4.1	28.6
1980	1,589	60.6	-4.8	4.1	19.5	23.2	-5,320.7	17,214	27,170	5.2	31.9
1985	2,150	91.1	5.4	6.2	10.0	29.8	-887.4	26,442	46,729	4.0	30.3
1990	5,659	251.8	9.3	4.7	10.0	37.5	-2,179.4	63,124	31,699	2.4	37.1
1995	10,823	451.7	9.0	3.2	15.6	36.5	-8,948	125,058	127,171	2.0	36.9
1996	11,380	480.2	67.1	3.9	15.8	33.8	-23,005	129,715	164,345	2.0	37.2
1997	10,307	437.4	5.5		14.1	33.4	-8,618	136,164	158,060	2.6	35.4
1998	6,823	443.1	-3.8	12.2	15.92	33.2	22,383	132,313	149,354	6.8	—

Sources: Byongrak Song, *The Korean Economy* (Hong Kong: Oxford University Press, 1994), pp. 60–61; The Bank of Korea (http://www.bok.or.kr), *Economic Statistics Yearbook 1997*; and The National Statistics Office (http://www.nso.go.kr).

postwar inflation and high unemployment severely undercut chances for economic recovery. Since 1954, South Korea launched extensive postwar reconstruction plans by not only restoring and expanding physical infrastructure with American assistance, but also by initiating an import substituting industrialization strategy in nondurable consumer sectors. Along with these measures, policy priority was given to macroeconomic stability in order to arrest chronic postwar inflationary pressures.

But these efforts did not bring about positive results. South Korea achieved an average annual growth rate of 4.4 percent during the period from 1954 to 1961, but this was a result more of American assistance than of endogenous economic development. Moreover, adoption of an import substitution industrialization strategy distorted the allocation of resources through political-economic collusion and rent-seeking behavior, while chronic inflation, structural unemployment, and pervasive corruption posed major obstacles to economic reconstruction. Social and political instabilities ensued through acute economic crises ultimately led to two major regime changes in 1960 and 1961, respectively. The April 19 Student Revolution in 1960 toppled the Syngman Rhee regime, giving birth to the Second Republic under Chang Myon. However, the Second Republic did not last long. Political paralysis resulting from the parliamentary system and factional politics, coupled with economic hardship and social instability, precipitated the May 16 military coup in 1961 led by Major General Park Chung Hee.[8]

Park's military rule during the 1961–1963 period did not improve economic conditions either. Despite his revolutionary pledge to eradicate poverty and famine, the first three years of his military rule were marred by a series of economic mishaps. Expansionary fiscal policies to coopt new support groups such as exemption for farm debts and initiation of extensive public projects, failed currency reform, and a stock market scandal aggravated economic conditions. A sharp reduction in American economic assistance further deteriorated the national economy under Park's military rule. The American government began to exert pressures on Park and his junta leaders for economic reforms by tying economic and food assistance to reform mandates.[9] The military government complied with American demands by adopting macroeconomic stabilization measures in 1963 and selective liberalization of foreign exchange and interest rates in 1964. And from 1965, the Park government began to initiate a full-fledged export-led economic growth strategy.[10]

The export promotion strategy, which was undertaken at the time of global economic expansion, turned out to be timely and effective. The annual average growth rate during 1963–1973 soared to almost 10 percent, and per capita income quadrupled from $100 in 1963 to $396 in 1973. Exports grew by forty times during the period from $86 million in 1963 to $3.2 billion in 1973. Along with this economic growth, unemployment rate declined from 8.2 percent in 1963 to 4.0 percent in 1973, while domestic savings and investments grew rapidly (see data in Table 8.1). But this economic ascension cannot be attributed solely to the adoption of a labor-intensive export promotion strategy. Massive inflow of foreign capital followed by diplomatic normalization with Japan in 1965, as well as the Vietnam War boom also made an important contribution to economic expansion during this period. It is also noteworthy that South Korea suffered sporadic economic downturns such as those in 1969–1970, accompanying serious sociopolitical instability.[11] Nevertheless, medium-term economic planning and an export-led growth strategy during the period from 1963 to 1973 produced the decisive momentum required to overcome the vicious cycles of poverty and underdevelopment in South Korea.

As with other countries in the region, the first oil crisis in 1973 dealt a critical blow to the South Korean economy. But South Korea's response was different from that of other East Asian countries. While Japan and Taiwan undertook contractionary policies to minimize the impact of the oil crisis, South Korea chose an ambitious path to heavy-chemical industrialization.[12] The South Korean government designated the steel, automobile, electronics, shipbuilding, and petrochemical industries as strategic sectors and made enormous investments between 1974 and 1978. Given that South Korea was still enjoying a competitive edge in labor-intensive sectors, this big push was not driven by shifting comparative advantage. It was to a great extent motivated by national security considerations; President Park opted for the big push because of its forward and backward linkages with the defense industry. Eroding American security commitment and increasing military provocation by North Korea forced him to achieve the national goal of self-defense by accelerating defense industrialization.[13] The annual average growth rate during the period of the big push (1974–1979) was over 10 percent, and in 1977, South Korea enjoyed its first balance of payments surplus amounting to $12.3 million by exceeding its export target of $10 billion.

However, the heavy-chemical industrialization strategy soon

encountered major setbacks. Duplication in investments, surplus capacity, and global economic recession revealed structural limitations to the big push. At the same time, excessive investments and the expansionary fiscal policy that disregarded inflationary consequences considerably jeopardized macroeconomic stability. In addition, rampant speculations in real estate and stock markets triggered by massive inflows of foreign exchange generated by the Middle East construction boom fueled inflationary pressures and turned the Korean economy into a bubble economy. After lengthy deliberations, the South Korean government announced major macroeconomic stabilization measures on April 17, 1979, but this time it was too late. The Korean economy was sliding into a deeper recession. Moreover, the assassination of President Park by Kim Jae-kyu, director of the Korean Central Intelligence Agency, on October 26, 1979, plunged South Korea into severe social and political turmoil. As Table 8.1 demonstrates, the South Korean economy suffered its worst economic downturn, recording the first negative growth (–3.74 percent) since 1956, the largest balance of payments deficit ($5.3 billion), snowballing foreign debts ($43 billion), high inflation (30 percent), and serious unemployment (5.2 percent).[14]

The Chun Doo Hwan government, which took political power, first through mutiny in the military and then by staging a military coup to take advantage of the power vacuum left by the death of Park Chung Hee, adopted and implemented assertive neoliberal economic reforms in order to overcome the crisis. Given the illicit genesis of the Chun regime, managing the crisis was vital to building his political legitimacy. The Chun government undertook sweeping macroeconomic stabilization measures through a mix of fiscal austerity, wage freezes, devaluation, realistic interest rates, and the removal of various subsidies such as the grain management fund and the fertilizer account. Along with these measures, it also accelerated privatization of state enterprises and the dismantling of various investment funds. Its neoliberal reforms were extended to structural adjustment. While heavy-chemical industrial sectors were realigned in order to cope with the problems of duplication and surplus capacity, the Chun government overhauled existing institutions governing industrial, banking and financing, trade and foreign investment, and competition policies. Liberalization, rationalization, and fair trade emerged as its new economic catchphrases.[15]

Chun's neoliberal reforms were successful. Growth rates rose from –3.7 percent in 1980 to 12.9 percent in 1986, while the balance of payment surplus hit a record high of $4.6 billion in 1986. The inflation rate also dwindled to 2.8 percent, and the unemployment rate decreased to below 4 percent (see Table 8.1). On the whole, macroeconomic stability was restored in a remarkable way. But structural adjustment measures did not show any signs of improvement. Measures to ease chaebols' economic concentration remained ineffective, and industrial rationalization efforts through the application of market logic did not bring about any visible outcomes. Although bilateral pressures from the United States fostered trade liberalization, a myriad of regulations were not lifted in the area of foreign direct investment. Most important, liberalization, rationalization, and internationalization of the banking and financial sector were not fulfilled as planned. Although the Chun government was successful in implementing macroeconomic stabilization, it fell far short of achieving its goal to restructure the economy, sowing the seeds for another major economic crisis.

Since democratic opening in 1987, the South Korean economy continued to enjoy an upswing. Despite social and political instability in the process of democratic opening and transition, its growth rate exceeded more than 12 percent per year, and its balance of payment surplus grew rapidly, turning South Korea into one of the major creditor nations. Government policies mattered, but the unprecedented economic boom benefited greatly from the international economy which was characterized by "three lows" (low interest rates, low oil prices, and low exchange rates). But the economic good times soon gave birth to a bubble economy. Record-high balance of payment surpluses led to an oversupply of money, overheating the national economy through widespread speculation in real estate and stock markets. Consequently, from 1989, the South Korean economy began to show a profound downswing. The growth rate declined from 12.4 percent in 1988 to 6.7 percent in 1989 and 9 percent in 1990. From 1990, balance of payments also turned into a deficit and the South Korean economy entered a long tunnel of recession.

The Kim Young Sam government, which was inaugurated in 1993, undertook expansionary measures to cope with the recessionary trend. It set a new goal of achieving per capita income of $10,000 and joining the Organization for Economic Cooperation and Development (OECD) through active pursuit of the globalization strategy. He portrayed *segyehwa (globalization)*[16] as "the shortcut which will lead us to building a first-class country in the twenty-first century."[17] However, the portrait proved to be false even before reaching the twenty-first century. A major setback to *segyehwa* took place during his tenure when the South Korean economy fell prey to a sudden collapse in November 1997, alarming the entire world. After a series of financial and foreign exchange crises, the Kim Young Sam government filed for national economic bankruptcy by asking the International Monetary Fund (IMF) for $57 billion in bail-out funds on December 3, 1997. The myth of the South Korean economic miracle was shattered, and national shame prevailed.

Table 8.2 presents data on the dark side of the South Korean economy under the Kim Young Sam government. During his term in office, South Korea's foreign debts increased from $43.9 billion to $160.7 billion in 1996 and $153 billion in 1997, while foreign reserve assets dwindled from $20.2 billion in 1993 to $12.4 billion in 1997. At the peak of the currency crisis, foreign reserves held by the central bank were less than $8 billion, spreading the fear of default. With foreign reserves being depleted, the Korean currency rapidly depreciated. In 1993, the won/dollar exchange rate was KW808.1, but the Korean won devalued by almost two times by the end of 1997, posting an exchange rate of 1,415 won/dollar. At one point, the exchange rate reached 2,000 won/dollar.

More troublesome was the private sector. As Table 8.2 illustrates, the banking and financial sector as well as the corporate sector showed their worst performance in recent history. The stock price index is generally considered the most reliable barometer of economic vitality. In South Korea, the average annual stock price index was 808.1 in 1993 and 1,027.4 in 1994. But it continued a downward slide throughout 1995 and 1996, falling to 375 by the end of 1997, its lowest level since the opening of the securities markets. Falling stock prices amidst rapid currency devaluation have drastically reduced the value of South Korean firms' assets. According to an analysis by the *Financial Times*, the total assets of all 653 South Korean firms listed on the Korean Securities Exchange Market were estimated to be only KW66.3 trillion as of the end of 1997, which was the equivalent of assets held by one European company, ING Group, a Dutch banking and financial firm ranked as the seventieth largest firm in the world.[18]

Another important indicator of microeconomic health is the size of nonperforming loans since it illustrates the magnitude of corporate bankruptcies. Total nonperforming loans were KW2.4 trillion in 1993 and KW1.9 trillion in 1994. By the end of September 1997, this figure rose to KW4.8 trillion. Given the avalanche of corporate bankruptcies including major *chaebols* such as Hanbo,

Table 8.2
Korean Economic Crisis and Major Economic Indicators

	1992	1993	1994	1995	1996	1997	1998
Growth Rate (%)	4.7	.8	8.6	9.0	7.1	5.5	-3.8 (Feb)
Stock Price index (KOSPI: 80.1 = 100)	678.4	866.2	1,027.4	882.9	651.2	376.3	297.9 (Jun)
Current Balance ($ million)	-4,529	385	-4,531	-8,948	-23,005	-8,168	22,383 (Jun)
Foreign exchange rate Won(\)/$	788.4	808.1	788.7	774.7	844.2	1415.2	1236.0 (Jul)
\/¥100	631.98	772.49	790.68	749.23	726.51	1,0873.77	873.77 (Jul)
Foreign exchange holding ($ million)	17,154	20,262	25,673	32,712	33,237	20,410	43,020 (Jul)
Dishonored ratio of checks and bills	0.12	0.13	0.17	0.20	0.17	0.40	0.42
Debt/GDP(%) ratio	19.17	17.07	20.91	25.82	32.79	34.02	—
Liberalization rate of capital market	4.65	4.88	9.11	12.58	15.03	6.97	—

Sources: The Bank of Korea, *Economic Statistics Yearbook*, each year; Samsung Economic Research Institute (http://www.seri-samsung.org/english/statist/statist.html).

Kia, Jinro, Daenong, Newcore, and Halla,[19] the size of nonperforming loans was much higher than 4.8 trillion Won. In fact, the IMF estimated that nonperforming loans amounted to KW 32 trillion, about 7 percent of GDP, in 1997.[20] A sharp increase in non-performing loans literally paralyzed the banking and financial sector, precipitating the financial crisis. Nonperforming loans accounted for 6.8 percent of total bank loans as of the end of September 1997. In addition, most firms in South Korea, especially small and medium-size enterprises, have traditionally relied on discount of corporate bills such as promissory notes to raise corporate funds. Thus, a high ratio of dishonored corporate bills implies a severe liquidity shortage and greater corporate delinquency. In the first three quarters of 1996, the ratio of dishonored corporate bills was 0.24 percent, a dramatic increase from 0.13 percent in 1993.

The economic crisis led to the first peaceful transfer of political power in fifty years. Opposition political leader Kim Dae Jung defeated the candidate from the ruling party in the December 1997 presidential election. The Kim Dae Jung government, which was inaugurated in February 1998, implemented IMF conditionalities methodically. Most structural adjustment measures, such as banking and financial reform, reform of big business, and labor reform, all of which were conceived of as early as the 1980s, but delayed for political reasons, were implemented within one year of his reign. And the South Korean economy began to demonstrate a remarkable pace of recovery. At this stage, it would be too premature to make any decisive assessment of Kim Dae Jung's reform efforts, but the specter of the economic crisis has disappeared, and the Korean economy is enjoying an unusual normalcy.[21]

In the preceding section, we have made a comprehensive overview of the historical trajectory of the South Korean economy. The most important finding is that the South Korean miracle is not permanent. As with other countries, its economy is also subject to rise and decline. Thus, it would be misleading to be preoccupied by success stories, while ignoring economic crises and failures. What, then, can account for the rise and decline of the South Korean economy?

Accounting for the Rise and Decline
of the Korean Economy

Four major variables have been identified in accounting for South Korea's economic transformation: the international system, market, the state, and networks. These variables have been traditionally regarded as the determinants of economic success. But we argue that they are equally useful predictors for economic crisis and decline, for they are not static, but variable. Parametric changes in these variables have influenced both the success and failure of the South Korean economy.

The International System and the Korean Economy

South Korea's economic ascension cannot be separated from the geopolitical calculus of the Cold War structure. American hegemonic engagement was vital to its rapid economic transformation. The United States virtually implanted the capitalist ideology and institutions in South Korea by not only removing socialist resistance, but also by cultivating procapitalist social forces during the American military government (1945–1948). American economic assistance played a pivotal role in reconstructing the South Korean economy from the ruins of the Korean War. Aid finance from the United States covered nearly 70 percent of total imports and 75 percent of total fixed capital formation between 1953 and 1961. Therefore, capitalist development in South Korea could have been considerably delayed without American intervention based on the Cold War logic of containment. At the same time, American security commitment and military assistance eased South Korea's fiscal burden by reducing the share of defense spending in government expenditure. The American role was also extended to policy intervention to foster outward-looking development. Were it not for American pressures, South Korea's transition to an export-led growth strategy could have been further delayed. Finally, access to American domestic markets contributed to the shaping of the South Korea's economic success.[22]

Another dividend from the Cold War structure was diplomatic normalization between Japan and South Korea and subsequent benefits therefrom. Immediately following Japan-Korea normalization in 1965, there was a rush of Japanese direct investments in South Korea. Moreover, newly formed regional economic networks involving the United States, Japan, and South Korea provided South Korean firms with unprecedented opportunities to achieve global reach for their exports as well as to accelerate the country's economic growth.[23] Favorable international economic environments were also a plus factor for the South Korean economy. At the time of South Korea's transition to an export-led growth strategy, the world economy was in boom, and world trade was rapidly expanding. The annual average growth rate for world exports reached almost 9 percent between 1960 and 1973, which in turn boosted South Korea's export of manufactured products.[24] In addition, the Vietnam War and the Middle East construction boom also helped the South Korean economy during the critical period of its economic transformation. While special demands created by the Vietnam War absorbed a great chunk of labor-intensive items such as garments (military uniforms), the Middle East construction boom facilitated South Korea's ability to overcome the acute foreign exchange crisis precipitated by the first oil crisis.[25]

Likewise, the international system was conducive to the rise of the South Korean economy. Yet international environments were not always benevolent. As the South Korean economy became larger and further integrated into the world economy, it began to face new challenges from the international system. The most notable challenge was bilateral and multilateral pressures for trade liberalization. Since the mid-1980s, South Korea began to enjoy considerable trade surpluses with the United States. In order to correct deficits, the United States exerted enormous bilateral pressures on South Korea to open its market through the application of the principle of strategic reciprocity. Along with this U.S. pressure, the ratification of the Uruguay Round also forced South Korea to open its domestic import markets.[26] While the United States and other countries in the North squeezed South Korea through import market restrictions and pressures for market opening, China and the second-generation Newly Industrial Countries (NICs) such as Thailand, Malaysia, and Indonesia were catching up with South Korea, undercutting its traditional export markets. South Korea was literally sandwiched between the protectionist threats from the North and export competition from the second-generation NICs.[27]

One of the most visible impacts of this dual pressure was a worsening balance of payments position. While exports were stagnant due to tough competition from new market entrants, opening domestic markets to foreign goods and services contributed to mounting trade deficits. South Korea recorded a modest trade surplus ($989 million) in 1993, but the trade balance began to deteriorate from 1994. The trade deficit rose from $6.3 billion in 1994 to $10 billion in 1995, $20.6 billion in 1996, and $8.4 billion in 1997. The deficits, which reflected the eroding international competitiveness of South Korean firms, were financed through foreign borrowing. In tandem with trade deficits, total external liabilities increased from $56.8 billion in 1994 to $104.7 billion in 1996 and $154 billion in 1997.[28]

The globalization strategy also entailed a new structure of vulnerability. South Korea aggressively liberalized its financial and capital markets as part of its globalization strategy, and overseas financing by South Korean banks and firms also became easier.[29] However, capital and financial liberalization did not improve the traditionally skewed pattern of external financing. South Korea's dependence on foreign borrowing continued.[30] While the inflow of foreign equity investments was still limited, foreign loans grew exponentially. The composition of foreign borrowing was more problematic, in which short-term loans constituted the lion's share of external financing. In 1985, short-term loans accounted for only 23 percent of total external liabilities. Since the globalization campaign, however, its share rose to 53.5 percent in 1994, 57.8 percent in 1995, and 58.2 percent in 1996. In good times, borrowing short-term loans do not pose any problems. In fact, it can be rather beneficial in terms of both favorable interest rates and enhanced capital mobility. However, in hard times, short-term liabilities can become self-defeating because of the panic potential they entail.[31]

South Korea was indeed a victim of the panic emanating from the dynamic interplay of domestic financial instability and contagion effects of the Southeast Asian countries' foreign exchange crises. In the first half of 1997, South Korea enjoyed a high degree of normalcy. But the chain reaction of bankruptcies of major chaebols starting in September 1997, the mounting size of nonperforming loans, and the weakened positions of South Korean banking and financial institutions triggered the panic behavior on the part of the international investment community. International lenders began to refuse to roll over short-term debts held by South Korean banks and firms. The roll-over rate plunged from an average of 90 percent before the crisis to the 30-percent level during the crisis, aggravating an already precarious situation. In December 1997, the roll-over rate hit rock bottom at 26.3 percent.[32] Borrowing new money and rolling over old loans became all the more difficult because of foreign exchange and financial crises, which had already swept the Southeast Asian region.

The wealth of problems faced by South Korea show that the international system is Janus-faced. While the geopolitical dynamics of the international system were a blessing during South Korea's economic take-off, deeper integration into the international and regional system through globalization made South Korea vulnerable to the transmission of external pressures and turbulence. The economic crisis and decline of South Korea since 1997 reflects its failures to cope with the challenges of fierce international competition, bilateral and multilateral pressures for market opening, and financial and capital market liberalization.

Corporate Failures and the Korean Economic Crisis

According to the market perspective, the real hero of the South Korean epic to economic ascension was the private sector. It is private firms who took maximum advantage of market-conforming economic institutions and policies, and turned shifting comparative advantage into their own competitive edge. In this regard, the paramount role of *chaebols* (business conglomerates) should not be underestimated. They served as innovative, assertive, and entrepreneurial agents of industrialization and export growth. For example, the top ten *chaebols* had total sales of over $65 billion in 1986, accounting for more than 65 percent of South Korea's GNP, and the revenue of the top five *chaebols* reached $116 billion in 1991, a figure equivalent to just under half of the country's GNP.[33] The top ten *chaebols* accounted for 40 percent of all bank credit in South Korea, 30 percent of value added in manufacturing, and roughly 66 percent of the value of all South Korean exports in 1987.[34] Likewise, chaebols gave an impressive performance as an engine of export-led growth.

But a closer examination reveals that corporate failure involving *chaebols* was one of major causes of economic downturn and crisis. Since the early 1990s, *chaebols* were rapidly losing their international competitiveness due to changes in factor prices. Democratic opening in 1987 triggered an intensive demand for high wages and better working conditions, resulting in wage increases of approximately 22 percent during 1988–1990.[35] Capital costs were also high, when compared with other competitors in the region such as Japan and Taiwan. As of 1994, the average interest rate was 11.4 percent in South Korea, while in Japan and Taiwan it was 4.8 percent and 7.2 percent, respectively. Among the three, South Korea has the highest financial burden ratio measured in terms of financial cost as a share of net sales. Such high capital costs led to eroding international competitiveness, low corporate profits, and low facility investment.

In coping with the new competitive environments and changes in factor prices, chaebols did not undertake corporate restructuring and downsizing. On the contrary, they aggressively engaged in corporate expansion through mergers and acquisitions as well as excessive investments in production facilities with borrowed money. In 1993, the top four leading *chaebols* (Samsung, Hyundai, Daewoo, LG) borrowed KW12.4 trillion from commercial and merchant banks, which rose to KW25.5 trillion as of June 1997. The amount of bank loans given to the top thirty *chaebols* also increased from KW59 trillion in 1992 to KW76.7 trillion in June 1997. Short-term debts accounted for most of these loans (63.3 percent). Consequently, the debt-equity ratio for major firms reached a perilous average of 300 percent in 1996. Cutthroat competition, weakening export prices, and the high financial expense of short-term debts began to eat into the profitability of corporations. As of the end of 1996, the top thirty *chaebols'* operating profit margin after deducting capital expenses was only 2.8 percent. The situation was much worse for other firms.

Consequently, starting with Hanbo Steel, several *chaebols* (Sammi, Jinro, Daenong, Kia, Newcore, Halla) went bankrupt in 1997. Unlike in the past, the government failed to prevent their collapse because their debts were too large to bail out. The domino effects of one corporate bankruptcy after another then caused panick in major lending institutions, which were stuck with the immense burden of nonperforming loans. Realizing that they were witnessing a major financial crisis, international credit rating agencies such as Standard & Poors and Moody's began to downgrade South Korea's overall creditworthiness. Banking and financial institutions, which relied heavily on short-term loans from the overseas banking community, could not borrow any more, which strained domestic financial and foreign exchange markets. To cope with the liquidity crisis caused by nonperforming loans and the cutoff of overseas loans, domestic commercial and merchant banks rushed to collect their loans en masse and suspended any further loans. Money pipelines for firms quickly dried up, fostering their collapse, and foreign exchange markets turned extremely unstable. Poor international credit ratings also precipitated an exodus of foreign investors from South Korea's security markets, triggering a sharp decline in stock prices, while interest rates skyrocketed. Several merchant banks and securities firms went bankrupt, and corporate bonds were left idle. The entire South Korean economy crumbled, making the pursuit of an IMF bailout inevitable in order to avoid a default on debt servicing.

Judged from the above, the economic crisis of 1997 can be

attributed to poor corporate performance. Reckless excessive investment with borrowed money sowed the seed of the financial crisis. However, South Korea's banking and financial sector cannot avoid the blame either. As the IMF aptly pointed out in its memorandum with the Korean government, financial institutions poorly priced risks and were willing to finance an excessively large portion of investment plans in the corporate sector, resulting in high leverage. Financial institution's lack of market orientation and moral hazard, coupled with lax prudential supervision, contributed to worsening the financial crisis. But ironically, the market failures evidenced through failing corporate performance and the crippled banking and financial sector were in part products of government failures. Excessive government intervention, the old inertia of industrial policy and government bailout, and the structural collusion between the government and big business all contributed to precipitating corporate and banking failures.

The State, Structural Rigidity, and Economic Crisis

As developmental statists have argued, the South Korean state played the most critical role in shaping the country's economic miracle. Armed with the hegemonic ideology of "rich nation, strong army," the South Korean state actively intervened in the market to guide, discipline, and coordinate the private sector through strategic allocation of resources and the discretionary use of diverse policy instruments. Strategic intervention by the state and its success were ensured by rational and competent bureaucrats who were insulated from contending political and social pressures. It is through the dynamic interplay of developmental ideology, strategic intervention, and the unique organizational structure of the state that enabled and sustained South Korea's stellar economic performance.

The triumph of the developmental state has come to an abrupt end, however, defying its positive causal links with economic performance. In fact, the genesis of the current economic downturn can be traced back to the negative externalities and breakdown of the developmental state.[36] First, Krugman's skeptical view of the East Asian miracle appears to be correct in the South Korean context. Input-driven industrialization disregarding total factor productivity reached the point of diminishing return, resulting in economic downturn. More important, the investment-led economic boom, which was partly associated with massive input of physical capital stocks, rather than their productive use, created bubbles, misguiding the direction of the national economy. All this was partly an outcome of state strategies geared toward the size principle and the need to play catch-up through big push industrialization. Simply put, South Korea failed to adapt to the transformation of market forces from input-driven to knowledge-driven parameters. Lack of adaptive capacity and subsequent structural rigidity constituted the core of the current economic crisis.[37]

Second, government failures also mattered. Rigid policy management, bureaucratic fragmentation, poor monitoring and supervision, and incompetent political leadership were all responsible for the economic downturn and crisis. The most noticeable policy failure can be found in the government's foreign exchange rate management.[38] As early as June 1996, mounting pressures for devaluation of the Korean currency can be found, but the government did not take any action. Fear of inflation, disciplining the corporate sector, and lobbying by banks, firms, and state enterprises which benefited from heavy foreign borrowing prevented the government from making a timely devaluation of the Korean currency.[39] Overvaluation of the Korean won depressed exports, while encouraging imports, eventually contributing to a worsening balance of payments.

There were also grave decisional mistakes in the process of the crisis.[40] At the end of 1996, the current account deficit reached 5 percent of GDP, and foreign reserves held by the Bank of Korea were $30 billion, which could pay for only three months' worth of imports. Despite such indicators, the government was optimistic about the future, citing the health of macroeconomic fundamentals. More important, during the height of the crisis (November 11–21), the Bank of Korea's disposable foreign reserves were reduced to $19.5 billion. Yet, the BOK wasted $6.7 billion defending the Korean currency. Consequently, foreign reserves dwindled to $12.7 billion by the end of November, aggravating the crisis. The worst mistake was that the government wasted time in calling for the IMF rescue financing. Since mid-October 1997, IMF officials had been urging the South Korean government to ask for rescue financing. But the government wasted almost a month before it did so, partly because of bureaucratic politics, and partly because of political factors. Those close to President Kim Young Sam did not want him to be viewed as a disgraced president who filed for state bankruptcy.

Serious mistakes on the part of the economic bureaucracy were equally critical. Among others, bureaucratic indecisiveness,

particularly in the handling of the Kia Motors situation, contributed to triggering the entire financial crisis. Kia Motors, the
seventh largest business conglomerate, was on the verge of bankruptcy in the summer of 1997. The government's original plan was
to let Kia go bankrupt. But two factors delayed its final decision.
One was public criticism, and the other a conflict of interest involving Kyung-shik Kang, then Deputy Prime Minister in charge of
finance and economy. It was public knowledge that the plight of Kia
Motors was engineered by the Samsung Group, which had long
attempted a takeover of the company. In the Kia-Samsung bout, the
public sided with Kia, making the latter's bankruptcy politically
difficult. Meanwhile, Kang, while serving as a national assemblyman representing Pusan before his appointment as Deputy Prime
Minister, was instrumental in bringing Samsung's new auto plant
to the Pusan area. Thus, Kang's initial efforts to let market logic
prevail over Kia were interpreted as a conspiracy to deliver Kia to
Samsung on a plate. Kang was hesitant, and after a three-month
delay, the government announced that it would turn Kia into a public enterprise. The government's prolonged indecision and its ultimate decision to bail out Kia Motors betrayed the expectations of
foreign investors and significantly damaged the government's credibility.[41]

An interagency feud also undermined the effectiveness of government's handling of the crisis. In the middle of the economic crisis, two leading economic agencies, the Ministry of Finance and
Economy (MOFE) and the Bank of Korea (BOK), engaged in a fierce
bureaucratic battle over a legislative bill on the central bank.
MOFE was trying to pass a new law that would fundamentally
limit the power and authority of BOK as the central bank by taking away its supervisory functions. BOK employees staged street
demonstrations to oppose the bill, while MOFE officials were lobbying National Assemblymen to push for its passage. The interagency feud virtually paralyzed the mechanism of crisis management.

The government's failure to monitor and supervise on the
banking sector was another significant factor. Financial and capital
liberalization in 1994 triggered overseas rush by Korean commercial and merchant banks.[42] They were inexperienced in international banking and finance, but they, nevertheless, aggressively
ventured into high-risk, high-yield capital games by investing with
borrowed short-term loans in high risk bonds in Southeast Asian
countries, Russia, and Latin America (Brady Bond).[43] When these

countries too experienced economic hardships, South Korean banks and financial institutions lost their money. Mobile international capital also made it difficult for the South Korean government to track capital movements. Apart from short-term loans, overseas financing by Korean firms could also not be accounted for. In a sense, the South Korean economic crisis was a crisis of monitoring, supervision, and accountability.

Finally, political leadership failure also factored in. Lack of competence and knowledge on the part of the top leadership was a further critical element allowing the precipitous escalation of the financial and foreign exchange crisis. President Kim Young Sam was ignorant of economic policies and left their management to his aides. But his aides were divided on the diagnosis of and prescriptions for the impending crisis. The Bank of Korea alerted President Kim to the danger of a foreign exchange crisis as early as July 1997, but the Ministry of Finance and Economy and the presidential economic secretary downplayed it, emphasizing the "healthy fundamentals" of the macroeconomy. It is known that Kim was not aware of the severity of situation until President Bill Clinton phoned him about the necessity of IMF rescue financing in late November, 1997. Kim's aides thought they could put off the IMF bailout until the end of Kim's tenure as president in February 1998. His poor monitoring and mismanagement aggravated the crisis by losing the timing of effective intervention.

In sum, the economic downturn and crisis can be seen as a product of failures of the developmental state. While strategic intervention by the state amplified market distortion, unruly investments, and moral hazard, its organizational structure was no longer functioning effectively. Erratic policy, bureaucratic fragmentation, monitoring and supervision failures, inability to insulate economic decision-making, and incompetent political leadership signaled the demise of the developmental state, precipitating and deepening the economic crisis.

Networks, Rent-Seeking, and Economic Decline

A revisionist interpretation, which defies the primacy of the state, while emphasizing intrinsic values of social and policy networks in enhancing economic performance, has drawn a greater appeal. Indeed, South Korea's homogenous social fabric and the Confucian cultural tradition not only bred the prevailing consensus on corporate goals, but also cultivated dense social and policy networks, both of which nurtured trust and close cooperation between the state and the private sector. Such network arrangements minimized the risk of opportunism by individual utility maximizing actors, and considerably reduced transaction costs by facilitating the flow of information. The fusion of government and large private enterprises through the dense networks solved various market imperfections through "extended bounded rationality, reduced small-number indeterminacies, better information, and a group-oriented atmosphere."[44] Moreover, vertical coordination by the state and horizontal consultation and consensus between the state and the private sector removed antagonistic relationships between the two by preventing both the state's predatory behavior and the social capture of the state. The end results were efficient, coherent, and flexible economic (industrial) policies and their effective implementation, which in turn contributed to facilitating impressive economic performance in South Korea.[45]

Network dynamics was not always conducive to economic performance, however. Dense networks between the state and the private sector eventually spread structural corruption, rent-seeking, and moral hazard, which are known to be the primary causes of economic crisis in South Korea.[46] Mancur Olson has warned that a relative longevity of stable political order could breed cartelistic distributional coalitions, holding economic growth at bay.[47] His warning appears to be true in South Korea. Developmental coalitions between the state and big business, which were formed in the earlier stage of economic development and sustained throughout the past four decades, no longer remained "developmental," but were transformed into "rent-seeking" machines. They ultimately undermined the state's ability to insulate economic policy-making from rent-seeking private interests. Cozy ties between politics and business through formal and informal networks were turned into exclusive structural collusion during the stage of mature economy, reviving the specter of collective action dilemmas.

The problem of nonperforming loans exemplifies network failures par excellence. Although nonperforming loans remained a chronic problem throughout the period of the developmental state, the South Korean government as a supplier of credit attempted to minimize a backlash by providing private enterprises with continued loans contingent on two criteria: satisfactory performance, and accommodation of the state's developmental objectives.[48] Reduced transaction costs through developmental networks and the state's constant discipline of the private sector prevented the avalanche of nonperforming loans. But loose discipline and deformed networks began to aggravate the situation of delinquent loans at the onset of the economic crisis. The Hanbo bankruptcy case in 1997, which was recognized as a major trigger of the crisis, offers an outstanding example in this regard. Hanbo, built around a construction company, invested heavily in its steel operations by borrowing from South Korean banks. Despite bleak business prospects and a low ratio of self-owned capital (about KW300 billion), Hanbo Steel was able to borrow KW5 trillion for investment in a steel plant. It was later revealed that political influence was instrumental in securing loans for Hanbo. Kim Hyun-chul, son of President Kim Young Sam, and an array of politicians from both ruling and the opposition parties were implicated in exercising influence over banks' loan decisions. The Hanbo case represents just the tip of the iceberg. A great portion of bank loans had been arranged through political connections.

Likewise, policy and social networks, which functioned as vital assets in reducing transaction costs by cementing ties among the state, business, and banks, turned out to be major liabilities through the formation of exclusive distributional coalitions and subsequent rent-seeking behavior.

Conclusion

The examination of South Korea's economic rise and decline reveals several interesting theoretical and empirical implications. First, South Korea is not an exceptional state. It is an ordinary state which is also subject to the cycles of economic boom and bust. Thus, preoccupation with the "miracle" or economic success could be quite misleading. Economic failures, downturn, and crisis should be legitimate research agendas in the study of South Korea's political economy of development. An accurate picture of its economic transformation can be captured when both successes and failures and their determinants are properly elucidated.

Second, the state, networks, and the international system do not always work as positive factors in shaping the nature of economic performance in South Korea. Their configurations can change over time, bringing about diverse impacts. The international system seems no longer benign. Maturing economy and deeper integration into the world economy through globalization have exposed South Korea to greater external challenges and vulnerability. The state and networks also no longer remain developmental. While state intervention has increased market distortions, networks have become the sources of rent-seeking and structural corruption, undermining economic performance. Thus, it seems essential to trace parametric changes in the state, networks, and the international system over time in order to account for the rise and decline of the South Korean economy.

Third, market forces are not the sole determinant of economic performance. The big picture of an economic landscape is determined by market forces, but the finer lines are drawn by domestic and international politics. In so far as economy shapes the political fortunes of leaders and people, politics delimits the boundary and nature of economic transactions and their outcomes. Likewise, market and politics are closely intertwined through mutually reinforcing causal chains. This is where the importance of political economy in accounting for economic development is most evident.

Finally, structural rigidity appears to be a major barrier to economic performance in South Korea. While the old political order was responsible for the formation of a cartelistic distributional coalition, extensive democratic reforms since the mid-1980s have dealt a critical blow to the logic of the developmental state and networks by precipitating new collective action dilemmas. Expansion of civil society and proliferation of new interest groups such as labor unions have severely undermined the traditional foundation of the developmental state. Economic policy-making has increasingly become subject to contending social and political pressures, resulting in more erratic behavior in economic policy management. In the twilight zone of the old political order and new democratic mandates, structural rigidity of the South Korean society has become all the more pronounced. Capacity to deprogram the inertia, ethos, and institutions of the developmental state, to correct government and network failures therefrom, and to alleviate structural rigidity will ultimately determine the future of South Korea's economy.

Notes

1. Bella Balassa et al., *Development Strategies in Semi-industrial Economies* (Baltimore: Johns Hopkins University Press (for World Bank), 1982); Deepak Lal, *The Poverty of Development Economics* (London: The Institute of Economic Affairs, 1983); Anne O Krueger, "Free Trade Is the

Best Policy," in Robert Z. Lawrence and Charles L. Schultze (eds.) *An American Trade Strategy: Options for the 1990s* (Washington, DC: Brookings Institution, 1990); World Bank. *The East Asian Miracle: Economic Growth and Public Policy* (New York: Oxford University Press, 1993); Helen Huges, *Achieving Industrialization in East Asia* (Cambridge: Cambridge University Press, 1988).

2. Chalmers Johnson, *MITI and the Japanese Miracle* (Stanford, CA: Stanford University Press, 1982); Alice H. Amsden, *Asia's Next Giant: South Korea and Late Industrialization* (New York: Oxford University Press, 1989); Robert Wade, *Governing the Market: Economic Theory and the Role of Government in East Asian Industrialization* (Princeton: Princeton University Press, 1990); Stephen Haggard, *Pathway from the Periphery* (Ithaca, NY, and London: Cornell University Press, 1990); S. Haggard and Chung-in Moon, "The Korean State in the International Economy: Liberal, Dependent, or Mercantile?," in John Ruggie (ed.) *Antinomies of Interdependence* (New York: Columbia University Press, 1983); S. Haggard and C. Moon, "Institutions and Economic Policy: Theory and a Korean Case Study," *World Politics* 42(2), 1990, pp. 210–37.

3. Alice H. Amsden, *Asia's Next Giant.*

4. Peter Evans, *Embedded Autonomy: States and Industrial Transformation* (Princeton: Princeton University Press, 1995); Francis Fukuyama, *Trust: The Social Virtues and the Creation of Prosperity* (New York: The Free Press, 1995); Chung H. Lee, "The Government, Financial System and Large Private Enterprises in the Economic Development of South Korea," *World Development* 20, 1992, pp. 187–197.

5. For the dependencia school, see Hyun-chin Lim, *Dependent Development in Korea, 1963–79.* (Seoul: Seoul National University Press, 1985) and Dae-Keun Lee, *Han'guk Chunjangkwa 1950nyundaeui Jabonchookcheok* [The Korean War and Capital Accumulation in 1950s] (Seoul: Kachi, 1987). As to the geopolitical perspective, see Bruce Cumings, "The Origins and Development of the Northeast Asian Political Economy," *International Organization* 38(1), 1984, pp. 1–40. For an overview, see Stephen Haggard and Chung-in Moon, "The State, Politics, and Economic Development in Postwar South Korea," in Hagen Koo (ed.) *State and Society in Contemporary Korea* (Ithaca: Cornell University Press, 1993), pp. 51–93.

6. Cumings, "The Origins and Development," op. cit.

7. See Chung-in Moon, "Hanil Jungchikyungje Bikyoboonsuk" ["An Comparative Analysis of the Political Economy of Korea and Japan"], *The Journal of Asiatic Studies* 42(1), 1999, pp. 167–228.

8. S. Haggard, D. Kang, and Chung-in Moon, "Japanese Colonialism and Korean Development: A Critique," *World Development* 25(6), 1997; Bruce Cumings, *The Origin of the Korean War I* (Princeton: Princeton Uni-

versity Press, 1991); C. J. Eckert, *Offspring of Empire: The Koch'ang Kims and the Colonial Origins of Korean Capitalism, 1876–1945* (Seattle: University of Washington Press, 1991); Chung-in Moon and Sang-young Rhyu. "Overdeveloped State and the Political Economy of Development in the 1950s: A Reinterpretation." *Asian Perspective* 23(1), 1999, pp. 179–203. Jong-chul Park "Je 1 Konghwakukui Kukgagujowa suipdaechesanupui Jungchigujo" ["The State Structure of the First Republic and Political Structure of ISI"] *Han'guk Jungchihakhoibo* [Korean Political Science Review] 22(1), 1988, pp. 97–118; Dae-Keun Lee, *Han'guk*.

9. S. Haggard, B. K. Kim and Chung-in Moon, "The Transition to Export-Led Growth in South Korea: 1954–1966." *Journal of Asian Studies* 50(4), 1991, pp. 850–973.

10. Junkyungryun [The Federation of Korean Industries], *Han'guk Kyungjejungchak 30nyunsa* [Korean Economic Policies: The Thirty Year History] (Seoul: Sahoisasangsa, 1976). Kyungjekihoiwon [Economic Planning Board], *Kaebalyundaeui Kyungjejungchak: Kyungjekihoiwon 30 nyunsa* [Economic Policies during the Developmental Period: The Thirty Year History of EPB. Vol 1.] (Seoul: Miraesa, 1982).

11. Hyug Baeg Im, "The Rise of Bureaucratic-Authoritarianism in South Korea." *World Politics* 39(2), 1987, pp. 231–257.

12. In-won Jo, *Kukgawa Suntaek* [The State and Choice]. (Seoul: Kyunghee University Press, 1996); Kyun Kim, "Han'guk junghwahakkonguphwawa Kukgagaeipui Yangsangkwa Kwikyul" ["Heavy-Chemical Industrialization and Characteristics and Consequences of the State Intervention in Korea"], in The Association of Korea Industry Studies ed. *Oneului han'gukjabonjuuiwa Kukga* [Contemporary Korean Capitalism and the State] (Seoul: Hangilsa, 1988); Kwangseok Kim, "Han'guk Kyungjeui Kodosungjangyoin 1963–1978" ["Elements of High Economic Growth in Korean Economy"]. *Han'guk Kaebal Yongu* [Korean Development Studies], 1st Issue, 1979.

13. Jung-Ryum Kim, *Kim Jung-Ryum Hoigorok* [Kim Jung-Ryum's Memoirs: The Thirty Year History of Korean Economic Policy] (Seoul: Joongang Ilbo and Joongang Kyungje Sinmoonsa, 1990).

14. S. Haggard and Chung-in Moon, 1983. Ibid; Han'guk Kaebalwon [Korea Development Institute], Kunggi Anjunghwasichak Jaryojip [Research Resources for Stabilization Policy] (Seoul: Korea Development Institute, 1981).

15. Haggard and Moon, "Institutions . . ."; Chung-in, Moon. "The Demise of a Developmental State? Neoconservative Reforms and Political Consequences in South Korea," *Journal of Developing Societies* 4, 1988, pp. 67–84; Vittorio Corbo and Sang-Mok Suh, *Structural Adjustment in a Newly Industrialized Country: The Korean Experience*. (Baltimore: The Johns Hop-

kins University Press, 1992); Kyungjekihoiwon [Economic Planning Board], *Jayulhwasidaeui Kyungjejungchak—Kyungjekihoiwon 30nyunsa* [Economic Policy in the Age of Autonomy and Open-Door: The Thirty Years History of Economic Planning Board] (Seoul: Miraesa, 1994).

16. *Segyehwa* was the leading doctrine for national governance during the Kim Young Sam government. It pursued a more diversified international network, a more active role in multilateral cooperative efforts, and universally accepted values such as democracy, human rights, environmental protection, and social welfare.

17. *Korea Herald*, Janurary 7, 1995.

18. *The Financial Times*, December 29, 1997.

19. The number of corporate bankruptcy cases rose from 9,502 in 1993 to 12,000 cases as of October 1997. See *Wolgan Chosun* [Weekly Chosun] (January 1, 1998), p. 98.

20. The International Monetary Fund. "Korea-Memorandum on the Economic Progress." December 3, 1997, Seoul, p. 1.

21. Jongryn Mo and Chung-in Moon, "Korea after the Crash." *Journal of Democracy* 10 (3), 1999, pp. 150–164.

22. The U.S. government promised to provide continued aid contingent on South Korea's willingness to change its development orientation toward a greater role for exports and more openness to direct foreign investment. See Haggard, Kim, and Moon, "The Transition to Export-led Growth"; Cumings, "The Origins."

23. Cumings (1984), "The Origins"; Peter Katzenstein and T. Shirashi, *Network Power: Japan and Asia* (Ithaca: Cornell University Press, 1997); Kent Calder, "The North Pacific Triangle: Sources of Economic and Political Transformation," *Journal of Northeast Asian Studies* 7:2 (1989).

24. Gary Gereffi, "Paths of Industrialization: An Overview," in G. Gereffi and Donald Wyman (eds.) *Manufacturing Miracles: Paths of Industrialization in Latin America and East Asia* (Princeton: Princeton University Press, 1990), p. 21.

25. Chung-in Moon, *Political Economy of Third World Bilateralism: The Saudi Arabian-Korean Connection, 1973–1983*. Unpublished Ph. D. dissertation (University of Maryland, 1984).

26. Chung-in Moon, "In the Shadow of Broken Cheers: The Dynamics of Globalization in South Korea," in Aseem Prakash and Jeffrey Hart (eds.), *Coping with Globalization* (New York: Routledge, 2000).

27. Tun-jen Cheng and S. Haggard, *Newly Industrializing Asia in Transition*. (Berkeley: University of California, Institute of International

Studies, 1987); Walden Bello and Stephanie Rosenfeld, *Dragons in Distress: Asia's Miracle Economies in Crisis* (San Francisco: Institute for Food and Development Policy, 1990).

28. *Han'guk Eunhang* [The Bank of Korea]: Chung-in Moon. (1998), p. 15.

29. Rudiger Dornbush and Y. C. Park, "Financial Integration in Second-Best World: Are We Still Sure about Our Classical Prejudices," in R. Dornbush and Y. C. Park (eds.) *Financial Opening: Policy Lessons for Korea* (Seoul: Korea Institute of Finance, 1995); Sang-mun Hahm, *Jabonjayulhwawa Jungchakdaeeunge Daehan Yungu* [A Study on the Impacts of Capital Liberalization and Policy Responses], (Seoul: Korea Institute of Finance, 1995).

30. Han-young Chung, *Urinara Oichaeui Hyoyuljuk Kwanribangan.* [On Effective Management of Korea's Foreign Debts] (Seoul: Korea Institute of Finance, 1998).

31. S. Radelet, and J. Sachs. "The Onset of the East Asian Financial Crisis." Harvard Institute for International Development, March 30, 1998.

32. Jaejungkyungjewon [The Ministry of Finance and Economy], *Kyungjebaeksu* [Economy White Paper], (Seoul, 1998).

33. Karl J. Fields, *Enterprise and the State in Korea and Taiwan* (Ithaca: Cornell University Press, 1995), p. 35.

34. David I Steinberg, *The Republic of Korea: Economic Transformation and Social Change* (Boulder, Colorado: Westview Press, 1989).

35. Soon Cho, *The Dynamics of Korean Economic Development* (Washington D.C.: Institute for International Economics, 1994), p. 88.

36. Paul Krugman, "The Myth of Asia's Miracle," *Foreign Affairs* 73(6), 1994, pp. 62–78; Chung-in Moon and Sang-young Rhyu, "The State, Structural Rigidity, and the End of Asian Capitalism: a Comparative Study of Japan and South Korea," presented at an international conference on 'From Miracle to Meltdown: The End of Asian Capitalism?' (August 20–22, 1998, Murdoch University, Australia); Jongryn Mo and Chung-in Moon, "Democracy and the Origins of the 1997 Korean Economic Crisis," in Jongryn Mo and Chung-in Moon (eds.) *Democracy and the Korean Economy* (Stanford: Hoover, 1999).

37. Linda Weiss, *The Myth of the Powerless State* (Ithaca, NY: Cornell University Press, 1998). Chap. 3.

38. Chung-in Moon and Song-min Kim, "Democracy and Economic Performance in South Korea," in Larry Diamond and Byung-Kuk Kim (eds.) *Korean Democracy in Transition* (Boulder: Lynn Rienner Press, 2000).

39. Devaluation also had political and symbolic implications. Devaluation could compromise the government's goal of maintaining and upgrading per capita income to $10,000. Thus, devaluation was opposed for political reasons too.

40. *Donga Ilbo*, April 11, 1998.

41. The decision was also politically motivated. Facing the presidential election in December, the ruling Grand National Party did not want Kia's bankruptcy since its plants were located along the west-coast industrial belt, which was traditionally considered the stronghold of opposition parties. Likewise, electoral factors made the government indecisive in dealing with the Kia case.

42. Chung (1998)

43. Chung (1998); *Chosun Ilbo*, January 8, 1998.

44. Chung H. Lee, "The Government, Financial System, and Large Private Enterprises in the Economic Development of South Korea," *World Development* 20, 1992, p. 193.

45. Evans (1995), "Embedded."

46. Allen Booze and Hamilton. *Report on Korea* (Seoul: Maeil Business Newspaper, 1997); Roubini, Nouriel, *http://www.stern.nyu.edu/~nrobini/asia/asiahomepage.htm.* 1998.

47. Mancur Olson, *The Rise and Decline of Nations: Economic Growth, Stagnation and Social Rigidities* (New Haven, CT, and London: Yale University Press, 1984).

48. See Chung H. Lee, "The Government, Financial System . . . ," pp.187–197.

9

ॐ

The Foreign and Unification Policies of the Republic of Korea

Byung Chul Koh

If foreign policy is defined as state policy toward all external entities, its importance becomes quite plain. In an increasingly interdependent world, how a state manages its relations with other states and international organizations can affect its security and well-being in a tangible fashion.

A number of factors have helped to increase the stakes of foreign policy for the two Korean states—the Republic of Korea (ROK) and the Democratic People's Republic of Korea (DPRK)—alike. First, the Korean peninsula has served historically as a strategic crossroad in East Asia, frequently becoming an object or an arena of competition and conflict among the great powers surrounding it. This situation has forced Korea to pay special attention to its external environment.

Second, the emergence of two mutually hostile states on the peninsula at the end of World War II, claiming exclusive legitimacy respectively, has magnified the importance of foreign policy for both states. Their mutually incompatible claims not only necessitated the cultivation and strengthening of support from patron states but also spawned fierce diplomatic competition in the world arena.

Third, the Korean War of 1950–1953 had the effect of further internationalizing the Korean peninsula. Even though the war began as a fratricidal civil war, it quickly escalated to an international conflict. The United Nations, which had played a pivotal role in the establishment of the ROK, promptly intervened, creating the first and only UN combat force in that organization's history, to which 16 UN member states and South Korea, a non-UN member, contributed. With the addition of North Korea and the People's Republic of China (PRC), the number of countries participating in the war as belligerents totaled nineteen. The emergence of an entangling network of military alliances—a legacy of the war—has enhanced the international complexion of the peninsula.

The definition of foreign policy given above is broad enough to encompass South Korea's policy toward North Korea, for the two are distinct political entities operating as sovereign states in the world arena. Inasmuch as South Korea's policy toward the North is all but indistinguishable from its unification policy, one can argue that foreign policy subsumes unification policy. Given the latter's importance, however, it makes sense to treat it as a separate category.

In the remainder of this chapter, we will first examine the major themes in South Korea's foreign policy. The themes—quest for legitimacy, quest for security, and quest for development—reflect a continuity in Seoul's policy. We then discuss the change in South Korea's foreign policy under the rubric of autonomy, pragmatism, and efficacy. Turning to South Korea's unification policy, we begin by sketching in broad strokes of continuity and change in the policy. Next, we probe the unification policies of the Sixth Republic (1988–1993) and the "Civilian Government" (1993–1998), assessing both the numerous initiatives taken by the Sixth Republic under the leadership of President Roh Tae Woo and those of his successor, President Kim Young Sam. We conclude the chapter by pondering briefly on the implications of South Korea's foreign and unification policies.

Themes in South Korea's Foreign Policy

To provide an overview and facilitate a conceptual understanding of the dizzying array of events and decisions that dot the annals of South Korean diplomacy, we propose to identify and elaborate on the major themes in Seoul's foreign policy during the past four and a half decades. Such an approach, it should be stressed, necessarily entails an oversimplification of the complex reality.

Quest for Legitimacy

Under normal circumstances a state's legitimacy does not loom large in its foreign policy objectives. However, neither the

ROK nor the DPRK had the luxury of operating under normal circumstances. Indeed, the manner in which the two were created was far from normal.

The principal backdrop for their emergence was the division of the peninsula into two occupation zones in the aftermath of Japanese surrender. The inability of the two occupying powers—the United States in the south of the Thirty-Eighth Parallel and the Soviet Union in the north—to reach an agreement on how to bring about a viable political structure on the peninsula led to the intervention of the UN, an intervention that was confined to the U.S. occupation zone due to the refusal of the Soviets to allow a UN team into their zone.

Consequently, UN-observed elections were held only in the south, paving the way for the establishment of the ROK. In a resolution adopted in December 1948, the UN General Assembly declared:

> that there has been established a lawful government (the Government of the Republic of Korea) having effective control and jurisdiction over that part of Korea where the Temporary Commission was able to observe and consult and in which the great majority of the people of all Korea reside; that this Government is based on elections which were a valid expression of the free will of the electorate of that part of Korea and which were observed by the Temporary Commission; and that this is the only such Government in Korea.[1]

The preceding resolution lends itself to varying interpretations. One is that the UN General Assembly has recognized the ROK government as the only "lawful government" that meets two crucial conditions—(1) "having effective control and jurisdiction over that part of Korea where the [UN] Temporary Commission was able to observe and consult," namely, the U.S. occupation zone in the south and (2) "being based on elections which were a valid expression of the free will of the electorate of [the same part of Korea]."

More expansive than the preceding is the interpretation that the UN General Assembly has recognized only the ROK government in Korea as meeting the criteria of a lawful government; hence it is the "only lawful government" on the Korean peninsula. Needless to say, this is the interpretation that has been enthusiastically embraced by the South Korean government.

The ROK's claim to exclusive legitimacy on the peninsula,

however, encountered a frontal challenge from its northern rival on September 9, 1948, only three weeks after the ROK made its debut. The DPRK claimed that it had been organized on the basis of "free elections" held throughout Korea in which practically all eligible voters in the Soviet occupation zone and an overwhelming majority in the U.S. occupation zone allegedly participated. Labeling the ROK a "puppet" of the United States, the DPRK proclaimed itself to be the "only true and lawful government" on the peninsula.[2]

The existence of two rival regimes in Korea meant that the legitimacy of neither was secure. The Korean War could be viewed as DPRK's abortive attempt to settle the legitimacy issue once and for all. When the war ended in a stalemate, both the ROK and the DPRK found it necessary to turn to the diplomatic arena to buttress their respective legitimacy. Both placed high priority on inducing as many countries as possible to extend *de jure* recognition; since the goal was to have their claims of exclusive legitimacy confirmed, neither would accept dual recognition—that is, recognition by the same state of both. Known as the Hallstein doctrine—named after a West German foreign minister who had initiated a similar policy—the policy was strictly adhered to by Seoul for many years until it was effectively nullified by Pyongyang's concerted diplomatic campaign.

It was not until the 1960s that Seoul succeeded in outperforming Pyongyang in the legitimacy war. At the end of the 1950s, the scoreboard had been a virtual tie: Seoul had established ambassadorial-level diplomatic relations with fourteen countries, Pyongyang with thirteen. The Park Chung Hee regime, launched in the aftermath of a military coup in May 1961, the first in the ROK's history, however, stepped up efforts to increase the roster of diplomatic partners, reaping spectacular results: a total of 67 countries established full diplomatic relations with Seoul. This represented a sixfold increase in the number of countries that had extended to the ROK exclusive *de jure* recognition. Although Pyongyang was by no means idle in the diplomatic arena, it managed to add only 20 countries to its own roster of diplomatic partners.[3]

Seoul's edge in its diplomatic competition with Pyongyang, however, was blunted in the 1970s, when North Korea launched a major offensive in the world arena with impressive results. What Pyongyang did in the 1970s was to replicate Seoul's feat in the preceding decade: the DPRK added 68 countries to the roster of its diplomatic partners, whereas the ROK added exactly half that number to its own roster. The gap between Seoul and Pyongyang in terms of number of diplomatic partners had closed.

In trying to catch up with Seoul in the realm of diplomatic relations, Pyongyang had little choice but to woo the states with which Seoul had already established diplomatic relations. Since most countries would not heed Pyongyang's plea for derecognition of Seoul, they ended up having full diplomatic relations with both the ROK and the DPRK. As a result, whereas in 1962 not a single country simultaneously recognized both Seoul and Pyongyang, in 1976 a total of 49 countries did so. In short, intense competition between the two Korean states in the diplomatic arena led not to the enhanced recognition of the exclusive legitimacy of either state but to the simultaneous acceptance of their separate existence by a growing number of states.

A key factor that enabled Pyongyang to make a significant diplomatic inroad in the 1970s was the initiation of dialogue between Seoul and Pyongyang. Although short-lived, the dialogue signaled the advent of a new era of detente on the Korean peninsula, which in turn made it easy for Seoul's diplomatic partners to respond favorably to Pyongyang's overtures. It was against such a backdrop that North Korea made a significant breakthrough in 1973: for the first time ever, it succeeded in establishing ambassadorial-level diplomatic relations with a number of Western European countries, namely Sweden, Finland, Norway, Denmark, and Iceland. Switzerland and Portugal followed suit in 1974 and 1975, respectively.

Perhaps the most significant development in the 1970s as far as the legitimacy war was concerned was DPRK's entry into the UN system. In May 1973, the DPRK, overcoming stiff opposition by the ROK and its allies, was admitted to the World Health Organization (WHO), which conferred for the first time on Pyongyang the customary privilege of applying for observer status. Pyongyang lost no time in applying for that status, which was promptly granted; the DPRK permanent observer missions made their debuts in Geneva and New York in June.

This marked the beginning of the end of ROK dominance in the arena of UN diplomacy. Seoul could no longer count on the UN General Assembly to pass resolutions supportive of its position. In the fall of 1973, when the twenty-eighth session of the UN General Assembly convened, its First Committee (Political and Security Affairs) extended an unconditional invitation to the DPRK to send observers to its deliberations of the Korean question. Previously, invitations to North Korea had been contingent on its acceptance of the authority of the UN to deal with the Korean question. Contending that the UN, as a co-belligerent in the Korean War, had forfeited any right to play the role of an impartial arbiter on the Korean question, Pyongyang had steadfastly refused to accept the condition, thus allowing Seoul virtually a free hand in conducting its UN diplomacy.

The entry of the North Koreans to the scene changed the situation markedly. In 1973, all that the UN managed to do was to adopt a "consensus statement" on the Korean question. In 1974, North Korea came very close to scoring a victory: a draft resolution, sponsored by its allies, calling for withdrawal of UN forces—read: U.S. forces—from South Korea was narrowly defeated in the First Committee by a vote of 48 to 48, with 38 abstentions. Then in 1975, North Korea finally scored a symbolic victory: in an unprecedented move, the First Committee, and later the General Assembly as a whole, adopted two conflicting resolutions on Korea—one cosponsored by North Korea's allies and another cosponsored by South Korea's allies.[4]

Since the two resolutions canceled each other out, neither Seoul nor Pyongyang gained anything substantive. Nonetheless, the symbolic gain for North Korea was considerable, since it marked the first time that the UN General Assembly had passed a pro-DPRK resolution. By conveniently ignoring the pro-ROK resolution, North Korea could claim victory and urge the United States to honor the former, which called for withdrawal of all foreign troops from South Korea. As far as Seoul was concerned, the usefulness of the UN in bolstering its legitimacy had, for all practical purposes, evaporated.

In the ensuing years, the UN ceased its annual ritual of debating the Korean question. In fact, a significant milestone was reached in September 1991, when both Korean states became full-fledged members of the world organization. If exclusive legitimacy has receded into the background as a foreign policy goal, however, relative legitimacy—in the sense of generating more support for oneself than for one's rival in the world arena—has continued to shape not only Seoul's foreign policy, but Pyongyang's as well.

Quest for Security

Another theme in South Korea's foreign policy is the top priority Seoul has placed on ensuring its national security through all available means. The goals of legitimacy and security, in the

Korean context, are closely intertwined. Pursuit of legitimacy, particularly exclusive legitimacy, by the DPRK has posed the greatest threat to the security of the ROK. The Soviet-backed invasion of the South by North Korea in June 1950, as noted, bespoke Pyongyang's attempt to settle the legitimacy issue by force.

Following the signing of the armistice agreement in July 1953, North Korea has continued to threaten South Korea's security: it has dispatched armed agents to the South; beefed up its armed forces; dug underground tunnels across the Demilitarized Zone (DMZ); deployed a sizable proportion of soldiers and equipment in forward bases close to the DMZ in what Seoul sees as an offensive posture; precipitated incidents large and small involving the use of violence against the South; openly incited a forcible overthrow of the ROK government.

South Korea has responded to this continuing threat from the North by coupling its campaign to buttress its legitimacy on the global stage with an all-out effort to strengthen its defense capability vis-à-vis North Korea. There are two key components in Seoul's security policy: (1) the maintenance of American deterrent power in the form of both its treaty commitments to Seoul and military presence in the South, and (2) the modernization of South Korea's own military arsenal with U.S. assistance. In the 1970s, Washington's moves to scale down and even phase out its military presence in Korea spurred Seoul to build up its own defense industry with a view to attaining a self-reliant defense capability.

It is worth noting that Washington's commitment to Seoul's security in the post-armistice period materialized under unusual circumstances. U.S. President Eisenhower had initially rebuffed ROK President Syngman Rhee's request for a mutual defense treaty; in the end, however, Washington's need to secure Rhee's acquiescence to the armistice produced such a treaty. Rhee had not only opposed a cease-fire but also threatened to take unilateral military action against North Korea; his defiant act of unilaterally releasing 28,000 "anticommunist" prisoners of war, moreover, had nearly torpedoed the armistice.[5]

For his intransigence, Rhee came perilously close to being overthrown in what would have been a United States-sponsored coup d'état. An American contingency plan to topple Rhee, codenamed "Ever-ready," however, was never implemented.[6] In addition to the promise of a mutual defense treaty, Rhee extracted from Washington "$1 billion in economic aid over three years and equipment for an army of twenty divisions (about 700,000 soldiers)."[7]

Seoul's quest for security has engendered a vicious circle, for it invariably leads to countermeasures by Pyongyang, which in turn triggers further action by Seoul. What emerges is a zero-sum game in which an increase in the perceived security of one side implies a corresponding decrease in the perceived security of the other side. To counterbalance South Korea's military alliance with the U.S., North Korea forged two sets of military alliances—one with Moscow and another with Beijing. During the Cold War era the Korean peninsula thus had the dubious distinction of being the only area in the world where three sets of military alliances—the U.S., Russia, and China—intersected.

Seoul's *Nordpolitik* (northern diplomacy), a policy of wooing Communist countries initiated by President Roh Tae Woo in 1988, was fueled in large part by its desire to bolster its security by neutralizing the threat posed, albeit indirectly, by Pyongyang's principal allies. The policy proved to be a phenomenal success. Seoul and Moscow established full diplomatic relations in September 1990; six summit meetings were held between the two countries, with both former Soviet President Mikhail Gorbachev and Russian President Boris Yeltsin visiting South Korea. During his first state visit to the ROK in November 1992, Yeltsin indicated that Russia would consider repealing the article in the Moscow-Pyongyang treaty that provides for military intervention in the event of a war. He revealed that Russia had all but terminated military assistance and sales to North Korea, citing as an example "the suspension of operation of a MIG-29 assembly plant in the North." He reportedly "voiced interest in selling military technology and equipment to South Korea."[8]

This means that the Moscow-Pyongyang alliance no longer poses a serious threat to Seoul's security. In March 1999, in fact, Russia and the DPRK initialed a new treaty on friendship and cooperation that would replace the defunct alliance treaty.[9] The speed with which the Seoul-Moscow normalization materialized owes not simply to Roh's *Nordpolitik* but, more important, to its convergence with Gorbachev's "new thinking," which paved the way for the collapse of socialism in Eastern Europe and the Soviet Union. Seoul's willingness to provide sizable economic assistance to Moscow—a package of loans and investments worth $3 billion— played a key role in the unfolding of events.[10]

The conjunction of Seoul's *Nordpolitik* and an upsurge of pragmatism in Beijing's foreign policy helps to account for a rapid increase in trade and other economic exchanges between the two, culminating in the establishment of full diplomatic relations in

August 1992. This stunning development can only undercut the efficacy of the Pyongyang-Beijing treaty of friendship and mutual assistance that has been in force since 1961. Seoul now believes the probability of Chinese military intervention in a conflict on the Korean peninsula is exceedingly low. Nor does China seem willing to fill the void left by Russia in the field of military assistance and sales to North Korea.

None of this means, however, that the quest for security has ceased to shape Seoul's foreign policy. Not only does Pyongyang continue to maintain what General Robert W. RisCassi, the former Commander of the United States Forces Korea (USFK), has called "a highly mobile, extremely lethal, offensive force,"[11] but it is also suspected of covertly trying to develop nuclear weapons. Pyongyang's refusal to allow the International Atomic Energy Agency (IAEA) to conduct "special inspections" of suspected nuclear facilities and its decision to withdraw from the Nuclear Non-Proliferation Treaty (NPT) in June 1993 increased fears that it might be closer to manufacturing nuclear weapons than had previously been surmised.

The signing of an "Agreed Framework" by the U.S. and the DPRK on October 21, 1994, helped to avert a showdown, opening the way for a peaceful resolution of the nuclear issue. Under the framework, North Korea is committed to (1) freezing its nuclear program, (2) dismantling all of its graphite-moderated reactors as well as reprocessing plant, (3) allowing the removal of 8,000 spent nuclear fuel rods to another country, and (4) permitting IAEA inspection of the two sites in Yongbyon suspected by the United States and the IAEA as being secret nuclear waste storage facilities. In return for all this, North Korea will get two 1,000 megawatt light water reactors (LWRs); 500,000 tons of heavy oil for heating and generation of electricity per year for five to ten years; relaxation of trade restrictions by the United States; and diplomatic normalization with the United States.[12]

Implementation of the agreement requires close collaboration among the United States, South Korea, and Japan. In March 1995, these three countries set up an international consortium known as the Korean Peninsula Energy Development Organization (KEDO). Even though the agreement on KEDO's establishment is silent on the matter, the understanding among its three "original members" is that the United States will play the leading role. Pursuant to that understanding, a U.S. citizen was named KEDO's first executive director, with two deputy executive directors being supplied by South Korea and Japan. Significantly, however, Article II of the

KEDO charter provides that the light water reactor project, which KEDO will finance and supply to North Korea, will consist of "two reactors of the Korean standard nuclear plant model with a capacity of approximately 1,000 MW(e) each."[13]

Since South Korea has agreed to shoulder the lion's share of the financial burden—about 70 percent of the estimated 4.5 billion dollars—it insisted on playing the "central role" in the LWR project, of which the most important is the installation of South Korean-model reactors. The KEDO charter has fully endorsed Seoul's position. A joint press statement issued by the U.S. and North Korea in Kuala Lumpur, Malaysia on June 13, 1995, however, obscures South Korea's role in the LWR project:

> The Korean Peninsula Energy Development Organization (KEDO), under U.S. leadership, will finance and supply the LWR project in the DPRK as called for in the Agreed Framework. As specified in the Agreed Framework, the U.S. will serve as the principal point of contact with the DPRK for the LWR project. In this regard, U.S. citizens will lead delegations and teams of KEDO as required to fulfill this role. The LWR project will consist of two pressurized light water reactors with two coolant loops and a generating capacity of approximately 1,000 MW(e) each. The reactor model, selected by KEDO, will be the advanced version of U.S.-origin, design and technology currently under production.[14]

Substantively, the preceding paragraph in the Kuala Lumpur agreement leaves no doubt that the reactors to be sent to North Korea will be South Korean models. No other reactors match the description given in the paragraph. Symbolically, however, North Korea succeeded in suppressing any explicit reference either to South Korea or to South Korean model reactors. On the contrary, North Korea could and did point to the repeated references to the United States in the joint press statement, ignoring or even denying outright South Korea's pivotal role in the project as its principal financier as well as the supplier of LWRs themselves. The decision to install South Korean model LWRs means, moreover, that hundreds, perhaps thousands, of South Korean engineers, technicians, and other personnel will be stationed in the North for many years to come.

In March 1996, the Korea Electric Power Company (KEPCO) became the prime contractor of KEDO for the LWR project, thus making South Korea's central role in the project official. When KEDO opened an office in Shinpo's Kumho district in July 1997, where the two LWRs will be installed, two ROK Foreign Ministry officials joined two U.S. and one Japanese government officials as the staff. This marked a milestone in inter-Korean relations, for never before in the forty-nine-year history of the two states had representatives of one been permitted to be posted on the other's territory.[15]

In the following month, a historic groundbreaking ceremony was held in Kumho district, officially launching site preparation work for LWR installation.[16] About 100 South Korean workers began working side by side with a comparable number of North Korean workers on the site.

The discovery in August 1998 by U.S. intelligence of a massive underground construction project in Kumchangni, about 40 kilometers from Yongbyon, however, fueled the suspicion that North Korea may have resumed its nuclear weapons development program in violation of the October 1994 Geneva accords. After four rounds of negotiations spanning four months, the United States and North Korea reached an agreement in March 1999 that would permit multiple visits by U.S. experts to the suspected site. Although not an official quid pro quo, North Korea would receive an estimated 600,000 tons of food aid and other assistance from the United States. U.S. economic sanctions on the North were to gradually be lifted and steps toward diplomatic normalization, beginning with an exchange of liaison offices, were to be taken.[17]

All this suggests that while threats to Seoul's security are likely to substantially decline in the years ahead, Seoul's need to work closely with its ally, the U.S., and other states with which it has forged friendly relations, particularly Japan, will remain undiminished.

Quest for Development

The importance of economic development for South Korea lies in its multiple functions: it allows the ROK to jettison the stigma of poverty and dependence, helps to raise the standard of living for all the people, and undergirds national security. Military capability requires a strong industrial base; even for a country that relies primarily on imported arms, a strong economy is a *sine qua non*, since state-of-the art military equipment is enormously expensive.

South Korea's decision, made during the formative stage of the Park Chung Hee era, to emulate the Japanese model of development—relying on exports as the primary vehicle of growth—

vastly enhanced the role of foreign policy in the developmental equation.

Two countries, the United States and Japan, have occupied and continue to occupy a special position in South Korea's "economic diplomacy." While American involvement in ROK affairs is not only as old as (actually older than) the latter's official founding in 1948, Japan's participation in the economic affairs of the ROK, as distinct from those of the Korean people, did not begin in earnest until diplomatic relations were normalized between the two countries in the mid-1960s.

The harsh Japanese colonial rule in Korea (1910–1945) had helped to spawn a long list of contentious issues between Seoul and Tokyo. They include (1) the status of Korean residents in Japan; (2) problems concerning property claims; (3) problems concerning the "Peace Line"—which extended South Korea's jurisdiction to 50 nautical miles from its coastline, thus barring Japanese fishermen from fishing within these waters; (4) Japanese possession of Korean art treasures; (5) conflicting territorial claims to Tokto (Takeshima to the Japanese); and (6) Japan's policy of repatriating Korean residents to North Korea.[18]

All but the Tokto issue were settled, with both sides making significant concessions, paving the way for the signing of five agreements in June 1965. Following their ratification by the two governments, which were preceded by bitter internal political struggles in both countries, the agreements entered into force in January 1966.[19]

The principal economic benefit of this diplomatic breakthrough consisted of Japan's commitment to provide a total of $800 million in "economic cooperation" to South Korea over a ten-year period—$300 million in grants, $200 million in government loans, and $300 million in private commercial credits.

Although relatively small—in the view of many South Koreans, the terms of the ROK-Japan normalization constituted a humiliating sellout by the Park regime[20]—Japan's aid package nonetheless played a key role in Seoul's economic growth. Economic ties between Seoul and Tokyo have grown steadily over the years. Japan is now only second to the United States as South Korea's most important trading partner; South Korea ranks either second or third among Japan's trading partners.

The ROK-Japan economic relationship, however, is strikingly asymmetrical. South Korea has consistently incurred deficits in its balance of trade with Japan, and these deficits usually cancel out surpluses in South Korea's trade accounts with other trading partners. Another perennial issue involves technology transfer. Fearing a "boomerang effect," Japanese firms have shown extreme reluctance to transfer state-of-the-art technology to their South Korean counterparts.

The place United States occupies in South Korean foreign policy is *sui generis*. No other country has as pivotal a role to play in the ROK's quest for all three foreign policy goals—legitimacy, security, and development. Washington actually eclipses Tokyo in terms of economic value. Unlike Japan, the U.S. market has been wide open to South Korean products, which helps to explain why it has remained South Korea's foremost export market. In the 1980s, Seoul had a surplus in its trade balance with Washington for a number of years; in 1987, for example, the surplus reached $9.8 billion. In the 1990s, however, the balance of trade has turned in Washington's favor. All this means that trade friction between South Korea and the United States is quite manageable from the standpoints of both.

Until the 1970s, the United States and Japan together accounted for over 60 percent of South Korean exports. However, South Korea's efforts to diversify its global market has steadily increased the importance of the other nations of the world; by the early 1980s, the share of South Korean exports by its two top trading partners had declined to the 40 percent range. In 1994, the United States accounted for 21.4 percent and Japan for 14.1 percent (a combined total of 35.5 percent) of South Korean exports. South Korea's third largest export market was the European Union (EU), whose member states together accounted for about 10 percent of South Korean exports. This indicates that the majority of South Korean exports were destined for Third World countries. Particularly notable was a phenomenal increase in exports to China.[21]

Although South Korea has largely attained its goal of ridding itself of the stigma of underdevelopment and has entered the ranks of medium economic powers, its economy has nonetheless encountered a wide range of problems. These are: an appreciable decline in the competitiveness of its export goods due to the combined effects of rising wage levels at home and increasing competition from abroad; growing protectionism on the part of its principal trading partners; an inability to make significant technological breakthroughs, and a growing external debt. In late 1997 a currency crisis pushed South Korea to the brink of default. A $58-billion emergency rescue plan crafted by the International Monetary

Fund helped South Korea avert a bankruptcy. By early 1999, however, the South Korean economy appeared on its way toward recovery. All this means that the quest for economic development will remain a key goal of South Korean policy, both domestic and foreign.

Changes in South Korea's Foreign Policy

Inasmuch as foreign policy must respond to the stimuli of change in a state's external environment, it cannot afford to stand still. Change can also emanate from internal factors, such as change in political leadership, growth in economic capability, and a growing maturity of the political system. Three dimensions of change we propose to examine below are (1) autonomy, (2) pragmatism, and (3) efficacy.

Autonomy

Although the ROK was created as an independent state, its ability to assert and, more important, practice independence has varied widely over the past five decades. In general, to the extent that it has been closely related to economic self-reliance, independence has grown steadily over the years in tandem with South Korea's spectacular economic growth.

There have been exceptions to this generalization, the most notable of which is Syngman Rhee's track record. Notwithstanding his regime's heavy dependence on the United States for economic aid and military support, Rhee was remarkably independent of Washington. We have already noted his most celebrated act of defiance vis-à-vis Washington: his unilateral release of 28,000 anti-Communist North Korean prisoners of war in June 1953. Paradoxically, it was Rhee's fierce independence that was largely instrumental in institutionalizing Seoul's heavy military dependence on the U.S.[22]

Since South Korea's economy experienced an accelerated rate of growth during his long tenure as the ruler of South Korea, the Park era (1961–1979) witnessed a marked increase in ROK autonomy. Park's successful quest for the normalization of relations with Japan both reflected and facilitated his pursuit of self-reliance, and hence independence. In the short and medium term, however, Park's developmental strategy had the effect of increasing, rather than decreasing, Seoul's reliance on external economic resources.

Park's reliance on authoritarian political controls, which became particularly draconian in the 1970s with the establishment of a new political structure known as the *Yushin* (revitalizing reforms) system in the fall of 1972, created difficulties for his regime in terms of foreign policy. The United States in particular continued to exert both overt and covert ("quiet diplomacy") pressure to stem Park's flagrant abuse of human rights. In a sense, Park's stubborn refusal to yield to external pressure was a manifestation of his independence.

The Roh Tae Woo regime's pursuit of *Nordpolitik*, while dictated to a large extent by Seoul's security concerns, was also emblematic of both its ability to act independently and to allow for a maximization of autonomy. Anyone who harbors lingering doubts about Seoul's autonomous capability in foreign policy needs only to be reminded that it was Seoul that gave the green light to Washington and Tokyo to adjust their respective policies toward Pyongyang in a pragmatic direction, not the other way around. Prior to Roh's celebrated statement on July 7, 1988, both the United States and Japan had refrained from making any overtures toward the DPRK in deference to ROK sensitivity on such matters.

If the press reports about initial disagreements between Seoul and Washington on how to respond to Pyongyang's decision, unveiled in March 1993, to withdraw from the Nuclear Nonproliferation Treaty (NPT) are true, then they too are evidences of Seoul's enhanced autonomy. The government under Kim Young Sam reportedly favored a moderate approach—that is, first relying on persuasion and then increasing pressure gradually—while the Clinton administration took a more hard-line approach. The two allies eventually agreed on the strategy of "diplomacy first, sanctions later," which was closer, perhaps even identical, to Seoul's initial position.[23]

Pragmatism

The steady increase in South Korea's ability to assert autonomy in its foreign policy has entailed a corresponding growth in the salience of pragmatism in foreign policy. This trend, it should be noted, is more apparent in the realm of operational direction and tactics than in the realm of strategy. Strategic goals of foreign policy have remained remarkably resilient over the years.

In its formative years, the ROK pursued a highly dogmatic foreign policy. Although widely credited as having been a skillful manager of South Korea's relations with the outside world, Syngman Rhee's foreign policy was actually marked by a high degree of dogmatism. His militant anticommunism, uncompromising posture toward Japan, quarrel with Washington over the issue of Korean armistice, and adherence to the Hallstein Doctrine are cases in point.

To be fair, however, one needs to empathize with Rhee's perspectives. Having experienced the North Korean invasion and the ensuing war, Rhee had every reason to be distrustful, even contemptuous, of the North Korean Communists and their principal patron states. His dispute with Washington was related to that factor. His distrust of and animosity toward Japan were rooted in his long record of struggle against the Japanese colonial rule in Korea. Given all the concessions he managed to extract from the United States, it is worth reiterating that his dispute with Washington over the Korean armistice proved to be beneficial to his regime.

Rhee's successors have appreciably diluted the dogmatic components of South Korea's foreign policy. Particularly noteworthy is the performance of Park Chung Hee who: normalized diplomatic relations with Japan; greatly expanded Seoul's diplomatic partners, particularly in the Third World; jettisoned the Hallstein Doctrine; engaged in dialogue with North Korea; and enunciated an "open door" policy toward Communist states. Although some of these measures did not represent policy initiatives in a strict sense, but rather adaptive responses to *faits accompli*, this point does not alter the fundamental reality—that Seoul's foreign policy under Park became markedly pragmatic.

Foreign policy pursued by Park's successor, Chun Doo Hwan, continued to display a large aspect of pragmatism. As evidence of the continuing ascendancy of pragmatism in Seoul's foreign policy under the Fifth Republic, one can point to the strengthening of ties with the United States and Japan through summit diplomacy; the upgrading of relations with Third World countries, particularly those of Association of Southeast Asian Nations (ASEAN); the formulation of a comprehensive proposal for peace and reunification in Korea; and the reaffirmation of the "open door" policy toward Communist states.

The trend noted above continued unabated in the Sixth Republic; President Roh scored a string of impressive victories in the diplomatic arena, many of which can be subsumed under his celebrated *Nordpolitik*. Most notable among them were the ROK-

USSR diplomatic normalization; the ROK-PRC diplomatic normalization; the admission of the ROK, along with the DPRK, to the United Nations; and summit diplomacy involving all the major powers surrounding the Korean peninsula. That Roh was given the rare privilege of addressing the UN General Assembly in September 1988, at a time when the ROK had not yet succeeded in upgrading its status at the UN from an observer to a full-fledged member, can only be described as a diplomatic coup of significant symbolic proportions. All this was clearly linked to the strong pragmatic thrust of Seoul's foreign policy.

The Kim Young Sam government did not deviate from the pragmatic foreign policy line of its predecessors. President Kim's pursuit of summit diplomacy was no less vigorous than that of his immediate predecessor. Like Roh Tae Woo, Kim visited all four powers with special interests in the Korean peninsula—the United States, Japan, Russia, and China. The leaders of all visited Seoul. The Kim Young Sam government displayed a striking measure of pragmatism in dealing with the North Korean nuclear issue—perhaps the most serious challenge to its security and foreign policy interests. Not only did it work closely with Washington and Tokyo, it accepted, albeit grudgingly, the role of bystander in the U.S.-DPRK negotiations. Had Seoul been less flexible vis-à-vis Washington and, indirectly, Pyongyang, the Agreed Framework of October 1994 would not have materialized.

Although an assessment of the Kim Dae Jung government's overall performance in foreign policy must await the passage of a few more years, its record during the first fourteen months in office indicates that it may well turn out to be the least dogmatic of all eight governments South Korea has experienced thus far. It has vigorously pursued the policy of separating politics from economics vis-à-vis the North. Its "Sunshine" policy—seeking engagement with the North without lowering vigilance against threats to security emanating from Pyongyang—reflects pragmatism par excellence. That has spawned a "role reversal" in ROK-U.S. relations, with Seoul advocating a more moderate approach toward Pyongyang than Washington. Notable gains in ROK-Japan relations—such as the revision of a fisheries agreement, the adoption of a joint declaration on a new partnership toward the twentieth century as well as an action program, and an increase in the frequency of summit diplomacy and other high-level contacts—also bespeak the ascendancy of pragmatism in the Kim Dae Jung government's foreign policy.

Efficacy

In most cases, pragmatism implies efficacy. In other words, a policy that has been guided primarily by pragmatic considerations is likely to be efficacious. Given the uncertainty of the real world, however, the actual outcome of policy may contain unanticipated consequences. Pragmatism does not, therefore, guarantee efficacy. With this caveat in mind, let us assess the efficacy of South Korea's foreign policy.

South Korea's policy toward its allies has thus far proved to be extraordinarily efficacious. Although there have been occasional strains—such as the dispute between Syngman Rhee and Washington over the Korean armistice, and Park Chung Hee's problems related to his political repression and lobbying activities in Washington—ROK-U.S. relations have by and large remained on solid footing and have grown conspicuously in recent years.

Like all bilateral relations, however, Seoul-Washington ties hinge not only on the efficacy of Seoul's diplomacy but also on Washington's own needs, interests, and proclivities. Fortunately for the South Korean people, Washington's assessment of its stakes in Korea has not wavered over the past half century. This has been instrumental in cementing the ROK-U.S. alliance, which in turn has helped to preserve peace and stability on the Korean peninsula. With spectacular growth in the South Korean economic capability during the past few decades, the basic character of Seoul-Washington relations has been transformed from an asymmetrical dependence to a growing interdependence.

South Korea's policy toward Japan can also be rated as most efficacious. The turning point came during the early years of the Park Chung Hee era. The diplomatic normalization between Seoul and Tokyo in 1965, as noted, paved the way for an influx of Japanese capital and technology, which undergirded South Korea's drive for accelerated economic growth.

As is the case with Seoul-Washington relations, Seoul-Tokyo relations have been far from symmetrical. South Korea has consistently incurred huge deficits in its trade with Japan; about 70 percent of all the trade deficits South Korea has incurred in its global trade is attributable to Japan.

In addition to creating strains, a lopsided pattern of trade inevitably fuels another source of friction that has occasionally marred Seoul-Tokyo relations: Japan's policy toward North Korea. From 1965 to 1988, Seoul pursued a policy of preventing or discouraging Japan from dealing with North Korea in any way that even indirectly bolstered Pyongyang's legitimacy or its policy goals. While scrupulously avoiding any official contacts with the DPRK until 1990, Japan nonetheless implemented its long-standing policy of *seikei bunri* (separation of politics from economics) vis-à-vis North Korea. Two-way trade between Japan and North Korea grew from $31 million in 1965 to $564 million in 1988—an eighteenfold increase.[24] Had it not been for North Korea's payment problems, the trade volume would probably have grown at a faster rate.

Inasmuch as a change in Seoul's policy served as a catalyst for change in Tokyo's policy toward Pyongyang, the initiation of direct negotiations between Japan and the DPRK for diplomatic normalization in late 1990 was officially welcomed by the ROK. South Korea nonetheless set forth a number of conditions, which Japan accepted. They included North Korea's acceptance of IAEA inspections of its nuclear facilities, to which were later added the implementation of mutual inspections between the two Korean states.

The measurable gains in South Korean diplomacy vis-à-vis the rest of the world, including its giant neighbors to the north, Russia and China, serve to bolster the conclusion that Seoul's foreign policy has been singularly effective. In Seoul's case, pragmatism has almost always been enormously productive.

Continuity and Change in South Korea's Unification Policy

Just as its foreign policy has not been static, South Korea's unification policy too has undergone notable changes over the past five decades. To begin with continuity, however, we need to take note of the resilience of the strategic goals pursued by the successive regimes in the ROK and the politicization of the unification issue.

All eight governments since 1948 have been committed, either explicitly or implicitly, to the strategic goal of hegemonic unification; that is, unification in which either the South Korean system, or a system embodying democratic values, prevails over the North Korean system.[25] None of them has either contemplated or left open the option of permitting the Communists to remain a significant force in a reunified Korea.

The maximum goal of all the republics has been to eliminate Communist influence altogether; their minimum goal has been to neutralize it. The transparency of the maximum goal, however, has varied with different political leaders. Syngman Rhee, who spoke openly of "marching north" to "obliterate the Communists," was such a diehard opponent of compromising with the Communists that he even tried to torpedo the armistice negotiations. Park Chung Hee, while engaging in negotiations with the North, nonetheless made clear his profound distrust of the latter, indicating that the only way to reunify the Korean peninsula was to "prevail over communism."

None of Park's four successors—Chun Doo Hwan, Roh Tae Woo, Kim Young Sam, and Kim Dae Jung—has explicitly embraced the goal of prevailing over communism (the Korean phrase, *sunggong t'ongil*, literally means "unification by winning a victory over communism"). Both Chun and Roh, however, openly articulated their distrust of the North Korean regime, insisting that the latter's goal—to communize the South—had not changed. Notwithstanding repeated disavowals, moreover, the Roh government never truly ruled out the option of "unification by absorption" (*hupsu t'ongil*). The long-term outcome of the scenario envisioned by Kim Young Sam's unification formula, to be examined shortly, was the ascendancy of South Korean democracy over North Korean communism. Kim Dae Jung parts company with all of his predecessors in explicitly disclaiming any intention to absorb the North. That, however, is not the same as condoning Communist influence, let alone ascendancy, in the unified Korea.

Another common denominator of the unification policies of the successive South Korean regimes is that unification has always remained a highly politicized issue. More important, virtually all regimes have used the issue to further their respective political ends. No one surpasses the late Park Chung Hee in the degree to which unification policy was politically exploited. Not only did he replicate Syngman Rhee's tactic of cloaking all manner of repression in the guise of countering the threat of Communist subversion or aggression, he also exploited the inter-Korean dialogue to legitimize sweeping political changes, the transparent goals of which were to enhance his own power and ensure his prolonged rule.

Chun Doo Hwan's unification policy, notably his proposal for a summit meeting with Kim Il Sung and his unification formula, was fueled by his need to bolster his shaky claim to legitimacy. The vigor with which Roh Tae Woo pursued his *Nordpolitik*, including his policy toward North Korea, was also linked to his political needs and desires. Unlike Chun, however, Roh did not labor under the crushing burden of the near absence of legitimacy; Roh, after all, had been elected to his position in a direct election, albeit by a plurality rather than by a majority of the effective vote.

As the first civilian president in thirty-three years and blessed with a margin of electoral victory substantially greater than Roh's, Kim Young Sam had the least incentive to abuse the unification issue to undergird his legitimacy; the politicization of the unification issue came to an end in the Civilian Government. The People's Government under Kim Dae Jung has not only disavowed any intention of using unification policy to further its internal political goals but actually implemented the policy of separating politics from economics in inter-Korean relations.

Turning from continuity to change, we can discern three noteworthy aspects: (1) the diversification of means used in quest of unification, (2) the formulation of a comprehensive strategy, and (3) the varying salience of unification. To elaborate first on the diversification of means, Syngman Rhee, as already noted, openly advocated war as the means of unification. War, however, was not the only means he embraced; he also supported UN-supervised elections based on the principle of proportional representation—that is, one person, one vote.[26] Given the South's two-to-one advantage over the North in population, the UN formula would guarantee the former's dominance in a unified government.

It was only after Rhee's downfall in April 1960 that South Korea explicitly ruled out war or violence as a method of unification. Huh Chung, who headed a caretaker administration for three months between Rhee's downfall and the inauguration of the Chang Myon regime, dissociated himself from "the clichés, the emotional decisions and the 'March North' oaths of yesterday," advocating "efforts to bring the division of Korea to a peaceful end in accordance with the principles set forth in UN resolutions."[27]

The Chang regime reaffirmed Huh's policy, declaring that the UN formula alone would guarantee establishment of "a democratic, anticommunist, and unified government . . . through expression of the free will of the people." It added that "such reckless policy as trying to unify Korea by force as advocated by the past Liberal Government [of Syngman Rhee] should now be discarded."[28] Succeeding regimes have reiterated the renunciation of force and committed themselves unequivocally to peaceful unification. In the early 1970s, dialogue entered the repertoire of means for Korean unification for the first time.

The second aspect of change in South Korea's unification pol-

icy concerns the formulation of a comprehensive strategy for unification. Syngman Rhee's bellicose posturing did not really amount to
a strategy, for he lacked the capability to "march north" and crush
the Communist regime. Neither the interim government of Huh
Chung nor the Chang Myon regime lasted long enough to develop,
let alone implement, a comprehensive unification strategy.

Park Chung Hee, whose eighteen-year-rule is the longest in
the annals of the ROK, did have a strategy of sorts: construction
first, unification later. Stressing that "national unification will
become attainable only after the fulfillment of the intermediate
goals of building a self-reliant economy and modernization," Park
stated that when South Korea surpasses the North in the political,
economic, social, scientific, and other fields, the road to "unification
by prevailing over communism" would be opened. He foresaw that
the preceding conditions might materialize in the latter half of the
1970s; South Korea would then be in a position to take the initiatives toward unification.[29] Park, however, was assassinated in October 1979 before unveiling any comprehensive strategies or proposals for unification.

It was Park's successors who filled that void in South Korean
policy. Chun Doo Hwan's January 1982 proposal for "national reconciliation and democratic unification" (*minjok hwahap minju
t'ongil pang'an*) was the first comprehensive proposal for unification by the ROK government. It envisaged the formation of a "consultative conference for national unification" consisting of representatives from North and South Korea, which would draft a
constitution for a unified Korea. When a draft should be approved
by the conference, it would be submitted to a referendum in all
parts of Korea.[30]

Elections will then be held in accordance with the provisions
of the new constitution with the aim of organizing a unified legislature, government, and state. Pending the realization of all these
measures, however, North and South must take steps to normalize
their bilateral relations and achieve national reconciliation. Chun
specifically proposed the conclusion of a "provisional agreement on
basic relations between South and North Korea" incorporating
seven principles. To cite but two of them, the two sides would recognize each other's existing political order and pledge not to interfere in each other's internal affairs, and they would exchange resident liaison missions headed by cabinet-rank representatives.

Roh Tae Woo followed suit by unveiling a comprehensive proposal of his own in September 1989. His proposal will be examined

in detail in the following section. The third change in South Korea's unification policy is related to the second—the growing salience of unification. The commitment to unification, as measured by a willingness to assign high priority to it, has varied from regime to regime in South Korea. As the level of commitment ostensibly peaked in the Sixth Republic, Roh Tae Woo's unification policy, therefore, merits a close examination.

The Unification Policy of the Sixth Republic

The inauguration of Roh Tae Woo as President of the ROK on February 25, 1988 marked the first peaceful transfer of power since the founding of the republic in August 1948. Roh was the first popularly elected president in sixteen years. Having won the presidential election of December 1987 with less than 37 percent of the effective vote, however, Roh could claim neither a solid mandate nor indisputable legitimacy. The need to produce tangible results, therefore, was no less pressing for Roh than it was for his predecessors.

Roh seemed to have decided to place top priority on both democratization and inter-Korean relations. Having committed himself to the goal of democratization in the historic declaration of June 29, 1987, as well as during the presidential campaign, Roh was honor-bound to press ahead with that task. Improving inter-Korean relations, preferably achieving a breakthrough, was a goal Roh apparently set on his own. He made that plain in a series of acts, beginning with his inaugural speech and culminating in the unveiling of the "Korean national community unification formula" in September 1989.

In his inaugural speech in February 1988, Roh proclaimed the beginning of an "era of dialogue and cooperation between South and North Korea." He indicated a willingness to "visit anywhere in the world and to engage in a sincere dialogue with anyone" in order to ensure peace on the Korean peninsula and expedite its reunification. He also vigorously stated his intention to pursue "northern diplomacy" with a view toward creating an environment conducive to Korean unification. Two months later, during his first press conference as president, Roh made explicit his determination to "pave the way for peaceful unification through reconciliation and cooperation between South and North Korea" during his term of office.[31]

Then, on July 7, 1988, Roh took the first significant step

toward achieving his goal: in a special statement, he outlined a policy aimed at transforming inter-Korean relations from confrontation to cooperation. Stressing the need for the two parts of the divided peninsula to work together to build a genuine *minjok kongdonch'e* ("national community"), Roh declared that South Korea would take a series of measures: (1) it would pursue an exchange of people in all walks of life between North and South; (2) it would redouble efforts to assist separated family members to locate, communicate, and reunite with one another; (3) it would encourage inter-Korean trade, treating the latter not as interstate trade but as trade within the same nation; (4) it would no longer oppose trade involving nonmilitary goods between its allies and friends on one side and North Korea on the other; (5) it hoped to replace counterproductive diplomatic competition with North Korea in the world arena with cooperation in pursuit of common interests; and (6) it would be willing to assist North Korea to improve relations with the United States, Japan, and other states that are friendly with Seoul. Seoul, for its part, would seek improved relations with the Soviet Union, China, and other socialist countries.[32]

Of the foregoing, the most productive proved to be the last item, which became the core of the Sixth Republic's *Nordpolitik*. As already noted, the latter's success owed to a conjunction of circumstances—impressive growth in South Korea's economic capability; the upsurge of pragmatism in China, the Soviet Union, and Eastern European countries; and the opportunities and publicity generated by the Seoul Olympic Games, which were held from September 19 to October 2, 1988.

Against the preceding backdrop, Roh unveiled a comprehensive proposal for unification in a speech to the ROK National Assembly on September 11, 1989. Officially labeled the "Korean National Community Unification Formula," it became the second comprehensive blueprint for unification in the ROK's history. It was predicated on the premise that the building of a true national community must precede any serious attempt at the creation of a single political entity. The Korean National Community (KNC) formula envisages an interim stage in which North and South Korea will form a loose union, to be called the *Nambuk yonhap* (Korean Commonwealth).[33]

The Korean Commonwealth will have a number of executive and administrative organs: a Council of Presidents, a Council of Ministers, a Council of Representatives, a joint secretariat, and resident liaison missions. The Council of Presidents, consisting of the chief executives of the two Korean states, will be the highest decision-making organ. The Council of Ministers will consist of approximately ten cabinet ministers from each side, including prime ministers. Working through five standing committees—(1) humanitarian affairs, (2) political affairs and diplomacy, (3) economic affairs, (4) military affairs, and (5) social and cultural affairs—the Council will deal with the whole gamut of problems ranging from the reunion of separated family members to arms control.

The Council of Representatives, which will comprise about 100 legislators from each side, will draft a constitution for a unified Korea, devise methods and procedures to attain unification, and advise the Council of Ministers. After the Council of Representatives has agreed on a draft of the constitution of a unified Korea, it was to be "finalized and promulgated through democratic methods and procedures." That was to be followed by general elections to "form a unified legislature and a unified government." The joint secretariat, which will be located in a Peace Zone within the Demilitarized Zone, will provide logistical support to the various organs and oversee the implementation of decisions made by them. Resident liaison missions will be established in Seoul and Pyongyang, respectively.

The KNC formula sets forth a number of basic guidelines that would govern the unification process. First, unification shall be guided by three principles: independence, peace, and democracy. Second, the unified Korea shall be "a single national community in which every citizen is his own master, that is to say, a democratic nation that guarantees the human rights of every individual and his right to seek happiness." The unified Korea, moreover, must be a single nation in every sense of the word, not a confederation of two states with differing ideologies and political systems. Third, the legislature of the unified Korea shall be a "bicameral parliament composed of an upper house based on regional representation and a lower house based on population."

To no one's surprise, North Korea has categorically rejected the KNC formula, asserting that its own formula—the proposal for the establishment of the Democratic Confederal Republic of Koryo—is the only realistic and reasonable blueprint for unification. Nonetheless, several features of the KNC formula can be said to have been indirectly incorporated in the inter-Korean agreements that materialized two years later.

In December 1991, Seoul and Pyongyang signed two agreements that may well have momentous consequences. A product of five rounds of "high-level talks"—in which both delegations were headed by their respective prime ministers—the first agreement, known as "the Agreement on Reconciliation, Non-aggression, and Exchanges and Cooperation Between the North and the South," laid the groundwork for the institutionalization of the inter-Korean dialogue, spawning many structures that are not too dissimilar from those envisaged by the KNC formula. The second agreement, the Joint Declaration on the Denuclearization of the Korean Peninsula, complements the first. Both entered into force in February 1992.[34]

The first agreement, which is usually referred to as the North-South basic agreement, resembles an international treaty, for it contains a preamble and numbered articles, and was signed by the prime ministers of both sides, and calls for an exchange of instruments of ratification before its formal entry into force. There is, however, a disclaimer in its preamble stating that the relations between North and South Korea are not interstate relations but "special relations that arise provisionally" in the process of working toward unification.

Noteworthy provisions include: the explicit recognition of each other's system, the acceptance of the principle of noninterference in each other's internal affairs, the pledge "not to engage in any act aimed at destroying or overthrowing each other," the commitment to work toward transforming the armistice into a state of peace and to abide by the armistice agreement pending attainment of that goal, and the pledge to cease confrontation and competition on the international stage and to work together in the common national interest.

The basic agreement also enumerates several concrete measures to promote mutual exchanges and cooperation. It expresses the common determination of both sides to engage in the joint development of resources, the exchange of goods, and other forms of economic cooperation. It provides for the linking of railways and highways as well as for the opening of sea and air routes between the two sides. It also calls for the establishment of postal and communication links and for "free travels and contacts" between the inhabitants of the two parts of Korea. It stresses the urgency of reuniting an estimated ten million family members who have been separated by the division and the war and of solving other humanitarian problems.

As mentioned previously, the basic agreement has spawned a number of structures—North-South liaison offices in Panmunjom;

subcommittees dealing with political affairs, military affairs, and exchanges and cooperation; and joint committees on military affairs and on economic exchanges and cooperation. To this list should be added the North-South Joint Nuclear Control Commission, which came into being pursuant to the denuclearization declaration.

In the latter both sides pledged (1) not to test, manufacture, receive, possess, deploy, or use nuclear weapons; (2) to utilize nuclear energy for peaceful purposes only; (3) not to possess either nuclear reprocessing facilities or facilities for enriching uranium; and (4) to allow mutual inspections of facilities chosen by each other in accordance with the mutual agreement and pursuant to procedures and methods to be determined by the North-South joint nuclear commission.

While all of these structures, save the joint military committee and the joint economic committee, have held numerous meetings, very little progress has been made in terms of substantive issues. In fact, the positions taken by the two sides in the joint nuclear control commission diverged so sharply that the commission found itself in a deadlock. The most intractable of all the issues was the nuclear inspection issue—namely, whether and how to conduct mutual inspections of each other's nuclear facilities. That impasse fueled the suspicions, shared by Washington and Seoul, about a clandestine North Korean program to develop nuclear weapons, prompting them to announce that they would resume their annual joint military exercise, code-named Team Spirit, in 1993 after suspending it in the preceding year.[35]

This in turn angered North Korea, leading it to suspend the high-level talks and all negotiations with South Korea under the rubric of the various subcommittees and joint committees. The situation deteriorated sharply in February 1993, when North Korea rebuffed an IAEA request to inspect two sites in Yongbyon, a nuclear complex about 60 miles north of Pyongyang, where, according to Western intelligence, "nuclear waste from the reprocessing of the plutonium may be buried." When the IAEA responded by demanding a "special inspection"—an extraordinary procedure to "compel the opening of a site that a country has not declared as part of any nuclear program"—Pyongyang not only rejected the demand but also announced that it would withdraw from the NPT altogether. The IAEA board then voted to refer the matter to the UN Security Council.[36]

It should be noted that the unfolding of the dispute over special inspections coincided with the political transition in Seoul.

While the decision to resume the Team Spirit exercise was made during the Sixth Republic, its actual implementation did not occur until after the inauguration of Kim Young Sam's Civilian Government. We now turn to a brief discussion of the latter's unification policy.

The Unification Policy of the
Kim Young Sam Government

In his inaugural address on February 25, 1993, the new ROK president Kim Young Sam pledged that he would spare no effort to realize national reconciliation and unification, the "tasks that have been entrusted to me by history and the nation." He hastened to add, however, that what South Korea needed most was not a sentimental preoccupation with unification but the building of a national consensus on unification.[37]

He then called on his counterpart in North Korea, using the latter's official title "President Kim Il Sung," to assume the posture of genuine cooperation. Noting that the world is entering an era of peace and cooperation in which multifaceted cooperation is occurring between different nations, Kim Young Sam reminded Kim Il Sung that neither allies nor ideology can surpass the bonds of ethnicity; he used the Korean word *minjok*, which is usually translated as "nation." "If President Kim [Il Sung] truly values the nation more [than anything else] and if he truly wants a genuine reconciliation between our brethren in the South and the North and unification," Kim Young Sam said, "we can meet anytime and anywhere to discuss these matters."

Kim Young Sam expressed confidence that he and the North Korean president could "solve all the problems" by approaching them from the standpoint of the same nation or common ethnicity. Kim Young Sam then predicted that "our fatherland will be unified and become the homeland of freedom and peace within this century."

While the generalities contained in an inaugural speech did not constitute a policy, what was clear is that neither drastic change nor bold initiatives were in store. Continuity, in other words, was the hallmark of the Kim Young Sam government's unification policy. As noted, the joint U.S.-ROK military exercise, Team Spirit, occurred on schedule. The new administration also explicitly reaffirmed its predecessor's policy of linking economic cooperation to the nuclear issue.

Signs of change, however, were not totally absent. In some ways, in fact, notable changes began to occur. In a word, the Kim Young Sam government initially struck a more conciliatory posture toward North Korea than its predecessors. Two examples will suffice. First, one of the first acts it took was to allow the repatriation of Yi In-mo to North Korea. Yi was a seventy-six-year-old former North Korean soldier who had spent over thirty-five years in South Korean prisons. Yi's refusal to renounce communism had been a key factor in his prolonged detention. After his plight was reported in the South Korean press, the North Korean authorities located his wife, daughter, and grandchildren in the North. North Korea's demand for his repatriation had been a contentious issue in the inter-Korean dialogue; Pyongyang even torpedoed an exchange of home-visiting groups in August 1992 in retaliation for Seoul's continuing refusal to meet its demand. Given this background, the Kim Young Sam government's decision to allow Yi's return to North Korea was a goodwill gesture of major proportions.

Another example of the Kim government's conciliatory posture concerns its initial handling of the crisis precipitated by Pyongyang's announcement on March 12, 1993, that it would withdraw from the Nuclear Non-proliferation Treaty. Since the treaty requires a three-month notice for withdrawal, there was still time to persuade Pyongyang to change its mind. And that was precisely the approach the Kim government took. Although the U.S. reportedly favored a hard-line response, the Kim government worked hard to convince both Washington and Tokyo that diplomacy should precede sanctions.

In this connection, it is worth noting that Kim Young Sam's first cabinet included former academics who were known to have relatively moderate views on how to deal with North Korea. The Minister of National Unification, who concurrently serves as a deputy prime minister, was Han Wan Sang, a former sociology professor at Seoul National University. The views Han had articulated while he was an academic were markedly moderate and conciliatory toward the North. Also reputed to be of moderate persuasion was Han Sung-joo, who served as Kim Young Sam's foreign minister for nearly two years. Han, who is not related to Han Wan-sang, was a former political science professor at Korea University.

The Kim Young Sam government's blueprint for unification, first unveiled in July 1993, was all but indistinguishable from the KNC formula of the Sixth Republic. It embraced a "three-phased approach to unification" guided by three principles. The three phases were (1) reconciliation and cooperation, (2) the Korean Commonwealth, and (3) one state, one nation. The three guiding principles were (1) democratic national consensus, (2) coexistence and coprosperity, and (3) national well-being.[38]

In August 1994, President Kim Young Sam introduced a slightly modified version of his government's unification formula. Renamed the "three-stage unification formula for the creation of Korean National Community," the new version retained the three stages but omitted any explicit reference to the three principles. It made clear, however, that there would be no place in the unified Korea Seoul envisions for North Korean–style socialism. For the values of "freedom, democracy and well-being for all" would become the foundation stone of the unified state.[39]

If we construe unification policy broadly so as to subsume the entire gamut of the two Korean states' policies toward each other, then there were other developments bearing on the Kim Young Sam government's unification policy worth noting as well. In a departure from the generally conciliatory approach it had taken toward the North, the Kim Young Sam government struck an unmistakably hard-line posture toward Pyongyang in the wake of Kim Il Sung's death in July 1994.

Not only did Kim Young Sam fail to issue any statement of condolences but dealt harshly with South Korean citizens who attempted to pay their respects to the deceased North Korean leader. On the very day when Pyongyang was holding a memorial service for Kim Il Sung, moreover, the Kim Young Sam government published Russian archival material proving that Kim Il Sung had been the principal architect of the Soviet-backed invasion of the South in June 1950. All this infuriated the North Korean leadership immensely. Its sense of outrage was magnified by a sharp contrast between Seoul's response to Kim Il Sung's death on the one hand and those of Washington and Tokyo on the other. Both President Clinton and Prime Minister Murayama expressed their condolences to the North Korean people for the death of their leader. Clinton went so far as to praise the late Kim Il Sung for his "leadership" in helping to resuscitate the U.S.-DPRK high-level talks on the nuclear issue.[40]

The death of Kim Il Sung had a chilling effect on inter-Korean relations. Were it not for his sudden death, an unprecedented summit meeting between him and Kim Young Sam would have materialized, which might have opened the way for a new era of amity and cooperation on the Korean peninsula. An agreement had been reached for such a summit in negotiations held in Panmunjom ten days preceding Kim Il Sung's death between Kim Yong Sun, the chairman of the Unification Policy Committee of the DPRK Supreme People's Assembly and Lee Hong Koo, the then deputy prime minister and unification minister of the ROK. According to the agreement, the first summit meeting was scheduled to occur in Pyongyang from July 25 to 27, 1994.[41]

In June 1995, a stunning development occurred, a first in the annals of inter-Korean relations. Pyongyang requested Seoul to provide free rice to deal with serious food shortages. Actually, what must surely have been a humiliating decision by Pyongyang had been dictated by a combination of dire necessity and Seoul's policy. Seoul had asked Tokyo, to which Pyongyang had initially turned for help, not to heed Pyongyang's request until and unless Pyongyang first received rice from Seoul. Inter-Korean dialogue, which had been suspended since July 1994, resumed in Beijing, producing an agreement for the provision of 150,000 tons of rice by Seoul. It was quickly followed by a Tokyo-Pyongyang agreement, signed in Tokyo, under which Tokyo would supply Pyongyang with 300,000 tons of rice, of which a half would be free and the remainder would be sold on a deferred payment basis.[42]

During the implementation of the Seoul-Pyongyang rice deal, however, two incidents erupted that served to dampen the prospects for a new inter-Korean rapprochement. First, a South Korean ship carrying the first shipment of rice to the North was forced by the North Korean authorities to replace a South Korean flag with a North Korean flag before entering the port of Ch'ongjin. After North Korea apologized for the incident, South Korea resumed its shipment of rice. Then, a month later, North Koreans perpetrated another incident in Ch'ongjin. A South Korean ship that had just delivered rice was detained, with its entire crew, on grounds that a crew member had taken photographs of Ch'ongjin harbor, an act defined by North Korea as espionage. This time it was South Korea that was compelled to wire an apology to North Korea in order to obtain the release and return of the ship and its crew. These incidents triggered an avalanche of outrage and criticism on the part of politicians, journalists, and ordinary citizens in the South. They helped to dim the chances not only of Seoul's providing more rice to Pyongyang, which the latter wanted, but also of government-level economic cooperation and exchanges between the two sides, which Seoul would have liked to see develop.[43]

In the aftermath of a severe flood which, according to Pyongyang, adversely affected 5.2 million people and caused damage estimated at 1.5 billion dollars, North and South resumed dialogue in Beijing in late September. Seoul, however, set preconditions for discussing the issue or additional supply of rice and aid to flood victims: the release of a South Korean fishing vessel and its crew being detained in the North as well as an inquiry into what the South suspects is a kidnapping of a South Korean clergyman from Yanbian, China by North Korean agents. Pyongyang's refusal to meet these conditions led to an impasse.[44]

In sum, the unification policy of the Kim Young Sam government was a continuation of its predecessor's. If any change was detectable, it was a movement in the direction of moderation, reconciliation, and responsiveness vis-à-vis the North. The bottom line, however, was that the Civilian Government was no less committed to the overriding goal of national security and peace than any of its predecessors.

The "Sunshine" Policy of the
Kim Dae Jung Government

The emergence of the Kim Dae Jung government in February 1998 marked a new watershed in South Korea's transition to democracy. For the first time in the fifty-year history of the ROK, power was transferred from the ruling party to the opposition camp in a peaceful fashion. Not only did this stunning development trigger a metamorphosis of the structure and dynamics of power in South Korea but it also paved the way for change in South Korea's posture and policy toward the North.

Kim Dae Jung was and remains proponent of a "three-stage unification" formula. Upholding three principles of "self-reliance, peace, and democracy," the formula posits the stages of (1) confederation, (2) federation, and (3) the formation of either a centralized system of government or several autonomous regional governments on the model of the United States or Germany. The first stage in this formula resembles the Korean commonwealth in the proposals of Kim's predecessors, while the second stage has some similarties with Pyongyang's proposal for the establishment of a Democratic Confederal Republic of Koryo.[45]

Against this background, Kim Dae Jung unveiled his "Sunshine" policy—a policy aimed at inducing change in North Korean policy toward the South through conciliation and displays of good-will. Such a policy is clearly distinguishable from one of trying to force change in North Korean policy by pressure, display of force, and other hard-line measures. The idea and phrase are derived from an Aesopian fable in which, in a contest to determine which was the stronger, the Sun, not the Wind, succeeds in getting a man to take off his heavy coat. The policy, according to Kim Dae Jung, is guided by three principles:

> First, we will never tolerate armed provocation of any kind.
> Second, we do not have any intention to undermine or absorb North Korea.
> Third, we will actively pursue reconciliation and cooperation between the North and the South beginning with those areas which can be most easily agreed upon.[46]

Any arguments that the sunshine policy was a continuation of the policy of Kim's predecessors was quickly dispelled when the Kim Dae Jung government took steps to facilitate nongovernmental exchanges between the North and the South. It began to lift or reduce restrictions on travel and investments in the North by South Korean citizens. The most dramatic example of such policy was a sharp increase in the number of South Korean visitors to the North. With the opening of the scenic *Kumkang* (diamond) mountain to South Korean tourists, tens of thousands of South Korean citizens are visiting the North every month. The North has a huge financial stake in the tourist program operated by Hyundai group, for it earns $25 million a month—which may well be the largest single source of foreign exchange earnings for the cash-starved DPRK.[47]

Official contacts between Seoul and Pyongyang, however, remained minimal. Direct negotiations have not produced any tangible results. Participation in multilateral negotiations in the context of KEDO and the four-party talks involving the two Korean states, the United States, and China has thus far failed to bring about any measurable gain for inter-Korean relations at the governmental level.

Notwithstanding the absence of reciprocity, however, the Kim Dae Jung government patiently pursued its sunshine policy with the support of its principal ally, the United States, and major "partner," Japan. Should the North persist in spurning the South's overtures, however, a modification, even a jettisoning, of the policy cannot be ruled out.

Conclusion

How do the foreign and unification policies of South Korea examined in the preceding pages stack up against the policies of other states? While foreign policy is a *sine qua non* for all states, unification policy, obviously, is necessary only for divided nations, of which only two remain in the post–Cold War era: Korea and China.

To consider foreign policy first, the resilience of the strategic goals—legitimacy, security, and development—in South Korean policy is somewhat unusual, even though the same is true of North Korean policy as well. In most states legitimacy is not a major factor in foreign policy. While security is the common concern of all states, its salience is a function of the threat each state faces. Finally, development becomes a major foreign policy goal only for developing countries, provided that its leadership is development-oriented and willing to make the necessary sacrifices to attain it.

Pursuit of legitimacy and security by Seoul and Pyongyang alike has produced a zero-sum game in which one side can gain only at the expense of the other. Quest for security, in particular, has spawned a vicious circle of arms race, with deleterious consequences for both sides in terms of utilizing their limited resources.

This is why unification policy, of which the short-term goal is the reduction of tensions and promotion of exchanges and cooperation, is so important for both Korean states. While changes in Korea's external environment have been and continue to be the major variables in the equation, internal developments in South Korea have also helped measurably to increase the pragmatism and efficacy of its policy. The impasse in inter-Korean relations that has developed since late 1992 may be but a passing phenomenon. The marked increase in the moderation of Seoul's policy under Kim Dae Jung's "people's government," coupled with the continuing economic difficulties bedeviling the North as well as the latter's capacity for pragmatic adaptation, creates the hope that the Korean peninsula, too, will soon enter the post–Cold War era.

Notes

1. U.S. Department of State, *The Record of Korean Unification, 1943–1960: Narrative Summary with Principal Documents*, Department of State Publication No. 7084, Far Eastern Series No. 101 (Washington, DC: Government Printing Office, 1961), pp. 10–11, 76.

2. Choson Minjujuui Inmin Konghwaguk Kwahagwon Yoksa Yon'-guso [History Research center of DPRK], *Choson t'ongsa* [A General History of Korea] (Pyongyang: Kwahagwon Chulpansa, 1959), 3 vols., pp. 109–110. This official history calls the May 1948 elections in the south, which elected a constituent National Assembly that in turn elected Syngman Rhee as the first ROK president, a "complete shame." The elections that were held in the north in August 1948, on the other hand, were "free and fair," drawing 99.97 percent of eligible voters in the north and 77.52 percent of qualified voters in the south, this source asserts.

3. For a chronological list of countries with which the ROK and the DPRK established diplomatic relations from 1948 to 1983, see Byung Chul Koh, *The Foreign Policy Systems of North and South Korea* (Berkeley: University of California Press, 1984), pp. 11–13.

4. For the texts of the two resolutions, see United Nations documents, A/C.1/L.709, 24 September 1975 and A/C.1/L.708/Rev.1*, 13 October 1975.

5. Koh, *The Foreign Policy Systems of North and South Korea*, p. 211.

6. Ibid.

7. Donald S. Macdonald, *The Koreans: Contemporary Politics and Society*, 2nd ed. (Boulder, CO: Westview Press, 1990), p. 51.

8. *The Korea Newsreview*, November 28, 1992, pp. 4–5.

9. *Joongang Ilbo*, March 11, 1999.

10. This has prompted North Korea to bemoan what it saw as both a sellout and a betrayal by an erstwhile great power and friend. Nonpyongwon, "Ttalla-ro P'algo Sanun 'Oegyo Kwan'gye'" ["Diplomatic Relations'" That Are Sold and Bought with Dollars], *Nodong Sinmun* [Labor News], October 5, 1990. *Nodong Sinmun* is the daily organ of North Korea's ruling party, the Workers' Party of Korea.

11. U.S. Senate, Armed Services Committee, "Briefing Remarks by General Robert W. RisCassi, Commander United States Forces Korea, Commander In Chief United Nations Command, Commander in Chief Combined Forces Command, before the Armed Services Committee United States Senate, 4 March 1992," p. 10.

12. For the text of the framework agreement, see *Korea Focus* 2:3 (Sept.–Oct. 1994), pp. 166–68; for a Korean language version, as translated by North Korea, see T'ong'il Sinbo, Oct. 19, 1994, p. 1.

13. See the text of the agreement on KEDO in *Nambuk Taehwa* [South-North Dialogue], no. 62 (July 1995) (Seoul: Office of the South-North Dialogue, National Unification Board, 1995), pp. 85–101.

14. Ibid., pp. 58–59.

15. *Chosun Ilbo* (Seoul), July 29, 1997.

16. Ibid., August 20, 1997.

17. Jun Kwan-woo, "North Korea Settlement Eases Tension, Heralds Another Series of Negotiations," *Korea Herald*, March 18, 1999.

18. Youngnok Koo, "The Conduct of Foreign Affairs," in Edward R. Wright, ed., *Korean Politics in Transition* (Seattle: University of Washington Press, 1975), p. 221.

19. Ministry of Foreign Affairs, *Han'guk Oegyo Samsimnyon:1948–1978* [Thirty Years of South Korean Diplomacy: 1948–1978] (1979), pp. 117–118.

20. For an analysis of the widespread domestic opposition to the diplomatic normalization, see Kwan Bong Kim, *The Korea-Japan Treaty Crisis and the Instability of the Korean Political System* (New York: Praeger Publishers, 1971).

21. Statistics Office, *Han'guk Chuyo Kyongje Chipyo* [Major Statistics of the Korean Economy] (Feburary1995), pp. 242–48.

22. For an insider's account of Rhee's stormy relations with the United States, see Robert T. Oliver, *Syngman Rhee and American Involvement in Korea, 1942–1960* (Seoul: Panmun Book Co., 1978), especially chapters 18–20. Oliver was an adviser to Rhee for many years.

23. *New York Times*, March 30 and April 22, 1993; *Hanguk Ilbo*, March 31, 1993.

24. Japan, Ministry of Foreign Affairs, Asia Bureau, Northeast Asia Division, *Kankoku keizai kankei deta-shu* [A Collection of Data Relating to the Korean Economy] (July 1989).

25. The eight governments are as follows: the First Republic (1948–1960), the Second Republic (1960–1961), the Third Republic (1963–1972), the Fourth Republic (1972–1979), the Fifth Republic (1980–1988), the Sixth Republic (1988–1993), the Civilian Government [*Munmin Chongbu*] (1993–1998), and the People's Government [*Kingmin-ui Chongbu*] (1998–).

26. Ministry of Foreign Affairs, *Han'guk Oegyo Samsimnyon: 1948–1978* [Thirty Years of South Korean Diplomacy: 1948–1978] (1979), pp. 62–75.

27. W. D. Reeve, *The Republic of Korea: A Political and Economic Study* (London: Oxford University Press, 1963), p. 147.

28. Han-Kyo Kim ed., *Reunification of Korea: Fifty Basic Documents* (Washington, DC: Institute for Asian Studies, 1972), pp. 45–46.

29. Ministry of Foreign Affairs, *Han'guk Oegyo Samsimnyon 1948–1978*, pp. 78–79.

30. The text of Chun Doo Hwan's speech to the ROK National Assembly on January 22, 1982 in which he unveiled the proposal was published by Kukt'o T'ong'il-won, Nambuk Taehwa Samuguk [The Office of South-North Dialogue], *Nambuk Taehwa Paekso* [White Paper on the South-North Dialogue] (1988), pp. 481–85.

31. Unification Board, T'ong'il Chongch'aek-sil, ed. *1990 T'ong'il paekso* [1990 White Paper on Unification] (1990), pp. 45–46. In 1990, the ROK National Unification Board dropped "national" from its name. In Korean, its name changed from *Kukt'o T'ong'il-won* to *T'ong'il-won*.

32. Ibid., pp. 300–302.

33. Kukt'o T'ong'il-won, *Hanminjok Kongdongch'e Tong'il Pang'an: Iroke T'ong'il Hajanun Kosida* [The Korean National Community Unification Formula: This Is How We Can Attain Unification] (1989), pp. 40–48. As we shall see below, pending its revision by the Kim Young Sam government, the KNC formula remains as a key component of Seoul's unification policy; hence we are using the present tense here.

34. National Unification Board, Nambuk Taehwa Samuguk [The Office of the South-North Dialogue], ed. *Nambuk Taehwa* [South-North Dialogue], no. 54 (1992).

35. See the joint statement of the Twenty-Fourth Security Consultative Meeting between the United States and the ROK held in Washington on October 7 and 8, 1992 in *Korea Herald*, October 9, 1992.

36. *New York Times*, February 1, 6, 11, and 14, 1993; April 2, 1993.

37. *Hanguk Ilbo*, February 25, 1993, evening edition. The full text of Kim's speech appears on p. 2.

38. *Nambuk Taehwa* [South-North Dialogue], no. 58 (Oct. 1993), pp. 5–20.

39. Ibid., no. 60 (Oct. 1994), pp. 47–72; 127–38.

40. *New York Times*, July 10, 1994. For Pyongyang's condemnation of the Kim Young Sam government for what it called "inhuman" (*pan-illyunjok*) acts in the wake of Kim Il Sung's death, see *T'ong'il sinbo*, July 30 and August 6, 1994.

41. *Nambuk Taehwa* [South-North Dialogue], no. 60 (May–September 1994), pp. 7–35.

42. Ibid., no. 62 (December 1994–June 1995), p. 30; *Japan Times Weekly International Edition*, July 3–9, 1995, p. 3.

43. *Hankuk Ilbo*, June 30 and 31, July 3, August 9–10, 1995.

44. Ibid., September 28–30, 1995.

45. Kim Dae Jung, *"Three Stage" Approach to Reunification: Focusing on the South-North Confederal Stage*, Translated by Rhee Tong-chin (Los Angeles: Center for Multiethnic and Transnational Studies, University of Southern California, 1997), pp. 1–5.

46. Chong Wa Dae, *Che 15–dae Taet'ongnyong Ch'wi'imsa: Kungnan Kokbokkwa Chaedoyak-ui Sae sidae rule Yopsida* [The Inaugural Address by the Fifteenth President: Let Us Open a New Era in Which We Overcome Our National Difficulties and Make a Leap Anew] (February 25, 1998).

47. Ministry of Korean Unification, *'98 nyondo Taebuk Chongch'a P'yongka* [An Appraisal of the Policy Toward the North during 1998] (January 4, 1999).

10

ह&

Understanding the
North Korean Political Framework

Sung Chul Yang

*Utopian socialism differed from "scientific" social-
ism in degree rather than in kind.*

—Joseph A. Schumpeter[1]

*"When I think about socialism, the image that comes
to mind is an abyss between ideology and its implementation," another (Polish high school senior) student wrote. . . . The imprint on Central Eastern
Europe of forty years of socialism is nothing like
what communism's intellectual founder, Karl Marx,
had in mind. His utopian ideology has been virtually obliterated as a motivating force.*

—Dan Fisher[2]

Approaches to the Study of North Korean Politics

Directly and indirectly, the current North Korean political system has been greatly impaired by the metamorphosis of communism in Eastern Europe and the former Soviet Union, as well as by
the Chinese economic reforms that had begun more than a decade
earlier.

The ongoing metamorphosis of communism differs fundamentally from the earlier reform initiatives led by Tito and Khrushchev,

or Deng Xiaoping.[3] If the early revisionist efforts were political and economic measures to correct the failings of the socialist system without questioning the basic tenets of orthodox Marxism and Leninism, the present transformation of erstwhile socialist countries in Eastern Europe and the former Soviet Union began with the sober realization that some seventy-year old Marxist-Leninist political and economic experiments had abjectly failed. In brief, if the earlier reform or revisionist measures were communist *system-defensive*, the present changes are *system-replacing*. A towering irony is that contrary to the orthodox Marxian materialistic interpretations of history, the current transition is from socialism to capitalism, not the reverse. Whether we distinguish, as Burawoy asserts, Marxism from "Soviet Marxism, its most degenerate form," and further separate "the demise of state socialism" from "the viability of Marxist project,"[4] the direction and the content of political and economic changes in the former Soviet Union and Eastern Europe certainly resemble the embryonic forms of democratic pluralism and free market system.

The four remaining communist countries—China, Vietnam, North Korea, and Cuba—still cling, officially at least, to the "socialist path"; but in reality they, too, have been changing. China since the late 1970s and Vietnam since the late 1980s have cast off their erstwhile militant revolutionary paths, although their one-party political dictatorships still sputters along. Meanwhile, only North Korea's Kim Jong Il and Cuba's Fidel Castro appear more defiant in their rhetoric, but they, too, are at a crossroads. The question, then, is will a defiant communist "gang of four" survive or will it sooner or later meet the same fate as the fallen communist stars, Eastern Europe and the former Soviet Union? Explanations for the collapse of communism abound, although the future of the remaining four is uncertain. Take, for example, the October 1991 issue of *World Politics,* which dealt with the demise of communism in Eastern Europe and the former Soviet Union. None of the six authors in the issue raised, let alone explained, the reasons for the apparent durability of the four remaining communist states. Some common features the four share can be illuminated as partial explanations for their durability. First, their communist systems are, with the exception of North Korea, primarily *indigenous*. The communist regime in North Korea, like the former communist states in Eastern Europe, came into being under the auspices of the Soviet military authorities. Kim Il Sung was not simply a Soviet puppet, however. All absurd exaggerations and outright fabrications aside, Kim was involved verifiably in anti-Japanese guerrilla activities for decades, granting him respectable credentials for his rule. The Comintern and the former Soviet Union directly or indirectly assisted these four nations to achieve communist triumph, but again with the exception of North Korea, they won the communist victory primarily through protracted internal struggles.

Second, all three Asian communist states possess a long tradition of "Oriental despotism," making Western democratic ideas and political traditions new and alien to their political history. When compared to their Eastern European and Soviet counterparts, these countries lack democratic political experience, experimentation, and movements.

Third, all three remaining Asian communist states have deep-rooted Buddhist and Confucian traditions. Though introduced, Christianity was, like democratic ideas and thought, a relatively modern addition to old religious practices and belief systems.

Finally, with the exception of Cuba, the countries' geographic contiguity and their relatively intimate historical, cultural, and ethnic affinity need to be pointed out. The traditional Chinese center-periphery framework, manifested in terms of "middle kingdom and barbarian states," was replaced by the new communist patron-client arrangement.[5] The Chinese proclivity to claim hegemony in the region stems from a deep-rooted historical legacy. The Sino-Soviet and Sino-Vietnamese conflicts can be understood from this perspective: as long as the present Chinese political system persists, so will the Vietnamese and the North Korean systems. It is unlikely that China will sit idly while its two remaining "fraternal" contiguous socialist states become politically extinct. In China, the "Long Marchers" of the Chinese Revolution, including Deng Xiao Ping, have passed away or have been replaced by second- and third-generation leaders, and similar generational leadership changes are occurring in Vietnam and North Korea. Uncertainties surrounding these leadership changes will undoubtedly bear profound implications. This is evident in the context of succession politics in North Korea. The death of Kim Il Sung in 1994 opened a new era under Kim Jong Il, but still no significant political changes have emerged. The North Korean political system persists for now, although precariously.

Turning to the issue of North Korean studies, pro-North Korean propaganda materials, published and disseminated by the North Korean publishing houses, abound. Numerous anti-North Korean publications have been printed in South Korea as well.

Despite the proliferation of pro-and anti-North Korean propaganda materials and "studies," an objective, scholarly analysis of the North's political system has yet to be developed. Nevertheless, four approaches to the study of North Korean political system can be identified: historiographic studies, factional models, system analysis, and totalitarian approaches.

Historiographic studies on the North Korean political system, by far the most abundant, take a basically historical and descriptive approach. The trailblazing works of Chang-sun Kim, Dae-sook Suh, Chong-sik Lee, and others are notable.[6] The approach is, by definition, rich in historical details but lacks explicit analytic framework and rigor. Still, the contributions of the historiographic studies are significant in that they serve as the basic materials for more rigorous analytic studies.

Factionalism as an explanatory model of North Korean politics is not new; it is one of the salient features of Korean politics. Factionalist approaches may vary among scholars in their emphasis and interpretations. Some see factionalism in North Korean politics as the corporatist manifestation of traditional Korean political culture.[7] Others view it as a variant of political conflict among power elite.[8] While the former stresses certain cultural and social traits of groups and individuals, the latter focuses on the dynamics of power itself. Still others interpret factionalism as a by-product of communist political culture.[9] The factionalist approaches are by definition limited in that they may be able to explain the political behavior of the ruling elite in North Korea (and South Korea), but cannot analyze the North Korean political system.

The systems approach denotes the studies on North Korean politics that apply to the systems model.[10] Unlike the factionalist model, the systems approach explains the North Korean political system as a whole in a coherent and comprehensive manner, but underestimates both the peculiarities and the unique attributes of the communist political system. Still, studies on North Korean politics based on the systems approach, though very few in number, are by far analytically the most rigorous.[11]

As an alternative to the three approaches outlined above, I would like to suggest a totalitarianism model.

Totalitarianism as a Model

The North Korean political system represents a classical example of Wiatr's *monoparty* system or Sartori's *totalitarian uni-*

partism in that only the Workers Party of Korea (WPK) is legally permitted to exist.[12] On paper, two other "fraternal parties" exist—the *Ch'ondoist Ch'ong-u* party and the Korean Social Democratic Party—but they do not contest elections. In this sense, the WPK can be classified as being what Wiatr coins a *hegemonic* party. In fact, the WPK is the only party that governs North Korea; the "fraternal parties," along with other parapolitical organizations, have been nothing more than propaganda outfits (see Table 10.1).

In socialist states, opposition parties are either outlawed or eclipsed by the ruling parties. As Rush points out, while communism does not sanction an *opposition* (a group that stands just outside the portals of power and actively restrains the government), it cannot always prevent the existence of an *alternative* to the government (a group of prestigious individuals that stands ready to replace the government and has a basis of support).[13] Since the late 1960s, such an alternative in North Korea has virtually disappeared. When Kim Il Sung took power, he purged actual and potential political rivals within the WPK. By the late 1960s, all factions—the Soviet Group, the Yonan Group, the Workers' Party of

Table 10.1
Parties and Parapolitical Organizations in North Korea

Workers' Party of Korea
Korean Social Democratic Party
Ch'ondoist Ch'ong-u Party
Central Committee of the Democratic Front for the Unification of the Fatherland
Committee for the Peaceful Reunification of the Fatherland
General Federation of Trade Unions of Korea
League of Socialist Working Youth of Korea
Union of Agricultural Working People of Korea
Korean Democratic Women's Union
Korean General Federation of the Unions of Literature and Arts
Korean Journalists' Union
Korean General Federation of Industrial Technology
Central Guidance Committee of the Korean Ch'ondoists' Association
Korean Buddhist Federation
Consultative Council of Former South Korean Politicians in the North for the Promotion of Peaceful Reunification
Korean Democratic Lawyers' Association
Korean Students' Committee
Korean Committee for Solidarity with World People
Korean National Peace Committee

Source: Pyongyang Times, January 18, 1983

South Korea Group, and the domestic Group—were eliminated, except for Kim's own Partisan Group within the WPK. From this standpoint, the WPK's 1980 decision to groom Kim Il Sung's eldest son, Kim Jong Il, as the official successor to his father can be seen, among other things, as an attempt to fill the political vacuum created by the death of the senior Kim.

While North Korea shares several basic features with other erstwhile socialist countries, it also possesses unique political characteristics and practices that deviate significantly from its former fraternal socialist countries. In what follows, both common and deviant elements of the North Korean political system will be discussed in detail as they are related to its durability.

Common Elements: Promise versus Practice

The present North Korean political system is inherently a totalitarian socialist state. As in the remaining socialist countries, the governing party, the WPK, is the official party; no other parties are permitted to compete in the political arena. No political ideas or ideologies are allowed to circulate except for the governing ideology sanctioned by the WPK; Marxism-Leninism and Kim Il Sungism (or *juche* idealogy). At the core of Kim Il Sungism stands *juche*, Article 3 of the 1992 revised DPRK Socialist Constitution. The WPK's control of the armed forces, public security and intelligence apparatus, mass media and mass communication, education, and parapolitical mass organizations is nearly complete. State ownership of the means of production, centralized economic planning, management, production, investment, and distribution are elements that North Korea shares in common with other former socialist countries. In view of the above, the features of North Korea common to those of any socialist country can be identified as follows.

Marxism-Leninism

All socialist countries, past and present, have at one point declared Marxism-Leninism as their all-encompassing official ideology. Marxism-Leninism includes the dictatorship of the proletariat, the socialist ownership of the means of production, class struggle, the collectivist principle which is the leading and guiding role of the communist party, the principle of democratic centralism, the new socialist way of life, and proletarian internationalism.[14]

The North Korean Constitution proclaimed that the Communist Party—"the leading and guiding force of Soviet society and the nucleus of its political system and of all state organizations and public organizations"—was "armed with Marxism-Leninism" (Article 6). The 1972 DPRK Constitution stated that North Korea "is guided in its activity by the *juche* (self-reliance) idea of the Workers' Party of Korea, a creative application of Marxism-Leninism to the conditions of our country" (Article 4). This particular declaration allows North Korea to cling to the basic tenets of Marxism-Leninism while simultaneously justifying (as it has done) any political practices deviant from the orthodox Marxism-Leninism in the name of *juche*. Similarly, the Preamble to the 1982 Chinese Constitution proclaims that the Chinese people of all nationalities are "under the leadership of the Communist Party of China and the guidance of Marxism-Leninism and Mao Zedong Thought." Like Kim Il Sung's *juche*, Mao Zedong Thought was utilized as a rationale for political experiments divergent from orthodox communism. China demonstrated this particularly during the Cultural Revolution of the mid-1960s to early 1970s. However, as shown below, *juche* has gradually replaced Marxism-Leninism in North Korean propaganda rhetoric. The revised 1992 Constitution officially abandoned Marxism-Leninism. Article 3 of the 1992 Constitution simply states that "The Democratic People's Republic of Korea is guided by *juche*, a revolutionary ideology with a people-centered view of the world."

Socialist Rules of Conduct

The North Korean Constitution includes a chapter on "Fundamental Rights and Duties of Citizens," resembling chapters in the present Chinese and former Soviet constitutions. After listing the rights of the citizens—the right to work, the right to rest and leisure, health protection, housing, education, and others—all three constitutions include the following rather bone-chilling "duties" of their citizens:

> *Citizens must strictly observe the laws of the State and the socialist norms of life and the socialist rules of conduct (Article 81 of the 1992 DPRK Constitution). Work is the glorious duty of every able-bodied citizen. All working people in state enterprises and in urban and rural economic collectives should perform their tasks with an attitude consonant with their status as masters of the country. The state pro-*

*motes socialist labor emulation, and commends and rewards model
and advanced workers. (Article 42 of the 1982 PRC Constitution)
Citizens' exercise of their rights and freedoms is inseparable
from the performance of their duties and obligations. Citizens of
the USSR are obliged to observe the Constitution of the USSR and
Soviet laws, comply with the standards of socialist conduct, and
uphold the honor and dignity of Soviet citizenship. (Article 59 of
the 1977 USSR Constitution)*

The catch in North Korean, Chinese and Soviet citizens' rights
and freedom (for that matter, in all past and present socialist countries) lies in the phrases—"socialist rules of conduct," "socialist
labor," or "socialist norms of life." In essence, individual citizens
have neither the freedom from external control nor the freedom in
the capacity to act. The party, not individual citizens, determines
and defines proper socialist rules of conduct. The North Korean
Constitution is far more categorical in this regard: "The State elim-
inates the way of life left over from the old society and introduces
the new socialist way of life in all fields" (Article 42).

In exchange for the state's guarantee of work, housing, education, and public health, the citizens have surrendered their power
to decide on such intrinsically personal matters as where to work,
where to live, what to know, and what to learn. In brief, the loss or
absence of fundamental human freedom as a direct result of state-
controlled socialist rules of individual conduct stands out as one of
the most conspicuous common denominators of all past and present
communist states.

Socialist Economic System

North Korea is a socialist state (Article 1, 1992 Socialist Constitution of the DPRK) founded on socialist relations of production
and self-reliant national economy (Article 19). Thus, the state
"defends the socialist system against the subversive activities of
hostile elements at home and abroad" (Article 12). The DPRK Constitution is replete with such socialist phraseology as "building
socialism," "accelerate socialist construction," "develop socialist
property," among others. These constitutional stipulations of socialism are virtually identical to those of other socialist fraternal countries. For example, both the 1977 USSR Constitution and the 1982
Constitution of the People's Republic of China (PRC) declare that
their states are founded on socialism (cf. the 1977 USSR Constitution, Article 1 and the 1982 PRC Constitution, Article 1).

In theory, socialism as an economic system in socialist countries parallels capitalism in Western democratic states. In concrete terms, the North Korean economy is planned and managed by the state, and the means of production are owned by the state and cooperative organizations. State ownership of properties is unlimited. All natural resources, major factories and enterprises, ports, banks, transport, and communication establishments are owned solely by the state (Article 21). Cooperative organizations still own land, animals, farm implements, fishing boats, buildings, as well as small and medium-size factories and enterprises on a limited scale. However, the state has been developing the socialist cooperative economic system and transforming the property of the cooperative organizations into the property of the state. The right of private ownership, thus, does not exist in North Korea. Personal property is limited to earnings from work and other benefits, such as the small garden plots granted by the state. The North Korean economic system exemplifies a typical socialist command economy despite some marginal economic changes and reforms since the early 1980s.[15]

Dictatorship of the Proletariat

Consistent with Marxism, the symbolic cornerstone of the North Korean political system is the dictatorship of the proletariat. Article 4 of the 1992 DPRK Constitution proclaims that the sovereignty of the DPRK "rests with the workers, peasants, soldiers and working intellectuals." Furthermore, it stipulates that the working people exercise power through their representative organs—the Supreme People's Assembly (SPA) and local People's Assemblies at all levels. In reality, it is the ruling circles of the WPK that exercise power in the name of people; the representative organs are nothing but their rubber stamp. Article 10 is even more direct: the DPRK "exercises the dictatorship of the proletariat and pursues class and mass lines." Similar pronouncements-the "people's democratic dictatorship" (Article 1 of the PRC Constitution) and "the dictatorship of the proletariat" (Preamble to the 1977 USSR Constitution)—in past and present socialist constitutions are commonplace. In practice, the principle of the proletarian dictatorship has become the dictatorship of the WPK, and the proletariat—workers, peasants, soldiers and working intellectuals—are not their own sovereign masters. The proletariats have simply become its (Party's) *human* instruments. In the process of implementing the principle of proletarian dictatorship, dictatorship, but not a *proletarian* dictatorship, has managed to continue. In North Korea, the proletariats are not the masters of revolution and construction, as the official propaganda constantly declares. Rather, they have become the subjects of one-party father-son dictatorship.

Leadership of the Communist Party

In *What Is to Be Done* (1902), Lenin juxtaposes the spontaneity of the masses and the consciousness of the party members (i.e., the Russian Social-Democrats) and urges the necessity for the organization of "professional revolutionaries," that is, the Communist Party. He contends that: (1) no revolutionary movement can endure without a stable organization of leaders maintaining continuity; (2) the broader the popular mass drawn spontaneously into the struggle, the more urgent the need for such organization because all sorts of demagogues try to sidetrack the more backward sections of the masses; (3) such an organization must consist chiefly of professional revolutionaries; and (4) it should be manned mainly by the working class.[16] As a result, his idea of the Communist Party as the vanguard of the masses was born.

Article 11 of the DPRK Constitution states that North Korea is guided by the WPK. Similarly, the leading role of the Communist Party as the vanguard of the people is prefaced in the preambles of both the Chinese and the former Soviet constitutions. Contrary to Lenin's assertion of the spontaneity of the masses, the North Korean people have never been *spontaneously* drawn into the struggle. Rather, they have been *mobilized* by the WPK for its socialist construction and revolution. The WPK is not merely the leader or the vanguard of the masses, but the only party organization in the North Korean political arena. It is an example of monoparty or unipartism par excellence. Paradoxically, therefore, the communist party, which began as the party of "immense majority" to end the exploitation of the masses by the minority, be it the bourgeoisie or the feudal landlords, has become the minority party in the name of the majority working class. In essence, exploitation of the working class has not ended. The North Korean working masses have been suffering from the same Orwellian double-talk.

Principle of Democratic Centralism

The WPK has adopted Lenin's idea of democratic centralism[17] as its decision-making and organizational principle of government (Article 5). The bylaws of the WPK (Chapter II, Article 11) states that:

- *Every leadership organization of the party shall be democratically elected, and the elected leadership shall report its work periodically to party organizations.*

- *Party members shall obey the party organizations, the minority shall obey the majority, the lower party organization shall obey the higher party organizations, and all party organizations shall absolutely obey the Central Committee of the party.*

- *All party organizations should unconditionally support and carry out the party line and policies, and the lower party organizations must execute dutifully the decisions of the higher party organizations. The higher party organizations shall systematically direct and inspect the work of the lower party organizations, and the lower party organizations shall periodically report their work to the higher party organizations.*

With some minor variations, virtually all socialist countries have incorporated democratic centralism into their systems. The Chinese Communist Party (CCP) has upheld a principle of democratic centralism almost identical to the WPK's. The Constitution of the CCP adopted by the Twelfth National Congress on September 6, 1982 specifies six rules of the principle of democratic centralism (Chapter II, Article 10):

- *An individual party member is subordinate to the Party organizations, the minority is subordinate to the majority, the lower Party organizations are subordinate to the higher Party organizations, and all the constituent organizations and members of the Party are subordinate to the National Congress and the Central Committee of the Party.*

- *The Party's leading bodies at all levels are elected except for the representative organs dispatched by them and the leading Party members' groups in non-Party organizations.*

- *The highest leading body of the Party is the National Congress and the Central Committee elected by it. The leading bodies of local Party organizations are the Party congresses at their respective levels and the Party committees elected by them.*

- *Highest Party organizations shall pay constant attention to the views of the lower organizations and the rank-and-file members. Lower Party organizations shall report their work to highest Party organizations. Higher and lower Party organizations should exchange information and support and supervise each other. Party committees at all levels function on the principle of combining collective leadership with individual responsibility based on division of labor.*

- *All major issues shall be decoded upon by the Party committees after democratic discussion.*

- *The Party forbids all forms of personality cult.*

The principle of democratic centralism is also extended to the Chinese National People's Congress (NPC) and the local people's congresses, which are instituted, at least on paper, through democratic elections. They are responsible to the people and subject to the latter's supervision. All administrative, judicial, and procuratorial organs of the state are also created by the people's congresses to which they are responsible and under whose supervision they operate.

The division of functions and powers between the central and local state organs is guided by the principle of giving full play to the initiative and enthusiasm of the local authorities under the unified leadership of central authorities (Article 3 of the PRC Constitution). Similar principles of democratic centralism—the election of all bodies of state authority from the lowest to the highest, their accountability to the people, the obligation of the lower bodies to observe the decisions of the higher ones and combining central leadership with local initiatives and creative activity—have been included in the former Soviet Constitution and fundamental laws of other socialist countries (e.g., the former USSR Constitution, Article 3).

Two points are particularly noteworthy in North Korea's actual practice of the principle of democratic centralism. First, the principle has provided the theoretical rationale and device for Kim Il Sung cult-building (for that matter, the cult-building process of Stalin, Mao, Tito, and other heads of state in the socialist countries). Although the WPK by-law stops short of going beyond the rhetoric that "all party organizations shall absolutely obey the Central Committee of the party," absolute obedience to the higher party organs in reality does not end with the WPK Central Committee. The WPK Central Committee, in turn, obeys its Standing Committees, especially its Political Committee, Secretariat and Central Military Affairs Committee, and in turn these Standing Committees must obey their respective chairmen. In real terms, the people and the Party must pledge absolute loyalty to Kim Il Sung, and now Kim Jong Il. The senior Kim chaired all these key Standing Committees, while concurrently acting as the President of the DPRK, the President of the Supreme People's Assembly Central People's Committee, and the Chairman of the WPK Congress.

Herein lies the institutional basis for transforming one-party rule into a one-man rule. One-man rule, in turn, tends to generate a personality cult. The cult of Kim Il Sung may be partially explained by the (mis)application of the democratic centralism principle. Thus, it is no accident that the 1982 CCP Constitution appended a specific provision to the principle of democratic centralism which "forbids all forms of personality cult." It is still too early to tell whether or not this particular provision will actually prevent the CCP from its cult-building tendency. One thing is quite certain, nevertheless. As the cults of Stalin, Tito, Mao, Ceausescu, Kim Il Sung ("Great Leader"), and Fidel Castro ("Lider Maximo") have amply demonstrated, the tendency to centralize power in the central party organizations and ultimately in the hands of the chairman of the Party would be extremely difficult, if not impossible, to avoid.

Second, if "centralism" in the principle of democratic centralism tends to produce a personality cult in socialist systems, its "democratic" process tends to create a political farce. In the virtual absence of basic political freedoms enjoyed by the democratic states in Western Europe, North America, Oceania, and Japan, elections in socialist systems are nominal since the voters dutifully elect those candidates who are nominated by the party leadership. Media coverage of North Korean local elections in the 1980s dramatically illustrates this point. The captions on the front page of the *Pyongyang Times* on March 9, 1983, read: "Demonstration of Our People's United Strength" and "Elections to City and County People's Assemblies: 100% Voter Turnout, 100% Yes Votes." Under this caption, the following "news story" was printed.

Elections to the city and county people's assemblies took place from 9 A.M. to 8 P.M. on March 6. The elections were successfully carried out in strict accordance with the Regulation on the Elec-

*tions of Deputies to the People's Assemblies at all levels of the
Democratic People's Republic of Korea. According to the results of
the elections totalized at the city and county constituencies, one
hundred percent of the electors registered. For those now touring
abroad took part in voting and all of them cast their ballots for
the candidates registered at all the constituencies. The elections
powerfully demonstrated once again the invincible might of our
people, united rock-firm around the Central Committee of the
Party led by the Great Leader President Kim Il Sung, and the
superiority of our genuine socialist system. Elected deputies are
representatives of the workers, peasants and working intellectuals, who have worked devotedly with intense loyalty to the Party
and the leader for the prosperity of the socialist motherland and
the strengthening and development of our people's power. The
number of deputies elected to the city and county people's assemblies is 24,562.*

On February 25, 1985, the same caption—"100% Voter
Turnout, 100% 'Yes Votes'"—appeared on the front page of the
Pyongyang Times. The only changes in the content of the "news stories" were that the number of deputies increased from 24,562 in
1983 to 28,793 in 1985, the WPK's invincible "might" was replaced
by its "strength," and "Great Leader President Kim Il Sung" was
replaced by "Respected Comrade Kim Il Sung."

In contrast, the *Beijing Review* of February 25, 1980, reported
that voter turnout in China's Tongxiang County election was not
100 percent but 98.86 percent. Even in the election in the former
Soviet Union, the "yes" vote was 99.9 percent![18] In short, the North
Korean–style election of "100% Voter Turnout and 100% Yes Votes"
graphically exhibits North Korea's "democratic" centralism in
action. The 26 November 1991 issue of the *Rodong Shinmun*
reported that in the city-county People's Assembly elections, 99.89
percent cast 100 percent "yes" votes. The election results of the
Supreme People's Assembly (SPA), "the highest organ of the state,"
demonstrates (see Table 10.2) that this perfect electoral voting
behavior in North Korea's local elections is nothing but a carbon
copy of its national election. An interesting observation here is that
since the Ninth Election, the 10 percent voters—100 percent "yes"
voting pattern developed a small crack. Now the North Korean
media reports that only 99.7 percent took part in the election,
although it still claims 100 percent "yes" votes. In sum, despite
minor changes, North Korea's malpractice of democratic centralism
still persists.

Table 10.2
Election Results of the SPA

Term	Date	No. Seats	Voting (%)	Yes Vote (%)
1st	8/25/48	572 (360 + 212)	99.97	98.49
2nd	8/27/57	215	99.99	99.9
3rd	10/08/62	383	100.00	100.00
4th	11/26/67	457	100.00	100.00
5th	12/12/72	541	100.00	100.00
6th	11/11/77	579	100.00	100.00
7th	2/28/82	615	100.00	100.00
8th	11/02/86	655	100.00	100.00
9th	4/22/90	687	99.78	100.00

Source: Adapted from North Korea News, No. 107 (March 8, 1982); Pukhan Chonso (1980), p. 103. Yang Sung Chul, Bukhan Ch'ongch'iron [North Korean Politics] (Seoul: Park Yong-sa, 1991), p. 42.

Proletarian Internationalism

Another standard feature of all socialist systems is the idea of proletarian internationalism. The DPRK is to unite with all socialist countries and with all the people in the world to defeat imperialism and actively support and encourage their national liberation and revolutionary struggles. In order to accommodate these efforts, North Korea has incorporated into its constitution five elements of proletarian internationalism: equity, independence, mutual respect, noninterference in each other's internal affairs, and mutual benefit (cf. Article 170). These five factors nearly replicate the Five Principles of Peaceful Coexistence (Pancha Shila), which was originally written into the Indian-Chinese Agreement on Tibet on April 29, 1954. They are: mutual respect for sovereignty and territorial integrity, nonaggression, noninterference in each other's internal affairs, mutual benefits, equality, and peaceful coexistence (cf. Preamble to the PRC Constitution). The former Soviet Union had similar pledges in its constitution (cf. Article 29 and 30 of the former USSR Constitution). In reality, however, the PRC's "nonaggression" clauses have not deterred the PRC from its conquest of Tibet in 1950, intermittent hostilities in the Taiwan straits in the 1950s, Korean intervention (1950–1953), brief broader wars or skirmishes with India (1962), the former Soviet Union (1969 and 1971), and Vietnam (1978–1979), to list a few. Similarly, Soviet pledges did not prevent its direct invasion and intervention in Hungary (1956), Czechoslovakia (1968), and Afghanistan (1979).

Interestingly enough, the "nonaggression" clause is absent in the North Korean Constitution. Since North Korea invaded the South in June 1950, it may be inferred from the absence of the nonaggression clause that North Korea still has not ruled out the option of reunifying the country through military means. If this inference is correct, North Korea's constant propaganda rhetoric of reunifying the fatherland by peaceful means is patently false. In the midst of collapsing communism, North Korea now finds itself among a limited number of socialist fraternal countries, so its aim of reunifying the country is quickly becoming a pipe dream. In all practicality, even preserving and defending the system is becoming impossible.

Structure of the State

Finally, all present and past socialist states have shared the same basic formal political structures. The national legislative body is the highest organ of state power: North Korea's Supreme People's Assembly (SPA), China's National People's Congress (NPC), and the former Soviet Union's Supreme Soviet. Both the SPA and the NPC are unicameral, while the Supreme Soviet consists of the Soviet of the Union and the Soviet of Nationalities. The administrative or executive body—North Korea's Administration Council, China's State Council, and the former Soviet Union's Council of Ministers—is formed by the national legislative organ. Likewise, the national court and the Procurator's office are established by the national legislative body. Local legislative bodies form the executive and judicial branches of the government. On paper, therefore, the socialist political structures are set up on the principle of separation of powers. But in reality, they are run by the party based on the principle of *concentration of powers* in the hands of the party.

The Communist Party controls all the above political institutions, since its organizations correspond to all governmental apparatus from national to local levels, and its organizations at each level control their government counterpart. The crucial point is that the Communist Party in socialist states is an integral part of the governing structure. Unlike the competitive party systems in Western democracies, where parties *in* power and those *out of* power are in periodic competition with each other, the Communist Party continues to be *in* power with virtually no challenges from other political forces within. Nearly all socialist political systems are founded on the dictatorship of the Communist Party. As is clear from the foregoing, the North Korean political system exemplifies a Communist Party dictatorship. The fact that the WPK has been in power ever since the establishment of the DPRK graphically illustrates this point.

Deviations: Objective Conditions and Subjective Attributes

In view of the above, North Korea can be seen as an ordinary socialist country. However, it also demonstrates its own distinctive characteristics of a political system that deviates from mainstream socialist countries. They include: (1) ideological posture; (2) size principle; (3) echo; (4) siege mentality; (5) rationing syndrome; and (6) personality cult.[19]

Ideological Posture

Marxism-Leninism, along with Kim Il Sungism, is officially stipulated as North Korea's basic ideological tenet, although a gap exists between such symbolic posturing and the real political life in North Korea. The mere fact that the present North Korean political system emerged during the period of Soviet occupation indicates the inordinate influence of the former Soviet Union in North Korean politics. The North Korean political system is, however, not merely a facsimile of the Soviet model, or that of the Maoist formula. As indicated above, all three share a number of fundamental ideological principles in common, but the North Korean system possesses its own unique and peculiar elements.

It is interesting to note that the original DPRK Constitution adopted by the SPA on September 8, 1948, did not explicitly acknowledge Marxism and Leninism as the "official" ideology. Nor did it stipulate the WPK as the "official" party. Basic communist ideological and organizational principles—"the dictatorship of the proletariat," "democratic centralism," and "the building of a classless communist society"—were not cited anywhere. The original constitution even failed to empower the state with ownership and control of the means of production. Rather, ownership was divided into state ownership, cooperative ownership, and ownership by private natural or private juridical persons. Except for a garden plot (50 *pyong* or 0.04 acre), private ownership of any kind—of land, commerce, industry, and others—disappeared from North Korea by the end of 1958.

Nonacknowledgment of fundamental ideological principles in the original constitution does not mean that the DPRK did not endorse and practice them. To the contrary, Marxism-Leninism has been its "official" ideology; the WPK has been its "official" party since 1948; and the party, state, and military organization have been running largely in accordance with the principles of democratic centralism and of proletarian dictatorship. The WPK controls the mass media, mass communication, and all other literary, artistic, cultural, educational, scientific, and social enterprises. The military and other political control apparatus, such as security, public safety, and secret intelligence forces, are also under WPK control. In short, the North Korean political system possesses fundamental features of a communist dictatorship.

Nonendorsement of the basic principles and doctrines of communism in the original constitution was only a temporary political camouflage. North Korea explained that between 1948 and 1972 the country had been in a transition from the "anti-feudal, anti-imperialist, democratic revolution" to the socialist revolution. In the 1972 Socialist Constitution, North Korea launched its new phase—the consolidation and development of the socialist system.[20] The absence of certain ideological principles in the constitution reflected rather unfavorable political settings under which Kim Il Sung's Partisan Group initially had to stage a power struggle against the competing factional forces in the political arena.

At the beginning of the Republic, the Partisan Group was relatively small compared to the nationalist organizations and other political forces in North Korea. The Communist Party organizations had several competing factions. In addition to the Partisan Group, returnees from China (the Yanan Group), the Domestic Group, and the Worker's Party of South Korea vied for power in the early stages of North Korean communist politics. Kim's Partisan Group did not even constitute the majority among these rival communist factions. Under such circumstances, Kim and his group chose a broad coalition strategy until they consolidated power and gained strategic positions within the WPK, state, military, and other political control apparatus.

Herein lies the *evolutionary* character of the North Korean communist system. Kim's power was not absolute from the outset. His power increased gradually within the WPK. A steady and gradual consolidation of his power meant that other party factions had to be eliminated step-by-step. From this standpoint, the formal endorsement of Marxism-Leninism and *juche* as the fundamental tenets of North Korean ideology in the 1972 Constitution signified that Kim Il Sung and his group won the power struggles within the WPK: the absence of the endorsement for such official ideology in the 1948 Constitution indicated his rather weak leadership status. The exclusion of Marxism-Leninism and the sole inclusion of his *juche* ideology in the 1992 Constitution confirms the further consolidation of his and his son's power.

Size Principle

Another salient feature of North is the size principle. Its northern neighbors, China and the former Soviet Union, are two of the largest nations in the world. Compared with North Korea's 23 million people within 47,000 square miles of land area, China has the world's largest population (over 1.2 billion people) and the third largest land area (3.7 million square miles). The former Soviet Union has the world's third largest population (over 290 million) and the largest land area (8.6 million square miles). Compared to North Korea, China is nearly 53 times larger in population and 79 times bigger in size, while the former Soviet Union was 14 times larger in population and nearly 183 times bigger in size. In other words, North Korea and its population are much smaller than the average size and population of China's twenty-one provinces and five autonomous regions. It is less than a third of the average size of former Soviet Union's fifty-three subgovernmental units [union republics (15), autonomous republics (2), autonomous regions (8), and autonomous areas (10)] combined.

North Korea's population and size in relation to its two neighboring giants have had several ideological and political implications. First, being tiny can be tidy, so to speak. Since North Korea's 23 million people are virtually all ethnic Koreans, there are no nationality problems. By contrast, China has some fifty-four minority groups scattered over nearly 60 percent of its land area, with the Han Chinese constituting 94 percent of its total population and occupying mostly the fertile coastal areas. Only about 15 percent of China's land is arable, with the majority (nearly 85%) of the rural population concentrating on cultivation on only a sixth of its land mass. As Fairbank noted, a million villages are still generally beyond the reach of easy transportation by road, rail, or water, and lack marketing networks. Hence, the small-scale industrialization of the countryside is on a do-it-yourself basis and central direction is minimized.[21] Totalitarian control and planning notwithstanding, this illustrates the classic example of what Lucian Pye called the "penetration crisis."[22]

The former Soviet Union's enormous physical and demographic size has created no better, if not worse, situations than those of China. The former Soviet Union contained more than 110 ethnic and national minorities, with non-Slavic populations steadily on the rise, while the number of the so-called Great Russians and other Slavic populations declined.[23] Before the demise of the Soviet Union, the non-Slavic, especially Soviet Asians, approached 50 percent of the total population. Following the lead of the Baltic States, Estonia, Latvia, and Lithuania, other former republics under the loose political arrangement of the Commonwealth of Independent States (CIS) have also declared political independence and autonomy, eventually breaking up the CIS.

While the size of area and population in China and the former Soviet Union have posed problems of manageability, penetration, and integration, North Korea's size has worked to its advantage. The size principle, as demonstrated above, may explain the different performances in the socialist system. Why have these socialist countries produced different political and economic results when they have been applying basically the same socialist, political, and economic principles and programs? The answer may be found in the differences in their level or stage of economic and societal development, and in culture or in history. Beyond these, however, lies the physical and demographic size, which is an important factor explaining such divergent performances. Specifically, the socialist agricultural collectivization policy illustrates the classic example of the size principle. In the former Soviet Union, for example, two kinds of collectivized farms existed. There were some 26,000 multipurpose *kolkhoz* (collective farms), whose average size was 16,000 acres. On the one hand, typical collective farm had about 550 households. The state farms, *sovkhoz*, on the other hand, were more specialized, better mechanized, and larger in size. There were about 22,000 state farms whose size averaged 50,000 acres in 1985. The majority of the state farms specialized in certain agricultural products, such as grain, dairies, fruits, or vegetables. An average state farm employed about 550 people.[24] Before the collapse of the Soviet Union, the trend demonstrated the gradual increase of state farms and declining number of collective farms.

In North Korea, no collective or state farms of comparable size exist. All farmland in North Korea is divided into state-operated farms and agricultural cooperatives, whose average sizes are far smaller than the Soviet Union's state and collective farms. As in the former Soviet Union, North Korea's state farms are specialized to produce particular agricultural products. Presently, some 200 such farms, which constitute 12 percent of the total arable land, generate 20 percent of North Korea's entire agricultural products. When North Korea successfully completed the collectivization of agriculture in 1958, some 3,778 agricultural cooperatives with an average of 476 *chongbo* or 1,155 acres (1 *chongbo* = 2.45 acres) existed. An average agricultural cooperative has about 300 households.[25] In other words, North Korea's agricultural cooperatives are on the average fourteen times and forty-four times smaller, respectively, than their former Soviet counterparts, *kolkhoz* and *sovkhoz*.

The majority of farmers live in scattered villages, usually at the foot of mountains and valleys. A huge farming population in one particular region or location is rare. The size, topography, and demography of North Korea make Soviet-style collectivization inapplicable. Because North Korea's cooperative farms are relatively small in size and are usually located in or near the farming villages, they have managed greater efficiency and higher productivity than their former Soviet counterparts. Even to a casual visitor, many areas of uncultivated farmlands in China and the former Soviet Union are noticeable, but uncultivated land is very rare in North Korea. North Korea's physical size and resultant cooperative farm sizes have been a positive factor for management and production. Their relatively small sizes have contributed favorably to their centralized economic management in general and political control in particular. Still, North Korea's agriculture has not and cannot overcome the inherent limitations of the collectivized agricultural system. China, after agricultural reform in the late 1970s, has clearly demonstrated that North Korea's smaller agricultural land size has some advantages over the Chinese and the former Soviet Union's which is, however, nothing compared to the enormous benefits from the post-Mao decollectivization of agriculture, that is, the family-unit responsibility system.

Second, the size principle has security implications. Unlike the relationship between China and the former Soviet Union, whose respective sizes in territory, population, and other human and natural resources are comparable and, thus, make their rivalry inevitable, North Korea's relationship with China or with Russia has not created such rivalry. Despite North Korea's steadfast claims of mutual equality and independence, it has been a minor partner of its two giant socialist neighbors. China has challenged the for-

mer Soviet Union's ideological orthodoxy and politicomilitary hegemony, and both sides have clashed militarily over border issues.
These are not likely to cease in the future.[26] North Korea alone cannot challenge the hegemony of either of these two neighboring
giants, nor can it instigate military confrontations with either, even
on a limited scale. During the era of Sino-Soviet conflict, North
Korea played a political game by balancing one side against the
other, without reneging outright the relationship with one for the
other. Aside the rhetorical claims of independence and equality
under the banner of *juche,* herein lies the ultimate parameter of
North Korea as a military power and its political leadership role
within the socialist camp and the international community.

The findings of Dahl and Tufte on size and democracy
deserves attention in this connection. Among other things, they
found that "no single type or size of unit is optimal for achieving the
twin goals of citizen effectiveness and system capacity." By citizen
effectiveness and system capacity, they meant "citizens acting
responsibly and competently to fully control the decisions of the
polity," and "the polity has the capacity to respond fully to the collective preferences of its citizens."[27] Further, they posited that the
effectiveness of the citizen may be maximized if the unit is small
and homogeneous. At the same time, in such a unit the effectiveness of the dissenting citizens is minimized because they can be
easily detected, and their opposition crushed. They asserted that
the politics of diversity in the larger, more homogeneous unit may
better serve the dissenting citizen. Most important, they found that
the goal of maximizing citizen effectiveness can and does become
conflictual with the capacity of the system. In extreme cases, a citizen could be maximally effective within a system of minimal capacity when dealing with major issues or minimally effective within a
system of maximal capacity when dealing with major issues.[28]

The findings of Dahl and Tufte are relevant to the North
Korean political system. To employ their terminology, the socialist
political systems in particular are cases in which citizen effectiveness does not exist except in a nominal sense (election fanfares of
"100% voter turnout and 100% yes vote!"), while system capacity is
realized in full. North Korea represents the prime example of their
"extreme case," that is, minimal citizen effectiveness and maximal
system capacity. Again, North Korea epitomizes a case where the
effectiveness of the dissenting citizen is minimized. In the present
North Korean political system, the "dissenting citizen" is virtually
nonexistent. There have been "enemies of the people" such as "trai-

tors," "the lackeys of Japanese imperialism," "pro-Japanese and pro-American elements," "anti-Party factionalists," and others.[29] The "masses," not the "citizen" and "unity," nor "dissent," make up North Korea's standard political vocabulary. To borrow Kim Il Sung's own phraseology, "all Party (WPK) members . . . breathe the same air, speak the same words and act in unison." Again, in Kim's words, "never before have the whole Party and the entire people been so strongly knit together and united with a single ideology and will as they are now."[30] In short, in North Korea, the size principle helped Kim and his ruling elite to maximize system capacity in the virtual absence of "citizen effectiveness."

Echo Effect

Policy changes (symbolic or substantive) in the political, ideological, and security arenas of a socialist country (in any other country, for that matter) produce similar changes in other socialist countries. In reality, it is difficult to distinguish between the country that initiates or emulates such changes in line, policy, or program because such changes can take place simultaneously or sequentially. The problem of distinction between the initiator and emulator nations aside, the echo effect has been another variable that can explain the peculiarities of the North Korean political system.

The North's dialogue with South Korea in the early 1970s, 1980s, and 1990s corresponded to the U.S.-USSR and the U.S.-Chinese détente before, and to the demise of communism and the emerging new world order. North Korea, for example, announced that its doors are now open to foreign investment and technology transfer. This turnabout may be regarded as North Korea's new direction in economic strategy, which echoes China's adoption of new economic reform under Deng Xiaoping.

Specific examples, too, abound in this regard. North Korea's *Ch'ollima* (Flying Horse) Movement was comparable to China's Great Leap Forward in the late 1950s: although the latter ended in abject failure, the former still serves as the official developmental and mobilizational symbol. Another examples are Kim's *ch'ongsan-ri* in 1960 and Mao's *dazhai* in 1963 as the ideal models of North Korea's and China's respective cooperative farming methods.[31] Kim Il Sung's *juche* idea and Mao's doctrine of self-reliance (or, to stretch the comparison further, even Stalin's slogan of "socialism in one country") are literally, if not politically, analogous. North Korea's slogan of three great revolutions—the ideological, technological, and cultural—is akin to China's four modernizations of agriculture, industry, national defense, and science and technology. North Korea's Children's Guard, Young Red Guard, and Worker-Peasant Red Guards, too, are not a far cry from Mao's Red Guards. Building the Kim Il Sung cult and grooming Kim Jong Il as the official successor is comparable to the frenetic phase of the Mao cult during the Cultural Revolution and the designation of Lin Piao, the PRC defense minister, as Mao's official successor.

Generally, the success or failure of the initiator's line, policy, or program does not necessarily guarantee the same result for the emulator. The emulator may not obtain a similar result from adopting the initiator's programs, due to obvious additional factors characterizing each socialist country. Khrushchev's de-Stalinization Campaign, which began in the 1956 Twentieth Congress of the Communist Party of Soviet Union (CPSU), was, at least, temporarily successful. Yet it eventually ended with Khrushchev's own fall and Brezhnev's rise in 1964. Mao's cult, which peaked during the Cultural Revolution period of 1966–1968, died away under the post-Mao leadership in China. Mao's birthplace in the village of Sao San, in Hsisng T'an County, Hunan Province, south of Hankow on the Yangtze River, was once a mecca for Chinese and foreign tourists, particularly during the Cultural Revolution. It is no longer included in the "list." Mao's pictures and sayings have all disappeared from the public buildings and walls. De-Maoization was successful under Deng Xiaoping, even though there has been recurring nostalgia for Mao.

In contrast, the attacks on Kim Il Sung's personality cult by the Yonan Group within the WPK in the 1956–1957 period failed. Such attacks seem to have intensified the Kim cult.[32] Kim's pictures, statues, and monuments are still omnipresent; his sayings are displayed in all prominent public places and buildings; his birthplace, *Mangyondae,* on the outskirts of Pyongyang along the Daedong River, is still "first on the list" for North Koreans and foreign visitors. De-Kimization in the aftermath of de-Stalinization failed principally because the assault was made while he was alive with a firm grip on power. By contrast, Khrushchev attacked Stalin three years after his death. Deng, too, downgraded Mao after his death, in a piecemeal and cautious way. If the Soviet and Chinese experiences serve as a guide for North Korea's political future, a possibility of successful de-Kimization after Kim's death is not inconceivable. However, although three years have elapsed since his death, there are no signs of downgrading Kim. His idolization has, on the contrary, intensified along with the consolidation of his son's succession politics. Kim Jong Il has been ruling North Korea without any changes in the name of *Yuhun Tongchi* (rule by teachings of late Kim Il Sung). This truly underscores the North Korean anomaly.

Another example is China's so-called Ping-Pong Diplomacy in the early 1970s, which eventually led to rapprochement between China and the United States, Japan, and other noncommunist countries. However, "Ping-Pong" diplomacy in North Korea, where the World Table Tennis Championship was held in the spring of 1979, did not result in the opening of the DPRK to the West. It would be quite unfair to say, however, that North Korea alone was to blame for the failure. In the long run, the history of Sino-Korean relations reveals that changes in the former have a spillover effect on the latter in one form or another.[33] Here again, like the aforementioned size principle, there is a limit to the echo effect on North Korea's resistance. North Korea's current efforts to improve relations with Japan and the United States are cases in point.

To summarize, North Korea has not been and cannot be completely immune to the changes occurring in China, the former Soviet Union, or around the world. Because of North Korea's ideological affinity, physical proximity, and security linkage, it is extremely difficult to avoid the effects of changes in China and the former Soviet Union. It is true that North Korea is not, and has not always been, on the receiving end of such changes, and the former Soviet Union and China on the giving end. The roles of the initiator and the emulator have frequently been reversed. It is equally true, however, that North Korea, despite its vociferous claims of *juche*, has been more an emulator than an initiator.

Siege Mentality

The siege mentality[34] which is intricately intermingled with the size principle and the echo effect, is another peculiar ideological and political trait of North Korea. It refers to the belief held by the top-level party, state, military, and paramilitary leaders that North Korea is besieged by hostile and potentially threatening enemy countries. It is not merely xenophobia, but also a political instrument through which the North Korean power elite justifies the politics of intimidation and mobilization, and in the process, exaggerates foreign threats. A self-fulfilling prophecy has crept in to justify and rationalize their prolonged rule.

To the North, the former Soviet Union and China have been North Korea's ideological and security allies. At the eleventh hour of the Korean War, China sent its "Volunteers" to rescue North Korea from the UN counteroffensive led by the United States, which pushed the North Korean troops to the North Korean–Manchurian borders. After the cease-fire in 1953, China and the former Soviet Union offered assistance to North Korea to rebuild the country from the ashes of the war. Since 1961, North Korea has maintained friendship treaties with both; its economic and military ties with the two have been greater than those with any other former socialist countries. North Korea also played an adroit balancing act amid the Sino-Soviet schism in the early 1960s and 1970s.

Despite close relationships with China and the former Soviet Union, North Korea has been wary of these two northern neighbors. Pyongyang has been oversensitive to internal political interference by either China or the former Soviet Union. Kim's accentuation of *juche* and his relentless purging of the Soviet faction in the early and mid-1950s and pro-Chinese Yonan faction in the late 1950s uphold this point. The ruling circle's hypersensitivity and apprehension over Chinese and Soviet interference in North Korea's domestic politics stems basically from the overwhelming inequality in size and power existing between North Korea and its two giant neighbors. In that sense, the siege mentality is a minor partner's subjective feeling toward a major partner in the presence of an overwhelmingly unfavorable objective inequality between the two.

The North Korean ruling elite's siege mentality is abetted by three additional sources—self-imposed, system-imposed, and other-imposed isolation. The persistence of division and somewhat diminishing hostility between North and South Korea, the presence of U.S. military forces in the South, a lack of formal relationship with Japan, and the physical barriers presented by China and Russia in the northern border make North Korea feel locked in, uneasy and isolated.

The system-imposed encapsulation is even more fundamental. Beyond the fact that all socialist systems create a closed society, the current North Korean political system is indeed watertight. From the basic-level work team in the agricultural cooperatives, factories, and urban areas to the top-level central party, state, and military hierarchies, all are vertically and horizontally organized, coordinated, and controlled. Regimentation in North Korea is nearly total, and the militarization of its population and the fortification of the entire country are virtually complete. It is a garrison state without parallel.

The physical movements of people within the country or abroad are totally controlled.[35] Virtually no room exists for individual initiatives in education, job transfer and training, moving, traveling, and other ordinary human transactions. In that sense, the masses in North Korea are simultaneously mobilized and immobile. They are mobilized by the WPK, state, and military cadres for socialist construction work and for the fortification and defense of the fatherland, but they are immobile because they cannot travel freely, choose their place of residence, occupation, and the like.

The North Korean siege mentality is also self-imposed. The much propagandized *juche* idea substantiates this point. *Juche*, when applied to the area of foreign and international affairs, emphasizes North Korea's political independence and economic autarchy and discourages foreign transactions, trade, and investment. A rigid insistence on independence and autarchy in the world of political and economic interdependence has further isolated and encapsulated North Korea. It should be pointed out that in a time of acute international economic crises, such as the Arab Oil Embargo of 1974 and the worldwide recession in the late 1970s and the early 1980s, North Korea was relatively unaffected due to its autarchic economic structures. Still, an excessive self-reliance leads to self-isolation, which in turn breeds ignorance.

The North Korean siege mentality is also other-imposed. The presence of U.S. troops and arsenals in South Korea, the ROK-U.S.-Japan security arrangement, Japanese and American refusal (though some positive movements and bilateral talks are presently ongoing) to recognize the DPRK are the notable cases.[36] The North Korean leadership utilizes the siege mentality as a tool to control and mobilize the masses. The propaganda that North Korea is besieged by real and potential enemies, especially the capitalist United States and militarist Japan, supplies additional ammunition in mobilizing and militarizing the masses. As stated earlier, the siege mentality is a self-fulfilling prophecy. In the process of alerting the masses of actual or imagined foreign enemy aggressors and their puppets, the ruling party creates real threats. So the vicious circle of siege mentality continues.

North Korea's siege mentality is, in essence, a phobia, an isolation, and even an instrument. As a result of the fear of being beleaguered by foreign enemies the state develops a phobia of all "foreign" elements. Such phobia further secludes the people and the country from the outside world. The isolation from the outside world encourages fortification and militarization, which in turn cuts off outside contact and communication. Hence, the encapsulated country remains ignorant of the outside world that is equally in the dark about the former. Worse still, while the ruling elite initially used phobia and ignorance as an instrument of mass mobilization and control, it has become the victim of its own creation. Isolated and impoverished, North Korea must find a way out. It has shown much more flexible attitudes in dealing with the United States and Japan in the wake of recent developments, such as the nuclear crisis and food crisis. However, its authentic intention and explicit gesture have always been subject to skepticism. Kim Jong Il must escape this siege mentality in order to survive in the world of growing interdependence.

Rationing Syndrome

Another conspicuous element in North Korean politics is the rationing syndrome, or state control over the means of production and distribution under the banner of the socialist principle of equal and fair distribution. In the process of rationing goods and products to the masses by the state functionaries, these goods and products somehow have metamorphosed into gifts, perquisites, and privileges. These goods and products no longer represent what the masses have manufactured through their own labor and toil. The masses have, instead, become the recipients of these gifts, perquisites, and privileges distributed by the state functionaries. Rationing of food items and goods occur in nearly all former socialist countries, but rationing becomes a syndrome when the masses are led to believe that the rationed items are the largesse of the ruling elite, rather than an entitlement.

Perhaps an American farmer giving thanks to God for the food he produced can be similar to a North Korean farmer being grateful to the ruling functionaries for the rationed food. However, a fundamental difference separates the two in that while God has no political designs, the ruling elite has systematically utilized rationing as a mechanism of mass political control and manipulation.

Although the rationing syndrome is present in all past and present socialist systems, North Korea's variant is conspicuous because it is intertwined with the Kim Il Sung cult and the father-son succession scheme. In North Korea all food and general items are rationed in the name of the "Great Leader" Kim Il Sung and now in the name of "Dear Leader" Kim Jong Il. Not only general merchandise and food items but also special goods such as children's books, pencils, and uniforms are distributed in the name of the "Benevolent Leader" and "Dear Leader." The masses enjoy the benefits and privileges arising from all the new construction—buildings, dams, highways, museums, and monuments—and all the new cultural productions—music, movies, plays, operas, paintings, and sculptures—which are completed under the direction of Kim Il Sung and Kim Jong Il. The members of the WPK are given wristwatches, television sets, refrigerators, washing machines, and even apartment flats by the Great Leader and the Dear Leader in their "boundless generosity." In fact, some watches and TV sets are inscribed with the captions, "Gifts of the Great Leader Kim Il Sung or of the Dear Leader Kim Jong Il." The irony is that more often than not, these goods were made in Japan, Switzerland, or some other foreign country, but the foreign manufacturers' labels are removed and replaced with the senior or the junior Kim's inscription as if they had been produced in North Korea. On April 15, a national holiday celebrating the senior Kim's birthday, the "Great Leader" often appeared at school playgrounds to personally give school uniforms, books, and other school supplies to students, as if they were his birthday "gifts." Students often forgot that such gifts had been produced by their own parents' hard work.[37]

The rationing syndrome in North Korea stretches beyond physically tangible products such as food, clothes, housing, work, school, and domicile. It also extends to the psychological and political domains in the form of rationing information and intelligence in accordance with the hierarchy of power and position held by each recipient. As the goods are rationed according to the workers' grades and skill levels, information and intelligence are apportioned in relation to the party, state, and military functionaries' ranks and status. There are, for instance, six grade levels for agricultural workers, ranging from one, the lowest, to six, the highest. Third-grade-level agricultural workers receive a *saengwhalbi* (monthly living allowance) of about 100 North Korean Won ($1.00 equals 1.70 North Korean Won), and 160 Won is allotted to sixth-grade-level workers. Factory workers are divided into eight grade levels, and monthly allowances range from 70 Won to 120 Won. (These figures were given to me in the summer of 1981 by the cadres in one of the agricultural cooperatives and the factory complex I visited. The actual amount of an average farm and factory worker's allowance may vary).

North Korea is a rigidly stratified society. The workers are divided into eight salary grades (China has 24 salary grades in urban areas and 26 salary grades in rural areas, as compared with 18 grades of officialdom under the Qing Dynasty).[38] Interestingly enough, North Korea's grading and stratification is not based on need, but rather on ability, that is, both the workers' acquired skills and their capacity to demonstrate and convince the WPK that they are loyal to the Party. Accordingly, the socialist principle of "from each according to his ability: to each according to his needs" is perverted.

Information and privileges, too, are rationed according to each individual's grade, position, and power. Some have more access to intelligence and information than others in North Korea, where mass media and mass communication are tightly controlled and fed by the WPK. By contrast, the masses are fed "information" through loudspeakers installed in their homes by local party propaganda committees. Similarly, a majority of the middle-level cadres and functionaries receive the news at home and around the world through WPK-controlled TV or radio, or through governmental organs. Like other rationed items, the ruling elite controls the news.

In a way, information allocating is inherent in any socialist system where all information is party-controlled and where the function of the media is not the dissemination of the news and information to the public but the education, indoctrination, and propagandizing of party policies and programs. In Butterfield's words, the principle of rationing information is "to keep the leaders informed without contaminating the minds of the masses."[39] Apportioning information becomes a syndrome when the ruling elite use it as another mechanism of political control. It becomes a syndrome because the masses are deliberately kept in the dark on the premise that the ignorant, uninformed, and misinformed are easier to rule.

Even in Western democratic societies where mass media and mass communication are not monopolized by a single official party, the intelligent, articulate, and informed public are limited in number, and the majority of the people are not only uninformed, but uninterested in politics beyond their immediate personal matters and job concerns.[40] Democratic governments control and classify information and intelligence to a certain extent. The difference, then, lies not in the existence of an uninformed and inarticulate mass public, or in government-controlled information, but in how the government controls the classified information. In North Korea (and in other socialist countries), the masses are subject to the deliberate propaganda of the WPK-controlled mass media and mass communication, whereas the mass public in Western democratic societies select their own information for consumption in the absence of governmental control. The WPK not only regulates the information network, but also employs disinformation to manipulate and mobilize the masses. No such centralized controlling and manipulating agency of news and information exists in democratic societies, although centralized government control of classified intelligence and other intelligence activities may be found in both societies. No private or public news agencies compete for information in North Korea except for those organs controlled by the WPK, the Administration Council, and the People's Armed Forces.[41]

The Personality Cult

The cult of personality abounds in past and present socialist countries. The cults of Lenin, Stalin, Mao, Tito, and Ceausescu are just a few examples. North Korea's personality cult is new, unique, and peculiar in its scope, intensity, and duration. The cults of Lenin, Stalin, Mao, and Tito were all confined to the individual. Even at the zenith of the Mao cult during the period of the Cultural Revolution in the mid-1960s, his cult did not extend to his families and relatives. By contrast, the cult of Kim goes beyond Kim Il Sung himself. Kim is "father" of the nation; his father, Kim Hyong-jik, was "the devout Communist"; his mother, Kang Ban-suk, was the "mother" of Korea; his deceased first wife, Kim Chong-suk, was the "mother" of revolution; and his deceased brother, Kim Chol-ju, was the "revolutionary fighter." Kim Il Sung shines the brightest in his illustrious revolutionary family constellation. The official designation of his son to succeed him by the WPK Congress in October 1980 indicates the familial nature of his cult. In a strict sense, then, the Kim Il Sung cult in North Korea today is a family cult rather than a typical personality cult.[42]

The height of the Stalin cult in the late 1930s and the frenzy of the Mao cult in the mid-1960s cannot measure up to the Kim cult in North Korea today. Kim and increasingly his son have become omnipresent. Their pictures are everywhere, and their statues stand in the most prominent public places. Any public

place, farm, or factory they visit is adorned with a statue or picture
in their likeness; if they visit the same place several times, a corresponding number of plaques are placed on the wall. Virtually
everyone in North Korea and North Koreans overseas wear a Kim
Il Sung badge. No one makes a public speech without acknowledg-
ing the "Great Leader" and "Dear Leader." Their writings are
recited daily, their speeches are heard constantly, and their published works in Korean and foreign languages are prominently displayed in every library and in all the bookstores. No newspaper,
magazine, radio program, song, play, movie, or book is quite complete without direct or indirect tribute to the "genius" Kim and to
Kim junior.

From nursery school to university, all school buildings and
classrooms are saturated with pictures and plaques of Kim Il Sung
and Kim Jong Il. Nursery school children chant stories of Kim's
wunderkind years; primary school children memorize the activities
of his "superboy" years; secondary school students learn the revolutionary works of his youth; and college students study his anti-
Japanese guerrilla struggles. Kim, in short, serves not only as the
model for all age groups but is a corporeal god in North Korea. His
cult has reached a point of political aberration bordering on absur-
dity.[43]

His cult has lasted longer than that of any other socialist
leader, including Lenin, Stalin, Mao, and Tito. What is more, while
Marx, Engels, and Lenin received homage posthumously, the idola-
try of Kim (and Stalin and Mao) began with his approval. Four
points deserve attention in his connection. First, the Kim Il Sung
cult is neither an accident nor an overnight phenomenon. It has
grown since 1945, if not earlier. Kim rose gradually as the undis-
puted and unchallenged "supreme leader." His cult-building enterprise has been the symbolic facet of his political power struggles.
His cult has served, among other things, as the symbolic weapon
against his political rivals and enemies. Hence, his cult can be better understood and explained in the context of his power struggle
within the WPK. The last known purging of his "enemies" within
the WPK took place from 1968 to 1969. The Kim cult has also
served to promote unity—a rallying point for the ruling apparatus
and the masses.[44]

Second, the sources and substance of Kim's cult are not all
outright lies and groundless fabrications. Nor is his cult merely the
phenomenon of a pseudo-charismatic leader.[45] The problem with his
cult is one of *excess:* his personal leadership alone has been respon-

sible for the Korean communist revolution. Such exaggerated feats cannot be substantiated by any historical document on the Korean communist movement, the anti-Japanese armed struggles, or on post–War North Korean politics.

Third, the unprecedented intensity, scope, and duration of the Kim Il Sung cult notwithstanding, he has not been able to and cannot personally rule North Korea. His cult is so excessive that Kim seems to single-handedly rule North Korea. Quite to the contrary, the party, the state, the military and parapolitical, and paramilitary organizational apparatuses have been running the country. He is more of an ultimate mediator than a decision maker, more a legitimator than a formulator, and more an arbiter than an advocate. He is more like the chairman of the board than a chief executive officer—a nominal role as the symbol of national unity, the head of the state, and the ultimate rallying point of the party and the people.

Finally, if the history of personality cults in socialist countries can serve as a guide, the cult usually dies away with the death of the cult object and the cult may be *imitable* but not *inheritable*. As de-Stalinization and de-Maoization have amply demonstrated, the intensity of the *decultization* is generally proportionate to that of the cult itself. So far, Kim Il Sung's death has not brought about an end of his cult. On the contrary, his deification, with such symbolic adornments of the "immortal" revolutionary ideas of *juche,* has been reinforced. However, such deification cannot be perpetual. For all the succession of his son, his death will eventually be the iconoclasm of his own cult.[46]

Conclusion

Kim Il Sung died in July 1994, shortly before a scheduled summit meeting with South Korean President Kim Young Sam. His death precipitated widespread speculations on the impending collapse of North Korea. Chronic food crises, nuclear quagmire, and deepening economic hardships have further fueled its incoming demise. Despite three years of transitional uncertainties of succession politics, North Korea has not collapsed. The Kim Jong Il regime appears to have consolidated its power, and idolization of Kim Il Sung has further intensified. The developments in the North truly present an anomaly when judged by the objective criteria of the rise and decline of other socialist systems. In view of the contextual variables examined in this chapter, however, durability of the North Korean political system seems understandable. It is yet to be seen how long the Kim Jong Il regime will last. Yet it can be assured that the demise of the Kim Jong Il regime will be caused by changes in the internal parameters discussed above, rather than external pressures.

Notes

1.Joseph A. Shumpeter, *Capitalism, Socialism and Democracy*, 3rd ed. (New York: Harper Torch Books, 1962), p. 309.

2. *Los Angeles Times*, July 22, 1984.

3. Political reforms commensurate with a series of economic reforms initiated in 1978 under Deng's leadership have not been launched. Consequently, the Chinese economic reforms have created political dilemmas because the structure of political power remains basically unchanged. David Zwig, "Reforming China's Political Economy," *Harvard International Review* 11 (Spring 1989); Dorothy Salinger, "Economic Reform in China," *Harvard International Review* 11 (Spring 1989). Quoted in Joseph S. Nye, Jr., *Bound to Lead: The Changing Nature of American Power* (New York: Basic Books, 1990), p. 135. An in-depth analysis of the destined failures of reform efforts under the Soviet-type system is found in the January 1990 issue of the *Annals of the American Academy of Political and Social Science*, which focuses on privatizing and marketizing of socialism under special editorship of Jan S. Prybyla.

4. For details, see Michael Burawoy, "Marxism as Science: Historical Challenges and Theoretical Growth," *American Sociological Review 55* (December 1990), p. 792.

5. For a discussion of China's Chou Dynasty as a classic example of historic international systems, see K. J. Holsti, *International Politics: A Framework for Analysis*, 5th ed. (Englewood Cliffs: Prentice-Hall, 1988), pp. 25–36.

6. Chang-sun Kim, *Pukhan Siponyonsa* [Fifteen-Year History of North Korea] (Seoul: Chinmungak, 1961); Dae-sook Suh, *The Korean Communist Movement, 1918–1948* (Princeton: Princeton University Press, 1967); Robert A. Scalapino and Chong-sik Lee, *Communism in Korea* (Berkeley: University of California Press, 1972).

7. See for instance, Gregory Henderson, *Korea: The Politics of the Vortex* (Cambridge: Harvard University Press, 1968), pp. 312–333. I have examined Henderson's culturalist approach to the Korean politics in some detail. Bruce Cumings, for one, referred to the North Korean system as a

"corporatist socialism." For details, see his paper "Corporatism in North Korea," delivered at the 1981 APSA meeting, New York, September 3–6, 1981.

8. A majority of the works on North Korean politics published in South Korea belongs to this category. To name just a few: *Pukhan Chonggam*, 45–68 (Seoul: Kukdongmuncheyonkuso, 1980), pp. 157–168; Yong-Pil Rhee, "Characteristics of North Korean political system," *Unification Policy Quarterly* (Fall 1978), pp. 16–33; and Keuk-Sung Suh, "Reports on Party Congress and Power Elites in North Korea," *Unification Policy Quarterly* (1980), pp. 11–35. See also, Koon Woo Nam, *The North Korean Communist Leadership 1945–1965* (Birmingham: University of Alabama Press, 1974) and Dae-sook Suh and Chae-jin Lee, eds., *Political Leadership in Korea* (Seattle: University of Washington Press, 1977).

9. No systematic work on the North Korean political system based on this model is yet available. But Chae-wan Yim, for example, urged such an approach. See his, "Approach to the North Korean System in Terms of Political Culture," *Vantage Point* (September 1984), pp. 1–11. For the works on communist political culture in general, see, Archi Brown and Jack Gray, *Political Culture and Political Change in Communist States* (New York: Hilmes & Meier, 1977); Stephen White, *Political Culture and Soviet Politics* (London: Macmillan, 1979) and his "Political Culture in Communist States: Some Problems of Theory and Method," *Comparative Politics* (April 1984), pp. 351–366; Richard R. Fagan, *The Transformation of Political Culture in Cuba* (Stanford: Stanford University Press, 1969); Andrew J. Nathan, *Peking Politics, 1918–1923: Factionalism and the Failure of Constitutionalism* (Berkeley: University of California Press, 1976). Also, Robert Tucker, "Political Culture and Communist society," *Political Science Quarterly* 88:2 (June 1973), pp. 180–185; and Gabriel A. Almond, "Communism and Political Culture Theory," *Comparative Politics* 15 (January 1983): 127–138. Studies on factionalism in socialist countries are found in Andrew J. Nathan, "A Factionalism Model for CCP Politics," *China Quarterly* 53 (January-March 1973): 34–66; Lucian W. Pye, *The Dynamics of Factions and Censuses in Chinese Politics: A Model and Some Propositions* (Santa Monica: Rand Corporation, 1980).

10. For a full discussion of the systems model, see David Easton, *A System Analysis of Political Life* (New York: John Wiley and Sons, 1965).

11. A notable example is Yong-pil Rhee's edited volume of *Pukhan Chongchi* [North Korean Politics] (Seoul: Daewang-sa, 1982). See also, Young Whan Kihl, *Politics and Policies in Divided Korea: Regimes in Contest* (Boulder: Westview Press, 1984). Though theoretically less explicit, some earlier works also attempted to examine the North Korean political system *in toto*. For instance, Dong-wun Park, *Pukhan Tongchi Kigulon* [On the North Korean Governing Apparatus] (Seoul: Korea University Asiatic

Studies Center, 1964); Glen D. Paige, *The Korean People's Democratic Republic* (Stanford: Hoover Institution on War, Revolution and Peace, 1966). See also, Chun-a Lee, "A Study of Factors Sustaining the North Korean Political System," *Pukhan* (September 1982), pp. 206–221.

12. J. Wiatr, "The Hegemonic Party System in Poland," in S. Rokhan and E. Allardt, eds., *Mass Politics: Studies in Political Sociology* (New York: Free Press, 1970), pp. 281–290 and Giovanni Sartori, *Parties and Party System: A Framework for Analysis* (Cambridge: Cambridge University Press, 1979), p. 227.

13. Myron Rush, *How Communists States Change Their Rulers* (Ithaca: Cornell University Press, 1974), p. 85.

14. The theories developed primarily by Marx and Engels are dialectic materialism, the materialistic interpretation of history and class struggle, the dictatorship of the proletariat and withering away of the state, and the theory of surplus value. Lenin's theoretical contributions include the vanguard theory of party and democratic centralism, violent proletarian revolution, the weakest-link-in-the-chain theory of war, and the theory of imperialism. A good bibliography on Marx's own writing on these "theories" as well as other scholars' critical analyses of his works are found in Isaiah Berlin, *Karl Marx: His Life and Environment* (London: Oxford University Press, 1973), pp. 285–289. Also, William Ebenstein, *Great Political Thinkers: Plato to the Present* (Hillsdale: Dryden Press, 1969), pp. 977–985 and R. N. Carew Hunt, *The Theory and Practice of Communism* (Middlesex: A Pelican Book, 1971), pp. 293–306. A recent useful anthology of Lenin's works is edited by Robert C. Tucher, *The Lenin Anthology* (New York: W. W. Norton, 1975).

15. For an attempt to classify the various subtypes of communist economic systems, see John M. Montias, "A Classification of Communist Economic Systems," in Cammelo Mesa-Lago and Carl Beck, eds., *Comparative Socialist Systems: Essays on Politics and Economics* (Pittsburgh: University of Pittsburgh Press, 1975), pp. 39–51.

16. V. I. Lenin, *What Is To Be Done?* (New York: International Publishers, 1943), pp. 76–77.

17. For Lenin's discussion of democratic centralism, see *The Lenin Anthology*, ed., Robert C. Tucker (New York: W. W. Norton, 1975), pp. 84–96.

18. See Richard F. Starr, "Checklist of Communist Parties in 1983," *Problems of Communism* (March-April, 1984), pp. 41–51.

19. Issues of *juche*, succession politics, and the unification formula are equally important.

20. See Kim Il Sung, "Let Us Further Strengthen the Socialist System of Our Country," Speech given at the First Session of the Fifth SPA of the DPRK, December 25, 1977.

21. John Fairbank, *The United States and China* (Cambridge: Harvard University Press, 1979), p. 447.

22. The penetration crisis is one of six crises of political development. The other five are: legitimacy, participation, integration, identity, and distribution. For details, see the chapter by Lucian Pye in Leonard Binder et al., *Crises and Sequences in Political Development* (Princeton: Princeton University Press, 1971).

23. See, for instance, Richard Pipes, *Survival Is Not Enough: Soviet Realities and American Future* (New York: Simon and Schuster, 1984), pp. 179–186.

24. For details, see Vadim Medish, *The Soviet Union*, 2nd. rev. ed. (Englewood Cliffs: Prentice-Hall, 1985), pp. 148–151.

25. For an analysis of the North Korean agriculture, see So-haeng Lee, "Management of North Korean Cooperative Farms, I, II, III" (in Korean), *Pukhan* (September, October, December, 1981), pp. 70–81, 161–171, and 130–143, respectively. A short English version of his article is found in *Vantage Point 4* (December 1981). Also, Un-gun Kim, "An Estimate of North Korea's Agricultural Output (II)," *Vantage Point* (October 1985), pp. 1–11.

26. See, for instance, Seweryn Bialer, "The Sino-Soviet Conflict: the Soviet Dimension," in Donald S. Zagoria, ed., *Soviet Policy in East Asia* (New Haven: Yale University Press, 1982), pp. 93–120.

27. Robert A. Dahl and Edward R. Tufte, *Size and Democracy* (Stanford: Stanford University Press, 1973), pp. 20–21.

28. Ibid., p. 138.

29. For a detailed analysis of Kim's varying use of "enemies" as a political strategy, see S. C. Yang, *Korea and Two Regimes* (Cambridge: Schenknam, 1981), pp. 177–197.

30. Ibid., p. 187.

31. Kim's *Ch'ongsan-ri* method is found in S. C. Yang, op. cit., pp. 197–203. For a discussion of Mao's *Dazhai*, see Fox Butterfield, *China: Alive in the Bitter Sea* (New York: Bantam Books), pp. 403–405.

32. See S. C. Yang, "The Kim Il Sung Cult in North Korea," *Korea and World Affairs* 5:1 (Spring 1981), pp. 161–186 and "The Politics of Cult in North Korea," *Political Studies Review* (1985), pp. 27–52.

33. For a comparison of North Korean communism with Chinese communism, see Byung-joon Ahn, "North Korean Communism and Chinese Communism," *Pukhan* (January 1980), pp. 120–140.

34. George Kennan describes the Soviet neurotic siege mentality as follows: "It is a state of mind that assumes all forms of authority not under Soviet control to be wicked, hostile, and menacing while conjuring up the image of a Soviet regime uniquely endowed with insight, wisdom, and benevolence as it stands bravely against misguided and dangerous foreign forces, frustrating their evil designs and protecting its own grateful people. And its public pronouncements are characterized by "preposterous lapses of memory, shameless double-standards, claims of infallibility, cynical misuse of general terms such as 'democracy' and 'progressive' and 'imperialist,' and malicious distortion of the motives of others." George Kennan, *New Yorker*, September 1984. Quoted in *The Bulletin of Atomic Scientists* 41:1 (January 1985), p. 8. As it is quite clear from the above, Kennan's meaning of the Soviet siege mentality is largely analogous to the siege mentality of the North Korean ruling elite.

35. In 1983, for instance, 1,195,551 foreigners visited South Korea and 493,461 Koreans traveled abroad. Ten-year travel statistics from 1974 to 1983 are found in *Hankuk Ilbo*, February 17, 1984. Also, see *Korea Herald*, February 14, 1984. In 1990, 2,349,693 foreigners visited South Korea and 1,560,923 Koreans traveled abroad in *Korea Statistical Yearbook, 1991* (Seoul: Korean Statistical Association, 1991), pp. 64–66.

36. An example is the U.S. government's unprecedented act of issuing visas to three North Korean scholars who took part in a panel sponsored by the Mid-Atlantic Coast Conference of the Association of Asian Studies at the George Washington University on October 26, 1985.

37. The author saw a documentary film of this scene while visiting North Korea in the summer of 1981.

38. See, for instance, Butterfield, pp. 64–88.

39. Ibid., p. 38. In China, for instance, there are four layers of news. At the bottom comes a four-page tabloid-sized paper called the *reference news*, whose circulation is about 10 million; next is the *reference material*, which is available only to the party members and cadres through their *danwei* [unit]; the *internal reference* is available only to the officials above grade twelve on the ladder of twenty-four ranks, and finally, there is the *cable news*, which is limited to the members of the Central Committee and the commanders of the large military regions. For details, see pp. 383–405.

40. See, for instance, Philip E. Converse, "The Nature of Belief System in Mass Publics," in Norman Luttbeg, ed., *Public Opinion and Public Policy*, 2nd ed. (Homewood: Dorsey Press, 1974), pp. 300–344. In his recent

article, Converse stated that "state monopoly of information flows is a very central part of the blueprint for governance," in Marxist-Leninist governments, not just in wartime or under duress, but as a routine matter. By contrast, military dictatorships, while keen on monopolizing public information, "tend to come and go in rather short stints." He further lamented a severe lack of relevant theoretical literature on the relationship between power and information in Marxist-Leninist states. For details, see his "Power and the Monopoly of Information," *APSR* 88:2 (March 1985), pp. 1–9. Also, Angus Campbell, "The Passive Citizen," in Edward C. Dreyer and Walter A. Rosebaum, *Political Opinion and Behavior* (North Scituate: Duxbury Press, 1976), pp. 164–184.

41. North Korea's official publications include: *Rodong Shinmun* [Workers' Daily], a daily organ of the Workers' Party of Korea; *Minju Choson* [Democratic Korea], an organ of the DPRK government; *Kulloja* [Workers], a theoretical monthly organ of the WPK; *Nodong Chongnyon* [Working Youth], a daily organ of the Socialist Working Youth League of Korea; *Nodongja Sinmun* [Workers' News], an organ of the General Federation of Trade Unions published every two days; *Choson Inminkun Sinmun* [Korean People's Army News], a daily organ of the Ministry of People's Armed Forces; *Choguk* [Fatherland], a weekly by the Fatherland United Democratic Front; *Choguk Tongil Sinmun* [Fatherland Unification News], a biweekly by the Committee for the peaceful Reunification of the Fatherland; *Chollima* [Flying Horse], a monthly by Kunjung Munhwa [Mass Culture] Publishing House; *Pyongyang Sinmun* [Pyongyang News], a daily organ of the WPK Pyongyang Municipal Committee; and *Pyongyang Times*, an English paper.

42. For details, see S. C. Yang, "The Kim Il Sung Cult in North Korea," and "The Politics of Cult in North Korea."

43. Ibid.

44. Ibid.

45. The Kim Il Sung pseudo-charisma thesis is developed by Yong-pil Rhee. For details, see his *Pukhan Chongch'i* [North Korean Politics] (Seoul: Daewangsa, 1982), pp. 52–54.

46. For details, see S. C. Yang, "The Politics of Cult in North Korea."

APPENDIX 1

౭ಖ

Suggested Reading List

1. Introduction: Understanding Korean Politics

Cho, Soon-sung, *Korea in World Politics, 1940–1950: An Evaluation of American Responsibility* (Berkeley, University of California Press, 1967).

Cumings, Bruce, *Korea's Place in the Sun: A Modern History* (New York: Norton, 1997).

Gill, Barry K., *Korea Versus Korea: A Case of Contested Legitimacy (Politics in Asia Series)* (London: Routledge, 1996).

Hart-Landsberg, Martin, *The Rush to Development: Economic Change and Political Struggle in South Korea* (New York: Monthly Review Press, 1993).

Kihl, Young-hwan, *Politics and Policies in Divided Korea: Regimes in Contest* (Boulder: Westview Press, 1984).

MacDonald, Donald Stone and Donald N. Clark, *The Koreans: Contemporary Politics and Society* (Boulder: Westview Press, 1996).

U.S. Government Staff, *South Korea (Country Studies)*, 1996.

Yang, Sung Chul, *The North and South Korean Political Systems: A Contemporary Analysis* (Seoul: Seoul Press, 1994).

2. Korean Politics: Setting and Political Culture

Boyer, William W. and Byong Man Ahn, *Rural Development in South Korea: A Sociopolitical Analysis* (Newark: University of Delaware Press, 1991).

Helgesen, Geir, *Democracy and Authority in Korea: The Cultural Dimension in Korean Politics* (New York: St. Martin's Press, 1998).

309

Henderson, Gregory, *Korea: The Politics of the Vortex* (Cambridge: Cambridge University Press, 1968).

Kihl, Young Whan, "The Legacy of Confucian Culture and South Korean Politics and Economics," in Sang Young Choi, ed., *Democracy in Korea* (Seoul: Seoul Press, 1997).

Kim, Chong Lim, *The Legislative Connection: The Politics of Representation in Kenya, Korea, and Turkey* (Durham: Duke University Press, 1984).

Koo, Hagen, ed., *State and Society in Contemporary Korea* (Ithaca: Cornell University Press, 1993).

Palais, James B., *Politics and Policy in Traditional Korea* (Harvard East Asian Monographs, 159, 1992).

Pye, Lucien and Sidney Verba, eds., *Political Culture and Political Development* (Princeton: Princeton University Press, 1965).

Doh C. Shin, *Mass Politics and Culture in Democratizing Korea* (Cambridge: Cambridge University Press, 1999)

Wells, Kenneth M., *South Korea's Minjung Movement: The Culture and Politics of Dissidence* (Honolulu: University of Hawaii Press, 1995).

3. Development of Korean Politics—A Historical Profile

Cotton, James, *Politics and Policy in the New Korean State: From Roh Tae Woo to Kim Young Sam* (New York: St. Martin's Press, 1995).

Cumings, Bruce, *The Origins of the Korean War: Liberation and the Emergence of Separate Regimes, 1945–1947* (Princeton: Princeton University Press, 1981).

——, *Korea's Place in the Sun: A Modern History* (New York: Norton, 1997).

Eckert, Carter J., et al., *Korea Old and New: A History* (Cambridge: Harvard University, 1991).

Han, Sung-Joo, *The Failure of Democracy in South Korea* (Berkeley: University of California Press, 1974).

——, "South Korea: Politics in Transition," in Sang Young Choi, ed., *Democracy in Korea* (Seoul: Seoul Press, 1997).

Lee, Jung-Hoon and Young Sun Song, "Republic of Korea," in Charles Morrison, ed., *Asia-Pacific Security Outlook 1998* (Tokyo: Japan Center for International Exchange, 1998).

Lee, Manwoo, *The Odyssey of Korean Democracy: Korean Politics, 1987–1990* (New York: Praeger Publication Text, 1990).

MacDonald, Donald S., *The Koreans: Contemporary Politics and Society* (Boulder: Westview Press, 1990).

Nam, Koon Woo, *South Korean Politics: The Search for Political Consensus and Stability* (University Press of America, 1990).

Noerper, Stephen, *The Tiger's Leap: The South Korean Drive for National Prestige and Emergence in the International Arena* (Sofia: St. Kliment Ohridski University Press, 1996).

Steinberg, David I., *The Republic of Korea* (Boulder: Westview Press, 1987).

Vogel, Ezra, *The Four Little Dragons: The Spread of Industrialization in East Asia* (Cambridge: Harvard University Press, 1991).

4. The Institutional Foundations of Korean Politics

Amsden, Alice H., *Asia's Next Giant: South Korea and Late Industrialization* (New York: Oxford University Press, 1992).

Diamond, Larry, *Political Culture and Democracy in Developing Countries* (Boulder: Lynne Rienner Publishers, 1993).

Evans, Peter, Dietrich Rueschemeyer, and Theda Skocpol, eds., *Bringing the State Back In* (New York: Cambridge University Press, 1985).

Hwang, Kelley, "South Korea's Bureaucracy and the Informal Politics of Economic Development," *Asian Affairs* (June 1994), pp. 178–186.

Kim, Chong Lim, ed., *The Political Participation in Korea: Democracy, Mobilization, and Stability* (Santa Barbara: Clio Press, 1980).

Palais, James B. *Confucian Statecraft and Korean Institutions: Yu Hyong-won and the Late Choson Dynasty* (Korean Studies of the Henry M. Jackson School) (Seattle: University of Washington Press, 1996).

Rhee, Jong-Chan. *The State and Industry in South Korea: The Limits of the Authoritarian State* (London: Routledge, 1994).

Waldner, David. *State Building and Late Development* (Ithaca: Cornell University Press, 1999)

5. The Political Process in Korea

Han, Sung-joo, *The Failure of Democracy in South Korea* (Berkeley: University of California Press, 1974).

———, and Yung Chul Park, "South Korea: Democratization At Last," in James Morley, ed., *Driven By Growth: Political Change in the Asia-Pacific Region* (Armonk: M. E. Sharpe, 1993), pp. 163–191.

Huer, Jon, *Marching Orders: The Role of the Military in South Korea's 'Economic Miracle,' 1961–1971 (Contributions in Economics and Economic History, No. 92, 1989).*

Kim, C. I. Eugene and Young Hwan Kihl, eds., *Party Politics and Elections in Korea* (Silver Spring, MD: Research Institute on Korean Affairs, 1976).

Kim, Se-Jin, *Politics of Military Revolution in Korea* (Chapel Hill: University of North Carolina, 1971).

McNamara, Dennis L. ed. *Corporatism and Korean Capitalism* (Routledge Studies in the Growth Economies of Asia) (London: Routledge, 1999).

Pak, Chi-young, *Political Opposition in Korea, 1945–1960* (Seoul: Seoul National University Press, 1980).

Sohn, Hak-kyu, *Authoritarianism and Opposition in South Korea* (London: Routledge, 1989).

Wells, Kenneth M., *South Korea's Minjung Movement: The Culture and Politics of Dissidence,* (Honolulu: University of Hawaii Press, 1995).

6. Political Leadership and the Administrative Process in Korea

Caiden, Gerald E. and Bun Woong Kim, eds., *A Dragon's Progress: Development Administration in Korea* (Kumarian Press Library Management for Development, Seoul: Kumarian Press, 1991).

Cotton, James, ed., *Korea under Roh Tae Woo: Democratization, Northern Policy, and Inter-Korean Relations* (Canberra: Allen & Unwin, 1993).

Hahm, Sung Deuk and L. Christopher Plein, *After Development: The Transformation of the Korean Presidency and Bureaucracy* (Washington, DC: Georgetown University Press).

Hinton, Harold C., *Korea under New Leadership: The Fifth Republic* (New York: Praeger, 1983).

Kim, Bun Woong and Pan Suk Kim, *Korean Public Administration: Managing the Uneven Development* (New Jersey: Hollym International Corp., 1999)

Ro, Chung-Hyun, *Public Administration and the Korean Transformation: Concepts, Policies, and Value Conflicts (Kumarian Press Library of Management for Development)* (Seoul: Kumarian Press, 1993).

Suh, Dae-Sook and Chae-Jin Lee, eds., *Political Leadership in Korea* (Seattle: University of Washington Press, 1976).

7. The Political Economy of Democratic Changes in Korea

Ahn, Chung-Si, "Economic Development and Democracy in South Korea," *Korea and World Affairs* 15, no. 2 (Winter 1991), pp. 740–754.

Deyo, Frederic, ed. *The Political Economy of the New Asian Industrialism* (Ithaca: Cornell University Press, 1987).

Gills, Barry K., *Korea versus Korea: A Case of Contested Legitimacy* (London: Routledge, 1996).

Haggard, Stephan, *Pathway from the Periphery* (Ithaca: Cornell University Press, 1990).

Han, Sang-jin, "Economic Development and Democracy," *Korea Journal* (Summer 1995), pp. 5–17.

Kim, Chong Lim and Merkl, Peter, *Political Participation in Korea: Democracy, Mobilization, and Stability (Studies in International and Comparative Politics, 15)* (Santa Barbara: Clio Books, 1980).

Kim, Hak-Joon, *Democratization under the Sixth Republic* (Seoul: Korean Overseas Information Service, 1989).

Kwon, Huck-Ju, *The Welfare State in Korea: The Politics of Legitimation (St. Antony's Series)* (New York: St. Martin's Press in association with St. Anthony's College, 1998).

Lie, John, *Han Unbound: The Political Economy of South Korea* (Stanford: Stanford University Press, 1998).

Mo, Jongryn and Chung-in Moon, eds. *Democracy and the Korean Economy* (Stanford: Hoover Institution Press, 1998).

Moon, Chung-in and Jongryn Mo, eds., *Democratization and Globalization in Korea: Assessment and Prospects* (Seoul: Yonsei University Press, 1999).

Oh, John Kie-chang. *Korean Politics: The Quest for Democratization and Economic Development* (Ithaca: Cornell University Press, 1999).

Pae, Sung M., *Korea Leading Developing Nations: Economy, Democracy and Welfare* (Lanham, MD: University Press of America, 1992).

Ro, Chung-Hyun, *Public Administration and the Korean Transform Concepts, Politics, and Value Conflicts (Kumari Press Library of Management for Development)* (Seoul: Kumarian Press, 1993).

Robinson, Thomas W., ed., *Democracy and Development in East Asia: Taiwan, South Korea, and the Philippines (AEI Studies, 504)*, 1991.

Sakong, Il, *Korea in the World Economy* (Washington, DC: Institute for International Economics, 1993).

Wade, Larry L., *Economic Development of South Korea: The Political Economy of Success* (New York: Praeger, 1978).

White, Gordon, *Developmental States in East Asia* (New York: St. Martin's Press, 1988).

Woo, Jung-En. *Race to the Swift: State and Finance in Korean Industrialization* (Studies of the East Asian Institute) (New York: Columbia University Press, 1992).

8. The Foreign and Unification Policies of the Republic of Korea

Drennan, William, "Prospects and Implications of Korean Unification," *Northeast Asia Peace and Security Network Special Report*, Nautilus Institute, August 22, 1997, pp. 1–16.

Eberstadt, Nicholas, "Hastening Korean Unification," *Foreign Affairs*, 76, no. 2, (March/April 1997), pp. 77–92.

———, and Robert A. Scalapino, *Korea Approaches Reunification* 1995.

Gong, Gerrit W. et al., *Korean Peninsula Developments and U.S.–Japan–South Korea Relations* (Washington, DC: The Center for Strategic and International Studies, 1993).

Grinker, Roy Richard, *Korea and Its Futures: Unification and the Unfinished War* (New York: St. Martin's Press, 1998).

Han, Sung-Joo, *Korea in a Changing World: Democracy, Diplomacy, and Future Developments* (Seoul: Oruem Publishing House, 1995).

Hart-Landsberg, Martin. *Korea: Division, Reunification, and U.S. Foreign Policy* (New York: Monthly Review Press, 1998).

Hwang, In K., *One Korea via Permanent Neutrality: Peaceful Management of Korean Unification* (Cambridge: Schenkman Books, 1987).

Kwak, Tae-Hwan, Chonghan Kim, and Hong Nack Kim, eds., *Korean Reunification: New Perspectives and Approaches* (Seoul: Kyungnam University Press, 1984).

Kihl, Young Hwan, ed., *Korea and the World: Beyond the Cold War* (Boulder: Westview Press, 1994).

Kim, Hak-Chun, *Korea's Relations with Her Neighbors in a Changing World* (New Jersey: Hollym International Corp., 1993).

——, *The Unification Policy of South and North Korea* (Seoul: Seoul National University Press, 1977).

Kim, Young Jeh, *The Political Unification of Korea in the 1990s: Key to World Peace (Studies in World Peace, Vol. 3)* (Edwin Mellen Press, 1989).

Koh, Byung Chul, *The Foreign Policy Systems of North and South Korea* (Berkeley: University of California Press, 1984).

MacDonald, Donald S., *U.S.-Korean Relations from Liberation to Self-reliance: The Twenty Year Record* (Boulder: Westview Press, 1992).

Moon, Chung-in, ed., *Arms Control on the Korean Peninsula: International Penetrations, Regional Dynamics, and Domestic Structure* (Seoul: Yonsei University Press, 1995).

Noland, Marcus, "Why North Korea Will Muddle Through," *Foreign Affairs*, 76, no. 4 (July/August 1997), pp. 105–118.

Scalapino, Robert A., *The Problems of Division and Unification in Korea* (London: Audio Learning, 1983).

Sigal, Leon V., *Disarming Strangers: Nuclear Diplomacy with North Korea (Princeton Studies in International History Politics)* (Princeton: Princeton University Press, 1998).

Thompson, Kenneth W., ed., *Korea: A World in Change (Miller Center Series on a World in Change, Vol. 8)* (University Press of America, 1996).

9. Understanding the
North Korean Political Framework

An, Tai Sung, *North Korea in Transition: From Dictatorship to Dynasty* (Westport, CT: Greenwood Publishing Group, 1983).

Choe, In-su, *Kim Chong-il: The People's Leader* (Pyongyang: Foreign Languages Publishing House, 1983).

Hayes, Peter, "What North Korea Wants," *The Bulletin of the Atomic Scientists*, http://neog.com/atomic/issues/1994/so94/so94Albright.html.

Henriksen, Thomas H. and Jongryn Mo, *North Korea after Kim Il Sung: Continuity or Change?* (Stanford: Hoover Institution Press Publication, 1997).

Kim, Ilpyong J., *Communist Politics in North Korea* (New York: Praeger, 1975).

Kim, Samuel S., ed., *North Korean Foreign Relations in the Post–Cold War Era* (New York: Oxford University Press, 1998).

——, "Research on Korean Communism: Promise versus Performance," *World Politics* 32, no. 2 (January 1980).

Lee, Suck-Ho, *Party-military Relations in North Korea: a Comparative Analysis* (Seoul: Research Center for Peace and Unification of Korea, 1989).

Merrill, John, "North Korea in 1992: Steering Away from the Shoals." *Asian Survey* (January 1993).

——, *Korea: The Peninsular Origin of War* (Newark: University of Delaware Press, 1989).

Moon, Chung-in, ed., *Unraveling Regime Dynamics in North Korea* (Seoul: Yonsei University Press, 1998).

Park, Han S., *North Korea: Ideology, Politics, Economy* (Englewood Cliffs: Prentice Hall, 1996).

Segal, Leon. *Disarming Strangers: Nuclear Diplomacy with North Korea* (Princeton Studies in International History and Politics) (Princeton: Princeton University Press, 1998).

Scalapino, Robert A., *North Korea at a Crossroads* (Stanford: Hoover Institute Press, 1997).

Silvey, Jonathan and Tony Weiner, *The Other Korea: North Korea on the Eve of Change* (Pluto Press, 1990).

Smith, Hazel, ed., *North Korea in the New World Order* (New York: St. Martin's Press, 1996).

Snyder, Scott, *A Coming Crisis on the Korean Peninsula? The Food Crisis, Economic Decline, and Political Considerations* (Washington, D.C.: U.S. Institute of Peace, 1997).

Suh, Dae-Sook, *Korean Communism, 1945–1980: A Reference Guide to the Political System* (Honolulu: University Press of Hawaii, 1981).

———, and Chae-Jin Lee, *North Korea after Kim Il Sung* (Boulder: Lynne Rienner Publishers, 1998).

U.S. Governmental Staff, *North Korea (Country Studies)* 1995.

Yang, Sung Chul, *Korea and Two Regimes: Kim Il Sung and Park Chung Hee* (Cambridge: Schenkman Publishing Co., 1981).

APPENDIX 2

ಕ್ಕಿ

Map of Korea

ટ≱

Basic Facts on Korea and the Korean Peninsula

Republic of Korea, Korean Taehan Min'guk, country occupying the southern Korean peninsular in East Asia. South Korea is situated about 120 miles (193 km) northwest of the Japanese islands of Honshu and Kyushu and includes Cheju Island, which is located about 60 miles (97 km) south of the peninsular. The country is about 300 miles (480 km) long and about 135 miles (217 km) wide. It is bordered on the north by North Korea, in the east by the East Sea (Sea of Japan), on the south by the Korea Strait, and on the west by West Sea (Yellow Sea). The nation's capital is Seoul; its area is 38,830 sq m (99,274 sq km).

Basic Facts of Korea

Official name: Taehan Min'guk (Republic of Korea)

Form of government: Unitary multiparty republic with one legislative house (National Assembly [273 seats]).

Chief of state: President.

Head of government: Prime Minster.

Capital: Seoul.

Official Language: Korean

Official religion: none.

Monetary Unit: 1 won (W) = 100 chon; valuation (August 3, 1999) 1U.S.$ = W1,200

Demography

Population (1999): 46,430,000.

Density (1999): persons per sq mi 1,119.1, persons per sq km 463.

Urban-rural (1995): Urban 81.0%; rural 19.0%.

Ethnic composition (1990): Korean 99.9%; other 0.1%.

Religious affiliation (1995): Religious 50.7%, of which Buddhist 23.2%, Protestant 19.7%, Roman Catholic 6.6, Confucian 0.5%, Wonbulgyo 0.2%, Ch'ondogyo 0.1%, other 0.5%; Nonreligious 49.3%.

Major Cities (1998): Seoul population 10,321,496; Pusan 3,842,834, Taegu 2,504,645, Inch'on 2,498,404; Kwangju 1,342,009

Vital Statistics

Birth rate per 1,000 population (1995): 16.0 (world average 25.0)

Death rate per 1,000 population (1995): 6.0 (world average 9.3)

Natural increase rate per 1,000 population (1995): 10.0 (world average 15.7)

Total fertility rate (average births per childbearing woman, 1995): 1.8

Marriage rate per 1,000 population (1993): 7.0

Divorce rate per 1,000 population (1993): 1.1

Life expectancy at birth (1995): male 68.0 years; female 76.0 years.

Major causes of death per 100,000 population (1993): diseases of the circulatory system 149.0; malignant neoplasms (cancers) 105.9; accidents, poisoning, and violence 73.0; diseases of the digestive system 40.5; diseases of the respiratory system 24.1

National Economy

Budget (1997)

Revenue: W 95,511,700,000,000 (taxes on goods and services 32.4%, income taxes 28.5%, nontax revenue 15.5%, social security contributions 8.8%, taxes on international trade 6.3%, other taxes 8.5).

Expenditures: W 95.872,900,000,000

(defense 14.6%, education 17.6%, general public services 10.2%, social security and welfare 12.3%, economic services 25.5%, housing, transportation, and communication 8.0%, other 11.8%)

Public debt (external, outstanding, 1997): U.S.$159,237,000,000

Gross national product (1997): U.S.$437,400,000,000 (U.S.$9,511 per capita).

Foreign Trade

Imports (1997): U.S.$144,616,374,000

Exports (1997): U.S.$136,164,204,000

Education and Health

Educational attainment (1995). Percentage of population age 25 and over having: primary education or less 21.1%; secondary education 15.7%; high school education 37.5.%; college education 25.7%. Literacy (1990): total population age 15 and over literate 96.3%; males literate 99.15; females literate 93.5%.

Health (1997): physicians 62,609 (1 per 735 persons); hospital beds 164,588 (1 per 209 persons); infant mortality rate per 1,000 lives births (1995) 10.0

Food (1992): daily per capital caloric intake 3,285 (vegetable products 86%, animal products 14%); 14% of FAO recommended minimum requirement

Military

Total active duty personnel (1997): 690,000 (army 81.2%, navy 9.7%, air force 9.1%). Military expenditures as percentage of GNP (1995): 3.4% (world 2.8%); per capita expenditure U.S.$ 320.

APPENDIX 4

২৯

Korean Constitution

A Brief History of the Korean Constitution

The Constituent Assembly of the Republic of Korea was inaugurated on May 31, 1948. It adopted and promulgated a democratic Constitution on July 17, 1948, that stipulated a unicameral legislature and a presidential system of government. Under this Constitution, the first president of the Republic of Korea was elected by the Constituent Assembly and on August 15, 1948; the foundation of the Republic of Korea was proclaimed throughout the world.

The Constitution was amended nine times:

1. Amended on July 7, 1952
2. Amended on November 29,1954
3. Amended on June 15,1960
4. Amended on November 29,1960
5. Amended on December 26,1962 (wholly amended)
6. Amended on October 21,1969
7. Amended on December 27,1972 (wholly amended)
8. Amended on October 27,1980 (wholly amended)
9. Amended on October 29,1987 (wholly amended)

Constitution

This is a full text of the Constitution fully amended on October 29,1987.

PREAMBLE

We the people of Korea, proud of a resplendent history and traditions dating from time immemorial, upholding the cause of the

327

Provisional Republic of Korea Government born of the March First Independence Movement of 1919 and the democratic ideals of the April Nineteenth Uprising of 1960 against injustice, having assumed the mission of democratic reform and peaceful unification of our homeland and having determined to consolidate national unity with justice, humanitarianism and brotherly love, and

To destroy all social vices and injustice, and

To afford equal opportunities to every person and provide for the fullest development of individual capabilities in all fields, including political, economic, social and cultural Life by further strengthening the basic free and democratic order conducive to private initiative and public harmony, and

To help each person discharge those duties and responsibilities concomitant to freedoms and rights, and

To elevate the quality of life for all citizens and contribute to lasting world peace and the common prosperity of mankind and thereby to ensure security, liberty and happiness for ourselves and our posterity forever,

Do hereby amend, through national referendum following a resolution by the National Assembly, the Constitution, ordained and established on the Twelfth Day of July anno Domini Nineteen hundred and forty-eight, and amended eight times subsequently,

October 29, 1987.

Chapter I. General Provisions

ARTICLE 1 [DEMOCRACY]
(1) The Republic of Korea is a democratic republic.
(2) The sovereignty of the Republic of Korea resides in the people, and all state authority emanates from the people.
ARTICLE 2 [NATIONALITY]
(1) Nationality in the Republic of Korea is prescribed by law.
(2) It is the duty of the State to protect citizens residing abroad as prescribed by law.
ARTICLE 3 [TERRITORY]
The territory of the Republic of Korea shall consist of the Korean peninsula and its adjacent islands.
ARTICLE 4 [UNIFICATION, PEACE]
The Republic of Korea seeks unification and formulates and carries out a policy of peaceful unification based on the principles of freedom and democracy.

ARTICLE 5 [WAR, ARMED FORCES]
(1) The Republic of Korea endeavors to maintain international peace and renounces all aggressive wars.
(2) The Armed Forces are charged with the sacred mission of national security and the defense of the land and their political neutrality must be maintained.

ARTICLE 6 [TERRITORY]
(1) Treaties duly concluded and promulgated under the Constitution and the generally recognized rule of international law have the same effect as the domestic laws of the Republic of Korea.
(2) The status of foreigners is guaranteed as prescribed by international law and treaties.

ARTICLE 7 [PUBLIC OFFICIALS]
(1) All public officials are servants of the entire people and responsible to the people.
(2) The status and political impartiality of public officials is guaranteed as prescribed by law.

ARTICLE 8 [POLITICAL PARTIES]
(1) The establishment of political parties is free, and the plural party system is guaranteed.
(2) Political parties must be democratic in their objectives, organization, and activities, and have the necessary organizational arrangements for, the people to participate in the formation of the political will.
(3) Political parties enjoy the protection of the State and may be provided with operational funds by the State under the conditions as prescribed by law.
(4) If the purposes or activities of a political party are contrary to the fundamental democratic order, the Government may bring action against it in the Constitutional Court for its dissolution, and, the political party is dissolved in accordance with the decision of the Constitutional Court.

ARTICLE 9 [CULTURE]
The State tries to sustain and develop the cultural heritage and to enhance national culture.

Chapter II. Rights and Duties of the Citizens

ARTICLE 10 [DIGNITY, PURSUIT OF HAPPINESS]
All citizens are assured of human worth and dignity and have the right to pursue happiness. It is the duty of the State to confirm and guarantee the fundamental and inviolable human rights of individuals.

ARTICLE 11 [EQUALITY]

(1) All citizens are equal before the law, and there may be no discrimination in political, economic, social, or cultural life on account of sex, religion, or social status.

(2) No privileged caste is recognized or ever established in any form.

(3) The awarding of decorations or distinctions of honor in any form is effective only for recipients, and no privileges ensue therefrom.

ARTICLE 12 [PERSONAL LIBERTY, PERSONAL INTEGRITY]

(1) All citizens enjoy personal liberty. No person may be arrested, detained, searched, seized, or interrogated except as provided by law. No person may be punished, placed under preventive restrictions, or subject to involuntary labor except as provided by law and through lawful procedures.

(2) No citizens may be tortured or be compelled to testify against himself in criminal cases.

(3) Warrants issued by a judge through due procedures upon the request of a prosecutor have to be presented in case of arrest, detention, seizure, or search: Provided, that in a case where a criminal suspect is a apprehended in *flagrante delicto*, or where there is danger that a person suspected of committing a crime punishable by imprisonment of three years or more may escape or destroy evidence, investigative authorities may request an *ex post facto* warrant.

(4) Any person who is arrested or detained has the right to prompt assistance of counsel. When a criminal defendant is unable to secure counsel by his own efforts, the State assigns counsel for the defendant as prescribed by law.

(5) No person may be arrested or detained without being informed of the reason therefore and of his right to assistance of counsel. The family and other related persons, as designated by law, of a person arrested or detained shall be notified without delay of the reason for and the time and place of the arrest or detention.

(6) Any person who is arrested or detained, has the right to request the court to review the legality of the arrest or detention.

(7) In a case where a confession is deemed to have been made against a defendant's will due to torture, violence, intimidation, unduly prolonged arrest, deceit or similar action, or in a case where a confession is the only evidence against a defendant in a formal trial, such a confession may not be admitted as evidence of guilt, nor may a defendant be punished by reason of such a confession.

ARTICLE 13 [NULLA POENA SINE LEGE, DOUBLE JEOPARDY, RETROACTIVE LAW, FAMILY LIABILITY]

(1) No citizen may be prosecuted for an act which does not constitute a crime under the law in force at the time it was committed, nor may he be place d in double jeopardy.

(2) No restrictions may be imposed upon the political rights of any citizen, nor may any person be deprived of property rights by means of retroactive legislation.

(3) No citizen shall suffer unfavorable treatment on account of an act not of his own doing but committed by a relative.

ARTICLE 14 [RESIDENCE, MOVE]

All citizens enjoy the freedom of residence and the right to move at win.

ARTICLE 15 [OCCUPATION]

All citizens enjoy freedom of occupation.

ARTICLE 16 [HOME, SEARCH, SEIZURE]

All citizens are free from intrusion into their place of residence. In case of search or seizure in a residence, a warrant issued by a judge upon request of a prosecutor has to be presented.

ARTICLE 17 [PRIVACY]

The privacy of no citizen may be infringed.

ARTICLE 18 [SECRECY OF CORRESPONDENCE]

The secrecy of correspondence of no citizen may be infringed.

ARTICLE 19 [CONSCIENCE]

All citizens enjoy the freedom of conscience.

ARTICLE 20 [RELIGION, CHURCH]

(1) All citizens enjoy the freedom of religion.

(2) No state religion may be recognized, and church and state are to be separated.

ARTICLE 21 [SPEECH, PRESS, ASSEMBLY, ASSOCIATION, HONOR, PUBLIC MORALS]

(1) All citizens enjoy the freedom of speech and the press, and of assembly and association.

(2) Licensing or censorship of speech and the press, and licensing of assembly and association may not be recognized.

(3) The standard of news service and broadcast facilities and matters necessary to ensure the functions of newspapers is determined by law.

(4) Neither speech nor the press may violate the honor or rights of other persons nor undermine public morals or social ethics. Should speech or the press violate the honor or rights of other persons, claims may be made for the damage resulting therefrom.

ARTICLE 22 [LEARNING, INTELLECTUAL RIGHTS]

(1) All citizens enjoy the freedom of learning and the arts.

(2) The rights of authors, inventors, scientists, engineers, and artists are protected by law.

ARTICLE 23 [PROPERTY, PUBLIC WELFARE, EXPROPRIATION]

(1) The right to property of all citizens is guaranteed. Its contents and limitations are determined by law.

(2) The exercise of property rights shall conform to the public welfare.

(3) Expropriation, use, or restriction of private property from public necessity and compensation therefore are governed by law. However, in such a case, just compensation must be paid.

ARTICLE 24 [RIGHT TO VOTE]

All citizens have the right to vote under the conditions prescribed by law.

ARTICLE 25 [RIGHT TO PUBLIC OFFICE]

All citizens have the right to hold public office under the conditions prescribed by law.

ARTICLE 26 [PETITION]

(1) All citizens have the right to petition in writing to any governmental agency under the conditions prescribed by law.

(2) The State is obligated to examine all such petitions.

ARTICLE 27 [RIGHT TO TRIAL]

(1) All citizens have the right to be tried in conformity with the law by judges qualified under the Constitution and the law.

(2) Citizens who are not on active military service or employees of the military forces may not be tried by a court martial within the territory of the Republic of Korea, except in case of crimes as prescribed by law involving important classified military information, sentinels, sentry posts, the supply of harmful food and beverages, prisoners of war, and military articles and facilities, and in the case of the proclamation of extraordinary martial law.

(3) All citizens have the right to a speedy trial. The accused have the right to a public trial without delay in the absence of justifiable reasons to the contrary.

(4) The accused are presumed innocent until a judgment of guilt has been pronounced.

(5) A victim of a crime is entitled to make a statement during the proceedings of the trial of the case involved under the conditions prescribed by law.

ARTICLE 28 [FALSE IMPRISONMENT]

In a case where a criminal suspect or an accused person who has been placed under detention is not indicted as provided by law or is acquitted by a court, he is entitled to claim just compensation from the State under the conditions as prescribed by law.

ARTICLE 29 [STATE AND OFFICIAL'S LIABILITY]

(1) In case a person has sustained damages by an unlawful act committed by a public official in the course of official duties, he

may claim just compensation from the State or public organization under the conditions as prescribed by law. In this case, the public official concerned are not immune from liabilities.

(2) In case a person on active military service or an employee of the military forces, a police official, or others as prescribed by law sustains damages in connection with the performance of official duties such as combat action, drill, and so forth, he is not entitled to a claim against the State or public organization on the grounds of unlawful acts committed by public officials in the course of official duties, but only to compensations as prescribed by law.

ARTICLE 30 [VICTIMS]
Citizens who have suffered bodily injury or death due to criminal acts of others may receive aid from the State under the conditions as prescribed by law.

ARTICLE 31 [EDUCATION]

(1) All citizens have an equal right to receive an education corresponding to their abilities.

(2) All citizens who have children to support are responsible at least for their elementary education and other education as provided by law.

(3) Compulsory education is free of charge.

(4) Independence, professionalism, and political impartiality of education and the autonomy of institutions of higher learning are guaranteed under the conditions as prescribed by law.

(5) The State promotes lifelong education.

(6) Fundamental matters pertaining to the educational system, including schools and lifelong education, administration, finance, and the status of teachers are determined by law.

ARTICLE 32 [WORK]

(1) All citizens have the right to work. The State endeavors to promote the employment of workers and to guarantee optimum wages through social and economic means and enforces a minimum wage system under the conditions as prescribed by law.

(2) All citizens have the duty to work. The State prescribes by law the extent and conditions of the duty to work in conformity with democratic principles.

(3) Standards of working conditions are determined by law in such a way as to guarantee human dignity.

(4) Special protection has to be accorded to working women, and they may not be subjected to unjust discrimination in terms of employment, wages, and working conditions.

(5) Special protection has to be accorded to working children.

(6) The opportunity to work shall be accorded preferentially, under the conditions as prescribed by law, to those who have given distinguished service to the State, wounded veterans

and policemen, and members of the bereaved families of military servicemen and policemen killed in action.

ARTICLE 33 [UNIONS]

(1) To enhance working conditions, workers have the right to independent association, collective bargaining, and collective action.

(2) Only those public officials who are designated by law, have the right to association, collective bargaining, and collective action.

(3) The right to collective action of workers employed by important defense industries may be either restricted or denied under the conditions as prescribed by law.

ARTICLE 34 [WELFARE]

(1) All citizens are entitled to a life worthy of human beings.

(2) The State has the duty to endeavor to promote social security and welfare.

(3) The State endeavors to promote the welfare and rights of women.

(4) The State has the duty to implement policies for enhancing the welfare of senior citizen and the young.

(5) Citizens who are incapable of earning a livelihood due to a physical disability, disease, old age, or other reasons are protected by the State under the conditions as prescribed by law.

(6) The State endeavors to prevent disasters and to protect citizens from harm therefrom.

ARTICLE 35 [ENVIRONMENT, HOUSING]

(1) All citizens have the right to a healthy and pleasant environment. The State and all citizens shall endeavor to protect the environment.

(2) The substance of the environmental right is determined by law.

(3) The State endeavors to ensure comfortable housing for all citizens through housing development policies and the like.

ARTICLE 36 [MARRIAGE, FAMILY, MOTHERS, HEALTH]

(1) Marriage and family life are entered into and sustained on the basis of individual dignity and equality of the sexes, and the State must do everything in its power to achieve that goal.

(2) The State endeavors to protect mothers.

(3) The health of all citizens is protected by the State.

ARTICLE 37 [RESTRICTION, NO INFRINGEMENT OF ESSENTIALS]

(1) Freedoms and rights of citizens may not be neglected on the grounds that they are not enumerated in the Constitution.

(2) The freedoms and rights of citizens may be restricted by law only when necessary for national security, the maintenance of law and order, or for public welfare. Even when such restriction is imposed, no essential aspect of the freedom or right shall be violated.

ARTICLE 38 [DUTY TO PAY TAXES]
All citizens have the duty to pay taxes under the conditions as prescribed by law.
ARTICLE 39 [DUTY TO MILITARY SERVICE]
(1) All citizens have the duty of national defense under the conditions as prescribed by law.
(2) No citizen may be treated unfavorably on account of the fulfillment of his obligation of military service.

Chapter III. The National Assembly

ARTICLE 40 [PARLIAMENT]
The legislative power is vested in the National Assembly.
ARTICLE 41 [ELECTION]
(1) The National Assembly is composed of members elected by universal, equal, direct, and secret ballot by the citizens.
(2) The number of members of the National Assembly is determined by law, but the number may not be less than 200.
(3) The constituencies of members of the National Assembly, proportional representation, and other matters pertaining to National Assembly elections are determined by law.
ARTICLE 42 [TERM]
The term of office of members of the National Assembly is four years.
ARTICLE 43 [INCOMPATIBILITY]
Members of the National Assembly may not concurrently hold any other office prescribed by law.
ARTICLE 44 [IMMUNITY]
(1) During the sessions of the National Assembly, no member of the National Assembly may be arrested or detained without the consent of the National Assembly except in case of *flagrante delicto*.
(2) In case of apprehension or detention of a member of the National Assembly prior to the opening of a session, such member must be released during the session upon the request of the National Assembly, except in case of *flagrante delicto*.
ARTICLE 45 [INDEMNITY]
No member of the National Assembly can be held responsible outside the National Assembly for opinions officially expressed or votes cast in the Assembly.
ARTICLE 46 [DUTIES OF MEMBERS]
(1) Members of the National Assembly have the duty to maintain high standards of integrity.
(2) Members of the National Assembly must give preference to National interests and perform their duties in accordance with conscience.

(3) Members of the National Assembly may not acquire, through abuse of their positions, rights, and interests in property or positions, or assist other persons to acquire the same, by means of contracts with or dispositions by the State, public organizations, or industries.

ARTICLE 47 [SESSIONS]

(1) A regular session of the National Assembly is convened once every year under the conditions prescribed by law, and extraordinary sessions of the National Assembly can be convened upon the request of the President or at least one-fourth of the members.

(2) The period of regular sessions cannot exceed a hundred days, and that of extraordinary sessions, thirty days.

(3) If the President requests the convening of an extraordinary session, the period of the session and the reasons for the request must be clearly specified.

ARTICLE 48 [SPEAKERS]

The National Assembly elects one Speaker and two Vice-Speakers.

ARTICLE 49 [QUORUM, MAJORITY]

Except as otherwise provided in the Constitution or by law, the attendance of a majority of the total members, and the concurrent vote of a majority of the members present, are necessary for decisions of the National Assembly. In case of a tie vote, the matter is regarded as rejected.

ARTICLE 50 [PUBLICITY]

(1) Sessions of the National Assembly are open to the public: Provided, that when it is decided so by a majority of the members present, when the Speaker deems it necessary to do so for the sake of national security, they may be closed to the public.

(2) The public disclosure of the proceedings of sessions which were not open to the public is determined by law.

ARTICLE 51 [PENDING BILLS]

Bills and other matters submitted to the National Assembly for deliberation cannot be abandoned on the ground that they were not acted upon during the session in which they were introduced, except in a case where the term of the members of the National Assembly has expired.

ARTICLE 52 [INITIATIVE]

Bills may be introduced by members of the National Assembly or by the Executive.

ARTICLE 53 [PASSING BILLS]

(1) Each bill passed by the National Assembly shall be sent to the Executive, and the President shall promulgate it within fifteen days.

(2) In case of objection to the bill, the President may, within the period referred to in Paragraph (1), return it to the National

Assembly with written explanation of his objection, and request it be reconsidered. The President may do the same during adjournment of the National Assembly.

(3) The President may not request the National Assembly to reconsider the bill in part, or with proposed amendments.

(4) In case there is a request for reconsideration of a bill, the National Assembly reconsiders it, and if the National Assembly repasses the bill in the original form with the attendance of more than one half of the total members, and with a concurrent vote of two-thirds or more of the members present, it becomes law.

(5) If the President does not promulgate the bill, or does not request the National Assembly to reconsider it within the period referred to in Paragraph (1) it becomes law.

(6) The President promulgate without delay the law as finalized under Paragraphs (4) and (5). If the President does not promulgate a law within five days after it has become law under Paragraph (5), or after it has been returned to the Executive under Paragraph (4), the Speaker promulgates it.

(7) Except as provided otherwise, a law takes effect twenty days after the date of promulgation.

ARTICLE 54 [BUDGET]

(1) The National Assembly deliberates and decides upon the national budget bill.

(2) The Executive formulates the budget bill for each fiscal year and submits it to the National Assembly within ninety days before the beginning of a fiscal year. The National Assembly decides upon it within thirty days before the beginning of the fiscal year.

(3) If the budget bill is not passed by the beginning of the fiscal year, the Executive may, in conformity with the budget of the previous fiscal year, disburse funds for the following purposes until the budget bill is passed by the National Assembly:

1) The maintenance and operation of agencies and facilities established by the Constitution or law;

2) Execution of the obligatory expenditures as prescribed by law; and

3) Continuation of projects previously approved in the budget.

ARTICLE 55 [RESERVE FUND]

(1) In a case where it is necessary to make continuing disbursements for a period longer than one fiscal year, the Executive obtains the approval of the National Assembly for a specified period of time.

(2) A reserve fund is to be approved by the National Assembly in total. The disbursement of the reserve fund shall be approved during the next session of the National Assembly.

ARTICLE 56 [BUDGET AMENDMENT]
When it is necessary to amend the budget, the Executive may formulate a supplementary revised budget bill and submit it to the National Assembly.
ARTICLE 57 [CHANGES OF BUDGET BILL]
The National Assembly shall, without the consent of the Executive, neither increase the sum of any item of expenditure nor create any new items of expenditure in the budget submitted by the Executive.
ARTICLE 58 [ISSUING NATIONAL BONDS]
When the Executive plans to issue national bonds or to conclude contracts which may incur financial obligations on the State outside the budget, it needs the prior concurrence of the National Assembly.
ARTICLE 59 [TAXES]
Types and rates of taxes are determined by law.
ARTICLE 60 [CONSENT TO TREATIES]
(1) The National Assembly has the right to consent to the conclusion and ratification of treaties pertaining to mutual assistance or mutual security; treaties concerning important international organizations; treaties of friendship, trade and navigation; treaties pertaining to any restriction in sovereignty; peace treaties; treaties which will burden the State or people with an important financial obligation; and treaties related to legislative matters.
(2) The National Assembly also has the right to consent to the declaration of war, the dispatch of armed forces to foreign states, and the stationing of alien forces in the territory of the Republic of Korea.
ARTICLE 61 [INVESTIGATIONS]
(1) The National Assembly may inspect affairs of state or investigate specific matters of state affairs, and may demand the production of documents ' directly related thereto, the appearance of a witness in person, and the furnishing of testimony or statements of opinion.
(2) The procedures and other necessary matters concerning the inspection and investigation of state administration are determined by law.
ARTICLE 62 [GOVERNMENT IN PARLIAMENT]
(1) The Prime Minister, members of the State Council, or government delegates may attend meetings of the National Assembly or its committees and report on the state administration or deliver opinions and answer questions.
(2) When requested by the National Assembly or its committees, the Prime Minister, members of the State Council, or government delegates have to attend any meeting of the National Assembly and answer questions. If the Prime Minister or

State Council members are requested to attend, the Prime Minister or State Council members may have State Council members or government delegates attend any meeting of the National Assembly and answer questions.

ARTICLE 63 [RECOMMENDATION FOR REMOVAL]

(1) The National Assembly may pass a recommendation for the removal of the Prime Minister or a State Council member from office.

(2) A recommendation for removal as referred to in Paragraph (1) may be introduced by one third or more of the total members of the National Assembly, and passed with the concurrent vote of a majority of the total members of the National Assembly.

ARTICLE 64 [PROCEEDINGS, DISCIPLINARY ACTIONS]

(1) The National Assembly may establish the rules of its proceedings and internal regulations, provided that they are not in conflict with law.

(2) The National Assembly may review the qualifications of its members and may take disciplinary actions against its members.

(3) The concurrent vote of two-thirds or more of the total members of the National Assembly are required for the expulsion of any member.

(4) No. action may be brought to court with regard to decisions taken under Paragraphs (2) and (3).

ARTICLE 65 [IMPEACHMENT]

(1) In case the President, the Prime Minister, members of the State Council, heads of Executive Ministries, judges of the Constitutional Court, judges, members of the Central Election Management Committee, members of the Board of Audit and Inspection, and other public officials designated by law have violated the Constitution or other laws in the performance of official duties, the National Assembly may pass motions for their impeachment.

(2) A motion for impeachment prescribed in Paragraph (1) may be proposed by one-third or more of the total members of the National Assembly, and requires a concurrent vote of a majority of the total members of the National Assembly for passage: Provided, that a motion for the impeachment of the President shall be proposed by a majority of the total members of the National Assembly and approved by two-thirds or more of the total members of the National Assembly.

(4) Any person against whom a motion for impeachment has been passed is suspended from exercising his power until the impeachment has been adjudicated.

(5) A decision on impeachment does not extend further than removal from public office. However, it does not exempt the person impeached from civil or criminal liability.

Chapter IV. The Executive

Section 1. The President
Article 66 [Head of State]
(1) The President is the Head of State and represents the State vis-à-vis foreign states.
(2) The President has the responsibility and duty to safeguard the independence, territorial integrity, and continuity of the State and the Constitution.
(3) The President has the duty to pursue sincerely the peaceful unification of the homeland.
(4) Executive power is vested in the Executive Branch headed by the President.
Article 67 [Election]
(1) The President is elected by universal, equal, direct, and secret ballot by the people.
(2) In case two or more persons receive the same largest number of votes in the election as referred to in Paragraph (1), the person who receives the largest number of votes in an open session of the National Assembly attended by a majority of the total members of the National Assembly is elected.
(3) If and when there is only one presidential candidate, he shall not be elected President unless he receives at least one-third of the total eligible votes.
(4) Citizens who are eligible for election to the National Assembly, and who have reached the age of forty years or more on the date of the presidential election, are eligible to be elected to the presidency.
(5) Matters pertaining to presidential elections are determined by law.
Article 67 [Succession]
(1) The successor to the incumbent President is elected seventy to forty days before his term expires.
(2) In case a vacancy occurs in the office of the President or the President-elect dies, or is disqualified by a court ruling or for any other reason, a successor is to be elected within sixty days.
Article 69 [Oath]
The President, at the time of his inauguration, takes the following oath:
"I do solemnly swear before the people that I will faithfully execute the duties of the President by observing the Constitution, defending the State, pursuing the peaceful unification of the homeland, promoting the freedom and welfare of the people, and endeavoring to develop national culture."
Article 70 [Term]
The term of office of the President is five years, and the President cannot be reelected.

ARTICLE 71 [VACANCY]
If the office of the presidency is vacant or the President is unable to perform his duties for any reason, the Prime Minister or the members of the State Council in the order of priority as determined by law act for him.

ARTICLE 72 [REFERENDUM ON POLICY]
The President may submit important policies relating to diplomacy, national defense, unification, and other matters relating to the national destiny to a national referendum if he deems it necessary.

ARTICLE 73 [TREATIES, FOREIGN AFFAIRS]
The President concludes and ratifies treaties; accredits, receives, or dispatches diplomatic envoys; and declares war and concludes peace.

ARTICLE 74 [ARMED FORCES]
(1) The President is Commander-in-Chief of the Armed Forces under the conditions as prescribed by the Constitution and law.
(2) The organization and formation of the Armed Forces is determined by law.

ARTICLE 75 [DECREES]
The President may issue presidential decrees concerning matters delegated to him by law with the scope specifically defined and also matters necessary to enforce laws.

ARTICLE 76 [EMERGENCY POWERS]
(1) In time of internal turmoil, external menace, natural calamity, or a grave financial or economic crisis, the President may take in respect to them the minimum necessary financial and economic actions or issue orders having the effect of law, only when it is required to take urgent measures for the maintenance of national security or public peace and order, and there is no time to await the convocation of the National Assembly.
(2) In case of major hostilities affecting national security, the President may issue orders having the effect of law, only when it is required to preserve the integrity of the nation, and it is impossible to convene the National Assembly.

SECTION 2. THE EXECUTIVE BRANCH
SUBSECTION 1. THE PRIME MINISTER AND MEMBERS OF THE STATE COUNCIL

ARTICLE 86 [PRIME MINISTER]
(1) The Prime Minister is appointed by the President with the consent of the National Assembly.
(2) The Prime Minister assists the President and directs the Executive Ministries from active duty.
(3) No Member of the Military can be appointed Prime Minister unless he is retired from active duty.

ARTICLE 87 [MEMBERS OF STATE COUNCIL]
(1) The members of the State Council are appointed by the President on the recommendation of the Prime Minister.
(2) The Members of the State Council assist the President until the removal of a member of the State Council from office.
(3) The Prime Minister may recommend to the President the removal of a member of the State Council from office.
(4) No member of the military can be appointed a member of the State Council unless he is retired from active duty.

SUBSECTION 2. THE STATE COUNCIL
ARTICLE 88 [STATE COUNCIL]
(1) The State Council deliberates on important policies that fall within the Power of the Executive.
(2) The State Council is composed of the President, the Prime Minister, and other members numbering no more than thirty and no less than fifteen.
(3) The President is the chairman -of the State Council, and the Prime Minister is the Vice Chairman.
ARTICLE 89 [COMPETENCES]
The following matters are referred to the State Council for deliberation:
1) Basic plans for state affairs, and general policies of the Executive;
2) Declaration of war, conclusion of peace, and other important matters pertaining to foreign Policy;
3) Draft amendments to the Constitution, proposals for national referendums, proposed treaties, legislative bills, and proposed presidential decrees;
4) Budgets, settlement of accounts, basic plans for disposal of state properties, contracts incurring financial obligation on the State, and other important financial matters;
5) Emergency orders and emergency financial and economic actions or orders by the President, and declaration and termination of martial law;
6) Important military affairs;
7) Requests for convening an extraordinary session of the National Assembly;
8) Awarding of honors;
9) Granting of amnesty, commutation, and restoration of rights;
10) Demarcation of jurisdiction between Executive Ministries;
11) Basic plans concerning delegation or allocation of powers within the Executive;
12) Evaluation and analysis of the administration of State affairs;
13) Formulation and coordination of important policies of each Executive Ministry;

14) Action for the dissolution of a political party;

15) Examination of petitions pertaining to executive policies submitted or referred to the Executive;

16) Appointment of the Prosecutor General, the Chairman of the joint Chiefs of Staff, the Chief of Staff of each armed service, the presidents of national universities, ambassadors, and such other public officials and managers of important State-run enterprises as designated by law; and

17) Other matters presented by the President, the Prime Minister, or a member of the State Council.

ARTICLE 90 [ADVISORY COUNCIL OF ELDER STATESMEN]

(1) An Advisory Council of Elder Statesmen, composed of elder statesmen, may be established to advise the President on important affairs of State.

(2) The immediate former President becomes the Chairman of the Advisory Council of Elder Statesmen: Provided, that if there is no immediate former President, the President appoints the Chairman.

(3) The Organization, function, and other necessary matters pertaining to the Advisory Council of Elder Statesmen are determined by law.

ARTICLE 91 [NATIONAL SECURITY COUNCIL]

(1) A National Security Council is established to advise the President on the formulation of foreign, military, and domestic policies related to national security prior to their deliberation by the State Council.

(2) The meetings of the National Security Council are presided over by the President.

(3) The organization, function, and other necessary matters pertaining to the National Security Council are determined by law.

ARTICLE 92 [ADVISORY COUNCIL ON DEMOCRACY AND PEACEFUL UNIFICATION]

(1) An Advisory Council on Democratic and Peaceful Unification may be established to advise the President on the formulation of peaceful unification policy.

(2) The organization, function, and other necessary matters pertaining to the Advisory Council on Democratic and Peaceful Unification are determined by law.

ARTICLE 93 [NATIONAL ECONOMIC ADVISORY COUNCIL]

(1) A National Economic Advisory Council may be established to advise the President on the formulation of important policies for developing the national economy.

(2) The organization, function, and other necessary matters pertaining to the National Economic Advisory Council are determined by law.

SUBSECTION 3. THE EXECUTIVE MINISTRIES
ARTICLE 94 [HEADS OF MINISTRIES]
The Heads of Executive Ministries are appointed by the President
from among members of the State Council on the recommendation
of the Prime Minister.
ARTICLE 95 [ORDINANCES]
The Prime Minister or the head of each Executive Ministry may,
under the powers delegated by law or Presidential Decree, or *ex
officio*, issue ordinances of the Prime Minister or the Executive
Ministry concerning matters that are within their jurisdiction.
ARTICLE 96 [MINISTRY ORGANIZATION]
The establishment, organization, and function of each Executive
Ministry are determined by law.

SUBSECTION 4. THE BOARD OF AUDIT AND INSPECTION
ARTICLE 97 [BOARD OF AUDIT AND INSPECTION]
The Board of Audit and Inspection is established under the direct
jurisdiction of the President to inspect and examine the settlement of the revenues and expenditures of the State, the accounts
of the State, and other organizations specified by law and the job
performances of the executive agencies and public officials.
ARTICLE 98 [MEMBERSHIP, TERM]
(1) The Board of Audit and Inspection is composed of no less than
    five and no more than eleven members, including the Chairman.
(2) The Chairman of the Board is appointed by the President with
    the consent of the National Assembly. The term of office of the
    Chairman is four years, and he may be reappointed only once.
(3) The members of the Board are appointed by the President on
    the recommendation of the Chairman. The term of office of the
    members is four years, and they may be reappointed only once.
ARTICLE 99 [INSPECTION, REPORT]
The Board of Audit and Inspection inspects the closing of accounts
of revenues and expenditures each year, and reports the results to
the President and the National Assembly in the following year.
ARTICLE 100 [ORGANIZATION]
The organization and function of the Board of Audit and Inspection,
the qualifications of its members, the range of the public official's subject to inspection, and other necessary matters are determined by law.

Chapter V. The Courts

ARTICLE 101 [COURTS]
(1) Judicial power is vested in courts composed of judges.
(2) The courts comprise the Supreme Court, which is the highest
    court of the State, and courts at specified levels.

(3) Qualifications for judges are determined by law.

ARTICLE 102 [COURT ORGANIZATION]

(1) Departments may be established in the Supreme Court.

(2) There are Supreme Court justices at the Supreme Court: Provided, that judges other than Supreme Court Justices may be assigned to the Supreme Court under the conditions as prescribed by law.

(3) The organization of the Supreme Court and lower courts is determined by law.

ARTICLE 103 [INDEPENDENCE OF JUDGES]

Judges rule independently according to their conscience and in conformity with the Constitution and the law.

ARTICLE 104 [APPOINTMENT OF JUDGES]

(1) The Chief justice of the Supreme Court is appointed by the President with the consent of the National Assembly.

(2) The Supreme Court justices are appointed by the President on the recommendation of the Chief justice and with the consent of the National Assembly.

(3) Judges other than the Chief justice and the Supreme Court justices are appointed by the Chief justice with the consent of the Conference of Supreme Court justices.

ARTICLE 105 [TERM OF JUDGES]

(1) The term of office of the Chief justice is six years and he cannot be reappointed.

(2) The term of office of the Justices of the Supreme Court is six years and they may be reappointed as prescribed by law.

(3) The term of office of judges other than the Chief justice and Justices of the Supreme Court is ten years, and they may be reappointed under the conditions as prescribed by law.

(4) The retirement age of judges is determined by law.

ARTICLE 106 [SANCTIONS, EARLY RETIREMENT]

(1) No judge may be removed from office except by impeachment or a sentence of imprisonment or heavier punishment, nor may he be suspended from office, have his salary reduced, or suffer any other unfavorable treatment except by disciplinary action.

(2) In the event a judge is unable to discharge his official duties because of serious mental or physical impairment, he may be retired from office under the conditions as prescribed by law.

ARTICLE 107 [CONSTITUTIONAL REVIEW]

(1) When the constitutionality of a law is at issue in trial, the court requests a decision of the Constitutional Court, and judges according to the decision thereof.

(2) The Supreme Court has the power to make a final review of the constitutionality or legality of administrative decrees, regulations or actions, when their constitutionality or legality is at issue in a trial.

(3) Administrative appeals may be conducted as a procedure prior to a judicial trial. The procedures of administrative appeals are determined by law and are in conformity with the principles of judicial procedures.

ARTICLE 108 [COURT ADMINISTRATION]

The Supreme Court may establish, within the scope of law, regulations, pertaining to judicial proceedings and internal discipline and regulations on administrative matters of the court.

ARTICLE 109 [PUBLICITY]

Trials and decisions of the courts are open to the public: Provided, that when there is a danger that such trials may undermine the national security or disturb public safety and order, or be harmful to public morals, trials may be closed to the public by court decision.

ARTICLE 110

(1) Courts martial may be established as special courts to exercise jurisdiction over military trials.

(2) The Supreme Court has the final appellate jurisdiction over courts martial.

(3) The organization and authority of courts martial, and the qualifications of their judges are determined by law.

(4) Military trials under an extraordinary martial law may not be appealed in case of crimes of soldiers and employees of the military; military espionage; and crimes as defined by law in regard to sentinels, sentry posts, supply of harmful foods and beverage, and prisoners of war, except in the case of a death sentence.

Chapter VI. The Constitutional Court

ARTICLE 111 [COMPETENCE, APPOINTMENT]

(1) The Constitutional Court is competent to adjudicate the following matters:

1) The unconstitutionality of law upon the request of the courts;

2) Impeachment;

3) Dissolution of a political party;

4) Disputes about the jurisdictions between State agencies, between State agencies and local governments, and between local governments, and

5) Petitions relating to the Constitution as prescribed by law.

(3) The Constitutional Court is composed of nine adjudicators qualified to be court judges, and they are appointed by the President.

(4) Among the adjudicators referred to in Paragraph (2), three are appointed from persons selected by the National Assembly,

and three appointed from persons nominated by the Chief justice.

(5) The head of the Constitutional Court is appointed by the President from among the adjudicators with the consent of the National Assembly.

ARTICLE 112 [TERM, INCOMPATIBILITY]

(1) The term of office of the adjudicators of the Constitutional Court is six years, and they may be reappointed under the conditions as prescribed by law.

(2) The adjudicators of the Constitutional Court may not join any political party nor participate in political activities.

(3) No adjudicator of the Constitutional Court can be expelled from office except by impeachment or a sentence of imprisonment or heavier punishment.

ARTICLE 113 [MAJORITY, INTERNAL REGULATIONS]

(1) When the Constitutional Court makes a decision on the unconstitutionality of a law, impeachment, dissolution of a political party, or a petition relating to the Constitution, the J,concurrence of at least six adjudicators is required.

(2) The Constitutional Court may establish regulations relating to its proceedings and internal discipline and regulations on administrative matters within the limits of law.

(3) The organization, function, and other necessary matters of the Constitutional Court are determined by law.

Chapter VII. Election Management

ARTICLE 114 [ESTABLISHMENT]

(1) Election Management Committees are established for the purpose of fair management of elections and national referenda, and dealing with administrative affairs concerning political parties.

(2) The Central Election Management Committee is composed of three members appointed by the President, three members selected by the National Assembly, and three members designated by the Chief justice of the Supreme Court. The Chairman of the Committee is elected from among the members.

(3) The term of office of the members of the Committee is six years.

(4) The members of the Committee may not join political parties, nor participate in political activities.

(5) No member of the Committee can be expelled from office except by impeachment or a sentence of imprisonment or heavier punishment.

(6) The Central Election Management Committee may establish, within the limit of laws and decrees, regulations relating to

the management of elections, national referenda, and administrative matters concerning political parties and may also establish regulations relating to internal discipline that are compatible with law.

(7) The organization, function, and other necessary matters of the Election Management Committees at each level are determined by law.

ARTICLE 115 [INSTRUCTIONS]

(1) Election Management Committees at each level may issue necessary instructions to administrative agencies concerned with respect to administrative matters pertaining to elections and national referenda such as the preparation of the pollbooks.

(2) Administrative agencies concerned, upon receipt of such instructions, have to comply.

ARTICLE 116 [CAMPAIGNS]

(1) Election campaigns are conducted under the management of the Election Management Committees at each level within the limit set by law. Equal opportunity has to be guaranteed.

(2) Except as otherwise prescribed by law, expenditures for elections are not imposed on political parties or candidates.

Chapter VIII. Local Autonomy

ARTICLE 117 [LOCAL GOVERNMENTS]

(1) Local governments deal with administrative matters pertaining to the welfare of local residents, manage properties, and may enact provisions relating to local autonomy, within the limit of laws and regulations.

(2) The types of local governments are determined by law.

ARTICLE 118 [LOCAL COUNCILS]

(1) A local government has a council.

(2) The organization and powers of local councils, and the election of members, election procedures for heads of local governments, and other matters pertaining to the organization and operation of local governments are determined by law.

Chapter IX. The Economy

ARTICLE 119 [REGULATION AND COORDINATION]

(1) The economic order of the Republic of Korea is based on a respect for the freedom and creative initiative of enterprises and individuals in economic affairs.

(2) The State may regulate and coordinate economic affairs in order to maintain the balanced growth and stability of the

national economy, to ensure proper distribution of income, to prevent the domination of the market and the abuse of economic power, and to democratize the economy through harmony among the economic agents.

ARTICLE 120 [NATURAL RESOURCES]

(1) Licenses to exploit, develop, or utilize minerals and all other important underground resources, marine resources, water power, and natural powers available for economic use may be granted for a period of time under the conditions as prescribed by law.

(2) The land and natural resources are protected by the State, and the State establishes a plan necessary for their balanced development and utilization.

ARTICLE 121 [AGRICULTURE]

(1) The State endeavors to realize the land-to-the-tillers principle with respect to agricultural land. Tenant farming is prohibited.

(2) The leasing of agricultural land and the consignment management of agricultural land to increase agricultural productivity and to ensure the rational utilization of agricultural land or due to unavoidable circumstances, is recognized under the conditions as prescribed by law.

ARTICLE 122 [LAND LAWS]

The State may impose, as under the conditions prescribed by law, restrictions or obligations necessary for the efficient and balanced utilization, development, and preservation of the land of the nation that is the basis for the productive activities and daily lives of an citizens.

ARTICLE 123 [FARMING AND FISHING]

(1) The State establishes and implements a plan to comprehensively develop and support the farm and fishing communities in order to protect and foster agriculture and fisheries.

(2) The State has the duty to foster regional economies to ensure the balanced development of all regions.

(3) In order to protect the interests of farmers and fishermen, the State endeavors to stabilize the prices of agricultural and fishery products by maintaining an equilibrium between the demand and supply of such products and improving their marketing and distribution systems.

(4) The State fosters organizations founded on the spirit of self-help among farmers, fishermen, and businessmen engaged in small and medium industry and guarantees their independent activities and development.

ARTICLE 124 [CONSUMER PROTECTION]

The State guarantees a consumer protection movement intended to encourage sound consumption activities and improvement in the quality of products under the conditions as prescribed by law.

ARTICLE 125 [FOREIGN TRADE]
The State fosters foreign trade, and may regulate and coordinate it.
ARTICLE 126 [NO SOCIALIZATION]
Private enterprises may not be nationalized nor transferred to ownership by a local government, nor shall their management be controlled or administered by the State, except in cases as prescribed by law to meet urgent necessities of national defense or the national economy.
ARTICLE 127 [INNOVATION, STANDARDIZATION]
(1) The State strives to improve the national economy by developing science and technology, information and human resources, and encouraging innovation.
(2) The State establishes a system of national standards.
(3) The President may establish advisory organizations necessary to achieve the purpose referred to in Paragraph (1).

Chapter X. Amendments to the Constitution

ARTICLE 128 [INITIATIVE]
(1) A proposal to amend the Constitution can be introduced either by a majority of the total members of the National Assembly or by the President.
(2) Amendments to the Constitution for the extension of the term of office of the President or for a change allowing for the re-election of the President are not effective for the President in office at the time of the proposal for such amendments to the Constitution.
ARTICLE 129 [PUBLICATION]
Proposed amendments to the Constitution are presented to the public by the President for twenty days or more.
ARTICLE 130 [MAJORITY, REFERENDUM]
(1) The National Assembly decides upon the proposed amendments within sixty days of the public announcement, and passage by the National Assembly requires the concurrent vote of two-thirds or more of the total members of the National Assembly.
(2) The proposed amendments to the Constitution are submitted to a national referendum not later than thirty days after passage by the National Assembly, and are confirmed by more than one half of all votes cast by more than one half of voters eligible to vote in elections for members of the National Assembly.
(3) When the proposed amendments to the Constitution receive the concurrence prescribed in paragraph (2), the amendments to the Constitution is finalized, and the President promulgates it without delay.

Chapter XI. Enforcement Provisions

ARTICLE 1 [ENFORCEMENT]
This Constitution enters into force on 25 Feb 1988: Provided, that the enactment or amendment of laws necessary to implement this Constitution, the elections of the President and the National Assembly under this Constitution, and other preparations to implement this constitution may be carried out prior to the entry into force of this constitution.

ARTICLE 2 [FIRST PRESIDENTIAL ELECTION]
(1) The first presidential election under this constitution is held not later than forty days before this Constitution enters into force.
(2) The term of office of the First President under this Constitution commences on the date of its enforcement.

ARTICLE 3 [FIRST PARLIAMENTARY ELECTIONS]
(1) The first elections of the National Assembly under this Constitution are held within six months from the promulgation of this Constitution. The term of office of the members of the first National Assembly elected under this Constitution commences on the date of the first convening of the national Assembly under Constitution.
(2) The term of office of the members of the National Assembly incumbent at the time this Constitution is promulgated terminates the day prior to the first convening of the National Assembly under Paragraph (1).

ARTICLE 4 [PUBLIC OFFICIALS]
(1) Public officials and officers of enterprises appointed by the Government, who are in office at the time of the enforcement of this Constitution, are considered as having been appointed under this Constitution: Provided, that public officials whose election procedures or appointing authorities are changed under this Constitution, the Chief justice of the Supreme Court, and the Chairman of the Board of Audit and Inspection remain in office until such time as their successors are chosen under this constitution, and their terms of office terminate the day before the installation of their successors.
(2) Judges attached to the Supreme Court who are not the Chief justice or Justices of the Supreme Court and who are in office at the time of the enforcement of this Constitution are considered as having been appointed under this Constitution notwithstanding the provision of Paragraph (1).
(3) Those provisions of this Constitution which prescribe the terms of office of public officials or which restrict the number of terms that public officials may serve, take effect upon the dates of the first elections or the first appointments of such public officials under this Constitution.

ARTICLE 5 [OLD LAW]

Laws, decrees, ordinances, and treaties in force at the time this Constitution enters into force, remain valid unless they are contrary to this Constitution.

ARTICLE 6 [OLD ORGANIZATIONS]

Those organizations existing at the time of the enforcement of this Constitution which have been performing the functions falling within the authority of new organizations to be created under this Constitution, continue to exist and perform such, functions until such time as the new organizations are created under this Constitution.

APPENDIX 5

 è❧

Government Structure
of the Republic of Korea

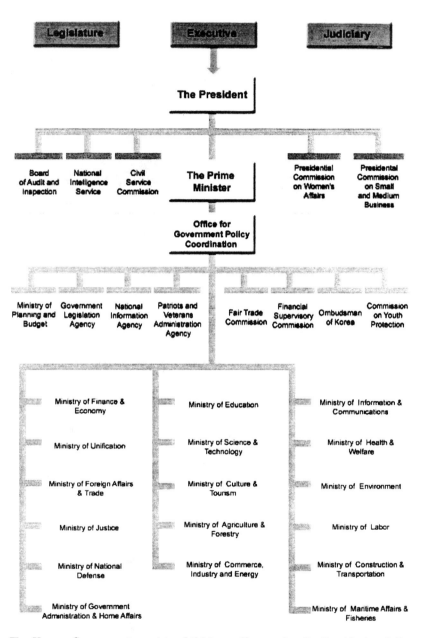

The Korean Government consists of thirteen offices under the President and the Prime Minister, and 17 ministries (as of May 17, 1999).

Contributors

About the Editors

Soong Hoom Kil (Ph.D., University of Michigan) was a member of the South Korean National Assembly and formerly a professor of political science at Seoul National University. He served as president of the Korean Political Science Association and has published numerous books and articles on Korean and Japanese politics. His most recent publications include *Contemporary Japanese Politics* (in Korean, 1998).

Chung-in Moon (Ph.D., University of Maryland) is the Dean of the Graduate School of International Studies and a professor of political science at Yonsei University. Prior to joining the Yonsei faculty, he taught at the University of Kentucky, Williams College, and the University of California at San Diego. He has published fourteen books and over one hundred and twenty articles in edited volumes and such scholarly journals as *World Politics*, the *Journal of Asian Studies*, and *International Studies Quarterly*. His most recent publications include *Economic Crisis and Structural Reforms in South Korea: Assessments and Implications* (2000), *Globalization and Democratization in South Korea: Assessments and Prospects* (1999), and *Democracy and the Korean Economy* (1999).

About the Authors

Woon-Tai Kim (Ph.D., Seoul National University) is professor emeritus of political science at Joong Ang University. He served

357

as president of the Korean Political Science Association and is a leading scholar on the political history of Korea. His publications include *Korean Politics* (in Korean).

David C. Kang (Ph.D., University of California, Berkeley) is assistant professor of government at Dartmouth College. He has published articles in *International Organization and World Development*.

Ki-shik S. J. Hahn (Ph.D., University of California, Berkeley) is professor emeritus of political science at Korea University. He is a leading scholar on the study of political leadership in South Korea. His publications include *Leadership Theory and Korean Politics* (in Korean) and *Leaders of Korean Politics* (in Korean).

Jung Bock Lee (Ph.D., University of Washington) is professor of political science at Seoul National University. He has published extensively in the areas of Korean and Japanese politics. His recent publications appeared in *Korean Political Science Review* (in Korean).

Dong-suh Bark (Ph.D., University of Minnesota) is professor emeritus of public administration at the Graduate School of Public Administration, Seoul National University. He served as president of the Korean Public Administration Association. His publications include *Administrative Reform Case of South Korea* (in Korean, 1999).

Byung Chul Koh (Ph.D., Cornell University) is professor of political science at the University of Illinois at Chicago Circle. His publications include *Administrative Elite in Japan and Foreign Policy System in North and South Korea*.

Sung Chul Yang (Ph.D., University of Kentucky) is the Korean Ambassador to the United States. He was a professor of political science at Kyunghee University and a member of the South Korean National Assembly. His most recent publications include *Comparative Political Systems in North and South Korea*.

Sunghack Lim (Ph.D., The Pennsylvania State University) is research professor of the Center for International Studies, Yonsei University. He has published in the areas of Korean and Taiwanese politics.

Index